1999

The Garden Tourist®

A Guide to Gardens, Garden Tours, Shows and Special Events

by Lois G. Rosenfeld

The Garden Tourist Press

THE GARDEN TOURIST® is a registered trademark of Lois G. Rosenfeld
ISSN 1062-6093
ISBN 0-9639082-7-8

Published by The Garden Tourist Press
330 West 72nd Street
New York, NY 10023

Printed in the United States of America

Contents

Introduction

The **Garden Tourist® 1999** celebrates its eighth year of publication with an all new and useful **Guide to Gardens**. In addition to our Calendar of Garden Events, you'll find this listing of botanical gardens and arboreta a perennially handy source of information wherever you travel, and whenever you want to see some wonderful gardens. Listed alphabetically by state, the *Guide to Gardens* gives descriptions, addresses, contact information and times of operation. So, if you're planning to attend some special garden event, you can now check for other great gardens in the area and visit those, too. And you can use the web addresses in our *Guide to Gardens* and *Events* entries to further check out what's new and what's been changed.

The calendar of events is now a selection of top events, listed by city and date. And please check us out at **www.gardencalendar.com** for events that set their dates after we went to press. You can use the links on this site to take virtual tours of many of the garden sites listed.

Our other new feature is **10 Great Garden Vacations for 1999** which gives you ideas for planning your garden travels. These articles are contributed by garden writers who really know what's special in their regions.

At the back of the book in **Far Away Places** you will find foreign tours sponsored by botanical gardens and horticultural societies, as well as some of the most important overseas events. The

Flower Shows section brings together all of the major shows in the U.S. and Canada by state and date.

Please let us hear from you if you have any suggestions or know of other events you like so we can share them with our readers. You can write to us or send us an e-mail to: gardentour@aol.com.

And remember: schedules do change, so always check ahead. Enjoy your garden touring!

Guide to Gardens & Selected Events

Nationwide

May-September
🌺 The Garden Conservancy

The Garden Conservancy, a non-profit organization which preserves America's great private gardens, will again make available its Open Days Directory for the 1999 season. Through this program private gardens in 26 states were open to the public in 1998 and the Conservancy plans to add several more regions in 1999. The Directory includes descriptions of each of the gardens, travel directions, and the dates and times each property is open to the public. Area public gardens are also listed. Proceeds from admission benefit the Garden Conservancy's preservation programs and donations are made by the Conservancy to not-for-profit organizations of the garden host's choice. To receive information about the 1999 Directory, membership in the Conservancy and its preservation projects, contact:

The Garden Conservancy, PO Box 219, Cold Spring, NY 10516
Email: gardencons@aol.com
(888)842-2442 or (914)265-2029

Alabama

Guide to Gardens

Bellingrath Gardens & Home
12401 Bellingrath Gardens Road
Theodore, AL 36582
Email: bellingrath@juno.com

(334)973-2217 *Fax:* (334)973-0540
🌺 The gardens comprise 65 acres of landscaping among towering live-oaks draped in Spanish moss. Special gardens include a rose garden, conservatory, great lawn, butterfly garden, rockery, formal gardens, oriental-American gardens and Mirror Lake. All ages enjoy the new ecological Bayou Boardwalk with a wonderful view of a southern bayou, home to countless varieties of birds, fish, other wildlife - even the occasional alligator.
Web: www.bellingrath.org/gardens/
Hours: 8am with seasonal closing hours
Fees: $7.50 Gardens; $13.95 Gardens & Home

Birmingham Botanical Gardens
2612 Lane Park Road
Birmingham, AL 35223
(205)879-1227 *Fax:* (205)879-3751
🌺 This 67-acre botanical garden has twelve special areas including a fine Japanese garden, a tea garden, Zen garden and bonsai exhibit. There is also a wildflower garden, fern glade, rhododendron garden, a 26-foot floral clock and a good collections or roses. The large conservatory houses cacti, succulents and orchids, and has seasonal exhibitions.
Web: www.bbgardens.org
Hours: Dawn-dusk
Fees: Free

Dismals Canyon
Route 3
Phil Campbell, AL
Mail: PO Box 281, Phil Campbell, AL 35581
(205)993-4559
🌺 A registered National Natural Landmark, Dismals Canyon has a natural arboretum of

twenty-seven different trees within a one hundred-foot radius, seven natural bridges and a winding stairway encased in natural rock. The canyon contains over 350 species of wildflowers and plants. The site offers a 2½-mile nature trail and a 6½-mile backpacker/mountain bike trail. Dismals Canyon offers guided 3-5 hour tours. Advance reservations needed.
Hours: Mar-Nov
Fees: Tours $4; $2 children up to sixth grade (by reservation)

Donald E. Davis Arboretum
Garden Drive
Auburn, AL
Mail: 101 Route LSB, Auburn University, Auburn, AL 36849
(334)844-5770 *Fax:* (334)844-1645
Founded in 1959, the Arboretum features a collection of plants native to Alabama. It includes a collection of trees found in North Alabama hardwood forests, an arbor planted with native vines and a pavilion with an open-air classroom. Under development are display areas for vegetation characteristic of Black-Belt soils, the prairies, coastal bog communities and sand dunes.
Hours: Dawn to dusk
Fees: Free

Dothan Area Botanical Gardens
214 East Main Street
Dothan, AL
Mail: PO Box 5971, Dothan, AL 36302
(334)793-3224 *Fax:* (334)793-5275
The Dothan Area Botanical Gardens are gardens in the making. Development began in 1995 with the clearing of a portion of the site, 50 acres of partially wooded, rolling land traversed by Cedar Creek and adjacent to Landmark Park. The Garden currently holds monthly Green Thumb Workdays, a Spring Garden Tour and Plant Sale, and other activities.
Web: www.dabg.com

The Hunstville-Madison County Botanical Garden
4747 Bob Wallace Avenue
Huntsville, AL 35805
(256)830-4447 *Fax:* (256)830-5314
The 5-acre central corridor planting contains aquatic, rose, daylily, fern, herb, perennial, annual and butterfly gardens. There are also nature trails, compost and vegetable demonstration areas. The Center for Biospheric Education and Research offers an audio/visual program and lunar greenhouse. Scheduled to open in 1999: Butterfly House and a new visitor's center.
Web: www.hsvbg.org
Hours: 8am-6:30pm Mon-Sat; 1-6:30pm Sun
Fees: $4; $3 seniors; $2 students; under 6 free

Jasmine Hill Gardens
3001 Jasmine Hill Road
Montgomery, AL
Mail: PO Box 6001, Montgomery, AL 36106
(334)567-6463 *Fax:* (334)567-6466
The 20 acres of Jasmine Hill are in bloom all year, with an extensive camellia collection during the winter, Japanese cherries in late March to early April, azaleas and flowering shrubs in the spring, crepe myrtles in summer, and annuals all the time. Throughout the Gardens are copies of Greek statuary, pools and fountains along native stone walks. A new Olympian Centre and a full-scale replica of the Temple of Hera ruins in Olympia, Greece are additional features.
Web: www.jasminehill.org
Hours: 9am-5pm Tues-Sun; Moon Strolls 6-10pm Thurs nearest full moon
Fees: $5; $3 children 6-12

Mobile Botanical Gardens
5151 Museum Drive
Mobile, AL
Mail: PO Box 8382, Mobile, AL 36608
(334)342-0555 *Fax:* (334)342-3149
❧ Located in the heart of Mobile, the Mobile Botanical Gardens encompass 64 acres of cultivated areas and nature trails. Highlights include native and exotic azaleas, camellia, hollies, magnolias and ferns. There is also a Rhododendron Garden and Herb Garden. Peak blooming season in MBG is late March and early April.
Hours: 8am-5pm
Fees: Free

University of Alabama in Huntsville Arboretum
Huntsville, AL
Mail: Facilities & Operations Building, Huntsville, AL 35899
(256)890-6482
❧ This Arboretum is situated on the University's 360-acre campus and contains more than 200 different deciduous trees and conifers, many of them labeled. Many of the trees are rare and not commonly seen outside of collections. About 100 of the specimens can be found around the lake area and an additional 40 to 50 around the Art Gallery.
Fees: Free

University of Alabama Arboretum
Pelham Loop Road
Tuscaloosa, AL
Mail: PO Box 870344, Tuscaloosa, AL 35487
(205)553-3278 *Fax:* (205)553-3278
❧ A 60-acre arboretum a few miles from the campus, with emphasis on indigenous trees, shrubs, and wildflowers. The garden is divided into four sections: native woodland, ornamentals, wildflower garden, and an experimental garden.

Web: www.uah.edu/admin/Fac/grounds/
Hours: 7am-5pm
Fees: Free

Selected Events

Birmingham

April 9, 10
❧ **Annual Fiesta Plant Sale**
A huge sale of plant material including annuals, bonsai, daylilies, ferns, herbs, hostas, iris, native plants, perennials, rhododendron, roses, orchids, exotic vegetable, tropical plants. books and gardening accessories.
Hours: 9am-5pm Fri; 9am-3pm Sat
Fee: Free
Birmingham Botanical Gardens *(See Alabama Guide to Gardens.)*

Dothan

April
❧ **Spring Garden Tour**
A tour of eight local gardens. Call for exact dates.
Hours: 2-5pm
For information: **Dothan Area Botanical Gardens** *(See Alabama Guide to Gardens.)*

Huntsville

April 15-18
❧ **Spring Plant Sale**
A huge sale of over 100,000 plants, including herbs, wildflowers, vegetables, annuals, perennials, shrubs and young trees. Held under tents on the Garden grounds. An annual event sponsored by The Garden Guild.
Hours: 10am-5pm Fri; 10am-6pm Sat; 1-5pm Sun
Fee: Free
The Hunstville-Madison County Botanical Garden *(See Alabama Guide to Gardens.)*

October 9, 10
✿ "Cornucopia" Fall Festival
An event for the whole family, with a plant and bulb sale, botanical art show and sale, a haunted house, Boo-tanical Boo-tique, food and entertainment .
Hours: 10am-5pm Sat; 1-5pm Sun
Fee: Admission $4; $3 seniors; $2 students; under 6 free
The Hunstville-Madison County Botanical Garden (See Alabama Guide to Gardens.)

November 24-December 31
✿ 1999 Galaxy of Lights
A drive-through light show billed as the Tennessee Valley's largest and most spectacular. More than 125 illuminated creations, from astronauts to Santa, throughout the Garden.
Hours: 5:30-9pm
Fee: $10 per car
The Hunstville-Madison County Botanical Garden (See Alabama Guide to Gardens.)

Mobile
See also Theodore

March 19-21
✿ Spring Plant Sale
Plants suitable for the hot, humid conditions of the Gulf coast, plus demonstrations and lectures on plants and planting.
Hours: 8am-5pm
Fee: Free
Mobile Botanical Gardens (See Alabama Guide to Gardens.)

March 25-28
✿ Flower Show
Festival of Flowers. Exhibits by top florists, landscape architects, designers and hobbyists, a display from Bellingrath Gardens, tablescape designs, plus plants, landscaping and garden products on sale. An annual event

benefiting the Providence Hospital Foundation.
Hours: 9:30am-5pm Thurs, Fri, Sat; 11am-5pm Sun
Fee: $6 in advance; $8 at door
Spring Hill College Campus, 4000 Dauphin Street, Mobile, AL 36602
(334)639-2050

May 9
✿ "Gallery of Gardens" Tour
A self-guided tour of some of Mobile's most interesting gardens.
Hours: 1-4pm Sun
Fee: $15
For information: **Mobile Botanical Gardens** (See Alabama Guide to Gardens.)

October 15-17
✿ Fall Plant Sale
A sale timed to the best planting season in the South, with speakers and seminars throughout the weekend.
Hours: 8am-5pm
Fee: Free; fee for keynote speech
Mobile Botanical Gardens (See Alabama Guide to Gardens.)

Theodore
20 miles from Mobile

November 26-December 31
✿ Magic Christmas in Lights
Millions of lights and seasonal displays throughout the grounds and home.
Hours: 5-9:30pm
Fee: Admission $7.50 Gardens; $13.95 Gardens & Home
Bellingrath Gardens & Home (See Alabama Guide to Gardens.)

Tuscaloosa

Mid May

Garden Celebrations! Tour

A tour of five or six local gardens. Call for exact date.
Hours: 1-4pm
Fee: $15
For information: **University of Alabama Arboretum** *(See Alabama Guide to Gardens.)*

Alaska

Guide to Gardens

Alaska Botanical Garden
Campbell Road off Tudor Road
Anchorage, AK
Mail: PO Box 202202 , Anchorage, AK 99520
Email: garden@alaska.net
(907)265-3165 *Fax:* (907)265-3180

Nestled is the foothills of east Anchorage along Campbell Creek in a quiet forest of birch and spruce is the Alaska Botanical Garden. Winding trails lead to the Demonstration Garden, the Perennial Garden and the Herb Garden. The Garden's master plan calls for 10% of the 110-acre site to be developed with ornamental plantings and the remainder to be preserved in its natural state.
Hours: Season starts May 15
Fees: Donation requested

Selected Events

Anchorage

June 26

2nd Annual Garden Fair

Includes displays, lectures, vendors, music and activities for the whole family.
Hours: 10am-8pm
Fee: $5; $10 family
Alaska Botanical Garden *(See Alaska Guide to Gardens.)*

August 7, 8

Anchorage Garden Tour

A tour of local gardens sponsored by the Anchorage Garden Club to benefit the Garden. Call (907)522-3490 for information.
Alaska Botanical Garden *(See Alaska Guide to Gardens.)*

Inland Passage

June 12-19

Wilderness Gardens of Alaska

A cruise aboard the clipper ship Yorktown sponsored by the American Horticulture Society.
For Information: **American Horticultural Society**, 7931 East Boulevard Drive, Alexandria, VA 22308
Email: info@haerttertravel.com
(800)942-6666

August 14-21

Alaska's Inland Passage Tour

A cruise aboard the clipper ship Yorktown sponsored by Holden Arboretum.
For information: **The Holden Arboretum**, 9500 Sperry Road, Kirtland, OH 44094
(440)256-1110 Education Department

Arizona

Guide to Gardens

Arboretum at Arizona State University
Tempe, AZ 85287
(602)965-8137 *Fax:* (602)965-9470

Situated in a pan-tropical area, the Arboretum has crested saguaro cacti and the largest variety of edible dates in North America.
Fees: Free

The Arboretum at Flagstaff
Flagstaff, AZ
Mail: PO Box 670, Flagstaff, AZ 86002
(520)774-1442 *Fax:* (520)774-1441
🌿 Located in a Ponderosa pine forest at an elevation of more than 7,000 feet, this site is a good place to see plants of the Colorado Plateau and cacti of northwestern Arizona.
Web: www.flagguide.com/arboretum/
Directions: 3.8 miles south of Old Route 66 on Woody Mountain Road
Hours: May-Oct 9am-4pm daily; mid-Mar-Apr & Nov-Dec 23 open Mon-Fri only; Dec 24-mid-March closed
Fees: $3;$1 youths 6-18

Arizona-Sonora Desert Museum
2021 North Kinney Road
Tucson, AZ 85743
(520)883-1380 *Fax:* (520)883-2500
🌿 The Desert Museum combines birds, beasts and botany. Exhibits recreate the natural landscape where mountain lions, prairie dogs, gila monsters, hawks and hummingbirds can be seen. The Gardens feature colorful desert gardens, pollinator gardens, and one of the area's best display of cactus and succulents.
Web: www.desert.net/museum/
Hours: Mar-Sept: 7:30am-6pm; Oct-Feb: 8:30am-5pm
Fees: $8.95; $1.75 children

Boyce Thompson Arboretum
37615 East US Highway 60
Superior, AZ 85273
(520)689-2811 *Fax:* (520)689-5858
🌿 Billed as Arizona's oldest and largest botanical garden, this Arboretum includes Cactus Garden, Queen Creek Canyon with mature-growth trees, the Memorial Herb Garden, and the High Trail with dramatic southwestern views. Featured are plants from the world's deserts. Nestled in scenic Queen Creek Canyon, it is one of Arizona's most spectacular nature spots.
Email: arboretum@ag.arizona.edu
Web: ag.arizona.edu/BTA/
Hours: 8am-5pm
Fees: $5; $2 children

Desert Botanical Garden
1201 North Galvin Parkway
Phoenix, AZ 85008
(602)941-1225; Hotline 24-hr (602)481-8134 *Fax:* (602)481-8124
🌿 This site includes a spectacular array of desert plants and flora from arid lands. The Garden has transplanted thousands of specimens to this 150-acre patch of desert land, including agaves, cacti, Desert Fern trees, aloes, yuccas and more. The height of the blooming season is from late March to May with unusual displays, such as the night-blooming cactus, into June and July. The Garden's 24-hour Hotline provides recorded updates on the best places in Arizona to see desert wildflowers and cactus blooms.
Web: aabga.mobot.org/AABGA/Member.pages/desert.html
Hours: May-Sept 7am-10pm; Oct-Apr 7am-sunset
Fees: $7; $6 seniors; $1 children 5-12

Tohono Chul Park
7366 North Paseo del Norte
Tucson, AZ 85704
(520)742-6455 *Fax:* (520)797-1213
🌿 Tohono Chul's numerous gardens display a wide variety of landscape materials, plants and design concepts, just moments from the busiest spot in Tucson. The Demonstration Gardens show how to conserve water and maintain a variety of water-loving and arid-adapted plants. The Park also features the Hummingbird Garden, the Garden for Children

and the Ethnobotanical Garden with examples of a variety of crops both grown by indigenous peoples and by New World explorers.
Web: www.azstarnet.com/~tcpark/
Hours: Grounds 7am - sunset
Fees: $2 suggested donation

Tucson Botanical Gardens
2150 North Alvernon Way
Tucson, AZ 85712
(520)326-9686 *Fax:* (520)324-0166
�$ Here, in an urban oasis, are displays of the variety of plants that thrive in southern Arizona: the Herb Garden, Tropical Exhibit, the Sensory Garden, Cactus and Succulent Garden, the Xeriscape Demonstration Garden, Wildflower Garden, a Barrio Garden, Butterfly Garden, Backyard Bird Garden and the Historical Garden.
Web: www.azstarnet.com/~tbg/
Hours: 8:30am-4:30pm
Fees: $4; $3 seniors; children under 12 free

Selected Events

Flagstaff

June 19, 20
🌿 **14th Annual Summer Plant Sale & Horticultural Fair**
A sale featuring hard to find native plants, plus expert advice, talks, displays and children's events.
Hours: 9am-4pm
Fee: $3; $1 children over 6
The Arboretum at Flagstaff *(See Arizona Guide to Gardens.)*

July 10
🌿 **Arboretum Open House**
A family event with themed tours of the garden, music and other activities.
Hours: 9am-5pm
Fee: Free

The Arboretum at Flagstaff *(See Arizona Guide to Gardens.)*

Phoenix

March, April & May
🌿 **Wildflower & Cactus Bloom Displays**
The prime months of the desert bloom, with wildflowers in March, the Saguaro generally in May.
Desert Botanical Garden *(See Arizona Guide to Gardens.)*

March 20, 21
🌿 **Spring Landscape Plant Sale**
More than 15,000 plants, trees and shrubs for arid landscapes, as well as smaller plants for patio container gardening.
Hours: 9am-5pm
Fee: Free entry to plant sale
Desert Botanical Garden *(See Arizona Guide to Gardens.)*

October 23, 24
🌿 **Landscape Plants & Used Book Sale**
More than 15,000 arid-land plants for sale plus a wildflower information center with advice for purchasing and preparing next spring's homegrown wildflower display. Book sale benefits the Garden's library.
Hours: 9am-5pm
Fee: Free
Desert Botanical Garden *(See Arizona Guide to Gardens.)*

December 3- 5
🌿 **Noches de las Luminarias**
An evening of music and refreshments in a garden glowing with 7000 luminaries. Event is a sell-out; advance ticket purchase required.
Hours: 5:30-9:30pm
Fee: $10; $4 children
Desert Botanical Garden *(See Arizona Guide to Gardens.)*

Superior

55 miles from Phoenix

February 13, 14
🌿 Flower Show

The Language of Flowers. A display of plants and blossoms with a theme - how flowers are used to communicate when words won't do. Plus a tasting of gourmet chocolates.

Hours: 8am-5pm
Fee: Admission $5, $2 children; Tastings $5 for 5
Boyce Thompson Arboretum *(See Arizona Guide to Gardens.)*

March
🌿 Wildflower Month

Displays of cultivated and native wildflowers throughout the month. Wildflower tours on Saturdays and Sundays. Call the Wildflower Hotline at (520)689-2811.

Hours: 8am-5pm
Boyce Thompson Arboretum *(See Arizona Guide to Gardens.)*

March 19-April 4
🌿 Spring Plant Sale

Thousands of drought-tolerant trees, shrubs, annuals, perennials, cacti and succulents plus expert advice on growing them. Guided tours each Saturday and Sunday at 1:30pm to see mature specimens of the plants.

Hours: 8am-5pm
Fee: Admission $5; $2 children
Boyce Thompson Arboretum *(See Arizona Guide to Gardens.)*

May 1
🌿 Herb Festival

A chance to learn about a variety of herbs. Includes tours of the herb garden, tastings, educational programs and activities for the whole family.

Hours: 11am-3pm

Fee: Admission $5; $2 children
Boyce Thompson Arboretum *(See Arizona Guide to Gardens.)*

October 15-November 1
🌿 Fall Plant Sale

Arid-land tolerant plants, including blooming plants, hard to find Arizona range plants, trees, shrubs, cacti and succulents. Horticulturists on hand each Saturday and Sunday at 11am.

Hours: 8am-5pm
Fee: Admission $5; $2 children
Boyce Thompson Arboretum *(See Arizona Guide to Gardens.)*

Tucson

February 15-April 16
🌿 Wildflower Tours

Guided tours through the desert at the height of the bloom.

Hours: 10am Mon, Wed, Fri
Fee: $2 suggested donation
Tohono Chul Park *(See Arizona Guide to Gardens.)*

March 13, 14
🌿 Plant Sale

A wide variety of arid-adapted plants for sale, plus mini-lectures, expert advice, a container garden workshop and a salsa recipe contest.

Hours: 9am-4pm Sat; 10am-4pm Sun
Fee: Free; fee for workshop
Tohono Chul Park *(See Arizona Guide to Gardens.)*

Late March
🌿 Wildflower Walks

Easy two-mile hikes guided by the Museum's naturalists to seek out and enjoy the wildflowers at the height of the bloom. Call for exact dates.

Arizona-Sonora Desert Museum *(See Arizona Guide to Gardens.)*

March 28
❧ Wildflower Festival & Picnic
A progressive dinner, plus wildflower walks, activities and musical entertainment.
Hours: 3:30-7pm
Fee: $40; $15 children
Tohono Chul Park *(See Arizona Guide to Gardens.)*

April 10, 11
❧ Tucson Home Gardens Tour
Visits some of the most intriguing gardens in Tucson, featuring everything from xeriscaping to wildflowers. Includes six home garden sites and a tour of the Tucson Botanical Gardens.
Hours: 10am-4pm
Fee: $12; children under 12 free
For information: **Tucson Botanical Gardens** *(See Arizona Guide to Gardens.)*

May 8
❧ Annual Herb Fair
A variety of herb plants and crafts for gardeners, cooks and enthusiasts, plus expert advice and herbal taste treats. Timed to coincide with the blooming of the Herb Garden,
Hours: 8am-2pm
Fee: Free
Tucson Botanical Gardens *(See Arizona Guide to Gardens.)*

June
❧ Night-Blooming Cereus & Plant Sale
A once-a-year event timed to the blooming of the cereus. Includes a sale of night-blooming plants, music and refreshments. Call for exact date.
Fee: Free
Tohono Chul Park *(See Arizona Guide to Gardens.)*

Late June-Early July
❧ Tohono O'odham Saguaro Harvest

A chance to gather saguaro fruits on the Museum's private off-site property in the traditional O'odham Indian manner. Call for exact date.
For information: **Arizona-Sonora Desert Museum** *(See Arizona Guide to Gardens.)*

October 2, 3
❧ Fall Plant Sale
Arid-adapted plants for sale, plus mini-lectures and workshops. Held in the Greenhouse parking lot.
Hours: 9am-4pm Sat; 10am-4pm Sun
Fee: Free
Tohono Chul Park *(See Arizona Guide to Gardens.)*

October 23, 24
❧ La Fiesta de los Chiles
An annual celebration of the chili pepper, with everything chili for sale: plants, fresh roasted chilies, ristras, salsas, jewelry, clothing, crafts and cuisine.
Hours: 10am-5pm
Fee: $3 in advance; $5 at gate
Tucson Botanical Gardens *(See Arizona Guide to Gardens.)*

December 3-5
❧ Luminaria Nights
An annual celebration with luminarias on the Garden paths and lights filling the trees.
Hours: 5:30-8pm
Fee: $5
Tucson Botanical Gardens *(See Arizona Guide to Gardens.)*

Yuma

December 12
❧ Annual Christmas Open House
An annual celebration with a Victorian theme.
Hours: 10am-4pm
Fee: Free

Arizona Historical Society, 240 Madison Avenue, Yuma, AZ 85364
(520)782-1841 *Fax:* (520)783-0680

Arkansas

Eureka Springs Garden
Highway 62 West
Eureka Springs, AR
Mail: Route 6 PO Box 362, Eureka Springs, AR 72632
(501)253-9244 *Fax:* (501)253-9244
🌺 Eureka Springs Gardens is a spectacular display garden on 33 acres of developed grounds which include the meadow and hillsides surrounding Blue Spring. The Spring, with peak flows of 38 million gallons per day, is the largest in Northwest Arkansas. Paths and walkways throughout the garden are planted with bulbs, annuals, perennials, wildflowers and flowering trees and shrubs.
Hours: May-Oct 9am-6pm; Mar-Apr & Nov 9am-5pm
Fees: $6.45; $4 children

Garvan Woodland Gardens
Hot Springs, AR
Mail: University of Arkansas, 230 Memorial Hall, Fayetteville, AR 72701
(501)623-8101 *Fax:* (501)262-2711
🌺 Donated to the Landscape Architecture Program of the University of Arkansas in 1985, these Gardens began as 210 acres of beautiful, unspoiled forested land on Lake Hamilton, near Hot Springs. Forty acres were opened in 1990. In addition to the native forest, there is a Border of Old Roses, Camellia Trail, Japanese Maple Hill with Tree Peonies, Rock Garden, Conifer Border, Woodland Walk, White Oak Walkout, Daffodil Hill. Reservations must be made in advance.

Web: www.byers-soft.com/tcg/
Hours: 9am-4pm Mon-Sat by appointment
Fees: $6; $10 for boat transportation to Gardens

Little Rock

February 19-21
🌺 **1999 Arkansas Flower & Garden Show**
Features eight creative demonstration gardens, nationally-known speakers, a major flower show of the Arkansas Federation of Garden Clubs and 75 booths exhibiting garden related products. Includes seminars and children's programs.
Hours: 9am-6pm; 10am-5pm Sun
Fee: $5; $3 seniors; $1 children 6-12; under 6 free
State House Convention Center, Markham & Main Street, Little Rock, AR 72201
(800)459-SHOW

Mountain View
120 miles from Little Rock

May 7, 8
🌺 **11th Annual Heritage Herb Spring Extravaganza**
A two-day seminar with nationally known specialists, plus a sale of herb plants, seeds and products.
Hours: 9am-5pm
Fee: $70 for two-day seminar, all inclusive
Ozark Folk Center State Park, Mountain View, AR
(870)269-3851 *Fax:* (870)269-2909

May 28-June 5
🌺 **Garden Glory Days**
Garden tours of the Heritage Herb Gardens, plus brief seminars on herb and organic gar-

dening topics and musical herb teas on Friday afternoon.
Hours: 10am-5pm; seminars in the garden at 11am & 3pm
Fee: $7.50
Ozark Folk Center State Park, Mountain View, AR
(870)269-3851 *Fax:* (870)269-2909

October 1, 2
⚜ Herb Harvest Fall Festival
Lectures and seminars, tours of the gardens and sale of crafts and products.
Hours: 9am-5pm
Fee: $70 for seminar
Ozark Folk Center State Park, Mountain View, AR
(870)269-3851 *Fax:* (870)269-2909

California

Guide to Gardens

Arboretum of Los Angeles County
301 North Baldwin Avenue
Arcadia, CA 91007
Email: contact-arboretum@arboretum.org
(626)447-8207 *Fax:* (626)447-3763
⚜ The Arboretum of Los Angeles County is a 127-acre horticultural and botanical museum, located in Los Angeles County in the San Gabriel Valley on the site of an original Rancho. It is known for its Tropical Forest, Tropical Greenhouse, Victorian Rose Garden, early California historical section and educational programs.
Hours: 9am-5pm
Fees: $5; $3 seniors and students; $1 children

Balboa Park & San Diego Botanical Garden
San Diego, CA

Mail: Visitors Center, 1549 El Prado, San Diego, CA 92101
(619)239-0512
⚜ Balboa Park is one of the unique urban parks in America, consisting of many different gardens and planted areas, in addition to museums and the San Diego Zoo, all managed and maintained by the City of San Diego. The Gardens include the Alcazar, the Desert Garden, Japanese Friendship Garden, Marston House garden, Palm Canyon, Rose Garden, San Diego Zoo Botanical Collection and the Zoro Garden for butterflies. There are free guided walking tours every Saturday.
Web: www.balboapark.org

Davis Arboretum
University of California
Davis, CA 95616
Email: arboretum@ucdavis.edu
(530)752-4880 *Fax:* (530)752-5796
⚜ The 100-acre Arboretum contains special collections of native plants from California, Australia and the Mediterranean. Features include eucalyptus, acacia, pine, cypress, as well as an oak grove, redwood grove, and perennial garden. The Arboretum specializes in drought-tolerant woody plants.
Web: arboretum.ucdavis.edu
Fees: Free

Descanso Gardens
1418 Descanso Drive
La Canada/Flintridge, CA 91011
(818)952-4401
⚜ Descanso Gardens is a 160-acre woodland garden famous for the largest camellia forest in North America. More than 60,000 camellia shrubs, some as tall as 20 feet, thrive in an oak forest. Descanso also offers a five-acre rose garden, lilacs, California native plants, masses of tulips and other spring-blooming plants and seasonal displays.

Web: www.descanso.com
Hours: 9am-4:30pm
Fees: $5; $3 seniors & youths; $1 children

Dunsmuir Botanical Gardens

Dunsmuir, CA
Mail: PO Box 636, Dunsmuir, CA 96025
(916)235-4740 *Fax:* (916)235-1974
🌺 The Dunsmuir Botanical Gardens, established in 1991, are located in the City Park. The City Park encompasses about ten acres of hilly, wooded acres bordering the Sacramento River. White dogwoods are prolific and showy in the spring. Unique to the area are Shasta lilies on the hillsides and the native azaleas along the river which can be viewed from the Park's walking trails.

The Elizabeth F. Gamble Garden Center

1431 Waverley Street
Palo Alto, CA 94301
(650)329-1356 *Fax:* (650)329-1688
🌺 The Gardens of the 2.3-acre estate, built in 1902 by Walter Hoff for Edwin Percy Gamble, display many turn-of-the-century features. In 1937, eleven years after her father's death, Elizabeth F. Gamble added the tea house and its surrounding gardens. Today the Gardens are divided into two parts: the formal gardens and the working gardens, used for experimental demonstrations and displays.
Web: www.mobot.org/AABGA/
Member.pages/elizgamble.gdnc
Hours: Daylight hours
Fees: Free

Filoli

86 Canada Road
Woodside, CA 94062
(650)364-8300 *Fax:* (650)366-7836
🌺 The garden at Filoli is a succession of garden rooms, designed by two well known native Californians, Bruce Porter and Isabella Worth.

It is arranged to take advantage of the natural surroundings and vistas, and blends formal and natural features. Filoli is a property of The National Trust for Historic Preservation. Tours of both the House and Garden are available.
Web: www.filoli.org
Hours: Mid Feb-early Nov 10am-2pm; closed Sun, Mon
Fees: $10; $1 children

Fullerton Arboretum

California State University, 1900 Associated Road
Fullerton, CA 92831
(714)278-3579 *Fax:* (714)278-7066
🌺 Since its opening in 1979, the 26-acre site has served as a resource for environmental, horticultural and historical education, and includes a selection of plants from around the world. A sale of plants propagated by the Potters, a volunteer support group, is held every Saturday and Sunday, except during August and September.
Web: arboretum.fullerton.edu
Directions: northeast corner of the California State University, Fullerton campus
Hours: 8am-4:45pm
Fees: Donation requested

Ganna Walska Lotusland

695 Ashley Road
Santa Barbara, CA 93108
(805)969-3767
🌺 This is a private garden, open by appointment only, designed by opera star Ganna Waleska. Unusual in concept and design, it contains large plantings of cacti, cycads and aloes, as well as a formal garden. Call for reservations.

Hakone Garden

21000 Big Basin Way
Saratoga, CA

Mail: PO Box 2324, Saratoga, CA 95070
(408)741-4994 *Fax:* (408)741-4993

🌷 This garden typifies the harmonious placement of plants, stones and water that are the essence of a Japanese garden. Each of the four gardens of Hakone represents a different style and perspective - the Hill and Pond Garden, the Tea Garden, the Zen Garden and Kizun-en or bamboo garden. Seasonal displays include flowering plums in January, flowering cherries in March, water lilies from May to September and more. Tea ceremonies take place the first Thursday of each month. Call for reservations.
Web: www.hakone.com
Hours: 10am-5pm Mon-Fri, 11am-5pm Sun
Fees: Free 1st Tues of month; admission fee at other times

Hortense Miller Garden
Laguna Beach, CA
Mail: PO Box 742, Laguna Beach, CA 92652
(949)494-6740

🌷 The 2.5-acre Garden is laid out on a 45 degree hillside and features a wildflower garden and footpaths.
Hours: Tues-Sat
Fees: Free

The Huntington Library, Art Collections & Botanical Gardens
1151 Oxford Road
San Marino, CA 91108
(626)405-2100 *Fax:* (626)449-1987

🌷 The 150-acre Botanical Gardens surrounding the Huntington Library and Museum contain more than 9,000 types of plants. The cacti and succulent specimens are among the best in the U.S. There are also excellent collections of cycads, palms, conifers and Australian plants. Special gardens include rose, Japanese, Shakespeare, herb and desert gardens.
Web: www.huntington.org

Fees: $8.50; $7 senior; $5 student

The Living Desert
47-900 Portola Avenue
Palm Desert, CA 92260
(760)346-5694

🌷 This 1200-acre desert preserve represents ten North American deserts and an African garden, and includes 400 animals representing 130 species.
Hours: 9am-5pm; closed August
Fees: $7.50; $6.50 seniors; $3.50 children

Luther Burbank Home & Gardens
Santa Rosa Avenue at Sonoma Avenue
Santa Rosa, CA 95402
(707)524-5445 *Fax:* (707)543-3030

🌷 The famed horticulturist, Luther Burbank, made his home in Santa Rosa for more than fifty years. This 1.6-acre Garden was dedicated as a memorial park by his widow. It is a tranquil area with formal gardens as well as cacti and succulents, and a greenhouse.
Web: aabga.mobot.org/AABGA/
Member.pages/Burbank/lbhg.html
Hours: Gardens open every day, all day;
Home, Greenhouse & Carriage House
Museum Apr-Oct Tues-Sun 10am-4pm
Fees: Gardens are free; tours $3

M. Young Botanic Garden
14178 West Kearney
Kerman, CA 93630
(209)846-7881 *Fax:* (209)846-9567

🌷 The 2.5-acre Garden specializes in shrubs from Australia, the Mediterranean, and southwest United States.
Hours: 9am-5pm Tues-Sun
Fees: Free

Mendocino Coast Botanical Gardens
18220 North Highway One
Fort Bragg, CA 95437

(707)964-4352 *Fax:* (707)964-4352
🌿 A 47-acre site by the sea with two miles of trails leading to the Pacific Coast and spectacular views, these Gardens include a formal Perennial Garden, many plantings of species and hybrid rhododendrons, plus collections of heather, succulents, ivies, fuchsia, dwarf conifers, heritage roses, dahlias and camellia. The property is sheltered by native coastal pine forests and planted groves of eucalyptus and Monterey cypress.
Hours: summer 9am-5pm; winter 9am-4pm
Fees: $6; $4 seniors & students

Mission San Juan Capistrano Gardens
San Juan Capistrano, CA
Mail: PO Box 697, San Juan Capistrano, CA 92693
(949)443-2060 *Fax:* (949)240-8091
🌿 The Gardens feature century-old pepper trees, Moorish fountains, cobbled pathways, bougainvillea, bird of paradise, rose gardens, hollyhocks, native herbs and more. The arched adobe structures of the Mission are the backdrop for this ten-acre garden containing 150 plant species from 50 countries.
Web: www.missionsjc.com
Hours: 8:30am-5pm; closed Thanksgiving, Christmas & Good Friday
Fees: $5; $4 children & seniors

Moorten Botanical Garden
1701 South Palm Canyon Drive
Palm Springs, CA 92262
(760)327-6555
🌿 The Garden has a special exhibition, the "World's First Cactarium," for close-up study of rare plants and insects.
Hours: 9am-4:30pm Mon-Sat, 10am-4pm Sun
Fees: $2; Children $.75

Mourning Cloak Ranch & Botanical Gardens
22101 Old Town Road
Tehachapi, CA 93561
Email: mcranch@lightspeed.com
(805)822-1661
🌿 The Mourning Cloak Ranch is so-named because of the abundance of Mourning Cloak butterflies that make it their home. Originally a rural ranch, this site of approximately 30 acres has been developed into an unusual garden, 4,000 feet above sea level in a mountain pass separating the Mojave Desert from the San Joaquin Valley. Because of its unique growing conditions, plant breeders and horticulturists use Mourning Cloak to test plants for cold hardiness.
Hours: May-Oct 9am-4pm by appointment

Oakland Museum & Gardens
1000 Oak Street
Oakland, CA 94607
(510)238-2200 or (888)625-6873 *Fax:* (510)238-2258
🌿 The Gardens of the Oakland Museum of California were a joint effort of the Museum's architect, Kevin Roche, the landscape designer Dan Kiley, and the late Geraldine Knight Scott, a Berkeley landscape architect. The design of the 7.5-acre site took advantage of the large cedars and redwoods already in place. Currently the Gardens provide a welcome refuge from city streets, with a screen of tall trees at the perimeter, smaller trees marking the elevations within the complex, and shrubs, flowering vines and perennials providing splashes of color.
Web: www.museumca.org

Oakland Municipal Park
Linda Vista Park
700 Jeanne Street
Oakland, CA 94612

Mail: 1520 Lakeside Drive, Oakland, CA 94612
(510)238-6643
This is the home of the Morcom Amphitheatre of Roses, Oakland's municipal rose garden. Recently refurbished, this historic garden typifies classic Edwardian design using many old cultivars, including roses from the hybrid teas of 1867, as well as modern plantings.

Quail Botanical Gardens
230 Quail Gardens Drive
Encinitas, CA
Mail: PO Box 230005, Encinitas, CA 92024
(760)436-3036 *Fax:* (760)632-0917
A world class collection of diverse and important plants, Quail Botanical Gardens includes California native plants, exotic tropicals, palms, bamboo and other unusual plant collections on 30 acres with scenic walks and trails.
Hours: 9am-5pm
Fees: $5; $4 seniors; $2 children 5-12

Rancho Los Alamitos
6400 Bixby Hill Road
Long Beach, CA 90815
(562)431-3541 *Fax:* (562)430-9694
Rancho Los Alamitos is a nationally recognized 7.5-acre historic site comprising a ranch house, four acres of historic gardens and five early twentieth-century agricultural structures. The site reflects almost every era of Southern California history. The gardens were designed in the 1920s and 1930s and include areas by the Olmsted Brothers and Florence Yoch.
Hours: 1-5pm Wed-Sun except holidays

Rancho Santa Ana Botanic Garden
1500 North College Avenue
Claremont, CA 91711
(909)625-8767 *Fax:* (909)626-7670
Located at an elevation of 1350 feet on the out-wash plain of the San Gabriel Mountains, this 86-acre Garden is laid out in three distinct areas. Indian Hill Mesa contains mature cultivars and wild species of California native plants, most prominently California Wild Lilacs and Manzanitas. This area also includes Riparian Woodland, Cultivar Garden, Basketry, and Oak Woodland Trails. The East Alluvial Gardens area includes the Desert Garden, Coastal Dune and California Channel Islands collections. The Plant Communities area displays some of the most impressive specimens of the entire collection, including the rare and endangered Crucifixion Thorn.
Web: www.cgs.edu/inst/rsa/
Hours: 8am-5pm
Fees: $2 per person, $5 per family suggested donation

Regional Parks Botanic Garden
Foot of South Park Drive & Wildcat Canyon Road
Berkeley, CA 94708
(510)841-8732 *Fax:* (510)848-6025
Within this large Park is a 7-acre arboretum of California plants. divided into special sections of dune, sea bluff, meadow, alpine and more Included are notable examples of Santa Cruz ironwood, California Nutmeg, Giant Sequoia, Redwood and wildflowers. The plantings are arranged by region, with paths leading from "Oregon" down to "Mexico." Every Saturday and Sunday guided tours are offered through the Garden's different regions.
Hours: 8:30am-5pm
Fees: Free

Regional Parks Botanical Garden
Tilden Park
Berkeley Hills, CA
Mail: 2950 Peralta Oaks Court, Oakland, CA 94605
(510)841-8732 *Fax:* (510)848-6025

The Garden emphasizes California native plants in a natural setting.
Directions: corner South Park Drive & Wildcat Canyon Road
Hours: 8:30am-5pm
Fees: Free

The Ruth Bancroft Garden

1815D Ygnacio Valley Road
Walnut Creek, CA
Mail: PO Box 30845, Walnut Creek, CA 94598
(925)210-9663 *Fax:* (925)944-9359
This private Garden thrives with minimal irrigation. African and Mexican succulents, New World cacti, Australian and Chilean trees, shrubs from California all grow side-by-side in the summer-dry Mediterranean climate of Walnut Creek. This is the first garden to be sponsored by The Garden Conservancy and can be seen by reservation only. Call for information and reservations.
Web: www.ruthbancroftgarden.org

San Luis Obispo Botanical Garden

Highway 1, El Chorro Regional Park
San Luis Obispo, CA
Mail: PO Box 4957, San Luis Obispo, CA 93403
(805)546-3501 *Fax:* (805)489-2575
The San Luis Obispo Botanical Garden is planned for a 150-acre site in El Chorro Regional Park. Today the Garden offers a one-acre preview of what's to come. On the second Saturday of every month, April to November, the Garden offers special events.
Web: www.fix.net/~cdills/slogarden/
Hours: 8am-dusk
Fees: Free

San Mateo Arboretum

San Mateo, CA
Mail: 101 9th Avenue, San Mateo, CA 94401

(650)347-7630
This is a 26-acre garden with Rose Garden, trees, shrubs, Japanese Garden and Greenhouse.
Directions: Between 5th & 9th Avenues near El Camino Road
Hours: 10am-3pm Tues, Thurs, Sat
Fees: Free

Santa Barbara Botanic Garden

1212 Mission Canyon Road
Santa Barbara, CA 93105
(805)682-4726 *Fax:* (805)563-0352
Located on 65 acres in the foothills just above the city, the Garden features over 1000 species of rare and indigenous California plants. It has meadows and canyons, a Redwood Forest and sweeping views of the Channel Islands.
Web: www.sbbg.org
Hours: 9am-5pm
Fees: $3; $2 seniors & students; $1 children; under 5 free

Sherman Library & Garden

2647 East Coast Highway
Corona del Mar, CA 92625
(949)673-2261 *Fax:* (949)675-5458
The Garden consists of a Tropical Conservatory, Rose Garden, Cactus Garden, Touch and Smell Garden, and fountains.
Hours: 10:30am-4pm
Fees: $3; free on Mon

Soka University Botanical Research Center

26800 West Mulholland Highway
Calabasas, CA 91302
(818)878-3703 *Fax:* (818)878-3795
The John and Julianna Hensley Demonstration gardens are dedicated to plants of the Santa Monica Mountains. Garden tours are given on the first Tuesday of the month.

Hours: 9am-5pm
Fees: Free

South Coast Botanic Garden
26300 Crenshaw Boulevard
Palos Verdes Peninsula, CA 90274
(310)544-1948 *Fax:* (310)544-1670
� The 87-acre Garden was developed from a landfill in 1960. It emphasizes native California species as well as Mediterranean and coastal plants. There is a large collection of roses, myrtles, proteas, flowering fruit trees and pines.
Fees: $5; $3 seniors & youths; $1 children

Strybing Arboretum & Botanical Gardens
Golden Gate Park, 9th Avenue & Lincoln Way
San Francisco, CA 94122
(415)661-1316 ext 354 *Fax:* (415)661-7427
🌲 Strybing Arboretum, located in Golden Gate Park, comprises 70 acres of what was once sand barrens, now transformed into various micro climates with many specimen trees. Collections of note are Malaysian Rhododendrons, Australian and New Zealand plants, echeverias, succulents, proteas crabapples, magnolias, among others. Special gardens include a Shakespeare garden, opera, Bible, rose, rock, native flora, Redwood, fragrance garden for the blind.
Web: aabga.mobot.org/AABGA/
Member.pages/strybing/

Theodore Payne Foundation for Wildflowers & Native Plants
10459 Tuxford Street
Sun Valley, CA 91352
Email: TheodorePayne@Juno.com
(818)768-1802; Hotline 24-hr
(818)768-3533
🌲 The Theodore Payne Foundation is committed to encouraging Californians to grow native plants in order to preserve and conserve the native wildflowers and landscape. Features include Flowerhill Trail which winds through acres of chaparral and wildflowers, and the Demonstration Garden which exhibits water-conserving plants and landscaping. The Plant Nursery offers a wide range of California native plants and seeds for sale. The Foundation maintains a Wildflower Hotline with a recorded message, updated weekly, on the best places to see wildflowers in California.
Directions: 3 miles from Burbank
Hours: 8:30am-4:30pm Wed-Sun
Fees: Free

Turtle Bay Museums & Arboretum on the River
800 Auditorium Drive
Redding, CA 96001
(530)243-8850 *Fax:* (530)243-8898
🌲 Turtle Bay is being developed as a major cultural and scientific center focusing on the Sacramento River watershed. The facilities to date include the Redding Arboretum by the River, Paul Bunyan Forest Camp. Redding Museum of Arts and History, Carter House Natural Science Museums - all located in downtown Redding at the hub of the Shasta Cascade region. The Arboretum includes 200 acres of beautiful oak savanna and wetlands, teeming with birds and wildlife. This is some of the last remaining riparian forest on the Sacramento River.
Web: www.turtlebay.org
Hours: Dawn to dusk
Fees: $2; $1 children (includes all Turtle Bay sites)

UC Berkeley Botanical Garden
200 Centennial Drive
Berkeley, CA 94720
(510)643-2755 *Fax:* (510)642-5045
🌲 The University of California's Botanical Garden displays over 13,000 types of plants

in 34 acres - most of wild origin. The Garden claims to have the largest collection of plants of any university garden in the country. For over a century, the Garden has been an important horticultural and botanical resource.
Web: www.mip.berkeley.edu/garden/
Hours: 9am-4:45pm; 9am-7pm Memorial Day-Labor Day
Fees: $3; $2 seniors; $1 children

UC Riverside Botanic Gardens
University of California
Riverside, CA 92521
(909)787-4650 *Fax:* (909)787-4437
🌱 The UCR Botanic Gardens are nestled in the Box Springs Mountains and cover nearly 40 hilly acres. There are over four miles of scenic trails and specially cultivated sites. Highlights include the Cactus and Succulent Gardens, the Iris Garden, Rose Garden, Geodesic Lath Dome housing a collection of cycads and palms, and Alder Canyon, filled with azaleas, camellia, ferns and buddleias.
Web: cnas.ucr.edu/~cnas/facilities/botanic.html
Hours: 8am-5pm
Fees: Free

Virginia Robinson Garden
1008 Elden Way
Beverly Hills, CA 90210
(310)276-5367 *Fax:* (310)276-5352
🌱 Set on a hillside, this Garden of 6.2 acres features terraced Italian gardens, a 2-acre palm grove, formal gardens and a rose garden. It is on the Register of Historic sites.
Hours: Tours 10am Tues-Fri, 1pm Tues-Thurs
Fees: $7; $4 seniros & students

Wrigley Memorial & Botanical Garden
1400 Avalon Canyon Road
Avalon, CA

Mail: PO Box 2739, Avalon, CA 90704
(310)510-2288
🌱 The 3-acre Garden is on a 35-acre site with many plants found only on Catalina and the other Channel Islands.
Hours: 8am-5pm

Selected Events

Anaheim

August 14-22
🌱 **Southern California Home & Garden Show**
A large show with theme gardens, a flower mart, garden festival, flower arrangements, merchandise for sale, antiques, pet pavilion and more.
Hours: noon-9pm Mon-Fri; 10am-9pm Sat; 10am-6pm Sun
Fee: $6.50; $5 seniors; $3 children
Anaheim Convention Center, Anaheim, CA
For information: **Southern California Home & Garden Show**, 2099 South State College Blvd, #410, Anaheim, CA 92806
Web: www.southex.com
(714)978-8888

Arroyo Grande
Halfway between San Francisco & Los Angeles

March 6, 7
🌱 **4th Annual Central Coast Orchid Show & Sale**
Orchid Rodeo. A judged show of the American Orchid Society. Includes a large sales area with vendors from across the Central Coast region, orchid culture demonstrations and experts to answer questions.
Hours: 9am-6pm Sat; 10am-5pm Sun
Fee: $15 in advance; $20 at door
South County Regional Center, 800 West Branch, Arroyo Grande, CA

For information: **Five Cities Orchid Society**, 1101 Ramona Avenue, Grover Beach, CA 93433
Email: duba@fix.net
(805)929-1791 Fax: (805)929-6682

Berkeley
San Francisco area

April 17
⚘ Annual Plant Sale
Native California plants, many not readily available elsewhere, at very reasonable prices.
Hours: 10am-3pm
Fee: Free
Regional Parks Botanic Garden (See California Guide to Gardens.)

April 24
⚘ Spring Plant Sale
Hundreds of plants from the Garden's collections, many not available elsewhere.
Hours: 10am-2pm
Fee: Free
UC Berkeley Botanical Garden (See California Guide to Gardens.)

September 25-October 17
⚘ Foods of the Americas
A Mesoamerican marketplace, focusing on the crops that originated in the Americas. Displays of growing specimens in the Crops of the World Garden, Tropical House and Cloud Forest.
Hours: 10am-4pm
Fee: Admission $3; $2 seniors; $1 children
UC Berkeley Botanical Garden (See California Guide to Gardens.)

September 26
⚘ Fall Plant Sale
Hundreds of plants from the Garden's collections, many not available elsewhere.
Hours: 10am-2pm
Fee: Free

UC Berkeley Botanical Garden (See California Guide to Gardens.)

Carmel

April 30, May 1, 2
⚘ Carmel Garden Show
Demonstration gardens from area landscape designers, seminars and workshops, a garden marketplace, floral and Ikeban designs, and a garden tour of three exceptional gardens in the Carmel Valley.
Hours: 10am-5pm Fri, Sat; 10am-4pm Sun
Fee: $18 in advance; $20 at door
Quail Lodge Resort, Carmel, CA
(831)625-6026

Claremont

March 7
⚘ Arbor Day Celebration
A celebration of California trees, with activity stations, information and tours.
Hours: 1-4pm
Fee: Free
Rancho Santa Ana Botanic Garden (See California Guide to Gardens.)

March 13-May 16
⚘ Wildflower Walks
Guided tours through the wildflower beds on Saturday and Sunday afternoons.
Hours: 2pm
Rancho Santa Ana Botanic Garden (See California Guide to Gardens.)

April 3, 4
⚘ Wildflower Show
A display of approximately 20 species of wildflowers from the Garden and local field regions. All specimens identified and labeled.
Hours: 10am-4pm
Fee: $2 per person, $5 per family suggested donation

Rancho Santa Ana Botanic Garden *(See California Guide to Gardens.)*

November 7, 8
🌱 21st Annual Plant Sale
Over 10,000 native and drought-tolerant plants, plus wildflower seeds and spring bulbs for sale, along with books, gifts and refreshments. Gardening experts on hand.
Hours: 11am-4pm Sat; 9am-1pm Sun
Fee: Free
Rancho Santa Ana Botanic Garden *(See California Guide to Gardens.)*

Coronado
5 miles from San Diego

April 17, 16
🌱 74th Annual Flower Show
Exhibits in horticulture and floral design, flower arrangements, miniatures, table arrangements, a youth section, various plant categories, educational programs and more. Sponsored by the Coronado Floral Association and the City of Coronado.
Hours: 1-5:30pm Sat; 10am-4pm Sun
Fee: $2; $1 children over 12
Spreckles Park, Coronado, CA
For information: **Coronado Floral Association**, PO Box 180188, Coronado, CA 92178

Costa Mesa
South of Long Beach

February 4-7
🌱 Fascination of Orchids International Show & Sale
A large regional show for all orchid and flower lovers, now in its 19th year.
Hours: 10am-9pm Thurs, Fri; 10am-7pm Sat, Sun
Fee: Admission

South Coast Plaza Crystal Court, 3333 Bear Street, Costa Mesa, CA
For information: **Orange County Cymbidium Society of America**, 21052 Cocobana Lane, Huntington Beach, CA 92646
Web: members.tripod.com\orchidsociety\
Email: orchidsociety@tripod.net
(714)962 8165 *Fax:* (714)964 3265

Davis

October 2
🌱 Plant Faire
A Sale of Uncommon Plants. More than 1000 varieties of garden plants, including many not available in nurseries, plus California native plants. Includes live music, refreshments and more. Held at Arboretum Headquarters, LaRue Road. Sponsored by Friends of the Davis Arboretum.
Hours: 8am-2pm
Fee: Free
Davis Arboretum *(See California Guide to Gardens.)*

El Cerrito
San Francisco area

May 16
🌱 Celebration of Old Roses
An annual event featuring hundreds of roses, old, modern and miniature, on display and for sale. Includes rose memorabilia, garden books, wreathes and bouquets, other perennials, food, and anything rose-related plus classes and a slide show. Lunch available.
Hours: 11am-4:30pm
Fee: Free
El Cerrito Community Center, Moeser Lane & Ashbury Avenue, El Cerrito, CA
For information: **Heritage Rose Group**, 925 Galvin Drive, El Cerrito, CA 94530
(510)526-6960

Encinitas

October
⚜ Basket Makers' Weekend
Workshops, demonstrations, an art exhibit, tours of the Gardens, and baskets, gourds and craft supplies for sale. Call for exact dates.
Hours: 9am-4pm
Fee: Charged for some classes
Quail Botanical Gardens *(See California Guide to Gardens.)*

October
⚜ Annual Plant Sale
A large selection of drought-tolerant plants, including some rare and unusual plants propagated from the Quail collection. Also for sale are dried plant material, books, home baked goods. Seminars and demonstrations.
Hours: 9am-3:30pm
Fee: Free
Quail Botanical Gardens *(See California Guide to Gardens.)*

Eureka

June 13
⚜ Annual Garden Tour
Call for information.
Hours: 9am-4pm
Fee: $10
For information: **Humboldt Botanical Gardens** *(See California Guide to Gardens.)*

Fort Bragg

Mid April
⚜ Annual Spring Plant Sale
Call for exact date.
Hours: 9am-5pm
Mendocino Coast Botanical Gardens *(See California Guide to Gardens.)*

Fullerton
60 miles from Los Angeles

April 24 25
⚜ Green Scene Garden Show
Over 90 exhibitors selling garden products and specialty plants, plus education exhibits, speakers, floral displays and children's garden activities.
Hours: 9am-4pm Sat; 10am-4pm Sun
Fee: $5; children under 18 free
Fullerton Arboretum *(See California Guide to Gardens.)*

June 5, 6
⚜ Orange County Herb Faire
An herbal celebration with over 30 herb and craft exhibitors, herb speakers, culinary competition, music, garden cuisine and lavender lemonade.
Hours: 10am-4pm
Fee: $5; children under 18 free
Fullerton Arboretum *(See California Guide to Gardens.)*

October 9, 10
⚜ Arborfest
Activities for the whole family, including apple pressing, butter making, children's crafts and plant and craft exhibits.
Hours: 10am-4pm
Fee: $5; children under 18 free
Fullerton Arboretum *(See California Guide to Gardens.)*

December 1-12
⚜ Victorian Christmas Tour
Weekday group tours through the Eastlake-style Heritage House by reservation. Candlelight tours, carriage rides, carolers and refreshments on December 4 and 5, at 5pm and 6pm. Call for weekday reservations: (714)278-3579. For candlelight evening reservations call (714)278-4792.

Fee: Weekday tours $2, $1 children; Candlelight evenings $15
Fullerton Arboretum *(See California Guide to Gardens.)*

Glendale
Los Angeles area

January 9, 10
✿ Glendale Rose Pruning & Garden Show
More than 60 vendors, popular speakers, seminars and participation by local societies. Sponsored by Glendale Parks and Recreation, Glendale Beautiful and The Pacific Rose Society and now in its 26th year.
Hours: 10am-5pm
Fee: $3
Glendale Civic Auditorium, 1401 North Verdugo Road, Glendale, CA
For information: **Glendale Beautiful**, PO Box 313, Glendale, CA 91203
(818)241-8040

La Cañada/Flintridge
Los Angeles area

January 16, 17 & 30, 31
✿ Camellia Shows
Hundreds of camellia blooms on display, advice from experts, plants for sale and guided tours through the famous camellia forest in Descanso. Sponsored by the Pacific Camellia Society (January 16,17) and the Southern California Camellia Council (January 30,31).
Hours: 1-4:30pm Sat; 9am-4:30pm Sun
Descanso Gardens *(See California Guide to Gardens.)*

April 9, 10
✿ Spring Plant Sale
A sale of thousands of plants, including lilacs, roses, perennials, irises, scented geraniums, cacti and succulents, trees and shrubs. Held in the Lake House Nursery at the Gardens.
Hours: 9am-4pm
Fee: Free
Descanso Gardens *(See California Guide to Gardens.)*

April 17, 18
✿ Garden Festival
A sale on the Main Lawn with many vendors. Horticultural society members on hand to give advice and answer questions.
Hours: 9am-4pm
Descanso Gardens *(See California Guide to Gardens.)*

May 1, 2
✿ Rose Festival
An old-fashioned fair with musicians, jugglers and magicians. Roses and rose-related items for sale.
Hours: 9am-4pm
Descanso Gardens *(See California Guide to Gardens.)*

October 16, 17
✿ Los Angeles Rose Society Show
Features thousands of rose blooms, arrangements and special displays.
Hours: 1-4pm Sat; 9am-4:30pm Sun
Descanso Gardens *(See California Guide to Gardens.)*

December 4-12
✿ Annual Christmas Celebration
A family event which includes a crafts sale, decorated Christmas trees, holiday entertainment and visits with Santa.
Hours: 10am-4pm daily
Descanso Gardens *(See California Guide to Gardens.)*

Lompoc

June 23-27
⚘ Lompoc Flower Festival
A five-day festival in the flower seed-producing Lompoc Valley, featuring self-guided tours of the more than 800 acres of flower fields, a flower show, and exhibits of the flower seed industry.
Hours: Noon-8pm
Fee: Free
Ryon Park, 800 West Ocean Avenue, Lompoc, CA
For information: **Lompoc Valley Festival Association**, 113 North I Street, PO Box 505, Lompoc, CA 93438
(805)735-8511

Los Angeles
See also Fullerton, Glendale, La Cañada/ Flintridge, Palos Verdes, Pasadena, San Marino

April 11
⚘ 40th Annual Garden Tour
A self-guided tour of five residential gardens in Santa Monica and West Los Angeles, plus a garden boutique and tea. Maps and tickets can be purchased in advance or on the day of the tour at any of the gardens. Benefits the Children's Hospital of Los Angeles.
Hours: 11am-4pm
Fee: $20
For information: **Santa Monica Bay Auxiliary**, 736 Claymont Drive, Los Angeles, CA 90049
(310)472-7762
Web www.childrenshospitalia.org/associates.html

October 7-10
⚘ 1999 Los Angeles Garden Show
Gardens for the New Millennium. More than 10 acres of designer gardens, a Plant Market, Marketplace, Cooking Pavilion, demonstrations and more.

Hours: 9am-7pm
Fee: $10
Arboretum of Los Angeles County *(See California Guide to Gardens.)*

Mill Valley
20 miles from San Francisco

May 1-9
⚘ 9th Annual Mt.Tamalpais Wildflower & Garden Festival
A week of lectures, hikes through the trails of Mt. Tamalpais, a walk through the garden of a noted rosarian and more. Benefits Mt. Tamalpais State Park and sponsored by the Mountain Home Inn.
For information: **Mt. Tamalpais Wildflower & Garden Festival**, 850 Chamberlain Court, Mill Valley, CA 94941
(415)388-3503 *Fax:* (415)956-2599

Oakland
San Francisco area

May 8, 9
⚘ 30th Annual California Wildflower Show
A profusion of native flowers gathered in the field and sorted and identified by botanists. Sponsored by the Museum, the California Native Plant Society, the University of California, Berkeley, and Jepson Herbarium.
Hours: 10am-5pm Sat; noon-5pm Sun
Fee: $6; $4 seniors & students
Oakland Museum & Gardens *(See California Guide to Gardens.)*

Pacific Grove
2 miles from Monterey

April 16-18
⚘ 38th Annual Wildflower Show
600 species and varieties of native wildflowers from Monterey County and the immediate vicinity, featuring rare and endangered species and

information on all specimens. Billed as the oldest and largest show of its kind in California.

Hours: 10am-5pm

Fee: $1 suggested donation

Pacific Grove Museum of Natural History, 165 Forest Avenue, Pacific Grove, CA 93950

Email: prmuseum@mbay.net

(831)648-3116 *Fax:* (831)372-3256

Palo Alto
San Francisco area

April 30, May 1
✿ Palo Alto Spring Gardens Tour

A tour of six outstanding private gardens plus the historic Gamble property. Lunch available.

Hours: 10am-4pm

Fee: $20 in advance; $23 at door; $15 lunch

For information: **The Elizabeth F. Gamble Garden Center** (*See California Guide to Gardens.*)

Palos Verdes
Los Angeles area

October 3
✿ 9th Annual Fall Plant Sale

A sale sponsored by the Garden Foundation.

Hours: 9am-4pm

South Coast Botanic Garden (*See California Guide to Gardens.*)

Pasadena
12 miles from Los Angeles

March 28
✿ Luxurious Living Home Tour

Guided tours of architecturally significant homes, from the early 1900s, and their gardens. Hosted by and benefits Pasadena Heritage.

Fee: $20

For information: **Pasadena Heritage**, 80 West Dayton Street, Pasadena, CA 91105

(626)441-6333

November 12-14
✿ Craftsman Weekend

Lectures, exhibits and a house and garden tour focusing on the Arts and Crafts period.

For information: **Pasadena Heritage**, 80 West Dayton Street, Pasadena, CA 91105

(626)441-6333

Petaluma
San Francisco area

May 22
✿ Through the Garden Gate Tour

Tour of ten private gardens in the Victorian town of Petaluma encompassing the variety of plant life supported in this wine country. Benefits the Petaluma Historical Museum.

Hours: 10am-4pm

Fee: $15

For information: **Petaluma Historical Museum**, 20 4th Street, Petaluma, CA 94952

(707)778-4398 *Fax:* (707)762-3923

Redding

April 3
✿ Redbud Festival

Call for information.

Turtle Bay Museums & Arboretum on the River (*See California Guide to Gardens.*)

April 24
✿ Annual Plant Sale

Call for information.

Turtle Bay Museums & Arboretum on the River (*See California Guide to Gardens.*)

Ripon
Near Stockton

February 26-28
✿ Almond Blossom Festival

At the height of the almond blossom bloom period, a festival with family and athletic events, displays, contests and more. Free

tours to nut growers, and an herb tour.
Hours: 10am-10pm
For information: **Ripon Chamber of Commerce**, 311 West First Street, PO Box 327, Ripon, CA 95366
(209)599-7519

Ross
San Francisco area

April 24, 25
✿ Spring Flower Festival
Sponsored by the Garden Society of Marin.
Fee: Free
For information: **Marin Art & Garden Center**, 30 Sir Francis Drake Blvd, PO Box 437, Ross, CA 94957
(415)454-5597

San Diego
See also Coronado

April 29-May 2
✿ Art Alive!
A kick-off to the city-wide *Buds 'n Bloom* celebration, a four-day exhibit of flowers and art, when the galleries are filled with floral displays created by professional designers and award-winning amateur exhibitors.
Hours: 11am-4:30pm Thurs; 9am-4:30pm Fri-Sun
Fee: $10; $8 seniors; $6 youth; $4 children
San Diego Museum of Art, Balboa Park, San Diego, CA
For information: **San Diego Museum of Art**, PO Box 122107, San Diego, CA 92112
(619)232-7931

Month of May
✿ Buds 'n Bloom
A major city-wide event featuring over 50,000 seasonal blooms throughout the Park, a major display of California wildflowers in Gold Gulch Canyon and the participation by more than 85

organizations, including museums, the Zoo and Balboa Park theater. Call for schedule.
For information: **Balboa Park** *(See California Guide to Gardens.)*

San Francisco
See also Berkeley, El Cerrito, Mill Valley, Oakland, Palo Alto, Petaluma, Ross, Santa Rosa, Walnut Creek

February 26, 27, 28
✿ 47th Pacific Orchid Exposition
A Symphony of Orchids. Over 100,000 orchids on display by individuals, societies and professional growers, symphonic music in the background, lectures and tours. Billed as the largest show of its kind on the West Coast.
Hours: 10am-6pm Fri; 9am-6pm Sat; 10am-5pm Sun
Fee: $10; $7 seniors & disabled
Fort Mason Center, Festival Pavillion, Marina Blvd at Buchanan, San Francisco, CA
For information: **San Francisco Orchid Society/Larose Group**, Hearst Building, Suite 707, San Francisco, CA 94103
Web: www.prmagic.com/orchid/
Email: larosegroup@prmagic.com
(415)546-9608

March 16-19
✿ "Bouquets to Art"
A display of floral arrangements which complement the art at the M.H. de Young Memorial Museum and the California Palace of the Legion of Honor. Lectures by internationally known speakers and luncheons available by reservation. Benefits the Fine Arts Museums of San Francisco
Hours: 9:30am-4:45pm; until 9pm Wed
Fee: $7; $5 senior; $4 youth; $25 lectures by reservation; lunch by reservation, fee charged
Held simultaneously at: **M.H. de Young Memorial Museum**, San Francisco, CA
and: **California Palace of the Legion of**

Honor, 100 34th Avenue, Lincoln Park, San Francisco, CA 94121
(415)750-3504

March 18-21
🌿 San Francisco Flower & Garden Show
25 show gardens created by some of the Bay Area's finest landscape architects and nurseries, more than 50 free seminars by well-known horticulturists, and 250 exhibitors in a large marketplace. A portion of the proceeds benefit the Friends of Recreation & Parks.
Fee: $10.50 in advance; $12.50 at door
The Cow Palace, San Francisco, CA
For information: **San Francisco Flower & Garden Show**, 26 South Park, San Francisco, CA 94107
Web: www.gardenshow.com
(800)829-9751 or (415)495-1769

March 20, 21
🌿 Annual Plant Sale
Rare and unusual plants, as well as many other plants for Bay Area gardening.
Hours: 10am-3pm
Fee: Free
Lakeside Park Garden Center, 66 Bellevue Avenue, Oakland, CA
For information: **California Horticultural Society**, c/o Academy of Sciences - Golden Gate Park, San Francisco, CA 94118
(415)566-5222

March-June
🌿 Bay Area & Wine Country Tours
Four tours of private gardens in the Bay Area and the Wine Country. For exact dates and more information, call (800)624-6633.
Strybing Arboretum & Botanical Gardens
(See California Guide to Gardens.)

April 24
🌿 Bamboo Festival & Sale
A sale and auction of rare and exotic bamboos, including some new introductions not available prior to this event. Included are clumping and running bamboos, giant bamboos, small decorative and variegated species, container bamboos.
Hours: Noon-2:30pm
Fee: Free
San Francisco County Fair Building, 9th Ave & Lincoln Way, San Francisco, CA
For information: **Northern California Chapter of the American Bamboo Society**, 480 West "I" Street, Benecia, CA 94510
Web: www.bamboo.org/abs/NoCalChapterinfo.html
(707)745-4091

June 5, 6
🌿 Open Garden Day
Over eighty community, school and urban market gardens throughout the Bay Area. Guided walking, bicycle or bus tour available or a map for self-guided tours.
Hours: 11am-4pm
Fee: Free
For information: **Center for Urban Education About Sustainable Agriculture**, 1417 Josephine Street, Berkeley, CA 94703
Web: www.igc.org/cuesa
(510)526-2788

San Juan Capistrano
South of Long Beach

June 12, 13
🌿 Annual Flower & Garden Festival
A family event featuring garden tours, lectures, demonstrations, a Children's Garden and food. Includes "Living History" characters from the Mission's 200 year history, an exhibit area with displays by over 60 vendors. Sponsored by the Gardening Angels Garden Club.
Hours: 8:30am-5:30pm
Fee: Admission $5; $4 children & seniors

Mission San Juan Capistrano Gardens *(See California Guide to Gardens.)*

San Luis Obispo

May 1, 2
�ును Annual Garden Festival

A landscape design competition, plant sale, speakers, arts and crafts booths, food, music and more.
Hours: 10am-4pm
Fee: $3
San Luis Obispo Botanical Garden *(See California Guide to Gardens.)*

October 9
🌸 Annual Fall Festival

A fall fruit and plant sale, pumpkin judging, speakers, arts and crafts booths, food, music and more.
Hours: 10am-4pm
Fee: $3
San Luis Obispo Botanical Garden *(See California Guide to Gardens.)*

San Marino

Los Angeles area, near Pasadena

February 13, 14
🌸 Camellia Show

Over 1000 blooms competing for honors. Sponsored by the Southern California Camellia Society.
Hours: 10:30am-4:30 pm
Fee: $8.50
The Huntington Library, Art Collections & Botanical Gardens *(See California Guide to Gardens.)*

March 27, 28
🌸 Bonsai Show

Over 100 specimens on display with demonstrations throughout the weekend. Sponsored by the California Bonsai Society, now in its

42nd year.
Hours: 10:30am-4:30pm
Fee: $8.50
The Huntington Library, Art Collections & Botanical Gardens *(See California Guide to Gardens.)*

April 16-25
🌸 Rose Festival

Tours, talks, demonstrations, plant sales and thousands of roses in the Gardens at the peak of their spring bloom.
Hours: noon-4:30pm weekdays; 10:30am-4:30pm Sat, Sun
Fee: $8.50
The Huntington Library, Art Collections & Botanical Gardens *(See California Guide to Gardens.)*

May 16
🌸 24th Annual Spring Plant Sale

The biggest event of the year at the Huntington, featuring thousands of plants propagated from the Garden's own collections.
Hours: 10am-4pm
Fee: Free
The Huntington Library, Art Collections & Botanical Gardens *(See California Guide to Gardens.)*

July 10, 11
🌸 Cactus & Succulent Society Show

The Cactus & Succulent Society of America's annual show and sale of hundreds of unusual specimens.
Hours: 10:30am-4:30pm
Fee: $8.50
The Huntington Library, Art Collections & Botanical Gardens *(See California Guide to Gardens.)*

November 11-14
🌸 Fall Plant Festival

Daily garden talks and an ongoing plant sale.
Hours: Sales noon-4:30pm weekdays;
10:30am-4:30pm Sat, Sun
Fee: $8.50
**The Huntington Library, Art Collections &
Botanical Gardens** *(See California Guide to
Gardens.)*

San Martin

30 miles south of San Jose

January-December
� Plant Sale
Sales on the first Friday of every month,
except holiday Fridays when its moved to the
second Friday. Benefits the Foundation.
Hours: 9am-3:30pm
Fee: Free
**Saratoga Horticultural Research
Foundation**, 15185 Murphy Avenue, San
Martin, CA 95046
(408)779-3303 *Fax:* (408)778-9259

San Simeon

April-October
🌿 Hearst Gardens, Grounds & Buildings Tour
Tour IV of the several given at Hearst Castle.
Covers nearly all of the estate's extensive gardens, terraces and walkways. Reservations
required.
Hours: 8:20am-3:20pm; longer in summer
Fee: $14; $8 youth 6-12
Hearst Castle, 750 Hearst Castle Road,
Highway 1, San Simeon, CA 93452
Web: www.hearstcastle.org
(800)444-4445

Santa Barbara

March 12-14
🌿 54th Annual Santa Barbara International Orchid Show
Romance of Orchids. Display and sale of thou-

sands of orchids by commercial and amateur
growers from as far away as the Pacific rim
and England. Coincides with open house at six
local nurseries, including Gallup & Stribling,
the world's largest grower of cymbidiums, and
Santa Barbara Estate, which specializes in
orchids that flourish outdoors. Billed as one of
the nation's largest and finest orchid shows.
Hours: 10am-5pm Fri; 9am-5pm Sat, Sun
Fee: $6; $5 seniors & students; $1 children
Earl Warren Showgrounds Exhibit Building,
101 & Las Positas Road, Santa Barbara, CA
For information: **Santa Barbara International
Orchid Show**, 1096 North Patterson Avenue,
Santa Barbara, CA 93111
Email: sborchid@aol.com
(805)967-6331

Santa Cruz

May 7-9
🌿 Cabrillo College Plant Sale & Spring Fair
20,000 plants representing 400-500 varieties, all grown by students in the Horticultural
Department. Foods, crafts and family activities. Benefits the College's vocational programs. Billed as the largest seasonal plant
sale on the Central Coast.
Hours: 9am-5pm Fri, Sat; 9am-noon Sun
Fee: Free
Cabrillo Community College , Football
Stadium, 6500 Soquel Drive, Aptos, CA 95003
(408)479-6241

Santa Rosa

North of San Francisco

June 26
🌿 Garden Exposition
A family-orientated day, with displays, educational programs, experts on hand and children's activities.
Hours: 10am-4pm

Fee: $5; children free
Luther Burbank Home & Gardens (See California Guide to Gardens.)

July 27-August 9
⚜ Sonoma County Fair & Exposition Flower Show
Participants include Northern California nurseries, florists, landscape architects, professional, amateur and junior gardeners. Part of the large county fair.
Hours: 10am-9pm
Fee: $5; $3 seniors; $2 children
Sonoma County Fairgrounds, 1350 Bennett Valley Road, Santa Rosa, CA 95402 (707)545-4200

December 4, 5
⚜ Holiday Open House
A turn-of-the-century celebration with holiday greenery, fruits and flowers throughout the Home and Greenhouse. Free refreshments.
Hours: 10am-4pm
Fee: Free
Luther Burbank Home & Gardens (See California Guide to Gardens.)

Sonora

May-June
⚜ Garden Tour
Six private gardens located in Tuolomne County in the Sierra foothills. Contact sponsor for exact date.
Hours: 11am-6pm
Fee: $5; $10 family
For information: **UCCE Master Gardeners**, 2 South Green Street, Sonora, CA 95370

Sun Valley
3 miles from Burbank

April 3
⚜ Poppy Day

Open House with tours of the garden, hikes through the trails and Wildflower Hill, plant sale and show. Call to confirm date.
For information: **Theodore Payne Foundation for Wildflowers & Native Plants** (See California Guide to Gardens.)

Tehachapi

August 29
⚜ St. Fiacre Day Dinner
A feast to honor the Patron Saint of gardeners in the form of a progressive dinner, with various courses served in different Mourning Cloak gardens. Reservations required.
Fee: $4; $6 lunch
Mourning Cloak Ranch & Botanical Gardens (See California Guide to Gardens.)

Upland
West of LA in the San Bernardino Mountains

May 1
⚜ Inland Valley HerbFest
A day filled with herbs, herb crafts and gardening with speakers, demonstrations and an herbal food contest. An annual event, now in its 3rd year.
Hours: 9am-4pm
Fee: Free
Highland Garden Center, 1885 North Campus Avenue, Upland, CA
For information: **Olde Thyme Gardens**, PO Box 1328, Upland, CA 91785
Email: herbs4u@gte.net
(909)318-5785 Fax: (909)579-0355

Walnut Creek
20 miles from San Francisco

January-March
⚜ Ruth Bancroft Winter Garden Tours
Tours of this private garden, not normally open to the public, on the first and third Saturdays of these months by reservation only.

Hours: 1pm
Fee: $5
The Ruth Bancroft Garden *(See California Guide to Gardens.)*

May 8
⚘ Open Day
One of the few days during the year when this private garden is open to the public.
Hours: 2-4pm
Fee: $4
The Ruth Bancroft Garden *(See California Guide to Gardens.)*

July17-October 16
⚘ Evening Tours
Guided tours of the Garden every Saturday during this time.
Hours: 6pm Sats only
Fee: $5
For information: **Ruth Bancroft Garden** *(See California Guide to Gardens.)*

October 16
⚘ Open Day & Iris Sale
One of the few days during the year when this private garden is open to the public. Includes a sale of bearded iris from Mrs. Bancroft's collection.
Hours: 2-4pm
Fee: $4
The Ruth Bancroft Garden *(See California Guide to Gardens.)*

November-December
⚘ Ruth Bancroft Winter Garden Tours
Tours of this private garden, not normally open to the public, on the first and third Saturdays of these months by reservation only.
Hours: 1pm
Fee: $5
The Ruth Bancroft Garden *(See California Guide to Gardens.)*

Colorado

Guide to Gardens

Betty Ford Alpine Garden
Ford Park, South Frontage Road
Vail, CO
Mail: Vail Alpine Garden Foundation, 183 Gore Creek Drive, Vail, CO 81658
(970)476-0103 *Fax:* (970)476-8702
⚘ This garden of one acre is the highest public garden in North America and a fine example of what can be grown in the mountains. More than 1,500 species bloom in the perennial garden. Special features include a collection of roses that do well in alpine settings, and the Meditation Garden featuring thymes and a mountain stream.
Web: www.vail.net/summer/garden/
Email: alpinegarden@vail.net
Hours: May-Sept Dawn-dusk
Fees: Free

Chatfield Arboretum
8500 Deer Creek Canyon Road
Littleton, CO 80120
(303)973-3705
⚘ The Aboretum of the Denver Botanic Garden, this site features trees and shrubs of the Rocky Mountains.

Denver Botanic Gardens
1005 York Street
Denver, CO
Mail: 909 York Street, Denver, CO 80206
(303)331-4000 *Fax:* (303)331-4013
⚘ The 23 acres of Denver Botanic Gardens provides an oasis in an urban setting. Features include the Rock Alpine, the Japanese, Water, Vegetable, Scripture, Romantic and Water-Smart Gardens. The Boettcher Memorial Conservatory houses an extensive collection of tropical plants, flower-

ing orchids and bromeliads.
Web: aabga.mobot.org/AABGA/
Member.pages/Denver/denver.html
Hours: 9am-5pm
Fees: $4; $2 seniors, children

Yampa River Botanic Park
Steamboat Springs, CO
Mail: PO Box 776269, Steamboat Springs,
CO 80477
(970)879-4300
🌿 At an altitude of 6,820 feet, this Park has
a unique and challenging environment. The
area has an average growing season of 51
days with low summer humidity. The long-term
goal of the Park, which opened in 1997, is to
display flowers, shrubs, trees and grasses
adapted to the northwest Colorado mountains
and arid valleys.
Hours: Dawn-dusk, spring until first heavy snow
Fees: Free

Selected Events

Denver

February 6-21
🌿 Botanical Illustration Show
A judged show of more than one hundred
botanical illustrations from all over the coun-
try. Many available for purchase.
Hours: 9am-5pm
Fee: Admission $4; $2 seniors, children
Denver Botanic Gardens *(See Colorado
Guide to Gardens.)*

February 6-14
🌿 Colorado Garden & Home Show
A large show with flowering gardens and
exhibitors of home and garden-related products and services.

Hours: 10am-9pm Sat; 10am-6pm Sun; 3-
9pm Mon-Fri
Fee: $8
Colorado Convention Center, 700 14th
Street, Denver, CO 80202
Web: www.gardeningcolorado.com
(303)932-8100

May 7, 8
🌿 50th Annual Plant & Book Sale
More than one quarter of a million native, exot-
ic and traditional plants. One of the largest vol-
unteer-run plant and book sales in the country.
Hours: 10am-5pm
Denver Botanic Gardens *(See Colorado
Guide to Gardens.)*

December 4-January 2, 2000
🌿 Blossoms of Light Holiday Celebration
Illumination of the Gardens and buildings plus
decorative floral displays. Bell ringers, choral
groups or dancers every evening.
Hours: 9am-9pm
Fee: $5; $3 seniors & youth
Denver Botanic Gardens *(See Colorado
Guide to Gardens.)*

Vail

June 6
🌿 Annual Plant Sale
A wide selection of alpines, annuals, perennials
and hanging baskets, plus specimens from the
Betty Ford Alpine Garden. Garden workshops
and plant experts on site to answer questions.
Hours: 8am-2pm
Riverwalk Center, Edwards, CO
For information: **Betty Ford Alpine Garden**
(See Colorado Guide to Gardens.)

July 11
🌿 Vail Garden Tour
Six of Vail's most spectacular private gardens
with designers on site to answer questions.

Transportation included and lunch available. Proceeds benefit the Betty Ford Alpine Garden and the Colorado Ski Museum.

Hours: 9am-3pm

Fee: $25

For information: **Betty Ford Alpine Garden**
(See Colorado Guide to Gardens.)

Connecticut

Guide to Gardens

Bartlett Arboretum

UC Stamford, 151 Brookdale Road
Stamford, CT 06903
(203)322-6971 *Fax:* (203)595-9168
🌹 This 63-acre Arboretum has collections of dwarf conifers, rhododendrons, azaleas, witches brooms, nut trees, pollarded trees and other tree collections. There is a bog area, a natural woodland and a woody ornamentals demonstration garden.

Web: vm.uconn.edu/~www.barad

Hours: 8:30am-dark

Fees: Free

Connecticut College Arboretum

270 Mohegan Avenue
New London, CT
Mail: PO Box 5201, New London, CT 06320
(860)439-5020 *Fax:* (860)439-5482
🌹 The Arboretum comprises 750 acres of native trees and shrubs with many of them labeled on the adjacent 100-acre campus. There is also the 5-acre Caroline Black Garden established in the 1920s. From April 26 through October the Arboretum conducts free guided walks, starting from the Olin Science Center at 2pm.

Web: www.conncoll.edu/ccrec/greennet/arbo/welcome.html

Elizabeth Park

Prospect & Asylum Avenues
Hartford, CT
Mail: Friends of Elizabeth Park, 10 Hampton Lane, Bloomfield, CT 06002
(860)242-0017 *Fax:* (860)243-1586
🌹 The Rose Garden in Elizabeth Park, established in 1903, was the first municipal rose garden in the country, with some bushes almost one hundred years old. It is also the first test garden. The site includes a rock garden, large annual garden, wildflower and lilac collections, a perennial garden, as well as a greenhouse with seasonal displays.

Hours: Dawn to dusk

Fees: Free

Glebe House & Gertrude Jekyll Garden

Hollow Road
Woodbury, CT
Mail: PO Box 245, Woodbury, CT 06798
(203)263-2855 *Fax:* (203)263-6726
🌹 The Gertrude Jekyll Garden at Glebe House, site of the birth of the Episcopal Church in America, has the only existing Jekyll garden of the three she designed in this country. Her scheme and plant list for the garden, which was never installed, were found sixty years later in Beatrix Farrand's archives, and today the garden is laid out according to her original plan. A perennial border against a background of yew hedges runs along the front and sides of the lawn, full of cottage flowers. A rose alley leads to the rose and kitchen herb gardens.

Hours: Apr-Nov 1-4pm Wed-Sun; closed winter months

Fees: $5; $2 children

Selected Events

Greenwich

May 1

May Gardener's Market

Selected house plants, annuals and perennials raised in the Garden Center's own greenhouses, plus those from more than twenty other vendors. Food and entertainment throughout the day.

Hours: 9:30am-3:30pm

Fee: Free

Garden Education Center of Greenwich, Bible Street, Cos Cob, CT 06807
(203)869-9242

October 23, 24

Festive Tables

An exhibition of 40 table designs by designers and garden club members.

Fee: Free

Garden Education Center of Greenwich, Bible Street, Cos Cob, CT 06807
(203)869-9242

Guilford

10 miles from New Haven

June 12

Secret Gardens of Guilford Tour

A self-guided tour of private gardens in the area. Starts at the Guilford Green where maps and tickets are available. Sponsored by the ABC program to benefit academically talented inner city students

Hours: 10am-4pm

Fee: $12 in advance; $15 day of tour

For information: **ABC, Inc.**, PO Box 140, Guilford, CT 06437
(203)453-0069

Hartford

February 18-21

18th Annual Connecticut Flower & Garden Show

Eighteen landscape exhibits, floral crafts, exhibitions of the Federated Garden Clubs of Connecticut, many free seminars presented by the Nurserymen's Association, UCONN Cooperative Extension, Florist's Association, Connecticut Horticultural Society and the Elizabeth Park Foundation, and more.

Hours: noon-9:30pm Thurs; 9am-9pm Fri-Sun

Fee: $9

Connecticut Expo Center, Hartford, CT

For information: **Connecticut Flower & Garden Show**, 274 Silas Deane Highway, Weathersfield, CT 06109
(860)529-2123

Late March

Spring Flower Show

A large display of forced spring bulbs in the spacious Lord & Burnham greenhouse and outdoors. Call for exact date.

Fee: Free

Elizabeth Park *(See Connecticut Guide to Gardens.)*

April 10

Volunteer Planting Day

Opportunity to learn how to plant bare root roses. No experience necessary.

Hours: 9am-noon

Fee: Free

Elizabeth Park *(See Connecticut Guide to Gardens.)*

April 23

Spring Plant Auction

Donations and plants from members' gardens, greenhouses and nurseries.

Hours: 7pm

United Methodist Church, 1358 New Britain Avenue, West Hartford, CT
For information: **Connecticut Horticultural Society**, 150 Main Street, Wethersfield, CT 06109
(860)243-1630

June 9
🌷 Tulip Bulb Sale
Over 10,000 bulbs for sale.
Fee: Free
Elizabeth Park *(See Connecticut Guide to Gardens.)*

June 19, 20
🌷 Rose Sunday
A concert, poetry readings and the Connecticut Rose Society Annual Rose Show in the Pond House.
Hours: 2-4:30pm
Fee: Free
Elizabeth Park *(See Connecticut Guide to Gardens.)*

July-August
🌷 Elizabeth Park Gardens Tour
Guided tours of the Rose Garden, annual, perennial and rock gardens by members of the Friends of Elizabeth Park. Call for schedule.
Fee: Free
Elizabeth Park *(See Connecticut Guide to Gardens.)*

September 25
🌷 Fall Plant Auction
See Spring event.
Hours: 7pm
United Methodist Church, 1358 New Britain Avenue, West Hartford, CT
For information: **Connecticut Horticultural Society**, 150 Main Street, Wethersfield, CT 06109
(860)243-1630

Meriden

April 23-25
🌷 Annual Daffodil Festival
Family activities and open greenhouses (from 12:30pm on) at the peak of the season in Hubbard Park - over 500,000 daffodils and fifty-three varieties in bloom.
Hours: Fri evening; 10am-8pm Sat; 10am-5pm Sun
Fee: Free
Hubbard Park, West Main Street, Meriden, CT 06450
Directions: Exit 4 off I 691
(203)630-4259

New London

October
🌷 Plant Sale
Native trees, shrubs, choice woody plants, perennials and ornamental grasses. Call for exact date.
Hours: 9:30am-1pm
Connecticut College Arboretum *(See Connecticut Guide to Gardens.)*

Stamford

February 20, 21
🌷 Winterbloom '99
The Little Flower Show. Displays of forced bulbs in the greenhouse, designer display gardens in the University's multi-purpose room, demonstrations in the Arboretum's Education Building, and many children's activities. Dates are tentative, so call to confirm.
Hours: 11am-4pm
Fee: Free
Bartlett Arboretum *(See Connecticut Guide to Gardens.)*

May 8
🌷 Spring Garden Fair
Over 10,000 shrubs, trees, perennials and

annuals for sale, plus educational exhibits and demonstrations, and specialists to answer questions.
Hours: 10am-3pm
Fee: Free
Bartlett Arboretum *(See Connecticut Guide to Gardens.)*

Wilton

May 8
🌺 Annual Mother's Day Plant Sale
Thousands of plants for sale, including perennials, annuals, herbs, vegetables, rock garden plants, hanging baskets, shrubs and wildflowers.
Hours: 9am-1pm
Fee: Free
Wilton Town Green, Wilton Center, Wilton, CT
For information: **Wilton Garden Club**, Box 121, Wilton, CT 06897
(203)761-0633

Delaware

Guide to Gardens

Ashland Nature Center
Brackenville & Barley Mill Roads
Hockessin, DE
Mail: PO Box 700, Hockessin, DE 19707
Email: ashland@dca.net
(302)239-2334 *Fax:* (302)239-2473
🌺 The Native Plant Demonstration Garden at the Ashland Nature Center was dedicated in 1994 by the Delaware Nature Society. The garden is designed to exemplify the beauty of native species which are ideal for home gardens and for attracting birds and butterflies.
Web: www.dca.net/naturesociety/
Directions: 9 miles from Wilmington
Hours: Nature Center 8:30am-4:30pm Mon-Fri, 9am-3pm Sat; noon-4pm Sun
Fees: Trail use $2; $1 children

🌺 The Gardens Collaborative
The Gardens Collaborative is a consortium of some 30 gardens and historic houses in the Delaware Valley. The Collaborative offers a Guidebook and map to all the sites. The Brandywine area members include the Brandywine Conservancy, Brandywine River Museum, Longwood Gardens, Rockwood Museum, Winterthur and others. Send a check for $8.95 to The Gardens Collaborative and receive their Guidebook.
For information: **The Gardens Collaborative**, 9414 Meadowbrook Avenue, Philadelphia, PA 19118
(215)247-5777

Rockwood Museum
610 Shipley Road
Wilmington, DE 19809
Email: info@rockwood.org
(302)761-4340
🌺 May and June are the best months to visit the gardens at Rockwood. Special events include a Mother's Day Tea and a summer concert series on Fridays in June.
Web: www.rockwood.org
Hours: 10am-dusk
Fees: $5; $4 seniors; $children

University of Delaware Botanic Gardens
Newark, DE
Mail: College of Agriculture & Natural Resources, University of Delaware, Newark, DE 19717
(302)831-2531 *Fax:* (302)834-0605
🌺 Located on 10 acres of the University campus, these Gardens were initiated as a teaching resource for the undergraduate horticulture programs and have become an excellent collection of plants for Delaware Valley landscapes. Features include the Herbaceous Garden, the Meadow Garden, the Native Garden and the Emily B. Clark Garden which

includes the dwarf conifer collection and mature hollies.
Web: bluehen.ags.udel.edu/udgarden
Directions: 1.5 miles north of I95
Hours: 8am-5pm year round
Fees: Free

Winterthur Museum & Gardens
Winterthur, DE 19735
(800)448-3883 or (302)888-4600
🌿 Winterthur is set on the 1,000-acre estate of Henry Francis du Pont in the rolling hills and woodlands of the Delaware Valley. The Gardens feature rhododendrons and azaleas, especially beautiful in May when the bulbs are in bloom. There are summer blooms on Oak Hill and March Bank, and fall colors throughout the Gardens. The Pinetum is one of the top collections in America. The Gardens offer guided tours, courses and workshops.
Web: www.winterthur.org
Fees: $8; $6 seniors & students; $4 children

Selected Events

Milford

September 11
🌿 Yuletide Farm & Community Seed Swap
An exchange of perennials, seeds, bulbs, tubers, or house plants. Live music, herbal goodies to sample and Yuletide's own strawberry lemonade.
Hours: 1-4pm
Fee: Donation requested
Yuletide Farm, Cedar Beach Road, RR1, Box 500A, Milford, DE 19963
Directions: Route 36 to Milford, Slaughter Beach Exit; east 3 miles (toward beach) on left
Email: yuletidefm@aol.com
(302)422-2234

Wilmington
See also Winterthur

May 1, 2
🌿 Native Plant Sale
More than 10,000 potted plants with over 200 rare, unusual and favorite varieties of native wildflowers, shrubs, ferns and aquatics, including some introductions from nearby Mt. Cuba. Pre-order by phone or email and pick up your plants at the sale.
Hours: 9am-5pm Sat; 10am-3pm Sun
Fee: Free
Ashland Nature Center *(See Delaware Guide to Gardens.)*

May 1
🌿 Wilmington Garden Day
A tour of many private gardens and several residences in the greater Wilmington area. Visitors receive maps and booklets and may tour as they please, or take planned tours of various types. Tickets available at retail outlets throughout the Wilmington/New Castle area, from the Delaware Center of Horticulture or at most of the sites on Garden Day. As we go to press this event is still not confirmed. Please call to verify the date.
For information: **Delaware Center of Horticulture**
(302)658-6262

June 26
🌿 City Country Gardens Tour
An intimate look at special private gardens which are rarely open to the public.
Hours: 10am-4pm
Fee: $25
For information: **Delaware Center for Horticulture**, 1810 North DuPont, Wilmington, DE 19806
(302)658-6262

Winterthur
Near Wilmington

April 4
⚜ Easter Sunday
A family event.
Hours: Noon-3:30pm
Winterthur Museum & Gardens *(See Delaware Guide to Gardens.)*

April 24, May 8, June 26
⚜ Successful Gardener Series
A series of demonstrations by Winterthur staff members: April 24, seasonal shrubs in the Gardens with Linda Elhart, Curator of Plants; May 8, container gardening with Joe Lazorchak, Winterthur's resident Landscape Designer; June 26, garden pests and environmentally safe ways to control them with Horticulturist Dave Birk. Reservations required.
Hours: 10-11:30am
Fee: $13
Winterthur Museum & Gardens *(See Delaware Guide to Gardens.)*

District of Columbia

Guide to Gardens

Dumbarton Oaks
1703 32nd Street
Washington, DC 20007
(202)339-6401
⚜ The Dumbarton Oaks Gardens were designed by Beatrix Farrand in cooperation with her clients, Mr. & Mrs. Robert Woods Bliss. The goal was to create a garden in America with elements of the traditional French, English and Italian gardens admired by Mrs. Bliss that would still be original. The formal gardens occupy 10 acres, divided into a green garden, a star garden, an Italian garden, a pebble terrace garden, a beech terrace, Urn terrace, a forsythia dell, a rose garden, a fountain garden, boxwood walk, a walled perennial and annual garden and Melisande's Allée.
Hours: 2-6pm April-Oct; 2-5pm Nov-March

Kenilworth Aquatic Gardens
Anacostia Avenue & Douglas Street NE
Washington, DC 20019
(202)426-6905
⚜ Kenilworth is the only national park devoted to aquatic plants. Highlights of its collection are native bog plants, waterlilies and lotus. From mid-summer to late fall, night tours are available to see the night bloomers at their best. Call for information and dates.
Directions: Near junction of US 50 & 295
Hours: 11am-4pm
Fees: Free

U.S. National Arboretum
3501 New York Avenue NE
Washington, DC 20002
(202)245-2726 *Fax:* (202)245-4575
⚜ Located in the nation's Capital, the National Arboretum is a refreshing place just moments from downtown DC. Plantings include the azalea, boxwood, daylily and native plant collections, the Asian Collection overlooking the Anacostia River, the Friendship Garden, the National Herb Garden, the Gotelli Collection of dwarf and slow-growing conifers, the National Bonsai and Penjing Museum, and the Court of Honor, featuring cultivars introduced by the National Arboretum.
Web: www.ars-grin.gov/ars/Beltsville/na/index.html
Hours: 8am-5pm
Fees: Free

United States Botanic Garden

Maryland Avenue & First Street SW
Washington, DC 20024
(202)225-8333 *Fax:* (202)225-1561
🌱 The United States Botanic Garden Conservatory will be closed for approximately two years to allow for a $33.5 million dollar renovation of the facility alongside a newly created, privately financed outdoor National Garden. For information on off-site events, call the garden or visit their web site.
Web: www.nationalgarden.org

Selected Events

March 4-7
🌱 **Washington Flower & Garden Show**
A Pretty Garden is Like a Melody. Designer landscaped gardens, each based on a song title, a large retail area, a major florist's competition, plus free demonstration and lectures.
Hours: 11am-9:30pm Thurs, Fri; 10am-9pm Sat; 11am-6pm Sun
Fee: $8; $3 children
The Washington Convention Center, 900 Ninth Street NW at New York Avenue, Washington, DC
For information: **Washington Flower & Garden Show**, 6017 Tower Court, Alexandria, VA 22304
(703)569-7141

April Sundays & Wednesdays
🌱 **Greenhouse Spring Garden Lectures**
Lectures on plant related topics, such as shade gardening, butterfly and hummingbird gardens, cut flower gardens and cooking with herbs.
Hours: 1pm Sun; 6:30pm Wed
Washington National Cathedral, Wisconsin & Massachusetts Avenues NW, Washington, DC 20016
(202)537-6263 *Fax:* (202)537-5775

Mid April
🌱 **White House Gardens Tour**
A tour of the White House and grounds, including the First Lady's Garden, Children's Garden and Rose Garden. Live military band music. Starts from the Visitor Entrance Building on the East side of the White House. Call for exact date.
Hours: 9am-noon & 2-5pm Sat; 2-5pm Sun
Fee: Free
The White House, Pennsylvania Avenue, Washington, DC 20502
Web: www.whitehouse.gov
(202)456-7041 24-hour info line

April 16-18
🌱 **Potomac Bonsai Show & Sale**
Nearly 100 bonsai, plus educational demonstrations by Association members and a sale of plants, tools and related products. Sponsored by the Potomac Bonsai Association.
Hours: 10am-5pm
U.S. National Arboretum *(See District of Columbia Guide to Gardens.)*

April 24
🌱 **Garden Fair & Plant Sale**
Thousands of plants and garden-related items, including ornamental and disease-resistant Arboretum introductions. Sponsored by the Friends of the National Arboretum.
Hours: 10am-3pm
Fee: Free
U.S. National Arboretum *(See District of Columbia Guide to Gardens.)*

May 1
🌱 **Herb Festival & Sale**
Educational activities and demonstrations on growing, cooking and using herbs in crafts by Society members. Sponsored by the Potomac Unit of the Herb Society of America.

Hours: 10am-3pm
Fee: Free
U.S. National Arboretum *(See District of Columbia Guide to Gardens.)*

May 8, 9
ꕔ Flower Mart
A sale and fair, sponsored by All Hallows Guild, on the grounds and in the greenhouse of the Cathedral.
Hours: 9am-5pm
Fee: Free
Washington National Cathedral, Wisconsin & Massachusetts Avenues NW, Washington, DC 20016
(202)537-6263 *Fax:* (202)537-5775

May 8
ꕔ 71st Annual Georgetown Garden Tour
A dozen or more private gardens in the Georgetown area open to tour participants. Optional minibus transportation included in the cost of tickets. Sponsored by Georgetown's Children's House. Advance reservations strongly recommended. Write for information.
Hours: 10:30am-5pm
For information: **Georgetown Children's House**, P.O. Box 3752, Washington, DC 20007

June 5, 6
ꕔ Sogetsu Ikebana Exhibition
More than 40 Ikebana arrangements in traditional, modern and avant-garde styles. Sponsored by the Maryland and Washington Branches of the Sogetsu School of Ikebana.
Hours: 10am-5pm
Fee: Free
U.S. National Arboretum *(See District of Columbia Guide to Gardens.)*

July 24
ꕔ 17th Annual Waterlily Founder's Festival
Garden walks, demonstrations, lectures and lots of family activities.
Hours: 11am-2pm
Fee: Free
Kenilworth Aquatic Gardens *(See District of Columbia Guide to Gardens.)*

September 12
ꕔ 15th Annual Kalorama House & Embassy Tour
A tour that starts from the Woodrow Wilson House and garden and visits six to ten residences and gardens in the Kalorama neighborhood, overlooking Rock Creek Park.
Hours: Noon-5pm
Fee: $18 in advance; $20 day of tour
For information: **Woodrow Wilson House Museum**, 2340 S Street NW, Washington, DC 20008
(202)387-4062

October 9-11
ꕔ Orchid Show & Plant Sale
A large display of orchids, plus educational programs on growing orchids and a sale of orchids and related products. Sponsored by the National Capital Orchid Society.
Hours: 10am-3pm
Fee: Free
U.S. National Arboretum *(See District of Columbia Guide to Gardens.)*

Mid October
ꕔ White House Gardens Tour
A tour of the White House and grounds, including the First Lady's Garden, Children's Garden and Rose Garden. Live military band music. Starts from the Visitor Entrance Building on the East side of the White House. Call for exact date.

Hours: 9am-noon & 2-5pm Sat; 2-5pm Sun
Fee: Free
The White House, Pennsylvania Avenue,
Washington, DC 20502
Web: www.whitehouse.gov
(202)456-7041 24-hour info line

Florida

Guide to Gardens

Alfred B. Maclay State Gardens
3540 Thomasville Road
Tallahassee, FL 32308
(850)487-4115 *Fax:* (850)487-8808
🌿 The azalea and camellia collections planted on this former estate, now a state park of
300 acres, are excellent. There are formal gardens and specimens of flowering trees, plus
demonstration gardens for camellia.
Hours: 9am-5pm
Fees: Jan-Apr, free except parking; May-Dec
$3

Bok Tower Gardens
11151 Tower Boulevard
Lake Wales, FL 33853
(941)676-1408 *Fax:* (941)676-6770
🌿 The Bok Tower Gardens were designed by
Frederick Law Olmsted, Jr., one of the designers of New York's Central Park. The Garden is
planted with camellias, azaleas and magnolias and contains an important collection of
palms. The nature observatory, Window by the
Pond, offers the opportunity to sit unseen and
watch the birds and wildlife around the pond.
Hours: Gardens 8am-5pm
Fees: $4; $1 children

Butterfly World
3600 West Sample Road
Coconut Creek, FL 33073

Email: gardens@butterflyworld.com
(954)977-4400
🌿 Butterfly World is a tropical garden of five
large screened aviaries that provide sanctuaries
for thousands of butterflies representing dozens
of species. Inside the gardens are waterfalls,
ponds, orchids, a Lakeside Botanical Gardens
and Secret Garden, and one of the largest collections of passion flowers.
Web: www.butterflyworld.com
Hours: 9am-5pm Mon-Sat; 1-5pm Sun
Fees: $11.95; $6.95 children

Eden State Gardens
181 Eden Garden Road
Point Washington, FL
Mail: PO Box 26, Point Washington, FL 32454
(850)231-4214 *Fax:* (850)231-2194
🌿 Eden State Gardens is part of Florida State
Parks and consist of the historic home and
gardens, property of the lumber magnate
William Henry Wesley 100 years ago. The
moss-draped live oaks, which dominate the
lawns, predate the Wesley development. From
October to May camellia and azaleas are
blooming, with peak bloom in March.
Web: www.dep.state.fl.us/parks/
Hours: 8am-sunset; Mansion 9am-5pm
Thurs-Mon
Fees: $2 park entrance; Mansion $1.50, $.50
children

Edison-Ford Winter Estates
2350 McGregor Boulevard
Ft. Myers, FL 33901
(941)334-7419 *Fax:* (941-332-6684
🌿 In 1885 Thomas Edison started spending his
winters in Fort Myers. His friend Henry Ford liked
to visit him there so much that he eventually
purchased the adjoining property. Continuous
tours of both properties are given every day. In-
depth horticultural tours of the great American
inventor's winter estate, lasting about three

hours, are given by advance reservation to three or more people. Approximately 200 plants and trees are viewed and discussed.
Web: edison-ford-estate.com
Hours: 9am-3:30pm Mon-Sat; noon-3:30pm Sun
Fees: Tours $16; $8 children; reservations required

Fairchild Tropical Garden
10901 Old Cutler Road
Miami, FL 33156
(305)667-1651 *Fax:* (305)661-8953
The 83-acre Garden displays tropical plants from around the world. Special features include the Gate House Museum of Plant Exploration Conservatory, Rainforest, Sunken Garden, Overlook and Bailey Palm Glade vistas. Narrated tram tours available.
Web: www.ftg.org
Hours: 9:30am-4:30pm
Fees: $8

Flamingo Gardens
3750 Flamingo Road
Davie/Ft. Lauderdale, FL 33330
(954)473-2955 *Fax:* (954)473-6669
These gardens are home to one of the largest collections of heliconias and the largest group of champion trees - 21 in all. Features include the rain forest, evergaldes and citrus groves.
Hours: Jun-Oct 9:30am-5:30pm; closed Mon
Fees: $10; $8 seniors & students; $5.50 children

Florida Cypress Gardens
2641 South Lake Summit Drive
Cypress Gardens, FL
Mail: PO Box 1, Cypress Gardens, FL 33884
(800)282-2123 *Fax:* (941)324-7946
Cypress Gardens is composed of more than 200 acres planted with tropical, subtropical and temperate plants.
Web: www.cypressgardens.com
Directions: Route 540 West off US 27
Hours: 9:30-5:30pm; some seasonal variations
Fees: $30.95; $26.30 seniors; $20.95 children 6-17; under 5 free; all fees are plus tax

Florida Tech Botanical Garden
150 West University Blvd
Melbourne, FL 32901
(407)768-8086 *Fax:* (407)726-8760
This 30-acre site is a natural preserve of different habitats, from sandy uplands of pines and palmettos, to a lush hammock of oaks, maples, hickories and other hardwoods, and a large collection of palms. The Botanical Garden is accessible from paths and wooden bridges on the outskirts of the Florida Tech campus or from within the landscaped grounds of the university.
Hours: 8am-6pm
Fees: Free

Harry P. Leu Gardens
1920 North Forest Avenue
Orlando, FL 32803
(407)246-2620 *Fax:* (407)246-2849
Harry P. Leu Gardens is located in the historic district in the heart of Orlando. The 50 acres of botanical collections feature camellia, roses, palms and tropical plants, The Leu House Museum, dating from the 1880s, is listed on the National Register of Historic Places.
Web: www.ci.orlando.fl.us/departments/leu_gardens/index.html/
Hours: Winter 9am-5pm; Daylight Savings Time 9am-8pm Mon-Sat, 9am-6pm Sun
Fees: $4; $1 children

Heathcote Botanical Gardens
210 Savannah Road

Ft. Pierce, FL 34982
(561)464-4672 *Fax:* (561)486-2748
🌺 Begun in 1985 in an effort to save important green space in an area of rapid urbanization, Heathcote Gardens is still under development. It now offers a Japanese Garden and subtropical flowers and foliage, both native and exotic, on its 3 1/2-acre site.
Hours: Nov-Apr 9am-5pm Tues-Sat, 1-5pm Sun
Fees: $2.50

The Kampong
4013 Douglas Road
Coconut Grove, FL 33133
(305)442-7169 *Fax:* (305)442-2925
🌺 Administered by the National Tropical Botanical Garden, this garden comprises 9 acres of tropical plantings. Guided tours are available by reservation.
Web: www.ntbg.org
Hours: Tours first Sunday of each month at 2pm and 3pm
Fees: Guided tour $10; $5 children 6-18; children under 6 free

Kanapaha Botanical Gardens
4700 SW 58th Drive
Gainesville, FL 32608
(352)372-4981 *Fax:* (352)372-5892
🌺 This 62-acre site contains many specialty gardens, including a Butterfly Garden, Spring Flower Garden, Palm Hammock collection, Florida's largest public Bamboo garden, a Vinery, and Hummingbird, Rock, Herb, Bog and Sunken gardens. The entire site is a wildlife sanctuary, home to many forms of wildlife, including bald eagles and alligators.
Web: hammock.ifas.ufl.edu/kanapaha
Hours: 9am-5pm Mon, Tues, Fri; 9am-dusk Wed, Sat, Sun; closed Thursday
Fees: $3; $2 children

The Marie Selby Botanical Gardens
811 South Palm Avenue
Sarasota, FL 34236
(941)366-5731 ext 10 *Fax:* (941)366-9807
🌺 Selby Gardens is perhaps best known for its living collection of more than 6,000 orchids. The 8.5 bay-front acres contain more than 20,000 plants, many collected in the wild by the Gardens' Research and Conservation Department. Selby has seven greenhouses and twenty distinct garden areas, including a butterfly garden, bamboo pavilion, banyan grove, succulent garden, cycad collection, bromeliad display, palm grove and the bay walk. The Tropical Display House contains exotic plants from all over the world and the Museum, with rotating exhibits of botanical illustrations.
Web: www.selby.org
Hours: 10am-5pm
Fees: $8; $4 children 6-12; under 6 free

McKee Botanical Garden
350 US Highway 1
Vero Beach, FL 32962
Email: mckeegdn@veronet.net
(561)794-0601 *Fax:* (561)794-0602
🌺 McKee Botanical Gardens is the major project of the Indian River Land Trust and has just been named to the National Register of Historic Places. The former McKee Jungle Gardens was an important tourist attraction in the Vero Beach area. It was developed by two visionary entrepreneurs, Arthur G. McKee and Waldo E. Sexton, and is one of the oldest botanical gardens in Florida. Founded in 1932, it became famous for its water lily and orchid collections and the hybridizing of tropical exotic plants. The McKee Botanical Gardens are now undergoing restoration and rehabilitation to modify the property and still retain its historic character.
Hours: Scheduled to open in 1999; current tours by appointment

Mounts Botanical Garden
531 North Military Trail
West Palm Beach, FL 33415
(561)233-1749 *Fax:* (561)233-1782
🌿 This 13-acre Garden is dedicated to education. In addition to native plantings, it has demonstration vegetable gardens.
Web: www.mounts.org
Hours: 8:30am-4:30pm Mon-Sat; 10am-5pm Sun
Fees: Donation requested

Pan's Garden
Preservation Foundation of Palm Beach, 356 South County Road
Palm Beach, FL 33480
(561)832-0731 *Fax:* (561)832-7174

Ravine State Gardens
1600 Twigg Street
Palatka, FL
Mail: PO Box 1096, Palatka, FL 32178
Email: ravine@gbso.net
(904)329-3721 *Fax:* (904)329-3718
🌿 Azaleas are the focus of this 85-acre park, with more than 100,000 bushes representing 50 varieties in bloom January through April. Other features include sub-tropical trees, shrubs and flowers, with the emphasis on native plants. There are also formal gardens and natural settings of streams and ponds. This is the site of the annual Azalea Festival. (See Florida Selected Events.)

Simpson Park Hammock
55 SW 17th Road
Miami, FL
Mail: 10110 SW 81st Street, Miami, FL 33173
(305)271-0735 *Fax:* (305)271-3375
🌿 The Simpson Park Hammock encompasses about 8.5 acres in downtown Miami and is the only remaining part of what was once a vast sub-tropical jungle. The conditions in the park parallel those of over one hundred years ago, with representative trees, plants and wildlife of South Florida. Since 1941 the Park has also provided a home for many plant societies, horticultural organizations and garden clubs at the Charles Torrey Simpson Memorial Garden Center.
Hours: 10am-5pm
Fees: Free

Sugar Mill Botanical Gardens
950 Old Sugar Mill Road, **Port Orange**, FL
Mail: PO Box 250791, Holly Hill, FL 32125
(904)767-1735
🌿 On an historic site donated to the county in 1963 and supported by the Botanical Gardens of Volusia, Sugar Mill Gardens were opened in 1988. Still a work-in-progress, the Gardens currently feature lilies, daylilies, azaleas, a bog trail, water garden, magnolia collection, Audubon Trail, camellia collection, hollies, gingers and the Xeriscape Garden. There's also Mother Nature's Forest, an area that is to be kept in its natural state without exotics, with its Ivy Lane and Hammock Trail.
Hours: Dawn-dusk
Fees: Free

University of Miami John C. Gifford Arboretum
San Amaro Drive & Robbia Avenue
Miami, FL
Mail: PO Box 249118, Coral Gables, FL 33124
(305)284-5364 *Fax:* (305)284-3039
🌿 A self-guided tour follows the historic trail which weaves through the original sections of the Gifford Arboretum. Plant families are highlighted with a brief description of some of the most interesting plants. The Arboretum includes major tropical tree families as well as a fully labeled set of the tropical trees native to southern Florida.

Web: fig.cox.miami.edu/Arboretum/gifford.html
Fees: Free

Cypress Gardens
Southwest of Orlando

March 15-May 15
🌺 Annual Spring Flower Festival
Uniquely designed floral topiaries depicting beautifully colored swans, tropical fish, peacocks and an 18-foot Easter rabbit, set amidst 35,000 annuals.
Hours: 9:30am-8pm
Florida Cypress Gardens *(See Florida Guide to Gardens.)*

November 8-21
🌺 Annual Mum Festival
More than three million chrysanthemums in bloom, with a 35-foot cascading waterfall of flowers as the centerpiece. Billed as the largest exhibit of its kind in America.
Hours: 9:30am-5:30pm
Florida Cypress Gardens *(See Florida Guide to Gardens.)*

November 25-January 9, 2000
🌺 Poinsettia Festival
More than 40,000 blooms in traditional red, white and pink as well as marbled varieties, with a 16-foot high poinsettia tree as a major focal point.
Hours: 9:30am-9pm
Florida Cypress Gardens *(See Florida Guide to Gardens.)*

Daytona Beach
50 miles east of Orlando

March 11-14
🌺 Garden & Leisure Lifestyles Show
Dreamscapes. A large garden and flower show with display gardens, decorator showcases, judged flower show, educational and professional seminars, chidren's activities, a marketplace and more. Sponsored by The Council of Garden Clubs of the Halifax District, The Florida Nurserymen Growers' Association, the Extension Service of the University of Florida, the Volusia County Florists' Association and other local groups.
Hours: 10am-5pm Thurs-Sat; 11am-5pm Sun
Fee: $2; $3 for Ocean Center parking
Ocean Center, 101 North Atlantic Ave (Route A1A), Daytona Beach, FL
For information: **Garden & Leisure Lifestyles Show**, 901 6th Street, Daytona Beach, FL 32114
Web: www.n-jcenter.com/garden/
(904)252-1511

Ft. Pierce
50 miles from West Palm Beach

November 20, 21
🌺 Annual Garden Festival
Plants for sale, plant clinics, demonstrations, an orchid show, crafts and more.
Hours: 10am-5pm Sat; 10am-3pm Sun
Fee: $2.50
Heathcote Botanical Gardens *(See Florida Guide to Gardens.)*

Gainesville

January 15-March 1
🌺 17th Annual Winter Bamboo Sale
Many species for sale on a dug-to-order basis from one of Florida's largest bamboo collections.
Hours: 9am-5pm Mon, Tues, Fri; 9am-dusk Wed, Sat, Sun
Fee: Free
Kanapaha Botanical Gardens *(See Florida Guide to Gardens.)*

March 27, 28
9th Annual Spring Garden Festival

Plants, garden-related merchandise, arts and crafts for sale, along with horticultural seminars, live entertainment, children's activities, food and more.
Hours: 9am-6pm Sat; 10am-5pm Sun
Fee: $4; $3 children
Kanapaha Botanical Gardens (See Florida Guide to Gardens.)

April 24
Moonlight Walk

Over 1000 luminarias, paper lanterns, floating candles, countless fireflies and the light of the full moon, plus entertainment and refreshments. Telescopes provided by the University of Florida Astronomy Club.
Hours: 7-11pm
Fee: $4; $3 children
Kanapaha Botanical Gardens (See Florida Guide to Gardens.)

July 1
Annual Giant Victoria Water Lily Sale

Offered for $25 on a first-come-first-served basis, these plants grow leaves that can reach a diameter of six feet. Available around July 1. For order information, call the Gardens.
Hours: 10am-5pm Sat; 10am-3pm Sun
Fee: $1
Kanapaha Botanical Gardens (See Florida Guide to Gardens.)

October 16
Open House & Fall Plant Show

Exotic and specialty plants for sale and informational displays by several plant societies.
Hours: 9am-dusk
Fee: Free
Kanapaha Botanical Gardens (See Florida Guide to Gardens.)

October 23
Moonlight Walk

Over 1000 luminarias, paper lanterns, floating candles, countless fireflies and the light of the full moon, plus entertainment and refreshments. Telescopes provided by the University of Florida Astronomy Club.
Hours: 7-11pm
Fee: $4; $3 children
Kanapaha Botanical Gardens (See Florida Guide to Gardens.)

Homestead
25 miles from Miami

January 9, 10
Annual Redland Natural Arts Festival

A celebration of Florida's pioneer spirit in which everything sold must be hand-made or home-made of natural materials. Tropical fruit trees, flowers and ethnic foods also available.
Hours: 10am-5pm
Fee: $3
Fruit & Spice Park, 24801 SW 187th Avenue, Homestead, FL 33031
(305)247-5727

March 6, 7
Asian Festival

Everything Asian - food, entertainment - plus tropical fruit and flowering trees for sale. Sponsored by the Asian American Federation.
Hours: 10am-5pm
Fee: $5
Fruit & Spice Park, 24801 SW 187th Avenue, Homestead, FL 33031
(305)247-5727

July 17, 18
Tropical Agriculture Festival

Tropical fruit trees and fruit for sale, plus an extensive mango display, agricultural and culinary lectures and demonstrations, and a sale of ethnic food.

Hours: 10am-5pm
Fee: $3; $1 children
Fruit & Spice Park, 24801 SW 187th
Avenue, Homestead, FL 33031
(305)247-5727

Key West

January 22, 23, February 12, 13 ,26, 27
☙ House & Garden Tour

Two-day tours featuring five private homes
and gardens per tour, selected for historic
value or unique design features. Sponsored
by the Old Island Restoration Foundation.
Hours: January tours 5-9pm; February tours
10am-4pm
Fee: $15 each tour
For information: **Old Island Restoration
Foundation**, PO Box 689, Key West, FL
33041
(305)294-9501

Lake Buena Vista

April 16-May 30
☙ Epcot International Flower
& Garden Festival

Demonstrations, guest speakers, workshops,
and more against a backdrop hundreds of
flower beds, millions of blossoms and topiary
displays. Now in its sixth year.
Walt Disney Epcot Center, Lake Buena Vista,
FL 32830
Web: www.disneyworld.com
(407)824-4321

Lake Wales

February 20-28
☙ International Carillon Festival

World-renowned carillonneurs performing on
the famous 57-bell Bok Tower carillon.
Lectures by guest artists and garden walks,
plus a special moonlight recital on Saturday
night, February 27, at 8pm.

Hours: Recitals 3 pm daily
Bok Tower Gardens *(See Florida Guide to
Gardens.)*

Miami

March 5-7
☙ 54th South Florida Orchid
Society Show

Magical Journey of Orchids. A major show
attended by orchidists from all over the world,
with exhibits, lectures, demonstrations and
materials for sale. Billed as the largest orchid
show in the country.
Hours: 10am-8pm Fri, Sat; 10am-6pm Sun
Fee: $9
Coconut Grove Convention Center, 2700
South Bayshore Drive, Coconut Grove, FL
For information: **South Florida Orchid
Society**, 10801 SW 124th Street, Miami, FL
33176
(800)654-4544 or (305)255-3656

March 19-21
☙ Flower Show & Sale

The Secret Hammock. A judged show, now in
its 44th year, featuring floral designs, horticultural displays, cut flowers, lectures, vendors
and more. Benefits Simpson Park, the only
natural hammock remaining in the City of
Miami.
Hours: 9am-2pm Fri; 10am-5pm Sat, Sun
Fee: $5
Simpson Park Hammock *(See Florida Guide
to Gardens.)*

June 6, 7
☙ 81st Annual Royal Poinciana Festival

A city-wide event coinciding with the blooming
of the flame-colored blossoms of the Royal
Poinciana trees. Features a large plant sale,
including Royal Poinciana seedlings, plant-
related lectures on June 7th, and a trolley tour
of trees (reservations required for this tour).

Funded by the City of Miami Beautification Committee.
Fee: Most events free; Trolley tour $15
The Museum of Science, 3280 South Miami Avenue, Miami, FL
For information: **Annual Royal Poinciana Festival**, 2472 SW 27 Terrace, Miami, FL 33133
(305)789-7539

July 10, 11
🌱 International Mango Festival
Tastings, a display of 150 cultivars, consultations with a mango medic, a Mango Auction, workshops and more.
Hours: 9:30am-4:30pm
Fee: Admission $8
Fairchild Tropical Garden (*See Florida Guide to Gardens.*)

November 6, 7
🌱 International Palm Society Show & Sale
Billed as the world's largest sale of rare and exotic palms. Sponsored by the South Florida Chapter of the International Palm Society.
Hours: 9:30am-4:30pm
Fee: Admission $8
Fairchild Tropical Garden (*See Florida Guide to Gardens.*)

November 13, 14
🌱 Annual Ramble: A Garden Festival
Exhibits and sales of culinary herbs, palms, flowering trees, heliconias, bromeliads and fruit trees. Food, arts and crafts, children's activities and more.
Hours: 9:30am-4:30pm
Fee: Admission $8; good for both days
Fairchild Tropical Garden (*See Florida Guide to Gardens.*)

Mt. Dora
30 miles from Orlando

October 30, 31
🌱 Mount Dora Plant & Garden Fair
Juried horticultural events, plants from specialty growers, garden-related work from fine craftsmen, butterfly and water gardens and more. Held in oak-shaded Donnelly Park, right in the center of Mt. Dora, recently called "The prettiest, most quaint and romantic small town (in Florida)."
Hours: 9am-5pm
Fee: Free
Donnelly Park, Mt. Dora, FL
Directions: Off US Highway 441, between Orlando and Ocala
For information: **Mt. Dora Plant & Garden Fair**, 37315 Beach Drive, Dona Vista, FL 32784
Web: www.mt-dora.com
(352)357-4116

Orlando

January 16, 17
🌱 Camellia Show
Award-winning blooms on display in one of the largest camellia collections in the southeast. Sponsored by the Central Florida Camellia Society.
Hours: 9am-5pm
Fee: Free
Harry P. Leu Gardens (*See Florida Guide to Gardens.*)

December 10-12
🌱 Winter Holidays
Holiday decorations in the museum, luminaries in the Gardens, music, visits by Mr. and Mrs. Claus, carolers and more.
Hours: House 10am-4pm; Gardens 6-9pm
Fee: Admission $4; $1 children

Harry P. Leu Gardens *(See Florida Guide to Gardens.)*

Palatka

45-60 miles from Jacksonville, Gainsville and Daytona Beach

March 11-14
❧ Azalea Festival

A week of events along the banks of the St. Johns River against a backdrop of azaleas in full bloom at Ravine State Gardens, with lots of entertainment, arts and crafts, and other activities. Some of the proceeds benefit Children's Miracle Network

Hours: Gates open 10am
Fee: Small fee
Ravine State Gardens, 1600 Twigg Street, Palatka, FL
For information: **Florida Azalea Festival**, PO Box 152, Palatka, FL 32178
Web: www.azalea.special.net
Email: arena@gbso.net
(904)328-0098

Pensacola

April 16-18
❧ 2nd Emerald Coast Flower & Garden Festival

A Standard Flower Show, garden related commercial vendors and craftsmen, lectures, demonstrations and refreshments. Coincides with Pensacola Junior College's Spring Fling.
Hours: 2-5pm Fri; 9-5pm Sat; noon-5pm Sun
Fee: Free
Pensacola Junior College, Pensacola, FL
For information: **Pensacola Federation of Garden Clubs, Inc.**, PO Box 2207, Pensacola, FL 32503
(850)432-6095

Sarasota

March 13-15
❧ Spring Plant Fair

Thousands of plants for sale, including the rare and seldom seen, often at bargain prices, plus free classes.
Fee: $3
The Marie Selby Botanical Gardens *(See Florida Guide to Gardens.)*

March 13, 14
❧ Flower Show

That's Entertainment. A judged flower show, with horticultural exhibits, educational exhibits and youth gardener displays. Sponsored by the nine Federated Circles of the Sarasota Garden Club to benefit the Butterfly Garden. Now in its 62nd year.
Hours: 1-5pm Sat; noon-5pm Sun
Fee: $3.50
Sarasota Garden Club, 1131 Blvd of the Arts, Sarasota, FL 34236
(941)955-0875

April 17, 18
❧ Sarasota Bromeliad Society Show & Sale

A judged show and sale of plants grown by Bromeliad Society members.
Fee: Admission $8; $4 children 6-12; under 6 free
The Marie Selby Botanical Gardens *(See Florida Guide to Gardens.)*

May 9
❧ Mother's Day Gardens Tour

A tour of private and public gardens representing a broad diversity of plants and landscapes.
Hours: Noon-5pm
Fee: $12
For information: **The Marie Selby Botanical Gardens** *(See Florida Guide to Gardens.)*

November 5, 6
❧ Sarasota-Bradenton Rose Society Show & Sale
More than 2,000 blooms from members' gardens, plus educational exhibits, demonstrations and a sale of cut roses and rose bushes.
Hours: 10am-4pm
Fee: Admission $8; $4 children 6-12; under 6 free
The Marie Selby Botanical Gardens (See Florida Guide to Gardens.)

November 13-15
❧ Fall Plant Fair
Thousands of native and tropical plants, including some rare and unusual, many at bargain prices.
Fee: $3
The Marie Selby Botanical Gardens (See Florida Guide to Gardens.)

December 1-January 3
❧ Holiday Celebration & Gardens by Candlelight
Seasonal floral displays on the grounds and in the Museum. Evening hours on December 3rd and 4th, with luminarias in the gardens, entertainment, food and fun for all ages.
Hours: 10am-5pm; 6-9pm Candleight evenings
Fee: Admission $8, $4 children 6-12, under 6 free; Candlelight evenings $10
The Marie Selby Botanical Gardens (See Florida Guide to Gardens.)

Tallahassee

April 24
❧ 6th Annual Garden Tour
A tour of private plantations and gardens in the area plus a lecture by Pamela Harper.
Fee: $35
For information: **Alfred B. Maclay State Gardens** (See Florida Guide to Gardens.)

West Palm Beach

February 19-21
❧ 5th Annual Palm Beach Tropical Flower & Garden Show
A Celebration of Gardening. A display of tropical gardening staged along the waterfront on Flagler Drive, West Palm Beach. Includes a blooming topiary exhibit from Cypress Gardens, an Orchid Extravaganza with displays from plant societies, growers and vendors, plus horticultural demonstrations, educational displays, activities and food.
Hours: 10am-6pm
Fee: $10; $8 seniors; reduced advance rates available
Flagler Drive, Intracoastal Waterway between Evernia & Banyan, West Palm Beach, FL
For information: **The Horticulture Society of South Florida**, 464 Fern Street, West Palm Beach, FL 33401
Web: www.palmbeachflowershow.org
(561)655-5522 Fax: (561)655-6007

March 14
❧ Festival
Garden Kaleidoscope. A spring festival for the whole family.
Hours: 11am-4pm
Fee: Free
Mounts Botanical Garden (See Florida Guide to Gardens.)

June 26
❧ Tropical Fruit Festival
Displays of tropical fruits gathered from all over South Florida, plus lectures given by fruit experts.
Hours: 10am-3pm
Mounts Botanical Garden (See Florida Guide to Gardens.)

November 7, 8
🌺 **Fall Plant Sale & Orchid**
   & Hibiscus Show
A show of orchids on Saturday; orchids and hibiscus on Sunday.
Hours: 9am-5pm Sat; 9am-4pm Sun
Mounts Botanical Garden *(See Florida Guide to Gardens.)*

Georgia

Guide to Gardens

Atlanta Botanical Garden
1345 Piedmont Avenue NE
Atlanta, GA 30309
(404)876-5859 *Fax:* (404)876-7472
🌺 Located on 30 acres in Piedmont Park, the Atlanta Botanical Garden features the Fuqua Conservatory as its centerpiece. More than 6,000 plant species from tropical and desert regions grow here, with priority given to rare and endangered plants. Birds fly freely, and poison-arrow frogs from the South American rain forests have been added. Other highlights of the Garden are the Rose garden, perennial, herb, wildflower, vegetable gardens, and a rock garden. A five-acre Upper Woodland has a camellia collection and a fern glade along with other southeastern native plants.
Web: aabga.mobot.org/AABGA/
Member.pages/Atlanta/atlanta.html
Hours: 9am-6pm Tues-Sun
Fees: $6; $5 seniors; $3 students & children 6-12; free after 3pm Thurs

Atlanta History Center
130 West Paces Ferry Road NW
Atlanta, GA 30305
(404)814-4000 *Fax:* (404)814-2041
🌺 In the heart of Atlanta's Buckhead neighborhood are thirty-three acres of gardens, woodlands and nature trails displaying the horticultural history of the Atlanta area. Surrounding the Atlanta History Museum is a landscape representing the natural succession of native plants in Piedmont Georgia. The Swan Woods Trail winds past study stations and through the Garden of Peace. There is also the Asian-American Garden with Japanese maples, hydrangeas and Satsuki azaleas, the Rhododendron Garden, the Quarry Garden, Farm Gardens and the Swan House Gardens with the recently restored Boxwood Garden.
Web: www.atlhist.org
Hours: 10am-5:30pm Mon-Sat, noon-5:30pm Sun
Fees: $7; $5 seniors & students; $4 children

Callaway Gardens
US Highway 27
Pine Mountain, GA
Mail: PO Box 2000, Pine Mountain, GA 31822
(800)282-8181 *Fax:* (706)663-5068
🌺 Callaway Gardens houses the Sibley Horticultural Center, an indoor/outdoor garden complex. There are 14,000 acres of gardens, woodlands and lakes with indigenous wildlife. Educational programs focus on conservation and ecology. Features include the Butterfly Center, the new 40-acre Azalea Bowl (in full bloom at the end of March), Mr. Cason's Vegetable Garden, a 7.5-acre demonstration garden with mixed rows of vegetables and flowers, plus a large herb garden. Callaway Gardens has been the site of episodes for PBS's *The Victory Garden* for more than a decade.
Web: www.callawaygardens.com
Hours: 8am-5pm; extended hours in warmer months
Fees: $10; $5 children

Elachee Nature Science Center

2125 Elachee Drive
Gainesville, GA 30504
(770)535-1976 *Fax:* (770)535-2302
�${}$ This woodland refuge and museum is designed to educate the public about the environment and how to protect it for future generations. It includes nature trails, native plant garden, museum, live animal displays, education programs and more.
Web: www.elachie.net
Hours: 10am-5pm Mon-Sat
Fees: $3; $1.50 children

Founders Memorial Garden

325 South Lumpkin Street
Athens, GA 30603
Email: gardenclub@peachnet.campus.mci.net
(706)542-3631
🌿 The Founders Memorial Garden is a living memorial to the twelve founders of the Ladies' Garden Club of Athens, the first garden club in America. The two and one-half acre series of gardens consists of a formal boxwood garden, two courtyards, a retrace, a perennial garden and an arboretum. The site serves as a museum of landscape design as well as a natural laboratory for botany, forestry and related disciplines.
Web: www.uga.edu/gardenclub/Founder.html

Lockerly Arboretum

1534 Irwinton Road
Milledgeville, GA 31061
(912)452-2112
🌿 Lockerly is an educational enterprise of about 50 acres, with rolling, uneven topography typical of the Piedmont. It is a horticultural laboratory rather than a showplace garden, with carefully labeled trees and shrubs from all over the world. It is of special interest to individuals and groups interested in botany, landscape gardening, horticulture and ecology.

Hours: Jun-Sep 8:30am-4:30pm Mon-Fri, Sat 10am-2pm; Oct-May 1-5pm
Fees: Free

Massee Lane Gardens

100 Massee Lane
Ft. Valley, GA 31030
Email: acs@mail.peach.public.lib.ga.us
(912)967-2358 *Fax:* (912)967-2083
🌿 Home of the American Camellia Society, Massee Lane Gardens comprise ten acres of camellias under the shade of towering pine trees where over 2,000 camellia plants bloom from November through March. The Gardens include a greenhouse, Japanese garden, roses and many spring bloomers, including dogwoods, azaleas and bulbs.
Web: www.acs.home.ml.org
Hours: 9am-5pm; 1-5pm Sun
Fees: $3

Rock City Gardens

1400 Patten Road
Lookout Mountain, GA 30750
(706)820-2531 *Fax:* (706)820-1533
🌿 On the Tennessee border, this is a 10-acre arboretum in which 400 species of native plants can be found. Its location is spectacular, in a sandstone formation of chasms and crevices, home to a wide variety of lichens.
Web: www.seerockcity.com
Hours: 9am-5pm
Fees: $9.95; $5.50 children

State Botanical Garden of Georgia

2450 South Milledge Avenue
Athens, GA 30605
(706)542-1244
🌿 This young garden, set in a preserve of over 300 acres, has an International garden, shade, rose, native flora, annual and perennial, dahlia, trial and herb gardens, as well as collections of rhododendron, ground covers

and native azaleas. There are five miles of nature trails.

Web: www.uga.edu/~botgarden/
Hours: 8am-sunset
Fees: Free

Selected Events

Athens
See also Bishop, Winterville

Early February
⚘ Wildflower Symposium
An opportunity to learn how to incorporate wildflowers into your garden. A cooperative effort of The Garden Clubs of Georgia, The State Botanical Garden and the Georgia Plant Conservation Alliance. Call for exact date.
Hours: 9:30am-3:30pm
Fee: $14
State Botanical Garden of Georgia *(See Georgia Guide to Gardens.)*

Mid April
⚘ Spring Plant Sale
A variety of plants to start off spring planting, including some rare natives. Call for exact date.
Hours: 9:30am-3:30pm
Fee: $14
State Botanical Garden of Georgia *(See Georgia Guide to Gardens.)*

Atlanta

January 28-31
⚘ Atlanta Garden & Patio Show
A large regional show with ten theme gardens, presentations, experts on hand to answer questions, and many exhibitors of garden products and services.
Hours: noon-9pm Thurs; 10am-10pm Fri, Sat; noon-6pm Sun
Fee: $8; $7 seniors; $2 children 7-12
Cobb Galleria Centre, Two Galleria Parkway,

Atlanta, GA
For information: **Atlanta Garden & Patio Show**, 1130 Hightower Trail, Atlanta, GA 30350
(770)998-9800

January 30, 31
⚘ African Violet Show
An exhibit, plus a sale and demonstrations on how to propagate and repot these house plants. Sponsored by the African Violet Society.
Hours: noon-6pm Sat; 9am-5pm Sun
Fee: Admission $6; $5 seniors; $3 students & children 6-12; free after 3pm Thurs
Atlanta Botanical Garden *(See Georgia Guide to Gardens.)*

February 17-21
⚘ Southeastern Flower Show
Salute to the Century - A Farewell with Flowers. An array of landscaped gardens and educational exhibits, plus free seminars with well-known experts, and a retail section with garden merchandise. Billed as the premier horticultural event in the region. Proceeds benefit the Atlanta Botanical Garden.
Hours: 9:30am-9pm Wed; 9:30am-7pm Thurs; 9:30am-9pm Fri, Sat; 9:30am-6pm Sun
Fee: $12; $10 in advance; $5 students & children
City Hall East Exhibition Center, 640 North Avenue, Atlanta, GA
For information: **Southeastern Flower Show**, 1475 Peachtree Street NE, Atlanta, GA 30309
(404)888-5638

April 9-11
⚘ Atlanta Dogwood Festival
A springtime celebration for the whole family in Piedmont Park among the dogwood blossoms.
Hours: 10am-8pm Fri; 10am-8pm Sat; noon-6pm Sun

Fee: Free
Piedmont Park, Atlanta, GA
For information: **The Atlanta Dogwood Festival**, 4 Executive Park Drive, Suite 1217, Atlanta, GA 30329
Web: www.dogwood.org
(404)329-0501

April 24, 25
Druid Hills Homes & Gardens Tour
A tour of the Druid Hills neighborhood and Park, both designed by Frederick Law Olmsted as his last project. A restoration of the Park is currently underway.
Hours: 10am-5pm Fri, Sat; 1-5pm Sun
Fee: $12 in advance; $15 day of tour
For information: **Druid Hills Civic Association**, 1208 Villa Drive NE, Atlanta, GA 30306
(404)524-TOUR

May 8, 9
Rose Show & Sale
The annual show of the Greater Atlanta Rose Society plus judged competitions, miniature rose plants for sale and the ABG's Rose Garden in peak bloom.
Hours: 2-6pm Sat; 9am-6pm Sun
Fee: Admission $6; $5 seniors; $3 students & children 6-12; free after 3pm Thurs
Atlanta Botanical Garden *(See Georgia Guide to Gardens.)*

May 8, 9
Gardens for Connoisseurs Tour
A Mother's Day weekend tour of private gardens in the Atlanta area benefiting the ABG.
Hours: 11am-5pm Sat; noon-6pm Sun
Fee: $20 tour; $5 per garden
For information: **Atlanta Botanical Garden** *(See Georgia Guide to Gardens.)*

May 22, 23
Bonsai Show
An exhibit of this ancient Asian art form, as well as a sale of bonsai plants, containers and tools. Presented by the Atlanta Bonsai Society.
Hours: 9am-5pm
Fee: Admission $6; $5 seniors; $3 students & children 6-12; free after 3pm Thurs
Atlanta Botanical Garden *(See Georgia Guide to Gardens.)*

June 19, 26, July 17, 24
12th Annual Tour of Ponds
A tour of more than thirty-five ponds in the Metropolitan Atlanta area. On June 19, Metro SW; on June 24, Metro NE; on July 17, Metro SE, on July 24, Metro NW.
Hours: 9am-7pm
Fee: $5
For information: **National Pond Society**, 3933 Loch Highland Pass, Roswell, GA 30075
Web: www.pondscapes.com
(800)742-4701

September 11
Lighted Ponds at Night Tour
Call for maps and information.
Hours: 8pm-midnight
Fee: $5
For information: **National Pond Society**, 3933 Loch Highland Pass, Roswell, GA 30075
Web: www.pondscapes.com
(800)742-4701

September 25
GardenFest '99
A day-long celebration of gardening and a plant sale sponsored by the Georgia Perennial Plant Association featuring historic and hard-to-find perennials, vines, woody plants, plus

demonstrations, gardening advice and tours of the gardens.
Hours: 11am-3pm
Fee: Free
Atlanta History Center (See Georgia Guide to Gardens.)

October 30, 31
🌼 Chrysanthemum Show
The 48th annual show of the Georgia Chrysanthemum Society.
Hours: Noon-6pm
Fee: Admission $6; $5 seniors; $3 students & children 6-12; free after 3pm Thurs
Atlanta Botanical Garden (See Georgia Guide to Gardens.)

December 5
🌼 Country Christmas
Lights and seasonal displays throughout the garden, carolers, entertainment, activities and gift items for sale. ABG's annual Christmas gift to the city.
Hours: Noon-5pm
Fee: Free
Atlanta Botanical Garden (See Georgia Guide to Gardens.)

Augusta

March 25-28
🌼 Sacred Heart Garden & Flower Show
Garden Whimsy. Displays by noted Augusta gardeners, lectures, workshops and more.
Hours: 7-9pm Thurs; 11am-5pm Fri, Sat
Fee: $5
Sacred Heart Cultural Center, 1301 Greene Street, Augusta, GA 30901
(706)826-4700

May 22, 23
🌼 Sacred Heart Garden Tour of Homes
A tour of some of the finest homes and gardens in Augusta, often called "The Garden City."

Hours: 11am-5pm
For information: **Sacred Heart Cultural Center**, 1301 Greene Street, Augusta, GA 30901
(706)826-9700

Bishop
12 miles from Athens

March 6
🌼 7th Annual Hellebore Day
See thousands of hellebores in full bloom at the nation's largest producer of hellebores. Plants will be for sale and you can take a self-guided tour of the display garden.
Hours: 10am-4pm
Fee: Free
Piccadilly Farm, 1971 Whipporwill Road, Bishop, GA 30621
(706)769-6516

Ft. Valley
30 miles from Macon

February 5-12
🌼 Camellia Festival
A week of special events celebrating the camellia and featuring a tour of historic homes, a Novice Camellia show, workshops, an art show, and activities for all ages and interests.
Massee Lane Gardens (See Georgia Guide to Gardens.)

December 6-31
🌼 Festival of Trees & Open House
A holiday celebration at the Fetterman building with Williamsburg-style fresh fruit and greenery and Fraser firs lining the halls, each decorated by a local organization. A free open House Sunday, December 7, 1-4pm, with refreshments, music and gifts for sale.
Hours: 9am-4pm except as noted above
Massee Lane Gardens (See Georgia Guide to Gardens.)

Gainesville
50 miles from Atlanta

March & April
🌱 Native Plant & Wildflower Sale
An ongoing sale of plants that attract hummingbirds, other birds and wildlife to the home garden. Brochure available for pre-order of native plants, shrubs and hard-to-find plants.
Elachee Nature Science Center *(See Georgia Guide to Gardens.)*

April 10
🌱 Wildflowers & Herb Day
Plant experts, garden walks and talks, focused on attracting birds and butterflies to home gardens. Wildflower and herb plant sales.
Hours: 11am-2pm
Fee: $3; $1.50 children
Elachee Nature Science Center *(See Georgia Guide to Gardens.)*

Macon
See also Ft. Valley

March 19-28
🌱 Cherry Blossom Festival
17th annual city-wide celebration of the cherry blossoms, with riding tours, house and garden tours, the Federated Garden Club's Spring Garden Show, Ikebana flower arrangements at Woodruff House, concerts, theater productions, sports events, fireworks and more.
For information: **Macon Cherry Blossom Festival**, 794 Cherry Street, Macon, GA 31201
Web: www.cherryblossom.com
(912)751-7429

Pine Mountain

January 22-24
🌱 Southern Gardening Symposium
A three-day gardening event featuring experts on gardening in the South, for both amateur

and professional gardeners.
Callaway Gardens *(See Georgia Guide to Gardens.)*

March 18-21
🌱 Plant Fair, Sale & Flower Show
A sale of rare and unique plants, plus a Southern Living seminar on March 19 and educational programs throughout the weekend.
Hours: 10am-6pm
Fee: $12; $6 children (registration for seminar required)
Callaway Gardens *(See Georgia Guide to Gardens.)*

Mid November - December
🌱 Fantasy in Lights
Billed as one of the world's largest light displays.
Fee: $10; $5 children
Callaway Gardens *(See Georgia Guide to Gardens.)*

Savannah

February 7
🌱 Annual Victorian Tea
An annual fund raising event in one of Savannah's elegantly restored mansions in the world-renowned Historic District.
Hours: 3-4pm, 4-5pm, 5-6pm (3 seatings)
Fee: $10
Held at: 326 Bull Street, Savannah, GA
For information: **Downtown Garden Club of Savannah**, 417 East Charlton Street, Savannah, GA 31401
(912)236-1070

March 25-28
🌱 64th Annual Savannah Tour of Homes & Gardens
Four days of tours and events focusing on the history and charm of this famous city. Features different walking tours each day, a

Country Tour, chamber concert and tea, Sunday dinner at Mrs. Wilkes' Boarding House, and Riverboat cruises. For complete information and reservations, as well as information and help regarding lodgings, contact the sponsor.

Hours: Vary with each tour
Fee: $30 starting fee
For information: **Savannah Tour of Homes & Gardens**, 18 Abercorn Street, Savannah, GA 31401
(912)234-8054

April 23, 24
🌺 NOGS Hidden Gardens Tour

A walking tour of at least eight private, walled gardens in Savannah's famed historic district, North of Gaston Street (NOGS). Tickets include "Simply Southern Tea" and tour of the Telfair Museum of Art.

Hours: 10am-5pm
Fee: $20
For information: **Garden Club of Savannah**, PO Box 13892, Savannah, GA 31416
(912)897-5177

Thomasville

April 23, 24
🌺 78th Annual Rose Show

Where Roses Reign – Memories Abound.
Attracts rose growers from Mississippi, Alabama, Georgia and Florida and features some 2000 roses in nursery, florist, youth and amateur categories. Billed as the oldest and largest show in the Southeast.

Hours: 1:30-6pm Fri; 9:30am-4pm Sat
Fee: $3
Thomasville Exchange Club Fairgrounds, Pavo Road, Thomasville, GA
For information: **Thomasville Garden Club**, 1002 East Broad Street, Thomasville, GA 31792
(912)226-0711

Winterville
Near Athens

June 25, 26
🌺 Marigold Festival Day

A week-long celebration culminating in a day full of varied events set against more than 7,000 marigolds planted all around this attractive town.
For information: **Marigold Festival**, PO Box 306, Winterville, GA 30683
(706)742-8600

Hawaii

Guide to Gardens

Allerton & Lawai Gardens

Lawai Beach Road on the south shore, Poipu
Kauai, HI
Mail: National Tropical Botanical Garden, PO Box 340, Lawai, HI 96765
(808)742-2623 *Fax:* (808)332-9765
🌺 Located on the south shore of Kauai island, these adjacent Gardens comprise 339 acres and are located directly across from scenic Spouting Horn. Guided tours are available by reservation.
Web: www.ntbg.org
Directions: 4 miles from Koloa on south shore of Kauai
Hours: 8:30am-5:30pm Mon-Sat
Fees: Guided tours $25 per person

Amy B. H. Greenwell Ethnobotanical Garden

Captain Cook, HI
Mail: PO Box 1053, Captain Cook, HI 96704
(808)323-3318 *Fax:* (808)323-2394
🌺 Located on the island of Hawaii, this 15-acre garden is landscaped to reflect the plant life of the area in the era before 1779, when Captain Cook sailed into Kealakekua Bay.

Web: www.bishop.hawaii.org/bishop/
greenwell/
Hours: Dawn-dusk
Fees: $2 suggested donation

Foster Botanical Garden
50 North Vineyard Blvd.
Honolulu, HI 96817
(808)522-7060 *Fax:* (808)522-7050
🌿 Foster Botanical Garden is a 14-acre oasis
in the heart of downtown Honolulu. Areas of
special interest are a collection of Old and
New World orchid species, a large collection
of palm trees, the Prehistoric Glen of primitive
plants gathered from around the world, a display of blooming hybrid orchids, and a collection of twenty-six trees designated "exceptional" and protected by law.
Hours: 9am-4pm
Fees: $5

Hawaii Tropical Botanical Garden
27-717 Old Mamaloha Highway
Hilo, HI
Mail: PO Box 80, Papaikou, HI 96781
(808)964-5233 *Fax:* (808)964-1338
🌿 The Garden is located on the island of
Hawaii, 8 1/2 miles north of Hilo. It displays a
large variety of palms, heliconias, gingers,
bromeliads and more.
Web: www.htbg.com
Hours: 9am-dusk
Fees: $16

Ho'omaluhia Botanical Garden
45-680 Luluku Road, Kaneohe
Oahu, HI 96744
(808)233-7323 *Fax:* (808)522-7050
🌿 The ethnobotanical garden of the Hawaiian
Botanical Gardens is located on the island of
Oahu and comprises 400 acres of wild tropical forest and a collection representative of
tropical areas around the world. There are no

formal plantings and the site is a natural forest preserve. Free two-hour tropical plant
nature walks are offered every weekend all
year, at 10am on Saturday and 1pm on
Sunday. Call for reservations.
Fees: Free

Kahanu Garden
1½ miles from Highway 360 on the east shore
Maui, HI
Mail: PO Box 95, Hana, HI 96713
(808)248-8912 *Fax:* (808)248-7210
🌿 Administered by the National Tropical
Botanical Garden, this garden comprises 124
acres on the east shore of Maui. Reservations
required for tours.
Web: www.ntbg.org
Directions: Ulaino Road & left at mile marker
#31
Hours: Afternoons Mon - Fri
Fees: Guided tour $10; children under 12 free

Kula Botanical Garden
Kekaulike Avenue, Highway 377, Kula
Maui, HI
Mail: RR2 PO Box 288, Kula, Maui, HI 96790
(808)878-1715
🌿 The Kula Botanical Gardens has been
developed in a natural setting of two stream
beds on the slopes of Haleakala Crater on
Maui. Easy walks wind through this garden of
tropical and native Hawaiian plants.
Directions: 20 miles east of Kahului
Hours: 9am-4pm
Fees: $4

Limahuli Garden
Near end of Highway #560
Kauai, HI
Mail: PO Box 808, Hanalei, HI 96714
(808)826-1053 *Fax:* (808)826-1394
🌿 Administered by the National Tropical
Botanical Garden, this garden comprises 17

acres on the north shore of Kauai.
Reservations required for guided tours.
Web: www.ntbg.org
Directions: 8 miles from Hanalei on the north shore of Kauai
Hours: 9:30am-4pm Tues-Fri & Sun
Fees: Guided tour $15; self-guided tour $10; children under 12 free

Lyon Arboretum

University of Hawaii, 3860 Manoa Road
Honolulu, HI 96822
(808)988-7378 *Fax:* (808)988-4231
☙ The Lyon Arboretum was started as a reforestation project by the Hawaii Sugar Planters Association in 1918 after World War I. In 1953 Dr. Harold Lyon helped to secure it for the University of Hawaii and shifted its emphasis from forestry to horticulture. The Arboretum has become a center for the rescue and propagation of rare and endangered Hawaiian plants. Among its many features are the Ethnobotanical garden, the Chinese-style Young Memorial Garden, an herb and spice garden and more. The Arboretum gives free guided one and one-half hour tours every month as follows: first Friday of each month at 1pm; third Wednesday of each month at 1pm; third Saturday of each month at 10am.
Hours: 9am-3pm Mon-Sat
Fees: Donation requested

Olu Pua Gardens

Kauai, HI
Mail: PO Box 518, Kalheo, Kauai, HI 96741
(808)332-8182 *Fax:* (808)332-5649
☙ This historic plantation estate features tropical gardens of flowers, trees, fruits and exotic plants from all over the world, including orchids, heliconias, bromeliads and other rare and endangered species.
Hours: 9am-5pm
Fees: $12; $6 children

Waimea Arboretum & Botanical Garden

59-864 Kamehameha Highway, Haleiwa
Oahu, HI 96712
Email: waimea@aloha.net
(808)638-8655 *Fax:* (808)638-0204
☙ This garden of 1800 acres contains thirty-four gardens areas.
Hours: 10am-5:30pm
Fees: $25

Selected Events

Honolulu

February 27
☙ **Spring Plant Sale**
The biggest collection of rare, endangered, native Hawaiian, Polynesian, and introduced species, plus herbs and fruit trees.
Hours: 10am-2pm
Fee: Free
Blaisdell Exhibition Hall, Ward Avenue, Honolulu, HI
For information: **Lyon Arboretum** *(See Hawaii Guide to Gardens.)*

Idaho

Guide to Gardens

Idaho Botanical Gardens

2355 North Penitentiary Road
Boise, ID 83712
Email: ibotgrd@micron.net
(208)343-8649 *Fax:* (208)343-3601
☙ Since its inception in 1984, the Idaho Botanical Garden has developed into twelve specialty gardens on 50 acres. The gardens include the Herb Garden, Heirloom Rose Garden, Alpine Garden, Contemporary English Garden, Butterfly/Hummingbird Garden, Historical Iris Garden, as well as Meditation,

Water, Cactus, Peony, Children's and Idaho Native Plant Gardens.
Hours: 9am-5pm Mon-Fri, 10am-6pm Sat-Sun
Fees: $3; $2 seniors, students

University of Idaho Arboretum & Botanical Garden

Between Nez Perce & West Palouse River Drive
Moscow, ID
Mail: 109-110 Alumni Center, Moscow, ID 83844
(208)885-6250 *Fax:* (208)885-4040
🌿 UI's Arboretum and Botanical Garden is situated on 63 acres of the university's holdings. The Master plan of 1980 is still being implemented, and five major sections are being developed: Asian, Western North America, Eastern North America, European and Display Gardens.

Selected Events

Boise

March 25-28
🌿 **U.S. Bank Boise Flower & Garden Show**
More than 150 garden and landscape related exhibits, seminars and other special events, including participation by the Idaho Botanical Gardens. Sponsored by the U.S. Bank and Idaho Nursery Association.
Hours: 5-9pm Thur; 10am-10pm Fri; 10am-9pm Sat; 10am-6pm Sun
Fee: $10
Boise Center on the Grove, Boise, ID
For information: **U.S. Bank Boise Flower & Garden Show** 4831 NE Fremont, Suite 3, Portland, OR 97213
(888)888-7631

June 6
🌿 **Boise Spring Gardens Tour**

A tour of 6-8 private gardens sponsored by Friends of the Gardens. Call to confirm date.
Hours: 11am-5pm
For information: **Idaho Botanical Gardens** *(See Idaho Guide to Gardens.)*

July
🌿 **Antique & Garden Show**
Call for exact date.
Hours: 10am-6pm
Fee: $10
Idaho Botanical Gardens *(See Idaho Guide to Gardens.)*

September 26
🌿 **Mad Hatter's Tea Party & Herb Faire**
Carnival games, a crazy hat contest, music, entertainment and a sale of herb products.
Hours: 10am-5pm
Fee: $3; $2 children
Idaho Botanical Gardens *(See Idaho Guide to Gardens.)*

October 24
🌿 **5th Annual Reef Tour**
A tour to see the captive coral reefs and the reef animals that live there in the private aquariums of five growers. Includes a visit to the Geothermal Aquaculture Research Foundation.
Hours: 10am-6pm
Fee: $5
For information: **Geothermal Aquaculture Research Foundation, Inc.**, 1321 Warm Springs Avenue, Boise, ID 83712
Web: www.garf.org
(208)344-6163

Meridian

September 25
🌿 **Idaho Herb Faire**
Booths with herbal crafts, foods, plants, fresh cut herbs. Plus free workshops and lectures.

Hours: 10am-5pm
Fee: Free
Storey Park, 215 East Franklin Road, Meridian, ID
For information: **Good Scents Herb Nursery**, 1308 North Meridian Road, Meridian, ID 83642
Web: netnow.micron.net/~basil/goodscents.html

Illinois

Guide to Gardens

Allerton Park & Conference Center

Monticello, IL
Mail: RR 2, PO Box 56, Monticello, IL 61856
(217)762-2721 *Fax:* (217)333-2774
Robert Allerton donated his private estate to the University of Illinois in 1946. It includes more than 1,000 acres of native flood plain and upland forest and over twenty miles of trails. The many formal landscaped garden areas contain a spring garden, brick walled garden, a gazebo, peony garden, annual, bulb, and sunken gardens, Chinese parterre and many sculptures. Early Spring through May is the peony bloom season with over 900 species of peonies, including historic varieties of French hybrids, some over 75 years old.
Web: www.ceps.uiuc.edu
Hours: 8am-5pm
Fees: Free

Anderson Gardens

340 Spring Creek Road
Rockford, IL 61107
(815)877-2525 *Fax:* (815)877-1525
Anderson Gardens is located on a five-acre site which contains an authentic Japanese pond-strolling garden, guest house, tea house, gazebo, stone lanterns and waterfalls - the classic elements of a Japanese Garden.
Hours: May-Oct 10am-4pm; noon-4pm Sun
Fees: $4; $3 seniors; $3 students

Cantigny

1 South 151 Winfield Road
Wheaton, IL 60187
(630)668-5161 *Fax:* (630)668-5332
Cantigny was the estate of Colonel Robert R. McCormack, former editor of the Chicago Tribune. The 10 acres of formal gardens are a portion of the 500-acre property and include a wide variety of trees, shrubs, flowering bulbs, annual and perennial flowers, and ground covers. The Idea Garden offers garden information and includes a Children's Garden.
Web: www.xnet.com/~cantigny/
Hours: 9am-sunset
Fees: $5 parking

Chicago Botanic Garden

1000 Lake Cook Road
Glencoe, IL 60022
(847)835-5440 *Fax:* (847)835-4484
The Chicago Botanic Garden encompasses 21 gardens that range from the English Walled Garden to the Fruit and Vegetable Garden, the Waterfall Garden and the Home Landscape Demonstration Gardens. Native habitat areas are exemplified by the "Prairie" and other restorations of historic Midwest landscapes. A center for education and research, the Garden contributes to plant breeding and conservation worldwide.
Web: www.chicago-botanic.org
Hours: 8am-sunset
Fees: Free; $5 weekday parking; $6 weekend & holiday parking

Garfield Conservatory

300 North Central Park Blvd
Chicago, IL
Mail: Chicago Parks District, 425 E McFetridge

Drive, 2nd floor, Chicago, IL 60605
(312)742-7737 *Fax:* (312)742-7736
The Garfield Conservatory, designed by Jens Jenson and considered revolutionary when it opened in 1907, is a Prairie-style structure which spans 5 acres and houses eight landscape gardens under glass with seasonal displays. These displays are held simultaneously at its sister institution, the Lincoln Park Conservatory, and both facilities are administered by the Chicago Parks District.
Web: www.garfield-conservatory.org
Hours: 9am-5pm
Fees: Free

Illinois Central College Arboretum
1 College Drive
East Peoria, IL
Mail: Horticulture Department, Illinois Central College, East Peoria, IL 61635
(309)694-8446 *Fax:* (309)694-5799
This 8-acre series of gardens at the entrance to the college contains a flowering crabapple collection, perennial garden, landscape arboretum and an All-America Selection display garden.
Hours: Dawn-dusk
Fees: Free

Klehm Arboretum & Botanical Garden
2701 Clifton Avenue
Rockford, IL 61102
Email: botanical@aol.com
(815)965-8146 *Fax:* (815)965-8155
Klehm consists of over 150 acres of trees and other plants with more than 400 tree species, many not typically found in the Midwest. For children, there is a Children's Garden complete with maze and interactive sundial. There are also community and special access gardening areas.

Ladd Arboretum & Ecology Center
2024 McCormack Blvd
Evanston, IL 60201
(847)864-5181 *Fax:* (847)864-9387
The Arboretum is comprised of 17 acres of woodland, including deciduous and evergreen trees, and features a Friendship Garden.
Hours: 9am-4:30pm
Fees: Free

Lincoln Memorial Garden
2301 East Lake Drive
Springfield, IL 62707
Email: lmgarden@inw.net
(217)529-1111 *Fax:* (217)529-0134
Located on 77 acres along Lake Springfield's southern shore and dedicated as a living memorial to Abraham Lincoln, the Garden was designed by noted landscape architect Jens Jenson, internationally famous for his naturalistic designs. Each season is celebrated with festivals, such as Indian Summer during the second weekend in October, the Holiday Market in mid-November, Blossom Time in the spring, and other seasonal events.
Hours: Garden sunrise-sunset; Nature Center 10am-4pm Tues-Sat, 1-4pm Sun
Fees: Free

Lincoln Park Conservatory
2400 North Stockton Drive
Chicago, IL
Mail: Chicago Parks District, 425 E McFetridge Drive, 2nd floor, Chicago, IL 60605
(312)742-7737 *Fax:* (312)742-7736
The Lincoln Park Conservatory is a whimsical Victorian-style structure of about two acres with three permanent gardens and a fourth housing annual seasonal shows. These seasonal displays are held simultaneously at its sister institution, the Garfield Conservatory, and both facilities are administered by the

Chicago Parks District.
Hours: 9am-5pm
Fees: Free

Luthy Botanical Garden

Glen Oak Park, 2218 North Prospect Road
Peoria, IL 61603
(309)686-3362 *Fax:* (309)685-6240
🌿 Four seasonal displays are held annually in the Conservatory: a spring display, a summer show of potted flowering plants, a fall show of chrysanthemums, the winter display of poinsettias, with candlelight tours in November and December.
Hours: Garden dawn to dusk; Conservatory 10am-4pm, noon-5pm Sun
Fees: Free

Montefiore

11250 South Archer Avenue
Lemont, IL 60439
(630)257-6576 *Fax:* (630)257-7440
🌿 A 28-acre estate with gardens modeled on those of Tuscany.
Hours: May 12-Sep 28 10am-6pm Tues only
Fees: Free

The Morton Arboretum

4100 Illinois Route 53
Lisle, IL 60532
(630)968-0074 *Fax:* (630)719-2433
🌿 The Morton Arboretum is an outdoor museum of trees, shrubs, and other plants. Established in 1922 by the founder of Morton Salt, it offers 1,700 acres of woodlands, prairies, ponds and gardens. It is organized by groups such as maples, oaks, azaleas and rhododendrons, and presents plant "cultures" in sections devoted to various regions. Its Schulenberg Prairie is one of the country's finest restored examples of the tall-grass prairies that once covered the Midwest. Other collections include thousands of bulbs, perennial beds, a crabapple collection and a hedge garden.
Web: www.mortonarb.org
Directions: Route 53 just north of I-88
Hours: 7am-7pm
Fees: $7 per car

Oak Park Conservatory

617 Garfield Street
Oak Park, IL 60304
(708)386-4700 *Fax:* (708)383-5702
🌿 The Conservatory contains three display houses, the Desert House, Tropical House and Fern House, with seasonal displays throughout the year. In addition, there is a prairie garden containing native Illinois flowers, an herb garden and a perennial garden.
Web: www.oakparks.com
Hours: 2-4pm Mon, 10-4pm Tues, 10am-6pm Wed-Sun
Fees: $2 suggested donation

Spring Valley Nature Sanctuary

1111 East Schaumburg Road
Schaumburg, IL 60194
(847)985-2100 *Fax:* (847)985-9692
🌿 The Sanctuary contains restored prairies, a demonstration "Backyard for Wildlife" garden with plantings for the homeowner, a peony display area adjacent to a restored 1928 peony farm, an heirloom garden, and an 1880 living history farm. It's administered by the Schaumburg Parks District.
Web: chicagotribune.com/link/schgarden
Hours: 9am-5pm
Fees: Free

Washington Park Botanical Garden

Corner of Fayette and Chatham Roads
Springfield, IL
Mail: PO Box 5052, Springfield, IL 62705
(217)753-6228 *Fax:* (217)546-0257
🌿 The Washington Park Botanical Gardens comprise 20 acres in the midst of a 150-acre

park, with a large Conservatory Dome. The Park was designed by landscape architect O.C. Simonds, well known for other Midwest sites such as Cranbrook and the Morton Arboretum, and is on the National Register for Historic Sites. There are changing seasonal displays in the Conservatory and out of doors. Special gardens include the Rose Garden, Shade Garden, Monocot Garden with an extensive iris collection, Daylily Garden, and the new rock garden.

Web: www.springfield-il.com/tourism/wash-gard.html
Hours: Noon-4pm Mon-Fri, noon-5pm Sat & Sun
Fees: Free

Selected Events

Bloomington
50 miles from Peoria

June 18-20
🌿 Glorious Garden Festival & Community Garden Walk
A self-guided tour of private gardens in the community and a free festival on the grounds of the historic David Davis Mansion, with a gardener's market, demonstrations, Mansion tours, carriage rides and refreshments.
Hours: 1-8pm Fri, 9am-4pm Sat, 11am-4pm Sun
Fee: Festival free; Garden Walk $10 in advance, $7 children; $12 day of Festival
David Davis Mansion, 1000 East Monroe, Bloomington, IL
For information: **Chestnut Health Systems**, 1003 Martin Luther King Drive, Bloomington, IL 61701
(309)828-1084 *Fax:* (309)828-3493

Chicago
See also Evanston, Highland Park, Oak Park, Rosemont

March 13-21
🌿 Chicago Flower & Garden Show
A large regional show with more than 40 garden displays offering ideas from small garden spaces to country mansions and everything in between. Free seminars and many garden-related items for sale.
Hours: 10am-8pm Mon-Sat; 10am-6pm Sun
Fee: Sat, Sun $10.50; $5 children; weekdays $10; $4 children
Navy Pier, Chicago, IL
For information: **Chicago Flower & Garden Show**, 2019 Lincoln, Evanston, IL 60201
(312)321-0077

April 10, 11
🌿 Illinois Orchid Society Show & Sale
A display and sale of orchids, plus lectures, workshops and video presentations.
Hours: 9am-5pm
Chicago Botanic Garden *(See Illinois Guide to Gardens.)*

May 1, 2
🌿 Sogetsu Ikebana Society Show & Sale
Over one hundred arrangements demonstrating the ancient Japanese art of flower arranging.
Hours: noon-5pm Sat; 10am-5pm Sun
Chicago Botanic Garden *(See Illinois Guide to Gardens.)*

June 20
🌿 Northern Chicagoland Rose Society Show & Sale
A display of modern hybrid tea roses, grandifloras, floribundas, old garden roses and shrub roses, plus miniature roses and cut flowers for sale and expert advice from Rosarians.
Hours: Noon-5pm

Chicago Botanic Garden *(See Illinois Guide to Gardens.)*

July 18
✿ 41st Annual Dearborn Garden Walk & Heritage Festival
Over fifty award-winning gardens open for visitors. Plus a neighborhood street festival with Marketplace, architectural walking tours of this historic Chicago neighborhood, live performances, food, children's activities, and more. Sponsored by and benefits the North Dearborn Association.
Hours: Noon-6pm
Fee: $5 suggested donation
Dearborn Street, Between Goethe & North Avenues, Chicago, IL
For information: **North Dearborn Association**, PO Box 10521, Chicago, IL 60610
(773)472-6561

July 24, 25
✿ 7th Annual Parade of Ponds
Open days at over 125 water gardens and private landscapes throughout the Chicago suburbs. Billed as the largest water gardening and landscape tour in the country. Write for information, tickets and the self-guided tour map.
Hours: 9am-5pm
Fee: $10
For information: **Aquascape Designs**, 1130-C Carolina Drive, West Chicago, IL 60185

August 14, 15
✿ Gardeners of the North Shore
A display and judged show of the best from local gardens, including annuals, perennials, potted plants, vegetables and more.
Hours: 1-4pm Sat; 10am-4pm Sun
Chicago Botanic Garden *(See Illinois Guide to Gardens.)*

August 20-22
✿ Midwest Bonsai Society Show & Sale
Attracts bonsai aficionados from across the country and features a judged competition of dwarf and miniature trees and shrubs, and a sales area offering plants, training tools and everything needed for growing and cultivating bonsai. One of CBG's most popular summer events.
Hours: noon-5pm Fri; 9am-5pm Sat, Sun
Chicago Botanic Garden *(See Illinois Guide to Gardens.)*

September 18
✿ Housewalk & Gardens Tour
A self-guided tour of six historic homes and gardens in NW Chicago. Purchase tickets and receive map at Mt. Olive Church, 3850 North Tripp Avenue.
Hours: 10am-4pm
Fee: $8 in advance; $10 day of tour
For information: **Irving Park Historical Society**, 4544 North Ayers Avenue, Chicago, IL 60625
(773)736-2143

October 16, 17
✿ Wisconsin & Illinois Lily Society Show
Hundreds of the Midwest's best lilies on display, plus tours of the Garden's lily collections, lectures and more.
Hours: 10am-5pm
Chicago Botanic Garden *(See Illinois Guide to Gardens.)*

East Peoria

September 11
✿ Landscape & Garden Day
Highlights the All-American selections and features seminars, tours and gardening information.
Hours: 9am-3pm
Fee: Free

Illinois Central College Arboretum *(See Illinois Guide to Gardens.)*

Evanston
Chicago area

May 14, 15
🌿 47th Annual Evanston Garden Fair
A fair at two sites organized by seven local garden clubs to benefit the community.
Hours: 9am-7pm
Raymond Park & Central Street, Evanston, IL
For information: **Evanston Garden Council**, c/o Environmental Association, 2024 McCormack Blvd, Evanston, IL 60201 (847)864-5181

June 27
🌿 10th Anniversary Garden Walk
A tour twelve private gardens throughout Evanston, plus one special public garden. Benefits the fund for environmental education. Transportation is required.
Hours: 1-5pm
Fee: $12 in advance; $15 day of walk
For information: **Keep Evanston Beautiful, Inc.**, 2100 Ridge Avenue, Evanston, IL 60201 (847)864-1311

Highland Park
Chicago area

July 18
🌿 Garden Walk
Call for information.
Hours: Noon-4pm
Fee: Free
For information: **Gardeners of the North Shore**, PO Box 283, Highland Park, IL 60035
Web: www.enternet.com/~gns/
(847)251-1774

LaFox

April-September
🌿 Prairie Hikes
Three-hour guided tours of the 40-acre prairie. Call for schedule.
Hours: 9am-noon
Fee: $5
Garfield Farm Museum, 3N016 Garfield Road, PO Box 403, LaFox, IL 60147
Web: www.elnet.com~garfarm/
(630)584-8485

August 29
🌿 Heirloom Garden Show
A display of antique varieties of vegetables, herbs and flowers exhibited by members of Seed Savers, the organization that seeks to preserve old varieties of plants. Produce is for sale and experts on hand with information.
Hours: 11am-4pm
Fee: $5
Garfield Farm Museum, 3N016 Garfield Road, PO Box 403, LaFox, IL 60147
Web: www.elnet.com~garfarm/
(630)584-8485

Lisle
25 miles from Chicago

April & May Weekends
🌿 Buds & Blooms
Plant and garden demonstrations, tram tours of the grounds, walking tours of spring blooms in the 24-acre Daffodil Glade and more. Free admission for Arbor Day celebration April 30-May 1 with tree planting and children's arts and crafts in addition to other activities.
Hours: 10am-4pm
Fee: Admission $7 per car
The Morton Arboretum *(See Illinois Guide to Gardens.)*

September & October Weekends
⚘ Fall Color Festival
Children's activities, fall color walking tours, tree planting demonstrations and more.
Hours: 10am-4pm
Fee: Admission $7 per car
The Morton Arboretum *(See Illinois Guide to Gardens.)*

Lombard
20 miles west of Chicago

May 1-16
⚘ Lilac Time
A celebration in this 8.5-acre Park, abloom with 1,200 lilacs of hundreds of varieties and 20,000 tulips. Includes a lilac sale, planting and care seminars, lilac walk, entertainers and family activities.
Hours: 9am and throughout day
Fee: $2; $1 seniors & children
Lilacia Park, Lombard, IL
Mail: Lombard Park District, 227 West Parkside Avenue, Lombard, IL 60148 (630)953-6000 Ext 27

Oak Park
8 miles from Chicago

March 16
⚘ Spring Open House
Floral displays of snapdragons, stocks, schizanthus, sweet peas and forced tulips plus live music.
Hours: Noon-4pm
Fee: Free
Oak Park Conservatory *(See Illinois Guide to Gardens.)*

May 1
⚘ Annual Herb & Scented Plant Sale
A sale of herb-scented plants and everlasting flowers sponsored by Friends of the Oak Park Conservatory.

Hours: 10am-3pm
Oak Park Conservatory *(See Illinois Guide to Gardens.)*

June 19
⚘ Garden Walk
A tour of ten private gardens in Oak Park and River Forest as well as the Oak Park Conservatory. Maps and garden guides available at Fox Center, Oak Park Avenue and Jackson Blvd. Sponsored jointly by the Friends of the Oak Park Conservatory and the Garden Club of Oak Park and River Forest.
Hours: 10am-3pm
Fee: $8 in advance; $10 day of walk
For information: **Oak Park Conservatory** *(See Illinois Guide to Gardens.)*

December 5
⚘ Holiday Open House
Holiday fun with refreshments, Santa Claus, live music, a craft fair and forced paperwhites for sale. Sponsored by the Friends of the Oak Park Conservatory and the Park District.
Hours: Noon-4pm
Oak Park Conservatory *(See Illinois Guide to Gardens.)*

Peoria

November19-January 2
⚘ Poinsettia Show & Candlelight Tours
Hundreds of poinsettias by candlelight. Candlelight tours on November 19, 20, 26, 27, December 3, 4, 10, 11, 17, 18.
Hours: 10am-4pm; 7-9pm candlelight tours
Luthy Botanical Garden *(See Illinois Guide to Gardens.)*

Rock Island

March 12-14
⚘ Lawn, Flower & Garden Show
Symphony in Bloom. A regional show spon-

sored by and benefiting the Quad City Symphony Orchestra.

Hours: 9am-9pm Fri, Sat; 9am-4pm Sun
Fee: $5 advance; $6 at door
QCCA Expo Center, 2621 4th Avenue, Rock Island , IL
(309)788-5912
Web: www.QConline.com/arts/qcso/
Email: qcsymphony@qconline.com
For information: **Quad City Symphony Orchestra**, 327 Brady Street, PO Box 1144, Davenport, IA 52805
(319)322-0931

Rockford

January 16, 17
🌿 Winter Woods Walk

A docent-led or self-guided tour through the firs, pines and other evergreens of the Arboretum. Includes refreshments and activities for children.
Hours: 10am-4pm
Klehm Arboretum & Botanical Garden *(See Illinois Guide to Gardens.)*

May 8, 9
🌿 Blossom Walk

Guided tours to see the crab apples and spring flowers in bloom. Also refreshments, children's activities and music.
Hours: 10am-4pm
Klehm Arboretum & Botanical Garden *(See Illinois Guide to Gardens.)*

June
🌿 Garden Fair

A plant sale, marketplace and activities for everyone on the grounds of the Arboretum. Call for exact date.
Klehm Arboretum & Botanical Garden *(See Illinois Guide to Gardens.)*

July 10, 11
🌿 Garden Glory Tour

A tour of 8-10 private gardens that benefits the Northern Illinois Botanical Society.
For information: **Klehm Arboretum & Botanical Garden** *(See Illinois Guide to Gardens.)*

October 2, 3
🌿 Autumn at the Arboretum

Annual woods walk to see the fall colors of the Arboretum. Also a boutique of dried arrangements, food, wagon rides, a Master Gardener on hand, music, and activities for everyone.
Hours: 10am-4pm
Klehm Arboretum & Botanical Garden *(See Illinois Guide to Gardens.)*

Rosemont
Near Chicago

February 10-14
🌿 Festival of Flowers & Homes

Two dozen garden displays, more than 200 booths featuring home and garden supplies and fifty seminars by well-known speakers and local experts. One of the largest home and garden shows in the Chicagoland area.
Rosemont Convention Center, Rosemont, IL
(847)888-4585 *Fax:* 847-869-1099

Schaumburg
30 miles from Chicago

April 25
🌿 Backyards for Nature Fair & Native Plant Sale

A celebration of Earth Day for the whole family. Includes a flower, tree and shrub sale, activities for children, demonstrations on planting home gardens to attract birds and wildlife.
Hours: 10am-2pm
Fee: Free

Spring Valley Nature Sanctuary (See Illinois Guide to Gardens.)

June 5
☙ 10th Annual Bulb & Plant Sale
Spring-flowering bulbs at bargain prices, plus perennial divisions and seedlings grown and donated by Garden Club members. Sponsored by the Schaumburg Community Garden Club.
Hours: 10am-3pm
Fee: Free
Schaumburg Community Recreation Center, 505 North Springinsguth Road, Schaumburg, IL

October 3
☙ Harvest Festival
A day on an 1880s working farm. Cooking, woodworking and handicrafts demonstrated by volunteers dressed in period attire. Food and handicrafts available for purchase.
Hours: 10am-4pm
Fee: Free
Heritage Volkening Farm , Spring Valley Nature Sanctuary, 1111 East Schaumburg Road, Schaumburg, IL
For information: **Schaumburg Community Garden Club**, 1111 East Schaumburg Road, Schaumburg, IL 60194
(847)706-6767 Fax: (847)985-9692

Springfield

February 20-March 14
☙ Maple Syrup Time
Guided tours and taping of sugar maple trees, followed by cooking the sap into real maple syrup.
Hours: 1pm, 2pm, 3pm Sat-Sun
Lincoln Memorial Garden (See Illinois Guide to Gardens.)

Late April-Early May
☙ Blossom Time Walks
Guided tours with a naturalist along woodland trails when the wildflowers, trees and shrubs are at their peak.
Hours: 1 & 3pm Sun
Lincoln Memorial Garden (See Illinois Guide to Gardens.)

Mid June
☙ Rose Festival
Call for exact date.
Hours: 1-3pm
Fee: Free
Washington Park Botanical Garden (See Illinois Guide to Gardens.)

October 9, 10
☙ Indian Summer Festival
Autumn delights and activities for the whole family, including walks through the fall woodland, games, food, music and more.
Hours: 10am-4pm
Fee: $3; $7 family
Lincoln Memorial Garden (See Illinois Guide to Gardens.)

Wheaton
35 miles west of Chicago

May 2
☙ Greenhouse Open House
Open house at the Cantigny Production Greenhouse when it's at its best, with about 160,00 annuals, perennials, collections of jade, succulents and topiaries. Staff on hand to answer questions and guide visitors.
Hours: 10am-4pm
Fee: Free
Cantigny (See Illinois Guide to Gardens.)

Indiana

Guide to Gardens

Foellinger-Freimann Botanical Conservatory

1100 South Calhoun Street
Fort Wayne, IN 46802
(219)427-6440 *Fax:* (219)427-6450
🌱 This modern Conservatory has three display houses: one features tropical plants, the second desert plants, the third is used for six seasonal shows. The winter show incorporates a garden-gauge railway, early spring features bulbs, April through June is an early summer display, then a summer display, chrysanthemums in October and November, a poinsettia show in late November through early January.
Hours: 10am-5pm Mon-Sat, noon-4pm Sun
Fees: $3; $2 students; $1.50 children

Garfield Park Conservatory

2505 Conservatory Drive
Indianapolis, IN 46203
(317)327-7184 *Fax:* (317)327-7268
🌱 This early Conservatory, established in 1872, is newly renovated. It maintains large collections of tropical plants and has four seasonal displays throughout the year. It is located in a park containing an historic garden which was just reopened in the fall of 1998.
Hours: 10am-6pm Tues-Sun
Fees: $3; $2.50 seniors; $2 children

Hayes Regional Arboretum

801 Elks Road
Richmond, IN 47374
(765)962-3745 *Fax:* (765)966-1931
🌱 This 355-acre site serves as a museum of living trees and includes hiking trails and nature center.
Hours: 9am-5pm Tues-Sat
Fees: $3 for car driving tour

Oakhurst Gardens

1200 North Minnetrista Parkway
Muncie, IN 47303
(765)282-4848 *Fax:* (765)741-5110
🌱 This Victorian garden has an English-style cottage garden, native wildflowers in woodlands accessed by mosaic pebble paths, a rock garden, herb garden and lily pond, all in a country environment in the middle of Muncie.
Hours: 10am-5pm Tues-Sat, 1-5pm Sun

Selected Events

Ft. Wayne

February 24-28
🌱 Ft. Wayne Home & Garden Show

A large regional show which includes exhibits by the Foellinger-Freimann Botanical Conservatory, plant societies, the State Florists Association, Garden Clubs of Indiana, professional landscapers and designers. Ongoing seminars and speakers, and Master Gardeners available for questions.
Hours: noon-10pm Wed-Fri; 10am-10pm Sat; 11am-6pm Sun
Fee: $6
Memorial Coliseum, 4000 Parnell Avenue, Ft. Wayne, IN
For information: **Ft. Wayne Home & Garden Show**, PO Box 26, Hope, IN 47246
(800)678-6652

Indianapolis

March 13-21
🌱 41st Annual Indiana Flower & Patio Show

More than 20 professionally landscaped gardens, a wide variety of garden-related merchandise and seminars. Participants include The Garden Club of Indiana, Indianapolis Landscape Association, State Florist's Association, plus other horticultural-related societies and clubs.

Hours: 10am-9pm Sat; 10am-6pm Sun; noon-9pm Mon-Fri
Fee: $7
Indiana State Fairgrounds, West & South Pavilions, 1202 East 38th Street, Indianapolis, IN
(800)215-1700 or (317)576-9933

April 30, May 1, 2
⚘ Spring Gardening Show
Orchard in Bloom. Gardens by top landscape designers, the Gardeners Market with garden and gift merchandise from over 100 retailers, a display of table settings and floral arrangements, a showcase of custom-built and planted window boxes, mini-seminars every day and a day-long seminar on May 1. Now in its 10th year. Benefits The Indy Parks Foundation and The Orchard School.
Hours: 10am-9pm Fri; 10am-5pm Sat; 11am-5pm Sun
Fee: $6 in advance, $8 at gate; children under 14 free
Holliday Park, 64th & Spring Mill Road, Indianapolis, IN
For information: **Orchard School Parents Association**, 615 West 64th St., Indianapolis, IN 46260
(317)290-ROSE

May 23
⚘ Opening of Oldfields Garden
Reopening of this 26-acre garden on the grounds of the Indianapolis Museum of Art after an extensive two-year restoration. See write-up in *10 Great Garden Vacations* for more information.
Oldfields at the Indianapolis Museum of Art, 1200 West 38th Street, Indianapolis, IN 46208
(317)923-1331

June 13
⚘ Opening of White River Gardens
Grand opening of a 3-acre conservatory and garden complex, a sister institution of the Indianapolis Zoo. See write-up in *10 Great Garden Vacations* for more information.
White River Gardens at the Indianapolis Zoo, 1200 West Washington Street, Indianapolis, IN 46222
(317)630-2001

September 11-25
⚘ 66th Annual Chrysanthemum Festival
Thousands of chrysanthemums of different varieties and colors, plus special events for everyone and a giant mum sale on Sunday.
Hours: 10am-8pm
Fee: $3; $2.50 seniors; $2 children
Garfield Park Conservatory *(See Indiana Guide to Gardens.)*

Madison
50 miles from Louisville & Cincinnati

April 24, 25, May 1, 2
⚘ Madison in Bloom Tour
Eight private gardens not normally open to the public. Bus tour available at additional fee.
Hours: 10am-4pm Sat; noon-4pm Sun
Fee: $7 until April 9; $9 thereafter
For information: **Jefferson County Historical Society**, 615 West First Street, Madison, IN 47250
Web: www.seidata.com/~jchs
Email: jchs@seidata.com
(812)265-2335

Muncie

June 5, 6
⚘ Garden Fair
Practical information and products for the home gardener, with speakers, demonstrations, vendors, food and more.

Oakhurst Gardens *(See Indiana Guide to Gardens.)*

October 9, 10
❧ Harvest Fair
Harvest displays, craft products made from natural materials, and fall and winter gardening tips.
Oakhurst Gardens *(See Indiana Guide to Gardens.)*

Iowa

Arie Den Boer Arboretum
Des Moines Water Works Park, 2201 Valley Drive
Des Moines, IA 50321
(515)283-8791 *Fax:* (515)283-8727
❧ This Arboretum of over 30 acres has a wonderful crabapple collection of 2,000 trees representing 215 species. Their peak bloom is in early May. There is also a small rare tree collection, many kinds of hostas, peonies, ornamental shrubs and greenhouses with cacti and succulents collections. The municipal park, home to the Arboretum, has lily ponds and lotus in fountains and pools.
Hours: 6am-10pm
Fees: Free

Bickelhaupt Arboretum
340 South 14th St
Clinton, IA 52732
Email: bickelarb@clinton.net
(319)242-4771
❧ Collections at this 14-acre Arboretum include dwarf and rare conifers, a Pinetum, oaks, maples, deciduous trees and shrubs, crabapples, lilacs, viburnums, shrub roses, hemerocallis, hostas, wildflowers and a restored prairie.

Hours: Dawn to dusk
Fees: Free

Des Moines Botanical Center
909 East River Drive
Des Moines, IA 50316
(515)242-2934 *Fax:* (515)242-2797
❧ This 14.5-acre garden has a spectacular greenhouse with over 1,000 species and cultivars from around the world. Six seasonal shows are held annually. There is a good bonsai collection.
Hours: 10am-6pm Mon-Thurs, 10am-9pm Fri, 10am-5pm Sat & Sun
Fees: $1.50; $.75 seniors; $.50 children and students; children under 6 free

Dubuque Arboretum & Botanical Gardens
Marshall Park
Dubuque, IA
Mail: 3125 West 32nd Street, Dubuque, IA 52001
(319)556-2100
❧ The only all-volunteer arboretum and botanical garden in the U.S., this 52-acre site has one of the largest public hosta gardens, as well as rose and seed-saver display gardens, a conifer collection, formal herb garden, and notable collections of iris, dahlias, and true lilies.
Directions: West 32nd & Arboretum Drive
Hours: May-Oct 8am-dusk; Nov-Apr 9am-5pm, 9am-1pm Sat, closed Sun
Fees: Free

The Garden of The Gardeners of America
5560 Merle Hay Road
Johnston, IA
Mail: The Gardeners of America, Inc., PO Box 241, Johnston, IA 50131
Email: tgoa.mgca.m@juno.com
(515)278-0295 *Fax:* (515)278-6245
❧ The Garden, headquarters of the National

Gardeners of America, Inc., has over 2000 annuals in decorative beds as well as perennial garden plots, a test vegetable garden, a rock garden and more. The public is welcome.

The Iowa Arboretum
1875 Peach Avenue
Madrid, IA 50156
Email: arbiowa@pionet.net
(515)795-3216 *Fax:* (515)795-2619
🌿 The Iowa Arboretum is located on 378 acres in the heart of Boone County. Highlights included gardens of herbs, native plants, roses, ornamental grasses, Siberian iris, daylilies and hostas. There are also woodland trails and a butterfly garden.
Hours: Sunrise-sunset
Fees: $2

Reiman Gardens
Iowa State University
Ames, IA 50011
(515)294-2710 *Fax:* (515)294-4817
🌿 The Reiman Gardens create an entrance to the University of Iowa and to the city of Ames. The 14-acre site contains an Herb Garden, Jomes Rose Garden which displays the All-America Rose Selections, the Campaniles Garden with its open expanse of flowering annuals, the Wetland Garden and the Dwarf Conifer Collection. Other features include the Fragrance Garden and the Annual Flower Trails.
Hours: 8am-dusk
Fees: Free

Stampe Lilac Garden
East Locust Street at Duck Creek Park
Davenport, IA
Mail: Davenport Horticultural Society, 920 College Avenue, Davenport, IA 52803
Email: hdd@revealed.net
(319)324-7841 *Fax:* (319)326-1325
🌿 The Stampe Lilac Garden was established in 1978 with 235 lilacs, 110 peonies, and approximately 30,000 spring bulbs. Current features include collections of flowering crabapples and beeches. The 5-acre garden was named "Best Small Garden" in 1985 by the International Lilac Society. A gazebo was constructed in 1983, and paved walkways added in 1996 to provide ADA accessibility.
Hours: 6am-dusk
Fees: Free

Vander Veer Park Botanical Center
215 West Central Park Avenue
Davenport, IA 52803
(313)326-7818 *Fax:* (319)326-7815
🌿 The Municipal Rose Garden at Vander Veer Park contains over 3,000 rose bushes representing some 130 varieties. The greenhouses contain seasonal displays, especially appreciated during the winter.
Hours: Dawn-dusk; Greenhouses 9am-5pm
Fees: Norminal fee

Selected Events

Cedar Rapids

May 16 (1998-update)
🌿 **Annual Plant Sale**
A variety of plants on sale in the greenhouse. Date is tentative so call to confirm.
Brucemore, 2160 Linden Drive SE, Cedar Rapids, IA 52403
(319)362-7375

Davenport
See also Rock Island, IL

May 9
🌿 **Annual Garden Walk & Plant Sale**
A walk through the Garden on Mother's Day when the lilacs are at peak bloom. A sale of hard-to-find cultivars plus thousands of plants

donated from members' home gardens. Refreshments available.
Hours: 9am-4pm
Fee: Free
Stampe Lilac Garden *(See Iowa Guide to Gardens.)*

June 13
❦ Gardens of East Bettendorf Garden Walk
A tour of ten private gardens plus crafts, music, dessert and beverages.
Hours: 10am-3pm
For information: **Vander Veer Park Botanical Center** *(See Iowa Guide to Gardens.)*

September 19
❦ Fall Festival
Call for information.
Vander Veer Park Botanical Center *(See Iowa Guide to Gardens.)*

Des Moines
See also Madrid

February 17-22
❦ Des Moines Home & Garden Show
Large demonstration gardens, bonsai and floral art displays, Iowa State Horticultural Society Good Earth Theater with hourly seminars, and more.
Hours: 4-9pm Wed; noon-9pm Thurs, Fri; 10am-10pm Sat; 10am-6pm Sun
Fee: $6; $2.50 children
Veterans Memorial Auditorium, 838 5th Avenue, Des Moines, IA
Directions: 5th & Crocker
Web: www.homeandgardenshow.com
(800)HOM-SHOW

Dubuque

April 24
❦ Arbor Day Celebration

The opening day of the season with a series of table clinics hosted by local experts.
Hours: 10am-noon; Arboretum 7am-dusk
Dubuque Arboretum & Botanical Gardens *(See Iowa Guide to Gardens.)*

June 18-20
❦ Rose Festival
Displays, a judged competition, lectures and concerts.
Hours: 9am-dusk
Dubuque Arboretum & Botanical Gardens *(See Iowa Guide to Gardens.)*

August 28, 29
❦ Tri-State Garden Club Show
Displays of flowers and produce, a judged competition, and music. Sponsored by the Tri-State Garden Club.
Hours: 9am-dusk
Dubuque Arboretum & Botanical Gardens *(See Iowa Guide to Gardens.)*

Madrid
Near Des Moines

April 30
❦ Arbor Day Celebration
Speakers, demonstrations, entertainment, and the planting of a commemorative tree. Catered lunch and tours available.
Hours: 9am-2pm
Fee: Fee for lunch only
The Iowa Arboretum *(See Iowa Guide to Gardens.)*

May 7, 8
❦ Rare & Unusual Plant Auction & Spring Plant Sale
Friday night preview and chance to bid on rare and unusual plants plus hundreds of hostas, Siberian iris and roses. Registration required. Sale of remaining plants plus herbs and perennials on Saturday. Free presentations at

the Saturday event.
Hours: 6:30-8:30pm Fri; 9am-5pm Sat
Fee: Free
The Iowa Arboretum (See Iowa Guide to Gardens.)

August 28
✿ Outrageous Fall Plant Sale
A wide selection of daylilies and hardy mums.
Hours: 9am-5pm
Fee: Free
The Iowa Arboretum (See Iowa Guide to Gardens.)

October 2
✿ Fall Fest
Prairie and woodland hikes to enjoy the fall colors, plant care demonstrations, apple cider pressing, a bake sale, hay rack rides and Fall crafts for children.
Hours: 9am-1pm
Fee: Free
The Iowa Arboretum (See Iowa Guide to Gardens.)

November 20-24
✿ Home Grown Holidays
A display of Iowa-grown Christmas trees, each decorated by area organizations using home crafted ornaments of garden-grown materials. Holiday gift items and hot cider available.
Hours: 10am-4pm
Fee: Free
The Iowa Arboretum (See Iowa Guide to Gardens.)

Orange City
40 miles from Sioux City

May 13-15
✿ Tulip Festival
Three days of special events celebrating Orange City's Dutch Heritage, including: floral displays at the Sioux County Historical Center, 120 3rd Street SW; blooming tulip gardens at the Orange City Century Home, 318 Albany Avenue NE; 6,000 imported tulips in a miniature Keukenhoff setting at the Vander Wel Tulip Test Garden, 212 Arizona Avenue SW; open garden days at private gardens.
Hours: 9am-8pm
Fee: $2 each attraction
Orange City Area, Orange City, IA
For information: **Chamber of Commerce**, 125 Central Avenue SE, PO Box 36, Orange City, IA 51041
Web: www.frontiercomm.net/~tulip
Email: tulip@orangecity.ia.frontiercomm.net
(712)737-4510

Pella

May 6-8
✿ Tulip Time Festival
An annual celebration of the city's heritage, including events of horticultural interest: tours of Pella's Tulip Lanes, Formal Tulip Gardens, Sunken Gardens and the Historical Village; the Pella Garden Club Flower Show.
Hours: 8:30am-9:30pm
For information: **Pella Historical Society**, 507 Franklin, PO Box 145, Pella, IA 50219
Web: www.kdsi.net/~pellatt
(515)628-4311

July 16, 17
✿ Garden Tour & Tea
Tour of four Pella area private gardens and three public gardens with a tea served in Scholte Church at the Historical Village.
Fee: $5 in advance; $8 day of tour; children under 13 free
For information: **Pella Historical Society**, 507 Franklin, PO Box 145, Pella, IA 50219
Web: www.kdsi.net/~pellatt
(515)628-4311

September 24, 25
❀ Pella Fall Festival
The Garden Club's Fall Flower Show, 20 open buildings in the Pella Historical Village plus the Village's own flower gardens in bloom with annuals. Displays, activities and refreshments for everyone.
Hours: 1-4pm Fri; 10am-4pm Sat
Fee: Donation requested
Pella Historical Village, Pella, IA
For information: **Pella Historical Society**, 507 Franklin, PO Box 145, Pella, IA 50219
Web: www.kdsi.net/~pellatt
(515)628-4311

Kansas

Guide to Gardens

Botanica, The Wichita Gardens
701 Amidon
Wichita, KS 67203
(316)264-0448 *Fax:* (316)264-0587
❀ Located on the banks of the Arkansas River in the heart of Wichita's cultural district, this 10-acre garden is home to flora native to Kansas and new introductions.
Web: www.botanica.org
Hours: 9am-5pm Mon-Sat, 1-5pm Sun & holidays
Fees: $4.50, $4 seniors; $2 students; under 6 free

Dyck Arboretum of the Plains
Hesston College
Hesston, KS 67062
(316)327-8127
❀ This 25-acre Arboretum specializes in native wildflowers and plants of the Great Plains and includes a prairie grass and native grass area.
Hours: Dawn-dusk
Fees: Free

Kansas Landscape Arboretum
488 Utah Road
Lakefield, KS 67487
(785)461-5760 *Fax:* (785)461-5322
❀ This 193-acre site includes a large flower garden, gazebo and picnic area, 350 memorial trees, nature trails, and a farm with antique farm machinery.
Hours: Dawn-dusk
Fees: Free

Overland Park Arboretum & Botanical Garden
8500 Santa Fe
Overland Park, KS 66212
(913)685-3604
❀ The Garden is still in the development stage. Currently there are five miles of trails through the nature preservation area, traversing different ecological environments. The Erickson Water Garden includes pools and a waterfall, surrounded by rock landscaping, ornamental grasses, wildflowers, groundcovers and ornamentals. There is also a Demonstration Garden for the homeowner.
Hours: Dawn-dusk
Fees: Free

Selected Events

Kansas City
See also Kingsville, Missouri

May 1
❀ Spring in the Garden
Opening of the Wyandotte County Master Gardeners Demonstration Gardens. Plants propagated by Master Gardeners for sale, including native plants, annuals, perennials, vines, shrubs and vegetables that are proven performers in this area. Workshops, demonstrations, activities for all and tips from the Kansas State University trained Master Gardeners of Wyandotte County.

Hours: 8am-4pm
Fee: Free
Wyandotte County Master Gardeners Demonstration Gardens Courthouse Annex, 9400 State Avenue, Kansas City, KS
For information: **Kansas City University Cooperative** Courthouse Annex, 9400 State Avenue, Kansas City, KS 66112
Web: www.oznet.ksu.edu/ex_wy
Email: cpl9538@msn.com

Wichita

March 4-7
⚜ 32nd Annual Wichita Lawn, Flower & Garden Show

Elaborately landscaped live gardens, over 150 commercial exhibits, a "Visions of Flowers" art exhibition, hourly gardening seminars and more. Acclaimed by House Beautiful as "one of the ten best in the USA."
Hours: 11am-9:30pm Thurs; 9:30am-9:30pm Fri, Sat; 11am-6pm Sun
Fee: $7; $6 seniors (Thurs only); children under 12 free
Century II Civic Center, Wichita, KS
For information: **Wichita Lawn, Flower & Garden Show**, 9505 West Central, Suite 103, Wichita, KS 67212
Web: www.oznet.ksu.edu/sedgwick/upcom.htm#LF&G
(316)721-8740

May 14
⚜ River Festival Garden Party

Music, flowers, food, and fun, plus flower potting and other activities for children. Part of Botanica's contribution to the Wichita River Festival.
Hours: 10am-8:30pm
Fee: Free with River Festival button
Botanica, The Wichita Gardens (*See Kansas Guide to Gardens.*)

June 5, 6
⚜ Butterfly Festival

A weekend celebrating the Butterfly and surrounding gardens. Demonstrations, exhibits and lots of butterfly-related craft opportunities for kids.
Hours: 9am-5pm Sat; 1-5pm Sun
Fee: Admission $4.50, $4 seniors; $2 students; under 6 free
Botanica, The Wichita Gardens (*See Kansas Guide to Gardens.*)

October 9, 10
⚜ Mum Festival

A spectacular display of more than 6,000 chrysanthemums growing throughout the Gardens. A full weekend of events to celebrate autumn.
Fee: Admission $4.50, $4 seniors; $2 students; under 6 free
Botanica, The Wichita Gardens (*See Kansas Guide to Gardens.*)

December 5, 6
⚜ Festival of Light

A holiday gift of light to the community from INTRUST Bank, with nearly 10,000 luminaries lining the paths of Botanica.
Hours: 6-9pm
Fee: Admission $4.50, $4 seniors; $2 students, under 6 free
Botanica, The Wichita Gardens (*See Kansas Guide to Gardens.*)

Kentucky

Guide to Gardens

Bernheim Arboretum & Research Forest
Highway 245
Clermont, KY
Mail: PO Box 130, Clermont, KY 40110

(502)955-8512 or Hotline (502)955-8822
Fax: (502)955-4039
🌿 Bernheim Arboretum and Research Forest contains collections of hollies, conifers, ornamental pears, dogwoods, beeches and more, plus gardens, lakes and 35 miles of hiking trails on its 15,000-acres site.
Web: www.win.net/bernheim
Hours: 7am-sunset
Fees: $5 per car weekends & holidays, free parking weekdays

Broadmoor Garden & Conservatory
U.S. Highway 60
Irvington, KY
Mail: PO Box 387, Irvington, KY 40146
(502)547-4200 *Fax:* (502)547-3100
🌿 Situated on 400 acres of a 2400-acre farm, Broadmoor features extensive water gardens with pools, fountains and waterfalls, a tropical plant conservatory, rose gardens, iris-lily gardens, a two-mile nature-wildflower trail and a picnic area.
Hours: Apr-Oct 15 by appointment
Fees: $7.50; discounts for seniors

Cave Hill Cemetery
701 Baxter Avenue
Louisville, KY 40204
(502)451-5630
🌿 This traditional cemetery, founded in 1849, is beautifully landscaped with mature trees and shrubs as well as new and unusual varieties.
Hours: 8am-9:30pm
Fees: Free

Selected Events

Clermont

October 16, 17
🌿 Colorfest
A family festival with activities and attractions for everyone, from pottery and raku to nature

discovery and pumpkin carving.
Hours: 10am-5pm
Fee: Admission $5 per car weekends & holidays, free parking weekdays
Bernheim Arboretum & Research Forest
(See Kentucky Guide to Gardens.)

Louisville

March 4-7
🌿 The Home Garden & Remodeling Show
A home show with about six garden areas.
Hours: 5-10pm Thurs; noon-10pm Fri; 10am-10pm Sat; noon-6pm Sun
Fee: $6
Kentucky Fair & Exposition Center,
Louisville, KY
For information: **Home Builder's Association**, 1000 North Hurstbourne Parkway, Louisville, KY 40223
Web: homeshow.hbal.com
(502)429-6000

April 17
🌿 Herb & Perennial Plant Sale
Many rare and unusual plants available, as well as one of the most comprehensive selections of herbs in the area.
Hours: 9:30am-3pm
Fee: Free
Farmington Historic Home, 3033 Bardstown Road, Louisville, KY 40205
(502)452-9920

May 7-9
🌿 Gardener's Fair at Historic Locust Grove
A wide selection of annuals and perennials for sale and the opportunity to collect new plants, tools and ideas from experts. Mother's Day Brunch available on Sunday and refreshments throughout the weekend.
Hours: noon-5pm Fri; 10am-5pm Sat; noon-5pm Sun

Fee: $5; $3 seniors (60+) and children; under 6 free
Locust Grove Historic Home, 561 Blankenbaker Lane , Louisville, KY 40207
Directions: Between River Road & Highway 42
Web: www.locustgrove.org
(502)897-9845

June 5
❧ Sunnyside Herb & Garden Festival
An indoor herb and garden plants and products sale with over twenty vendors plus a small outdoor Farmers Market.
Hours: 10am-5pm
Fee: Free
Floyd County 4-H Fairgrounds, 2828 Green Valley Road, New Albany , IN
For information: **Sunnyside Master Gardeners**, 136 River Road East, Charlestown, IN 47111
(812)293-3655 *Fax:* (812)256-6118

Paducah

April 12
❧ Opening of the Lighted Dogwood Trail
A kick-off reception at City Hall with music refreshments and at 7:30pm complimentary bus tours of the 12.5 mile lighted Trail which stays open as long as the Dogwoods are in bloom. This event is part of a festival of the arts which includes a flower show, an art show, theater production, music and guided tours and a bicycle tour. Call to confirm the date and for a complete schedule of events.
Hours: Reception starts at 6:30
Fee: Free
For information: **Paducah Visitor's Bureau**, 128 Broadway, PO Box 90, Paducah, KY 42002
(800)-PADUCAH

May 7, 8
❧ Perennial Plant Sale
A sale of plants from the gardens of the members of the Open Gate Garden Club. Funds used to support the Airport Viewing Garden at Fisher Road and U.S. 60.
Hours: 10am-4pm
Fee: Free
Marie's Gifts, Park Avenue, Paducah, KY
For information: **Open Gate Garden Club**, Paducah, KY
Email: gardener@sunsix.infi.net
(502)554-4466 or (502)442-3089

Louisiana

Guide to Gardens

The Gardens of The American Rose Center
8877 Jefferson-Paige Road
Shreveport, LA 71119
Email: ars@ars-hq.org
(318)938-5402 *Fax:* (318)938-5405
❧ This is the home of the American Rose Society, over 40 acres of roses, including the All-America Rose Selections, miniature roses, single petal roses, and the What's New plantings of the nation's newest hybrids.
Web: www.ars.org
Hours: Apr-Oct 9am-5pm Mon-Fri, 9am-dusk Sat, Sun
Fees: $4; $3 seniors; children under 13 free

Hodges Gardens & Wilderness
Highway 171 south of Many
Many, LA
Mail: PO Box 921, Many, LA 71449
(318)586-3523 *Fax:* (318)586-7111
❧ Hodges Gardens is a combination of natural scenic areas and formal gardens, tucked in the rolling pine lands of West Central

Louisiana. In addition to seasonal displays in nearly one hundred flower beds, there is a Rose garden, greenhouses, and the wonderful view from Observation Point across the 225-acre lake to East Texas.
Web: www.hodgesgardens.qpg.com
Hours: Feb-Aug 8am-4:30pm
Fees: $6.50; $5.50 seniors

Jungle Gardens
Highway 329
Avery Island, LA 70513
(318)365-8173 *Fax:* (318)369-6326
🌿 Jungle Gardens on Avery Island was founded by the owner of Tabasco, Edward McIlhenny, to save the snowy egret. It has developed into a unique sanctuary and preserve, home to a large collection of camellia, azaleas, wildflowers, plants from all over the world, and wildlife. Among the highlights are a marsh trail, live oaks, a sunken garden and a palm garden.
Hours: 8am-5:30pm

Longue Vue House & Gardens
7 Bamboo Road
New Orleans, LA 70124
(504)488-5488
🌿 On January 2nd, Longue Vue will open a new Discovery Garden geared to children ages 5-12, where they can dig, do and discover.
Web: www.longuevue.com
Hours: 10am-4:30pm Mon-Sat,1-5pm Sun
Fees: $7; $6 seniors; $3 students & children

Louisiana State Arboretum
4213 Chicot Park Road
Ville Platte, LA
Mail: PO Box 494 Route 3, Ville Platte, LA 70586
Email: arboretum@crt.state.la.us
(318)363-6287 *Fax:* (313)363-5616

🌿 The State's Arboretum is a 300-acre living museum of trees, featuring plants native to Louisiana. There are 2.5 miles of nature trails which lead through a mature Beech-Magnolia forest.
Hours: 9am-5pm
Fees: Free

New Orleans Botanical Garden
City Park, 1 Palm Drive
New Orleans, LA 70124
(504)483-9386 *Fax:* (504)483-9485
🌿 Louisiana's only botanical garden, the Botanical Gardens in City Park typify the 1930s Art Deco movement in architecture and sculpture and feature the floral diversity that thrives in New Orleans' mild climate. Highlights include the water lily pond, the Parterre, the secluded formal Rose Garden, the ancient live oaks, the Butterfly Walk and the Conservatory's collection of exotic tropical flora. There are also herb gardens, a ginger collection and a vegetable garden.
Hours: 10am-4:30pm Tues-Sun
Fees: $3; $1 children 5-12

Rip Van Winkle Gardens
5505 Rip Van Winkle Road
New Iberia, LA 70560
Email: rvw@1stnet.com
(800)375-3332 *Fax:* (318)365-3354
🌿 The 25-acre Gardens are planted so that different sections are at their peak in different seasons. There is a formal English garden, an Alhambra garden, a magnolia garden, a tropical glen and a woodland garden. Woodland paths connect the gardens. Excellent collections of camellia, Louisiana iris and specimen trees are found throughout the grounds. The greenhouses contain orchids, camellia and tropicals.
Web: www.rip.com
Hours: 9am-5pm

Fees: $9; $8.50 seniors; $7 students; $5.50 children

Rosedown Plantation & Gardens
12501 Highway 10
St. Francisville, LA 70775
(225)635-3332
🌺 One of the earliest of the 19th century historic gardens, these 28-acre Gardens represent 165 years of continuous gardening. This Louisiana plantation owner and his wife, Daniel and Martha Turnbull, were one of the earliest to import camellia, azaleas and cryptomeria. The site includes fern gardens, medicinal and kitchen herb gardens, annual and perennial gardens. A prime time to visit is March at the height of the blooming period for the century-old azaleas, dogwood and magnolia.
Directions: Highway 10 & 61 North
Hours: 9am-5pm
Fees: $10; $4 children

Shadows-on-the-Teche
317 East Main Street
New Iberia, LA 70560
(318)369-6446 *Fax:* (318)365-5213
🌺 The gardens of Shadows-on-the Teche reflect their long history and have both 19th and 20th century elements. It features ornamental plantings along the front, Main Street view, as well as secluded landscaped areas accessed by paths beneath the live oaks.
Hours: 9am-4:30pm
Fees: $6; $3 children

Zemurray Gardens
23115 Zemurray Garden Drive
Loranger, LA 70446
(504)878-2284 *Fax:* (504)878-2284
🌺 The 150-acre Garden includes collections camellias, dogwoods, wildflowers, Louisiana iris, and bulbs. There are woodland trails and greenhouses. This private garden is open to the public for six weeks from March to mid-April when the camellias and azaleas are in full bloom.
Hours: 10am-6pm March-mid-April
Fees: $4; $3 seniors & children

Selected Events

Many

July 4
🌺 **Independence Day Festival**
Arts and crafts, live entertainment and fireworks after dark to celebrate the 4th.
Fee: $4; $3 children
Hodges Gardens & Wilderness *(See Louisiana Guide to Gardens.)*

Monroe

March, April Weekends
🌺 **Plant Sales**
Four or five weekend sales to benefit the ongoing research work of the NLU Herbarium. Call for exact dates.
NLU Plant Research Center, 3907 Bon Aire Drive, Monroe, LA
For information: **Friends of the NLU Herbarium**, PO Box 82608, Monroe, LA 70884
Email: allenhere@earthlink.net
(318)342-1812

New Orleans

March 18-21
🌺 **New Orleans Spring Fiesta**
A parade of horse-drawn carriages through the French Quarter and tours of plantations, private homes and courtyards in and around historic New Orleans, including Bocage and L'Hermitage Plantations.

For information: **New Orleans Spring Fiesta**, 826 St. Ann Street, New Orleans, LA 70116
Email: jbcook108@worldnet.att.net
(800)550-8450 or (504)581-1367

April 10, 11
✿ Spring Garden Festival
Plant and garden products exhibits, educational programs and plant sales.
Hours: 10am-5pm
Fee: $4
New Orleans Botanical Garden *(See Louisiana Guide to Gardens.)*

October 2, 3
✿ Secret Garden Patio Tour
Tour of sixteen different privately-owned gardens in the French Quarter, eight different ones on each day.
Hours: Noon-4pm
Fee: $10 per day
For information: **Patio Planters**, PO Box 72074, New Orleans, LA 70172
(504)522-5524

October 16, 17, 18
✿ Fall Garden Festival
Plant and garden products exhibits, educational programs and plant sales.
Hours: 10am-5pm
Fee: $4
New Orleans Botanical Garden *(See Louisiana Guide to Gardens.)*

Shreveport

April 24-May 1
✿ Spring Bloom Festival
A ten-day celebration honoring the first bloom roses in the Gardens, home to more than 20,000 roses. Garden exhibits, live entertainment, educational seminars and more.
Hours: 9am-6pm
Fee: $5

The Gardens of The American Rose Center
(See Louisiana Guide to Gardens.)

November 26-January 2
✿ Christmas in Roseland
More than 1,000,000 lights in the gardens, plus model trains, toy soldiers and reindeer.
Hours: 5:30-10pm; closed Christmas and New Year's Days
Fee: $10 per car or $3 per person
The Gardens of The American Rose Center
(See Louisiana Guide to Gardens.)

Maine

Guide to Gardens

Beatrix Farrand Garden
College of the Atlantic, Route 3
Bar Harbor, ME 04609
(207)288-5015 *Fax:* (207)288-4126
✿ This rose garden was designed by Beatrix Farrand for Mrs. James Byrne and was a prototype for the famous rose garden at Dumbarton Oaks in Washington, D.C. Acquired by College of the Atlantic in 1973, the garden was restored by landscape architect Patrick Chasse to Farrand's original concept, updated for practical College use. Funds for the restoration came from the Garden Club of Mt. Desert and Mr. and Mrs. David Rockefeller.
Hours: Jun-Sep dawn-dusk
Fees: Free

Coastal Maine Botanical Garden
Barters Island Road
Boothbay, ME
Mail: PO Box 234, Boothbay, ME 04537
(207)633-4333 *Fax:* (207)882-4232
✿ This Garden is a work in progress on 128 acres purchased in 1995. The site includes 3,600 feet of tidal river frontage in an ever-

green and hardwood forest, with ledges, wet-lands and fresh water ponds. The land is full of native trees, shrubs, ferns, mosses, lichens and mushrooms. Initial development includes a Wetland Garden and bridge, a Shore Walk and a Fern Walk.

Merryspring Horticultural Nature Park
Conway Road
Camden, ME
Mail: PO Box 893, Camden, ME 04843
Email: merwprng@gwi.net
(207)236-4885 *Fax:* (207)230-0663
🌿 The Park includes the Herb garden, rose, perennial, hosta and heather gardens, a 10-acre arboretum and connecting trails.
Hours: Park dawn-dusk; Visitor Center & Library 9am-2pm Mon-Fri
Fees: Free

Pine Tree State Arboretum
Augusta, ME
Mail: PO Box 344, Augusta, ME 04332
(207)621-0031 *Fax:* (207)621-8245
🌿 The Arboretum is located on 224 acres directly across the Kennebec River from the Capitol Building. The plant collection includes trees and shrubs, a rock garden, rhododen-dron and lilac plantings, and one of the largest collections of hosta in New England.
Hours: Dawn-dusk
Fees: Free

Roger Clapp Greenhouses & All America Selections Trial Garden
University of Maine, College Avenue
Orono, ME 04469
(207)581-3112
🌿 The Garden includes extensive plantings of annuals, herbs and perennials, including cur-rent All America Selections winners. The Greenhouses contain many exotic species from the tropics to the desert.

Hours: Gardens dawn-dusk; Greenhouses 8:30am-4:30pm weekdays
Fees: Free

Thuya Garden & Asticou Azalea Garden
Northeast Harbor, ME
Mail: PO Box 1120, Northeast Harbor, ME 04622
(207)276-5130
🌿 Thuya Garden, a formal English-style garden of annuals and perennials, was recently restored by landscape architect Patrick Chasse. Exotic evergreens, rhododendron, kalmia and native trees make up the special collections.

Asticou Azalea Garden is a 2-acre garden designed by Charles K. Savage using many of the plants from Beatrix Farrand's Reef Point Gardens in Bar Harbor. It contains a Japanese sand garden and an excellent collection of aza-leas and rhododendrons.
Hours: mid Jun-mid Oct 9am-5pm; call in advance
Fees: Donation requested

Tidebrook Conservation Trust
38 Bartol Island Road
Freeport, ME 04032
(201)865-3856
🌿 The Tidebrook is a landscape garden sur-rounding a house, with lawns, trees, shrubs, flower beds and foundation plantings.
Hours: May-Oct weekday afternoons
Fees: Free

Wolfe's Neck Farm Gardens
University of Southern Maine, Wolfe Neck Road
Freeport, ME
Mail: The Stone House, PO Box 159, Freeport, ME 04032
(207)865-3428
🌿 The former estate of Mr. and Mrs. M. C. Smith now serves as a demonstration center for organic gardening. The flower beds and Stone House gardens are always open for viewing.

Augusta

September 25-27
🌿 Common Ground Fair

Displays of livestock, produce, flowers, all kinds of agricultural exhibits, vendors and entertainment for the whole family. Call for show location.

Hours: 9am-dusk
Fee: $6; $2 seniors & children (free on Fri)
For information: **Maine Organic Farmers & Gardeners Association**, PO Box 2176, Augusta, ME 04338
(207)622-3118

Belfast

July 9-10
🌿 9th Annual Garden Tour

A tour of seven to eight private gardens in Belfast, a coastal community located on Penobscot Bay.

Hours: 10am-4pm rain or shine
Fee: $8 in advance; $10 day of tour
For information: **Waldo County General Hospital**, 15 Seaside Drive, Belfast, ME 04915
(207)338-1104

Brunswick
Near Portland

July 7, 8
🌿 Gardening with Nature Tour

A tour of diverse private gardens in and around Brunswick, including shade gardens, seaside gardens, perennial and annual displays.

Hours: 10am-4pm
Fee: $15
For information: **Brunswick-Topsham Land Trust**, 103 Maine Street, Brunswick , ME 04011
(207)729-7694

Camden

July 15
🌿 52nd Annual House & Garden Tour

A tour of many homes and gardens in the Camden-Rockport area, including the Spite House Gardens. Call to confirm date.

Hours: 9am-4:30pm
Fees: $20
For information: **Camden Garden Club**, PO Box 1047, Camden, ME 04843
(207)236-7714

October 2
🌿 Windfall Fair & Apple Festival

Local produce, handicrafts, art, music and dancing, cider pressing, hayrides, games and contests.

Hours: 10am-6pm
Fee: $1
Merryspring Horticultural Nature Park *(See Maine Guide to Gardens.)*

Kennebunk

July 17
🌿 Private Gardens of the Kennebunks

A tour of eight private gardens benefiting the York County Child Abuse Council. Call to confirm date.

For information: **York County Child Abuse Council** PO Box 568, Biddeford, ME 04005
(207)284-1337

Lewiston

July 17
🌿 Lewiston-Auburn Garden Tour

A tour of six private gardens, usually three in Lewiston and three in Auburn. Benefits the Society. Contact them for advance ticket purchases.

Hours: 10am-4pm
Fee: $10 in advance; $12 day of tour

For information: **Maine Music Society** PO Box 711, Auburn ME 04210
(207)782-1403

Portland

See also Brunswick

March 11-14
⚜ Portland Flower Show

A regional show, sponsored by the Association of Maine Landscapers and Nurserymen.
Hours: 10am-6pm
Fee: $8; $5 seniors & children
Portland Company Complex, 58 Fore Street, Portland, ME
For information: **Association of Maine Landscapers & Nurserymen**, RR2, PO Box 1584, Turner, ME 04282
Email: sunnyside@tka.com
Fax: (207)225-3998

Rockland

July 18
⚜ Gardens in the Georges River Watershed Tour

The 8th annual tour of country gardens in the watershed towns of Warren, Union and Hope sponsored by the Georges River Land Trust. Tickets, brochure and map can obtained in advance at area bookstores or by writing to GRLT.
Hours: 10am-5pm
Fee: $12 at each garden day of tour; $10 advance
For information: **Georges River Land Trust**, 328 Main Street, Studio 206, Rockland, ME 04841
(207)594-5166

Standish

May-October
⚜ Marrett House Perennial & Herb Sale

Saturday sales offering a variety of old-fashioned perennials and herbs, including some from this historic garden. Free house tours during the sales. Call for exact dates.
Hours: 10am-4pm Saturday
Fee: Free
Society for the Preservation of New England Antiquities, Marrett House, PO Box 3, Standish, ME 04084
(207)642-3032

Maryland

Guide to Gardens

Brookside Gardens
1500 Glenallan Avenue
Wheaton, MD 20902
(301)949-8230 Fax: (301)365-8371
⚜ The 50-acre Garden contains many small gardens, including a Japanese garden, rose garden, a winter garden, formal garden with clipped hedges and more. There are many rare and unusual trees, plus greenhouses with seasonal displays.
Hours: 9am-5pm
Fees: Free

City of Baltimore Conservatory
Druid Hill Park, Gwynns Falls Parkway & Auchentoroly Terrace
Baltimore, MD
Mail: Department of Parks & Recreation, 4915 Greenspring Avenue, Baltimore, MD 21209
(410)396-0180 Fax: (410-367-8039
⚜ Located in Druid Hill Park, the Baltimore Conservatory has expanded from the original 1888 Palm House to include four greenhouses and outdoor gardens.

Hours: 10am-4pm Thurs-Sun
Fees: Free

Cylburn Arboretum
4915 Greenspring Avenue
Baltimore, MD 21209
(410)367-2217 *Fax:* (410)367-8039
⚘ A highlight of this 174-acre preserve is the large wildflower garden. The site also includes nature trails, formal gardens, herb garden, an All-America garden, a sensory garden, many good collections of flowering trees, and a boxwood collection.
Hours: 7:30am-3:30pm
Fees: Free; $2 parking donation requested

Ladew Topiary Gardens
3535 Jarrettsville Pike
Monkton, MD 21111
(410)557-9570 *Fax:* (410)557-7763
⚘ Ladew Topiary Garden has been sited as "the most outstanding topiary garden in America" by the Garden Club of America, with 15 thematic gardens on 22 acres.
Directions: 14 miles north of Baltimore
Hours: Apr 15-Oct 11 10am-4pm Mon-Fri, 10:30am-5pm Sat & Sun
Fees: House & Garden $8, $2 children; Garden $6, $1 children

William Paca Garden
Visitors' Center, 1 Martin Street
Annapolis, MD 21401
(410)267-7619 *Fax:* (410)267-6189
⚘ This is an 18th century Maryland garden of elegant plantings on two urban acres.
Web: aabga.mobot.org/AABGA/
Member.pages/williampaca.html
Hours: 10am-4pm, noon-4pm Sun
Fees: House & Garden $6; Garden $3

Selected Events

Statewide

April 18-May 30
⚘ The Annual Maryland House & Garden Pilgrimage
This well-known event takes place in April and May, when different communities hold tours of outstanding and historic homes and gardens in the various counties. Tickets can be purchased in advance from the Pilgrimage Headquarters or at the first house visited. Tour Books with full information will be available after March 15. For a copy, send name, address and $2 to Pilgrimage Headquarters. Six counties throughout the state are included on the tour. The schedule is as follows:
Saturday, April 17
Anne Arundel County
Friday, April 23
Baltimore City, Guilford area
Saturday, April 24
Kent County (Eastern Shore)
Sunday,April 25
Worcester County (Eastern shore)
Wednesday, May 5
Baltimore County
Saturday, May 8
Calvert County (Southern MD)
Wednesday, May 12
Carroll County (Western MD)
Hours: 10am-5pm
Fee: $20 per tour; $5 per house
For information: **Maryland House & Garden Pilgrimage**, 1105A Providence Road, Towson, MD 21286
Web: www.mhgp.org
(410)821-6933

Annapolis

May 15, 16
❧ William Paca Garden Spring Plant Sale
Native, rare and period plants grown on site from seeds in the collection of the historic William Paca Garden.
Hours: 10am-4pm Sat; noon-4pm Sun
Fee: Free
William Paca Garden (See Maryland Guide to Gardens.)

Baltimore

May 8
❧ Market Day
A large selection of plants, shrubs, vegetables, annuals and wildflowers for sale, plus a flea market and refreshments. Also crafts and children's activities.
Hours: 8am-2pm
Fee: $2 parking donation requested
Cylburn Arboretum (See Maryland Guide to Gardens.)

May 8
❧ Plant Sale
Unique cuttings, seedlings, topiary frames, annuals and perennials.
Hours: 10:30am-5pm
Ladew Topiary Gardens (See Maryland Guide to Gardens.)

June 19
❧ Solstice Celebration
A day of activities devoted to nature, gardening, recycling. Fun and learning for the whole family.
Hours: 8am-4pm
Fee: $1 suggested donation

Cylburn Arboretum (See Maryland Guide to Gardens.)

September 11
❧ Exotic & Native Plant Sale & All-America Selection Day
This is the major plant sale in the area. Sponsored by Cylburn Arboretum Association.
Hours: 8am-2pm
Fee: $2 parking donation requested
Cylburn Arboretum (See Maryland Guide to Gardens.)

October 10
❧ Festifall
Family fun with environmental and horticultural emphasis.
Hours: 10am-4pm
Fee: $2 parking donation requested
Cylburn Arboretum (See Maryland Guide to Gardens.)

October 10
❧ Fall Festival
A great day for the whole family with live music, pony rides, vendors and more.
Hours: Noon-5pm
Ladew Topiary Gardens (See Maryland Guide to Gardens.)

Bethesda

April 30-May 2
❧ Annual Landon Azalea Garden Festival
A chance to visit the world-famous azalea collection of over 100 varieties in full bloom in Landon School's Perkins Garden. Tours of the azaleas, wildflower and herb gardens, crafts and food, activities. A fund raiser for the school.
Hours: 10am-5pm
Landon School, 6101 Wilson Lane, Bethesda, MD 20817
(301)320-1066 Fax: (301)320-1133

Buckeystown

8 miles south of Frederick

July 10, 11
⚘ Lotus Blossom Festival

Acres of lotus in bloom, plus lectures, demonstrations on how to install a water garden, arts, crafts, kid's activities, and more. Benefits the Frederick Regional Youth Orchestra.
Fee: Donation requested
Lilypons Water Gardens, 7000 Lilypons Road, PO Box 10, Buckeystown, MD 21717
(800)999-5459

Frederick

See also Buckeystown

May 22, 23
⚘ Beyond the Garden Gates Tour

A tour of some nine private gardens and two church gardens in historic Frederick, Maryland. Proceeds used for beautification projects in downtown Frederick.
Hours: 1-5pm
Fee: $10
For information: **City of Frederick**, 4 West Seventh Street, Frederick, MD 21701
Web: www.cityoffrederick.com
(301)694-2489

Timonium

March 5-7 & March 12-14
⚘ Maryland Home & Flower Show

Romantic Gardens. Professionally landscaped gardens, garden and home merchandise, educational exhibits, plant society exhibits, seminars given by the Federated Garden Clubs of Maryland and others, healthy cooking demonstrations and more.
Hours: March 5 4pm-10pm Fri; other days 10am-10pm; 10am-6pm Sun
Fee: $8.50; $2 children 6-12; under 6 free
Timonium Fairgrounds, 2100 York Road, Timonium, MD 21093

Web: www.chesome.com/hmgarshow/
Email: slprod@erols.com
(410)863-1180 *Fax:* (410)863-1187

April 15-18
⚘ The Rites of Spring Home
   & Garden Exhibition

Exhibition gardens, plus a large selection of plants and accessories for sale from many boutiques and gardens. Benefits the Union Memorial Hospital.
Hours: 6-9pm Thurs; 10am-8pm Fri; 10am-6pm Sat; 10am-4pm Sun
Timonium Fairgrounds, 2100 York Road, Timonium, MD
Mail: Union Hospital Foundation, 201 East University Parkway, Baltimore, MD 21218
(410)554-2662

October 15-17
⚘ Fall Maryland Home & Garden Show

Gardens by top area landscapers plus a wide variety of home products and services, seminars, demonstrations and crafts for sale.
Hours: 10am-10pm Fri, Sat; 10am-6pm Sun
Fee: $6.50; $2 children
Timonium Fairgrounds, 2100 York Road, Timonium, MD 21093
Web: www.chesome.com/hmgarshow/
Email: slprod@erols.com
(410)863-1180 *Fax:* (410)863-1187

Wheaton

November 27-January 3, 1999
⚘ Garden of Lights

Garden and conservatories illuminated for the holidays.
Hours: 5-9pm Wed-Sun; closed Dec 24, 25
Fee: $3
Brookside Gardens *(See Maryland Guide to Gardens.)*

December 9-January 10, 1999

Winter Display

The Conservatory is decorated for the holidays with poinsettias, lights and fresh greens.

Hours: 10am-5pm

Brookside Gardens *(See Maryland Guide to Gardens.)*

Massachusetts

Guide to Gardens

The Arnold Arboretum

125 Arborway
Boston, MA 02130
(617)524-1718 *Fax:* (617)524-1418

The 265-acre Arnold Arboretum of Harvard University displays a premier collection of North American hardy trees, shrubs and vines on a site designed by its first director, Charles Sprague Sargent, and Frederick Law Olmsted. The plants are grouped by family and arranged in botanical sequence along the main drive. The Arboretum is a National Historic Landmark and is an integral part of the parklands known as the Emerald Necklace, a functioning unit of the Boston Parks Department.

Web: www.arboretum.harvard.edu
Hours: Sunrise-sunset
Fees: Free

Ashumet Holly & Wildlife Sanctuary

286 Ashumet Road
East Falmouth, MA 02536
(508)563-6390

Ashumet was planted by Wilfred Wheeler, "the Holly Man," who began planting hollies to protect them from fires, development and Christmas collecting. Ashumet is operated by the Massachusetts Audubon Society.

Web: www.massaudubon.org
Hours: Sunrise-Sunset
Fees: $3; $2 seniors & children

Berkshire Botanical Garden

Junction of Routes 102 & 183
Stockbridge, MA 01262
(413)298-3926 *Fax:* (413)298-4897

Established as an educational center in 1934, this 15-acre Garden contains a rock garden, herb garden with 90 kinds of culinary and medicinal plants, perennial garden, orchard, vegetable garden, vineyard and pond. Other features include collections of hostas, azaleas, daylilies, dwarf conifers, bog and water plants. There are also greenhouses, a lath house, demonstration and test gardens, and a garden for the handicapped.

Hours: May-Oct 10am-5pm
Fees: $5; $4 seniors; $3 students

The Botanic Garden of Smith College

Lyman Conservatory
Northampton, MA 01063
(413)585-2740

The entire campus of Smith College was designed by Frederick Law Olmsted one hundred years ago as a botanic garden and arboretum. The Lyman Conservatory houses additional plant collections and has seasonal displays all year. Nearby is one of the oldest rock gardens in America and the systematics garden. Other gardens around the campus include a Japanese viewing pavilion, wildflower garden, herb, rose, formal knot and gazebo gardens.

Web: www.smith.edu/garden
Hours: 8:30am-4pm daily
Fees: Free

Chesterwood

4 Williamsville Road
Stockbridge, MA
Mail: PO Box 827, Stockbridge, MA 01262
(413)298-3579 *Fax:* (413)298-3973

Chesterwood is the early 20th century summer studio, home and garden of Daniel Chester French, sculptor of the Lincoln Memorial and Minute Man statues. French transformed a traditional New England farm into a gentleman's estate, with a formal garden, woodland walks, vistas, and landscape structures. Chesterwood is a National Trust Historic Site.
Web: www.nthp.org
Hours: 10am-5pm
Fees: Grounds $5.50

Garden in the Woods
180 Hemenway Road
Framingham, MA 01701
(508)877-6574 *Fax:* (508)877-3658
The 45-acre Garden is devoted to the conservation of temperate North American flora. The Garden features ever-changing displays of naive and rare foliage and flowers, beginning in early spring and continuing through late fall. Special gardens include Rich Woodland Groves, Lily Pond, Sunny Bog, Pine Barrens, Western Garden, Rock Gardens and Meadow. It is owned and operated by the New England Wild Flower Society.
Web: www.newfs.org/~newfs
Hours: Apr 15-Oct 9am-5pm; May hours to 7pm
Fees: $6; $5 seniors; $3 children

Heritage Plantation
Grove Street
Sandwich, MA
Mail: PO Box 566, Sandwich, MA 02563
(508)888-3300
The Plantation has a holly dell, daylily garden with hundreds of varieties, an herb garden, a wildflower garden, and an outstanding collection of Dexter rhododendrons.
Hours: 10am-5pm
Fees: Charged

Isabella Stewart Gardner Museum
The Fenway
Boston, MA 02115
(617)566-1401
The Museum's three floors of galleries open onto an interior courtyard filled with changing displays of flowering plants. A walled outdoor garden is open to the public during warm weather.
Web: www.boston.com/gardner/
Hours: 11am-5pm Tues-Sun
Fees: $10; $7 seniors; $5 college students; free under 18

Lyman Estate, The Vale
185 Lyman Street
Waltham, MA 02154
(781)891-4882 ext 244 Greenhouses *Fax:* (781)570-9147
The Lyman Estate, a National Historic Landmark owned by the Society for the Preservation of New England Antiquities, includes the house, greenhouses and 37 acres of woodland, gardens and cultivated fields. The landscape, largely unchanged since 1839, is one of the few surviving examples of 18th-century naturalistic design. There are three greenhouses on the grounds: the Grape House with extensive vines from cuttings taken in 1870 from Hampton Court in England; the Camellia House with its 100 year old specimens; and the "new" greenhouse, added in 1930 to provide fresh flowers for the house.
Web: www.SPNEA.org
Hours: Greenhouses 9:30am-4pm Mon-Sat; Grounds 9am-5pm
Fees: Free

Sedgwick Gardens
572 Essex Street
Beverly, MA 01915
(978)524-1871 *Fax:* (978)921-1948

This 7-acre garden includes trees, shrubs and flowering plants.
Hours: Dawn-dusk
Fees: Free; donations accepted

Tower Hill Botanic Garden

11 French Drive
Boylston, MA 01505
(508)869-6111 *Fax:* (508)869-0314
Located on 132 rural acres, Tower Hill features a spectacular bulb display, a Lawn Garden with over 350 varieties of trees and shrubs, Secret and Cottage Gardens, a Vegetable and Wildlife Garden, an orchard of heirloom apple varieties, walking trails and panoramic views.
Web: www.towerhillbg.org
Hours: 10am-5pm Tues-Sun & holiday Mon
Fees: $7; $5 seniors; $3 youth; under 6 free

Selected Events

Ashfield

June 26, 27
12th Annual Farm & Garden Tour

Tour of some nine private farms and gardens in the area. Benefits the Franklin Land Trust, which seeks to preserve farm and agricultural land. Lunch available by reservation. The event often sells out, so it is advisable to write for tickets in advance. Travel and lodging information will be sent with tickets.
Hours: 10am-4pm
Fee: $12 (ticket holders can attend the tour on one or both days)
For information: **Franklin Land Trust**, PO Box 216, Ashfield, MA 01330
(413)628-4696

Barnstable

April 24
Annual Daffodil Tea & Open Garden Day

Tea in the English-style country garden of St. Mary's Church, amidst spring flowers in a woodland setting. Reservations required. Garden open all day to the public without reservation, with hundreds of daffodils, hyacinths, flowering shrubs and trees in bloom.
Hours: Tea 2-4pm
Fee: Tea $10
St. Mary's Episcopal Church, Route 6A, PO Box 395, Barnstable, MA 02630
(508)362-2205

Beverly Farms

June 13
Garden Tour of Eight Coastal Gardens

Visits gardens in Manchester, Beverly Farms and Prides Crossing on the North Shore.
Hours: 10:30am-4:30pm
For information: **North Shore Garden Club**, 809 Hale Street, Beverly Farms, MA 01915
(978)927-1709

Boston

March 13-21
128th New England Spring Flower Show

The oldest continuously operating horticultural event, with over 60 major exhibits and 40 life-sized gardens, plus hundreds of vendors and amateur entries. Includes educational programs for children and adults, demonstrations, competitions, a large gardeners' market, and many special events. Sponsored by the Massachusetts Horticultural Society.
Hours: 10am-9:30pm Mon-Sat; 10am-6pm Sun
Fee: Weekend $16; weekday discounts
Bayside Exposition Center, 200 Mt. Vernon, Boston, MA
For information: **Massachusetts Horticultural Society**, 300 Massachusetts Avenue, Boston, MA 02115

Web: www.masshort.org
Email: mhspa@masshort.org
(617)536-9280

April 27-29
✿ Art in Bloom '98
Flower arranging as an art form, with floral arrangements from over 70 New England garden clubs displayed beside selected masterpieces from the Museum's collection. Flower arranging demonstrations and noted speakers.
Hours: 10am-4:45pm Tues; 10am-9:45pm Wed, Thurs
Fee: Admission $10; $8 seniors
Museum of Fine Arts, 465 Huntington Avenue , Boston, MA 02115
(617)369-9300 ext 3395

May 16
✿ Lilac Sunday
The only day in the year when picnicking is allowed in the Arboretum, at the peak of the lilac bloom.
Hours: 10am-4pm
Fee: Free
The Arnold Arboretum *(See Massachusetts Guide to Gardens.)*

May 20
✿ Hidden Gardens of Beacon Hill Tour
A tour of twelve gardens, plus five ribbon gardens, which may be viewed but not entered, in this historic section of 19th century brick townhouses. Coffee served from 9-11am, and tea from 2:30-4:30pm. The 70th annual garden tour sponsored by the Beacon Hill Garden Club. Tickets are limited so call in advance.
Hours: 9am-6pm
For information: **Beacon Hill Garden Club** , c/o Ticket Chairman Charles Street Station, PO Box 302, Boston, MA 02114
(617)227-4392

June 19
✿ South End Gardens Tour
A self-guided tour of over 40 private and community gardens in the South End neighborhoods of Claremont and Chester Park. Benefits the South End/Lower Roxbury Open Space Land Trust, which owns and maintains twelve community gardens and pocket parks in the area and services five affiliated gardens. Call to confirm date and order tickets.
Hours: 10am-4pm
Fee: $12 in advance; $15 day of tour
*For information:***South End/Lower Roxbury Open Space Land Trust**, PO Box 180923, Boston, MA 02118
(617)536-2488

Boylston
10 miles from Worcester

May 5
✿ Seven States Daffodil Show
Hundreds of blooms on display. Sponsored by the American Daffodil Society.
Hours: 1-7pm
Tower Hill Botanic Garden *(See Massachusetts Guide to Gardens.)*

June 5
✿ Tower Hill Botanic Garden Plant Sale
Great selection of all kinds of plants, shrubs and trees, plus a silent auction, exhibitions by twelve plant societies, tools, books, gardening gifts, refreshments and information.
Hours: 11am-2pm
Fee: Free
Tower Hill Botanic Garden *(See Massachusetts Guide to Gardens.)*

June 6
✿ Siberian & Tall Bearded Iris Show
Sponsored by the Iris Society of Massachusetts, a show of cut stems and floral design.

Hours: 1-5pm
Fee: Free
Tower Hill Botanic Garden *(See Massachusetts Guide to Gardens.)*

July 10, 11
🌿 Lily Show
Displays of dozens of varieties of Asiatic, Oriental and Trumpet lilies suitable for Central Massachusetts gardens. Sponsored by the New England Lily Society.
Hours: 1-5pm Sat; 10am-5pm Sun
Fee: Free
Tower Hill Botanic Garden *(See Massachusetts Guide to Gardens.)*

October 9-11
🌿 Harvest Weekend
Tastings, tours of apple orchard, harvest displays, children's activities, heirloom apple varieties for sale.
Hours: 10am-5pm
Fee: $4; $3 senior; $2 youth
Tower Hill Botanic Garden *(See Massachusetts Guide to Gardens.)*

December 3-January 2
🌿 Holly Days
Decorated trees and holiday greenery, lights, unique horticultural creations and holiday music. Weekend decorating and cooking demonstrations plus garden tours at 1pm Saturday and Sunday.
Hours: 10am-5pm Tues-Sun; open til 8pm Wed
Fee: $4; $3 senior; $2 youth
Tower Hill Botanic Garden *(See Massachusetts Guide to Gardens.)*

East Falmouth
Cape Cod

December 3-5, 10-12
🌿 Wreath, Greens & Holly Sale

Holly Days. A sale of fresh cut greens, balsam wreaths, swags, fresh cut Cape Cod holly and hand crafted items, all made by the Friends of Ashumet and Cape area garden clubs. Chowder, mulled cider and other refreshments served.
Hours: 10am-3pm
Fee: Free
Ashumet Holly & Wildlife Sanctuary *(See Massachusetts Guide to Gardens.)*

Framingham

April 15
🌿 Opening Day
Plant sales, tours and gift shop specials to celebrate opening day at this largest collection of wildflowers in the Northeast.
Hours: 9am-5pm
Garden in the Woods *(See Massachusetts Guide to Gardens.)*

April 24
🌿 Earth Day Celebration
Garden tours every half hour from 9:30am-3:30pm, family activities and a slide show on how to grow wildflowers.
Hours: 9am-5pm
Fee: Free
Garden in the Woods *(See Massachusetts Guide to Gardens.)*

June 12
🌿 25th Annual Plant Sale
Billed as the largest sale of wildflowers in New England, with over 200 varieties of wildflowers, plus perennials, flowering trees and shrubs.
Hours: 10am-3pm
Fee: Free
Garden in the Woods *(See Massachusetts Guide to Gardens.)*

Greenfield

May 22
🌿 **4th Annual Extravaganza Plant Sale**
A plants, bulbs and baked goods sale sponsored by the Greenfield Garden Club for its community projects.
Hours: 8am-1pm
Fee: Free
Display Garden of Greenfield Garden Club, Trap Plain - Silver & Federal Streets, Greenfield, MA
For information: **Greenfield Garden Club Display Garden**, 252 Davis Street, Greenfield, MA 01301

July 10
🌿 **7th Annual Greenfield Garden Club Tour**
A self-guided tour of private gardens in the Greenfield area, starting at Trap Plain Display Garden. Plant sale and refreshments.
Hours: 9am-4pm
Fee: $8
Display Garden of Greenfield Garden Club, Trap Plain - Silver & Federal Streets, Greenfield, MA
For information: **Greenfield Garden Club Display Garden**, 252 Davis Street, Greenfield, MA 01301

Lenox

July 10
🌿 **Hidden Treasures of the Berkshires Tour**
A tour of private houses and gardens in Lenox. Call for reservations.
Hours: 10am-4pm
Fee: $20 in advance; $25 day of tour
For information: **Lenox Garden Club**, PO Box 552, Lenox, MA 01240
(413)598-3089

Leverett

June 12
🌿 **Leverett in Bloom Tour**
A self-guided garden tour of six to eight area gardens, plus a plant sale and a buffet lunch by advance reservation. Starts at Town Hall. Tickets on sale near the date at local locations.
Hours: 9am-3pm; Plant Sale 9-11am
Fee: $6 tour; $10 tour and buffet
For information: **Leverett in Bloom Garden Tour**, 6 Rattlesnake Gutter Road, Leverett, MA 01541
(413)548-9082 or (413)367-9562

Nantucket
Cape Cod

April 24, 25
🌿 **Annual Nantucket Daffodil Festival**
A competitive show judged by American Daffodil Society judges, featuring a large Junior Division.
Hours: 2-5pm Sun; 10am-5pm Mon
Fee: Free
The Point Breeze Hotel, 89 Easton Street, Nantucket, MA
For information: **Nantucket Garden Club**, PO Box 627, Nantucket, MA 02554
(508)228-0644

July 14
🌿 **Annual Community Green Thumb Flower Show & Sale**
Call for information.
Hours: 10am-5pm
Fee: Free
The Point Breeze Hotel, 89 Easton Street, Nantucket, MA
For information: **Nantucket Garden Club**, PO Box 627, Nantucket, MA 02554
(508)228-0644

August 11
🌺 45th Annual House & Garden Tour
Six houses and gardens in the village of Siaconset. Refreshments served.
Hours: Noon-5pm
Fee: $30
For information: **Nantucket Garden Club**, PO Box 627, Nantucket, MA 02554 (508)228-0644

Pittsfield

July 17, 18
🌺 Concealed City Gardens Tour
A self-guided tour of private gardens in the heart of the Berkshire Mountains.
Hours: 10am-4pm Sat; noon-4pm Sun
Fee: $12 in advance
For information: **Pittsfield Beautiful**, 243 North Street, Pittsfield, MA 01201 (413)442-2680 *Fax:* (413)442-4094

Salem

February 27, March 27, April 24
🌺 Greenhouse Tips
Sessions by Peabody Essex Landscape Manager on the secrets for cultivating the garden, raising plants from seed, greenhouse management. Call for reservations.
Hours: 9:30-10:30am
Fee: $40 series; $14 per class
The Peabody Essex Museum, East India Square, Salem, MA 01970
Web: www.pem.org
(978)745-9500 ext 3028

Somerset

June 19
🌺 Somerset Garden Tour 1999
Tour of eight private gardens in the Somerset area starting at the Congregational Christian Church in the center of town where maps and tickets will be distributed. Noon lunch at the Church Hall included.
Hours: 10am-3pm
Fee: $15; includes luncheon
Tour starts from: **Congregational Christian Church**, Route 138, Somerset, MA
For information: **Somerset Garden Club**, 51 Franklin Road, Somerset, MA 02726
Email: Mamafranjo@worldnet.att.net
(508)674-5573

Stockbridge

May 7-9
🌺 Plant Sale & Herb Fair
Thousands of plants ready for the garden, including annuals, perennials, rare and unusual plants, herbs, trees and shrubs, plus select garden items and tools.
Hours: 10am-5pm
Fee: Free
Berkshire Botanical Garden *(See Massachusetts Guide to Gardens.)*

August
🌺 Summer Festival & Flower Show
A flower show presented by the Berkshire Botanical Garden and local garden clubs, with food, entertainment and outdoor, nature and garden related activities for everyone. Call for exact date.
Hours: 10am-5pm
Fee: $5; $4 seniors; $3 students
Berkshire Botanical Garden *(See Massachusetts Guide to Gardens.)*

October 2, 3
🌺 65th Annual Harvest Festival
The Berkshire's oldest and best known community event, with fun, activities, entertainments, crafts and a giant tag sale.
Hours: 10am-5pm
Fee: $2 parking fee
Berkshire Botanical Garden *(See Massachusetts Guide to Gardens.)*

December 3-5
Marketplace

Windows & Doors. Wreaths and holiday decorative items for sale made from herbs, flowers and vegetable gardens, plus seasonal plants and greenery and garden-related gifts.

Hours: 10am-5pm
Fee: Free
Berkshire Botanical Garden *(See Massachusetts Guide to Gardens.)*

Sturbridge

June 5
Spring Gardens in Bloom

Demonstrations and talks on 19th century gardening topics, plus walking tours through historic spring gardens in full bloom.

Hours: 9am-5pm
Fee: Admission $16; $15 seniors; $8 children
Old Sturbridge Village, 1 Old Sturbridge Village Road, Sturbridge, MA 01566
Web: www.osv.org
(508)347-3362

August 7
Summer Garden Day

Sessions on historical gardening techniques with hands-on activities.

Hours: 9am-5pm
Fee: Admission $16; $15 seniors; $8 children
Old Sturbridge Village, 1 Old Sturbridge Village Road, Sturbridge, MA 01566
Web: www.osv.org
(508)347-3362

September 25, 26
An Early 19th Century Agricultural Fair

A recreated 1830s celebration, the forerunner of today's agricultural fairs. Call the Village, ext 325, to enter your own heirloom produce or flowers.

Hours: 9am-5pm

Fee: Admission $16; $15 seniors; $8 children
Old Sturbridge Village, 1 Old Sturbridge Village Road, Sturbridge, MA 01566
Web: www.osv.org
(508)347-3362

Waltham

January 19-February 13
Camellia Blooming Season

An extraordinary display of camellia trees in full bloom in the Camellia House, many more than a century old, plus a sale of camellias and other winter flowering plants.

Hours: 9am-4pm daily
Lyman Estate, The Vale *(See Massachusetts Guide to Gardens.)*

Weston

September 19
Plant Sale

A large number of rare and unusual trees, shrubs, vines and perennials, many propagated at the Arnold Arboretum and unavailable at commercial nurseries.

Hours: 9am-1pm
Fee: Free
Case Estates, 135 Wellesley Street, Weston, MA
For information: **The Arnold Arboretum** *(See Massachusetts Guide to Gardens.)*

Worcester

See also Boylston

March 25-28
Central Massachusetts Spring Flower Show

Over thirty major landscape displays and garden vignettes, plus lectures and workshops by leading horticultural authorities in the area. More than 100 vendors in the 19,000 square foot "Garden Shop" offering a wide range of products and services. Presented by Spag's

and the Telegram & Gazette in cooperation with the Worcester County Horticultural Society/Tower Hill Botanic Garden. **Centrum Centre**, 50 Foster Street, Worcester, MA
For information: **Central Massachusetts Spring Flower Show**, 319A Southbridge Street, Suite 250, Auburn, MA 01501 (800)533-0229 *Fax:* (503)832-0371

Michigan

Guide to Gardens

Anna Scripps Whitcomb Conservatory Showhouse

Conservatory Drive, Belle Isle
Detroit, MI 48207
(313)852-4064 *Fax:* (313)852-4074
🌼 This site is comprised of 10 acres of gardens and the Conservatory, built in 1904 and redesigned in the 1940s by Albert Kahn in the style of Jefferson's Monticello. The Conservatory houses rotating displays of its great collections, including orchids, tropical vines and flowers, cacti, a fernery and tropical fruit trees. The formal gardens outside were designed by Frederick Law Olmsted.
Hours: 10am-5pm
Fees: Conservatory $2, $1 seniors & children 2-12; Gardens are free

Cranbrook House & Gardens

380 Lone Pine Road
Bloomfield Hills, MI
Mail: PO Box 801, Bloomfield Hills, MI 48303
(248)645-3149 *Fax:* (248)645-3085
🌼 The Garden has 40 acres of formal gardens with fountains, scuplture, hedges and flowering ornamentals. The special gardens include a sunken garden, herb garden, rose garden, English garden, a wildflower collec-

tion, and annuals appropriate to the season. The entire garden is maintained by volunteers.
Hours: May-Aug 10am-5pm Mon-Sat; 11am-5pm Sun
Fees: Gardens $3; $2 seniors

Dow Gardens

West Street at Andrews & Eastman Avenues
Midland, MI 48640
(800)362-4874 *Fax:* (517)631-0675
🌼 This 60-acre estate includes formal and informal gardens. More than 600 species of shrubs and flowers can be found on the grounds, including fine specimens of oak, maple, dogwod, crabapple, pine, rhododendron, magnolia and viburnum.
Web: www.michigan.org/mi/dowgardens/
Hours: 10am-sunset
Fees: $3; $1 children

Fernwood Garden & Nature Center

13988 Range Line Road
Niles, MI 49120
(616)695-6491 *Fax:* (616)695-6688
🌼 The 100-acre Nature Center offers a large woodland area, tall grass prairie, and wilderness and marsh areas, all with good trails. In addition, there are many special gardens, including herb, rock, lilac, rose, boxwood, wildflower, groundcover, silver and blue foliage, a Japanese garden and a pioneer garden. Also has noteworthy collections of iris, hostas, peonies, ferns, shade and street trees.
Hours: May-Sep 10am-6pm; Oct-April 10am-5pm; longer hrs Sat; closed Mon
Fees: $4; $3 seniors; $2 students

Frederik Meijer Gardens

3411 Bradford NE
Grand Rapids, MI 49525
(616)957-1580 *Fax:* (616)957-5792
🌼 The 70-acre Frederik Meijer Gardens feature outdoor gardens designed by Oehme and

vanSweden, with paths throughout the natural wetlands, woodlands and prairies. The Conservatory is the largest in the State of Michigan and houses tropical plants from all over the world.
Web: www.meijergardens.org
Hours: 9am-5pm Mon-Sat; noon-5pm Sun
Fees: $5; $4 seniors; $2 children

Hidden Lake Gardens of MSU
6280 West Munger Road
Tipton, MI 49287
(517)431-2060
⚘ The Gardens comprise a 755-acre landscape arboretum on the campus of Michigan State University. They include natural and developed landscapes. More than six miles of paved drive connects areas of interest such as dwarf and rare conifers, hostas, ornamental tree and shrub collections. The conservatory houses tropical collections.
Hours: 8am-dusk
Fees: $3 weekends; $1 weekdays

Horticultural Demonstration Gardens
Michigan State University
East Lansing, MI
Mail: Department of Horticulture, A-240-A PSSB, East Lansing, MI 48824
(517)355-4800 *Fax:* (517)353-0890
⚘ Developed for educational purposes on the Michigan State campus, the Gardens have become a premier garden site in the state. There are five gardens: the Annual Trial Garden, the Foyer Garden, the Rose Garden, the Perennial garden, and the Idea Garden. The Clarence E. Lewis Arboretum, adjacent to the Gardens, is a 6-acre site featuring a fruit tree collection, a new central court garden and a diverse collection of spring blooming trees and shrubs, ornamentals perennials and groundcovers in a landscaped setting.
Hours: Dawn-dusk

Fees: $1; $.50 children

Leila Arboretum
928 West Michigan Avenue
Battle Creek, MI 49017
(616)969-0270 *Fax:* (616)969-0616
⚘ Leila Arboretum consists of 72 acres, with more than 3000 species of trees and shrubs dating back to the 1920s. It's laid out in the style of famous European gardens.
Hours: Daylight hours
Fees: Free

Matthaei Botanical Gardens
1800 North Dixboro Road
Ann Arbor , MI 48105
(734)998-7061 *Fax:* (743)998-6205
⚘ A major university facility of the University of Michigan, the Gardens occupy 350 acres of both landscaped and wild areas. Situated along Fleming Creek, the gardens include four nature trails, mature woodlands, wetlands, several ponds and a tall grass prairie. Special gardens include a rose garden, rock garden, a knot garden, medicinal plantings and fern collections. The Conservatory contains three display houses with a tremendous diversity of plants: tropical, warm temperate and arid.
Web: www.lsa.umich.edu/mbg/
Hours: 8am-dusk; Conservatory 10am-4:30pm
Fees: $2; $1 students

W.J. Beal Botanical Garden
West Circle Drive
East Lansing, MI
Mail: 412 Olds Hall, MSU, East Lansing, MI 48824
(517)355-7750 *Fax:* (517)432-1090
⚘ Established in 1873 by Professor William James Beal, the Garden is the oldest continuously operated botanical garden of its kind in the United States. More than 5,000 different kinds of plants can be found on the five-acre

site. Tours can be arranged to focus on basic botany, conservation, rare plants of the Great Lakes Region, economic botany and plant taxonomy. Call or write for information.
Web: www.cpp.msu.edu
Fees: Free

Selected Events

Ann Arbor

April 17, 18
⚘ Orchid Festival
An annual show featuring plant displays, lectures and vendors, sponsored by the Ann Arbor Orchid Society.
Hours: noon-5pm Sat; 10am-5pm Sun
Fee: Free
Matthaei Botanical Gardens (See Michigan Guide to Gardens.)

May 1, 2
⚘ Spring Perennial Sale
Over 30,000 perennials, ground covers, vines herbs, roses, grasses, aquatic plants and more. Also garden tools and supplies.
Hours: 10am-4:30pm
Fee: Free
Matthaei Botanical Gardens (See Michigan Guide to Gardens.)

May 9
⚘ Mother's Day Wildflower Day
An annual celebration of the Helen V. Smith Woodland Wildflower Garden. Guided tours, wildflower sales and afternoon tea.
Hours: Noon-3pm
Fee: Free
Matthaei Botanical Gardens (See Michigan Guide to Gardens.)

June 12
⚘ A Garden Walk
A tour of five private gardens. Rain date is June 13
Hours: 10am-4pm
Fee: $8
For information: **Woman's National Farm & Garden Association**, 3353 Craig Road, Ann Arbor, MI 48103
(734)769-0691

June 26
⚘ Gardenscapes Opening
A day at Matthaei to celebrate the opening of Gardenscapes. Call for information.
Matthaei Botanical Gardens (See Michigan Guide to Gardens.)

August 14
⚘ Herb Fest
Seminars on growing, harvesting and using herbs with demonstrations, lectures and a fresh herbal lunch. Reservations required.
Hours: 9:30am-2pm
Fee: $15
Matthaei Botanical Gardens (See Michigan Guide to Gardens.)

October 9, 10
⚘ Fall Festival
A Blast to the Past. Activities, crafts demonstrations, a marketplace, hiking and food.
Matthaei Botanical Gardens (See Michigan Guide to Gardens.)

Battle Creek

May 7, 8
⚘ Spring Plant Sale
One of the best selections of plants in the area. Held once a year and sponsored by the Leila Arboretum Society.
Hours: 9am-2pm
Fee: Free

Burnham Brook Center, 245 West Michigan Avenue, Battle Creek, MI
For information: **Leila Arboretum** *(See Michigan Guide to Gardens.)*

July 17, 18
❧ Garden Tour
A tour of approximately six private gardens in the Battle Creek area.
For information: **Leila Arboretum** *(See Michigan Guide to Gardens.)*

September 8
❧ Gardener's Market
An annual event with bulb sale, perennial exchange, Farmer's Market, ongoing demonstrations and more.
Leila Arboretum *(See Michigan Guide to Gardens.)*

Benton Harbor
Near South Bend, Kalamazoo, Grand Rapids

April 25-May 2
❧ Blossomtime Festival
A festival, now in its 93rd year, honoring agriculture, especially the fruit industry. A week of various local activities plus nine drive-yourself tours through the "Fruit Belt" in full bloom in Southwestern Michigan. Tour maps describing the ripe seasons for the fruits and vegetables along these routes.
Fee: Charged for some activities
For information: **Blossomtime Festival**, 151 East Napier Avenue, Benton Harbor, MI 49022
(616)926-7397

Bloomfield Hills
25 miles from Detroit, 2 miles from Birmingham

May 12, 13
❧ Spring Plant Sale
Michigan wildflowers such as trillium, blood-

root, hepatica, Jack-in-the-Pulpit, perennials, miniature roses, herbs, favorite annuals and greenhouse plants. This date is tentative so call to confirm.
Hours: 10am-5pm Wed; 10am-3pm Thurs
Fee: Free
Cranbrook House & Gardens *(See Michigan Guide to Gardens.)*

December 18
❧ Fall Plant Sale
Greenhouse plants, topiaries, dried flowers, bouquets, wreaths, potpourri, herbs, grapevines, floral trees and garden accessories. Call to confirm this date.
Fee: Free
Cranbrook House & Gardens *(See Michigan Guide to Gardens.)*

Bridgman

April 24, 25
❧ Michiana Orchid Society Show
A show featuring some of the area's best commercial and amateur orchid growers, plus a plant sale.
Hours: 10am-5pm
Cook Energy Information Center, Red Arrow Highway, PO 850, Bridgman, MI 49106
Directions: Exit 16 on I-94
(800)548-2555

June 17, 18
❧ Flower Show & Sale
A show targeted to the interests of the novice gardener, landscaper or florist, plus a sale of plants and plant material.
Hours: 10am-5pm
Cook Energy Information Center, Red Arrow Highway, PO 850, Bridgman, MI 49106
Directions: Exit 16 on I-94
(800)548-2555

Clawson

Near Troy & Royal Oak

May 29
❧ Spring Fling

A sale of plants dug from the members' own gardens, such as devil's paint brush and black hollyhock, known to be proven bloomers. Crafts, planted decorative items and baked goods also available.

Hours: 1-3pm
Fee: Free
Clawson Historical Museum, 41 Fisher Court, Clawson, MI
For information: **Clawson Garden Club**, 1141 Langley, Clawson, MI 48017
(248)435-0645

July 11
❧ The Garden Walk

A tour of five local gardens, plus a boutique at the Historical Museum with perennials, garden crafts and refreshments.

Hours: 1-4pm
Fee: $5
For information: **Clawson Garden Club**, 1141 Langley, Clawson, MI 48017
(248)435-0645

September 25
❧ The Fall Fest

A sale of perennials from member's own gardens, plus crafts, baked goods and even cookies for dogs!

Hours: 1-3pm
Fee: Free
Clawson Historical Museum, 41 Fisher Court, Clawson, MI
For information: **Clawson Garden Club**, 1141 Langley, Clawson, MI 48017
(248)435-0645

Detroit

See also Bloomfield Hills

February 13, 14
❧ Annual Orchid Display & Sale

A display of unusual and rare orchids from the private collection of Taylor Orchids' Ron Ciesinkski, plus an orchid sale and a slide lecture by the exhibitor.

Hours: 11am-4pm Sat; 12:30-4pm Sun; lecture noon Sat
Fee: $1
The Detroit Garden Center, Moross House, 1460 East Jefferson, Detroit, MI 48207
(313)259-6363

May 29
❧ Spring Plant Sale

Annual sale of perennials and annuals, with hostas, ferns, grasses, herbs and more. Held by the Belle Isle Botanical Society.

Hours: 10am-3pm
Fee: Free
Anna Scripps Whitcomb Conservatory Showhouse *(See Michigan Guide to Gardens.)*

December 11, 12
❧ Christmas Open House

Detroit's oldest brick house decorated for an old-fashioned Christmas, plus a Christmas decorating demonstration.

Hours: Noon-4pm; demonstration 1:30pm both days
Fee: $1
The Detroit Garden Center, Moross House, 1460 East Jefferson, Detroit, MI 48207
(313)259-6363

East Lansing

August 6, 7
❧ Garden Day

Well-known speakers plus workshops on perennials, herbs, roses, garden crafts and more. For complete information send self-addressed stamped envelope to: Sandy Allen, Dept. of Horticulture, PSSB, Michigan State University, East Lansing, MI 48824.
Fee: $45
Horticultural Demonstration Gardens *(See Michigan Guide to Gardens.)*

Fenton

July 18
Garden Tour
A tour of six theme gardens in the historic Fenton Linden area, plus free refreshments and chance to win a park bench! For complete information, write to the Club.
Hours: 10am-4pm
Fee: $6
For information: **Open Gate Garden Club**, PO Box 549, Fenton, MI 48430

Grand Rapids

See also Benton Harbor

March 6-April 18
Butterflies are Blooming
Hundreds of native and tropical butterflies fly free in the Conservatory in the largest temporary butterfly exhibition in the country. Special activities on the weekends.
Frederik Meijer Gardens *(See Michigan Guide to Gardens.)*

July
Steve's Garden Tour
A tour of area private homes and gardens to benefit the Gardens. Call for exact date.
For information: **Frederik Meijer Gardens** *(See Michigan Guide to Gardens.)*

Grosse Pointe Farms

July
Grosse Pointe Gardens Tour
A tour of five area gardens, ranging from small and intimate to large, formal estates, plus the Trial Gardens planted by area garden clubs, and the Grace Adams Harrison Garden for Children, located on the grounds of the War Memorial. Call for date and advance tickets.
Hours: 1-5pm
Fee: $8 in advance; $10 day of tour
For information: **Grosse Pointe War Memorial**, 32 Lake Shore Drive, Grosse Pointe Farms, MI 48236
(313)881-4594

Holland

May 6-15
Tulip Time Festival
A festival celebrating the blooming of millions of tulips, imported from the Netherlands, and planted in parks, gardens and lanes throughout the community. Activities include: a self-guided tour to see the miniature fields and special plantings of the Tulip Lanes; the display of blooms in Dutch settings at the Veldheer Tulip Gardens, 12755 Quincy & US 31, Holland, MI 49424 (616)399-1900.
Fee: Fee for some activities
For information: **Tulip Time Festival**, 171 Lincoln Avenue, Holland, MI 49423
(800)822-2770 or (616)396-4221

Kalamazoo

See also Benton Harbor

March 5-7
Kalamazoo County Flowerfest
A large regional show with display gardens from Leila Arboretum, garden centers and nurseries. Exhibitions by plant and horticultural

societies, seminars and demonstrations, vendors and more. Sponsored by the Kalamazoo Landscape Nurserymen's Association.
Hours: 10am-8pm Fri, Sat; noon-5pm Sun
Fee: $5
Wings Stadium, I-94, Sprinkle Road exit, Kalamazoo, MI
Wings Stadium, I-94, Sprinkle Road exit, Kalamazoo, MI
For information: **Kalamazoo County Flowerfest**, PO Box 986, Portage, MI 49081 (616)381-3597

Marshall

July 10, 11
⚘ Marshall Area Garden Tour
Welcome to My Garden. A tour of seven private gardens in the area of Marshall, a Historic Landmark District located in south central Michigan. Featured this year, the Jens Jensen garden behind the Brooks Mansion, recently purchased for restoration and open to the public for the first time.
Hours: 10am-4pm
Fee: $6 in advance; $8 day of tour
For information: **Marshall Area Garden Club**, 221 North Gordon, Marshall, MI 49068 (616)963-1448

Niles

December 2-30
⚘ Lights Before Christmas
Illumination of the gardens, shrubs and trees every Thursday through Sunday in December.
Hours: 6:30-9pm
Fee: $4
Fernwood Garden & Nature Center *(See Michigan Guide to Gardens.)*

Minnesota

Como Park Conservatory
1325 Aida Place
St. Paul, MN 55103
(651)487-8200 *Fax:* (651)487-8255
⚘ Como Park Conservatory is the largest Victorian-style glass domed botanical garden in the region. It features a Palm Dome, Fern Room, Gallery Garden, Bonsai Room, Sunken Garden with five seasonal displays every year, and a special display in the North Wing of tropical plants used in everyday life, such as coffee and cocoa. On the grounds near the Conservatory is the Ordway Memorial Japanese Garden.
Hours: 10am-4pm
Fees: $1; $.50 seniors & students; children under 6 free

Glensheen Historic Estate
UMN Duluth, 3300 London Road
Duluth, MN 55804
(888)454-4536
⚘ This formal garden and series of geometric flower beds surround a Jacobean revival style mansion built in 1908 on the shores of Lake Superior. Shrubs, perennials and annuals are all at their best during the summer months.
Web: www.d.umn.edu/glen/
Hours: May-Oct 9:30am-4pm; Nov-Apr 11am-2pm Fri-Sun
Fees: $4

Minnesota Landscape Arboretum
3675 Arboretum Drive
Chanhassen, MN
Mail: PO Box 39, Chanhassen, MN 55317
(612)443-2460 *Fax:* (612)443-2521
⚘ The Arboretum consists of 935 acres of rolling hills, native woods, a restored native prairie, a natural bog area, and formal display gardens, with a variety of plant and tree col-

lections. The grounds are accessible by hiking trails, paved paths, cross-country ski trail and a 3-mile drive.
Web: www.arboretum.umn.edu
Directions: 9 miles west of 494 on Highway 5
Hours: 8am-4:30pm
Fees: $5; 18 and under free

Selected Events

Chanhassen
30 miles southwest of Minneapolis

March 20, 21
ℳ Sugarbush Pancake Brunch & Maple Tour
Maple syrup tour and demonstrations both days, plus all-you-can-eat pancake brunch using Arboretum maple syrup. Call for advance ticket information.
Hours: 10am-3pm
Minnesota Landscape Arboretum *(See Minnesota Guide to Gardens.)*

May 15, 16
ℳ Arboretum Auxiliary Annual Plant Sale
Trees, shrubs, perennials, wildflowers, ornamental grasses, hostas, roses, ferns and annuals for sale.
Hours: 9am Sat; 10am Sun
Minnesota Landscape Arboretum *(See Minnesota Guide to Gardens.)*

September 18, 19
ℳ Arboretum Flower & Garden Show
A competitive show with many categories of flowers and vegetables open to gardeners of all ages including children. Judging on Saturday morning then show is open to the public. Sponsored by the Arboretum and now in its 17th year.
Hours: 1-4:30pm Sat; 11am-4:30pm Sun
Fee: $5; children & students under 18 free

Minnesota Landscape Arboretum *(See Minnesota Guide to Gardens.)*

September 25
ℳ Fall Festival
Cider-pressing, tram rides around the Arboretum, displays by environmental groups and plant societies, sales of fall bulbs, plants, dried flower arrangements, and apples from the Horticultural Research Center. An event for the whole family.
Hours: 9am-3pm
Minnesota Landscape Arboretum *(See Minnesota Guide to Gardens.)*

December 4
ℳ Auxiliary Holiday Sale
Large selection of wreaths, centerpieces, candles, ornaments, cards and swags, all from materials grown and hand-crafted by the Arboretum's Auxiliary.
Hours: 9am-3pm
Minnesota Landscape Arboretum *(See Minnesota Guide to Gardens.)*

December 8-January 2
ℳ Festival of Trees
Around the World, Past & Present. A holiday display of 15-20 fresh evergreens decorated with handmade and natural materials hand-crafted by garden clubs, herb societies and other groups.
Hours: Snyder Building 8am-4:30pm Mon-Fri, 11am-4:30pm Sat & Sun
Minnesota Landscape Arboretum *(See Minnesota Guide to Gardens.)*

Minneapolis
See also Chanhassen

March 3-7
ℳ Minneapolis Home & Garden Show
Landscaped gardens, floral displays, hundreds of exhibitors, plus hourly garden seminars by

the Minnesota Sate Horticultural Society, a Bonsai Gallery, Floral Sculpture and more.
Hours: 4-10pm Wed; 10am-10pm Thurs; 10am-10pm Fri, Sat; 10am-6pm Sun
Fee: $7; $3 children ages 6-12
Minneapolis Convention Center, 1301 South 2nd Avenue, Minneapolis, MN
For information: **Minneapolis Home & Garden Show**, 15235 Minnetonka Blvd., Minnetonka, MN 55345
Web: www.homeandgardenshow.com
(612)933-3850

June 29
❦ East Harriet Farmstead Neighborhood Garden Tour

A self-guided tour of ten private gardens, including boulevard, sun, shade and vegetable gardens, all in a ten-block area. Sponsored by the East Harriet Farmstead Neighborhood Association. Pick up tickets at the Park.
Hours: 10am-1pm
Fee: $4
For information: **Lyndale Farmstead Park**, 3900 Bryant Avenue South, Minneapolis, MN 55409
(612)370-4948

Rochester

June 26
❦ Historic Mayowood Mansion & Gardens Tour

A tour of the gardens and former home of Dr. Charles H. Mayo, co-founder of the Mayo Clinic. Includes a flower arranging display presented by the Rochester Garden and Flower Club and on view throughout the Mansion. Other gardens in the Rochester area also open to tour-goers. Sponsored in conjunction with the Olmsted County Master Gardeners.
Hours: 9am-3pm
Fee: $10

For information: **Historic Mayowood Mansion**, 3720 Mayowood Road SW, Rochester, MN 55902
(507)282-9447

St. Paul

August 26-September 6
❦ Minnesota State Fair Flower Shows

A series of two-day exhibitions by plant societies during the Minnesota State Fair, starting with an exhibition by the Minnesota Horticultural Society on August 26, 27.
Hours: 8am-11pm
Fee: Free
State Fair Grounds, Horticultural Building, Snelling at Como Avenue, St. Paul, MN
For information: **Minnesota State Horticultural Society**, 1755 Prior Avenue North, Falcon Heights, MN 55113
(800)676-6747 or (651)642-2200 for State Fair information

Mississippi

Guide to Gardens

The Crosby Arboretum
370 Ridge Road
Picayune, MS
Mail: PO Box 1639, Picayune, MS 39466
(601)799-2311 *Fax:* (601)799-2372
❦ This relatively new Arboretum, opened in the mid-1980s, specializes in plants of the local Pearl River basin. Many species of trees, shrubs, wildflowers and grasses have been planted and plans are underway for expansion.
Web: www.crosbyarboretum.org
Hours: 9am-5pm Wed-Sun
Fees: $4; $2 children

Mynelle Gardens
4736 Clinton Blvd

Jackson, MS 39209
(601)960-1894 *Fax:* (601)922-5759
This informal Garden dates from 1920. The 6-acre site contains thousands of azaleas, magnolias, gardenias, camellias, a rose garden, a Japanes-style area of the gardens and lots of spring-blooming bulbs and plants. Daylily hybridizing is a specialty.
Hours: Mar-Oct 9am-5:15pm; Nov-Feb 8am-4:15pm
Fees: $2; $.50 children under 12

Wister Gardens
500 Henry Road
Belzoni, MS 39038
(601)247-3025
The Gardens comprise 14 acres surrounding a colonial house. They include a small lake, 8,000 azaleas, rose gardens, tulips and spring bulbs, fruit trees, and Italian fountain and gazebo. In the fall there's an excellent display of chrysanthemums, both outdoors and in greenhouses.
Hours: 8am-5pm
Fees: Free

Selected Events

Jackson

March 27, 28
Annual Spring Celebration & Plant Sale
An annual celebration with a plant sale and Q&A with Master Gardeners on Saturday, and music, clowns, puppet shows for children on Sunday. Refreshments throughout the weekend.
Hours: Sale 9am-2pm Sat; party 2-4:30pm Sun
Fee: Free Sat; adults $.50 Sun
Mynelle Gardens *(See Mississippi Guide to Gardens.)*

Picayune

50 miles from New Orleans

March 20, 21
Spring Plant Sale
A huge stock of native plants for sale, including perennials, plants for butterflies and hummingbirds, and a large selection of Louisiana iris. Experts on hand to offer help in plant selection.
Hours: 10am-3pm
Fee: Free
The Crosby Arboretum *(See Mississippi Guide to Gardens.)*

May 8, 9
Wildflower Weekend
Tours, talks and thousands of wildflowers in bloom.
Hours: 10am-3pm
Fee: Free
The Crosby Arboretum *(See Mississippi Guide to Gardens.)*

June 19
Aquatic Plant Sale
Water lilies, pickerel weed, frog-bit, golden-club, swamp lily and water orchids. Experts in pond construction and maintenance on hand to answer questions.
Hours: 10am-3pm
Fee: Free
The Crosby Arboretum *(See Mississippi Guide to Gardens.)*

September 25, 26
Fall Plant Sale
A large selection of trees, shrubs, perennials, azaleas, butterfly plants, cypress trees and more.
Hours: 10am-3pm
Fee: Free
The Crosby Arboretum *(See Mississippi Guide to Gardens.)*

October 9, 10

⚘ Wildlife Weekend

Tours, talks and demonstrations focusing on the native plants and animals that make this part of the world unique.

Hours: 10am-3pm
Fee: Free
The Crosby Arboretum *(See Mississippi Guide to Gardens.)*

Missouri

Guide to Gardens

Hawks Grove Garden

26017 Stark Road
Peculiar, MO
Mail: PO Box 301, Harrisonville, MO 64701
(800)320-1463 *Fax:* (816)380-6089
⚘ Situated on 13 acres of open hills south of Kansas City, the five year-old site is the organic display garden of artist Ouida Touchon. The Garden includes a formal garden with antique roses, a blue garden, paint box flower beds, a woodland garden, apple allée, vegetable garden and water features. Advance reservations required.
Hours: May-Sep by reservation
Fees: $5

Missouri Botanical Garden

4344 Shaw Boulevard
St. Louis, MO 63110
(314)577-5100 *Fax:* (314)577-9598
⚘ This major Botanical Garden includes one of the largest collections of orchids in North America, as well as an azalea/rhododendron garden, a rose garden shaped like a wheel, and the Linnean House, a brick conservatory and one of the oldest continuously operating display greenhouses in the U.S. Special gardens include a bulb garden, scented garden

hosta walk, Geodesic Dome Conservatory, rock garden English Woodland garden, rose garden, Japanese and Nanjing Friendship gardens, boxwood, victorian, herb, maze and dry stream gardens.

Web: www.mobot.org
Hours: 9am-5pm; Memorial Day-Labor Day 9am-8pm
Fees: $5; $3 seniors

Powell Gardens

1609 NW US Highway 50
Kingsville, MO
Mail: Route 1, PO Box 90, Kingsville, MO 64061
(816)697-2600 *Fax:* (816)697-2619
⚘ These Gardens are comprised of 20 acres of developed gardens, terraced gardens, a wildflower meadow, rock and waterfall garden, perennial gardens, and a glass-domed conservatory with rotating seasonal exhibits.
Web: aabga.mobot.org/AABGA/ Member.pages/Powell/powell.html
Hours: 9am-dusk
Fees: $5; $4 seniors; $2 children

Shaw Arboretum

Gray Summit, MO
Mail: PO Box 38, Gray Summit, MO 63039
(314)451-3512 *Fax:* (315)451-5583
⚘ This 2400-acre site contains a rich diversity of plants and animals in restored and constructed habitats. Highlights include a wildflower garden with five acres of Missouri wildflowers, a 100-acre tall grass prairie, wetlands areas with boardwalk and observation blind, a restored 19th century home and 14 miles of hiking trails.
Web: www.mobot.org/arboretum/
Hours: 7am-sunset
Fees: $3; $2 seniors

Selected Events

Gray Summit
10 miles from Eureka

May 15
🌿 Native Plant Sale
A wide selection of plants native to the midwest offered by twelve nurseries in Missouri and Illinois. Hundreds of varieties of wildflowers, ferns, trees and shrubs for home landscaping, as well as seeds and plants of the prairie, wetland, woodland and savanna. Held at the Whitmore Wildflower Garden in the Arboretum.
Hours: 9am-4pm
Fee: Free
Shaw Arboretum *(See Missouri Guide to Gardens.)*

Hermann

May 22, 23
🌿 Hermann Spring Gardens Tour
A choice of two tours featuring roses, spring flowers and water gardens: the Town Tour, a walking tour of gardens in the Hermann Historic District, or the Country Tour of gardens in the surrounding hills by car. Take either or both. Other special events at local wineries and bed & breakfasts.
Hours: 10am-5pm
Fee: $5 for each tour
For information: **Hermann Garden Club**, 112 East First Street, Hermann, MO 65041 (800)932-8687

September 25, 26
🌿 Hermann Fall Gardens Tour
The same format as the spring tour, highlighting vineyard gardens and fall flowers. High tea available by reservation.
Hours: 10am-5pm
Fee: $5; tea $8

For information: **Hermann Garden Club**, 112 East First Street, Hermann, MO 65041 (800)932-8687

Kingsville
30 miles from Kansas City

May weekends
🌿 Spring Garden Fair
Lectures, entertainment and activities for the whole family every weekend, plus plant sales with annuals, perennials, herbs and unique items from the greenhouse.
Hours: 10am-5pm Sat; noon-5pm Sun
Fee: $6; $5 seniors; $3 children
Powell Gardens *(See Missouri Guide to Gardens.)*

St. Louis

January 8-10
🌿 St. Louis Flower Show
Because Life Should Be Beautiful.
Landscaped display gardens, floral displays, educational exhibits, a market place, speakers and tours. Hosted by the Junior League of St. Louis and now in its 9th year.
Hours: 10am-9pm Fri, Sat; 10am-6pm Sun
Fee: $6 adults in advance; $8 adults, $6 seniors, $3 children at door
America's Center, 701 Convention Plaza, St. Louis, MO
For information: **Junior League of St. Louis**, 10435 Clayton Road, St. Louis, MO 63131 (314)342-5036

April 17-May 9 weekends
🌿 GardenExpo
Plant society shows, special garden tours, information booths, hands-on workshops, demonstrations, vendors, children's activities, entertainment, food and special Garden Gate shop promotions.
Hours: 9am-5pm

Fee: Admission $5; $3 seniors
Missouri Botanical Garden *(See Missouri Guide to Gardens.)*

May 15, 16
⚘ 30th Annual House & Garden Tour
A self-guided tour of eight houses and gardens in the turn-of-the-century Kingsbury Place and Waterman Place neighborhoods.
For information: **Central West End Association**, 5 Maryland Plaza, St. Louis, MO 63108
(314)367-2220

June 5
⚘ Chinese Celebration Day
Chinese activities for the whole family, with special tours of the Chinese Garden in bloom, food, crafts and a dragon dance.
Missouri Botanical Garden *(See Missouri Guide to Gardens.)*

September 4-6
⚘ 24th Annual Japanese Festival
Japanese cultural activities, including drumming, kabuki, bonsai demonstration, tea ceremonies, ikebana and more.
Hours: 10am-6pm
Missouri Botanical Garden *(See Missouri Guide to Gardens.)*

October 2, 3
⚘ Best of Missouri Market
Country stands filled with Missouri farmer and food producer harvest. Arts and crafts, live stock, music, exhibits and more.
Hours: 9am-5pm
Fee: Fee charged
Missouri Botanical Garden *(See Missouri Guide to Gardens.)*

University City

April 24
⚘ Perennial Plant Sale
Perennials from gardeners own gardens at very reasonable prices, including some unusual varieties. Proceeds support this volunteer group's efforts to maintain over 300 local public gardens.
Hours: 9am-2pm
Fee: Free
For information: **UC City in Bloom**, 7146 Kingsbury Blvd, University City, MO 63130
(314)721-4647

Montana
Guide to Gardens

University of Montana Arboretum
Missoula, MT
Mail: Physical Plant Building, Missoula, MT 59812
(406)243-2183 *Fax:* (406)243-2335
⚘ This University of Montana Arboretum is the State Arboretum of Montana. It is home to over 300 varieties of trees, shrubs and perennial species.
Hours: 8am-4:30 Mon-Fri
Fees: Free; donations accepted

Nebraska
Guide to Gardens

Nebraska Statewide Arboretum
Lincoln, NE
Mail: Thompson Library, University of Nebraska, PO Box 830715, Lincoln, NE 68583
(402)472-2971 *Fax:* (402)472-8095
⚘ The Nebraska Statewide Arboretum is a network of arboreta, parks, historic properties and

other public landscapes in dozens of communities across the state. The NSA links together and supports these sites and makes them accessible to the public. Contact them for a complete list of affiliates or visit their web site.
Web: www.ianr.edu/nsa/index.html

Omaha Botanical Garden
5th & Cedar Streets near Zoo
Omaha, NE
Mail: PO Box 24089, Omaha, NE 68124
(402)346-4002 *Fax:* (402)346-1355
🌲 This young Garden of 75 acres was started in the 1980s. It currently includes an arboretum and four specialty gardens: a rose garden, herb garden, shade and hosta garden and children's garden.
Web: www.radiks.net/obg/
Hours: 9am-4pm
Fees: Free

UNL Botanical Gardens & Arboretum
1340 North 17th Street
Lincoln, NE 68588
(402)472-2679 *Fax:* (402)472-9615
🌲 The UNL Botanical Gardens have various special gardens, including the Cather Garden with native wildflowers, grasses, trees and shrubs, a sculpture garden, perennial borders framing the entrance to the City Campus at Love Memorial Library, perennial flower gardens at Andrews and Burnett Halls, the Donaldson Garden of exotic and unusual trees and shrubs, the Holling Garden. Gardens on the East Campus include an iris garden, the Porch and Old Rose Collection, the Old Mall of trees and herbaceous perennials, the South Meadow and the 5-acre Maxwell Arboretum.
Web: www.unl.edu/unlbga/
Hours: Dawn-dusk
Fees: Free

Lincoln

April 24
🌲 **Annual Spring Affair**
Free educational lecture, demonstration and exhibition series designed for the home owner and gardener, and a plant sale of over 200 varieties of perennials and herbs. Sponsored by UNL Botanical Garden & Arboretum, State Fair Park Arboretum and Nebraska Statewide Arboretum.
Hours: 9am-4pm
Fee: Free
State Fair Park , Lincoln, NE
For information: **UNL Botanical Gardens & Arboretum** *(See Nebraska Guide to Gardens.)*

Nevada

Arboretum of UNLV
4505 Maryland Parkway
Las Vegas, NV 89154
Email: arbor@ccmail.nevada.edu
(702)895-3392 *Fax:* (702)895-4173
🌲 This on-campus Arboretum includes hardy trees and shrubs from around the globe, as well as native desert plants. A brochure describing a self-guided tour is available.
Fees: Free

Desert Demonstration Garden
3701 West Alta
Las Vegas, NV 89153
(702)258-3205 *Fax:* (702)258-7146
🌲 The Garden dispels the notion that desert landscaping is limited to cacti and rocks, with more than 1,000 species of plants in eleven theme gardens. On the first Thursday of every month a seasonal garden tour is offered and

on the second Tuesday of each month, a Birds in the Garden tour.
Web: www.lvvwd.com
Hours: 8am-5pm; tours 1st Thurs & 2nd Tues at 9am (8am Jun-Aug)
Fees: Free

Ethel M Chocolate Factory & Cactus Garden
2 Cactus Garden Drive
Henderson, NV
Mail: PO Box 98505, Las Vegas, NV 89193
(702)458-8864
The 3-acre Garden has a good collection of cacti and succulents.
Directions: 8 miles from Las Vegas
Hours: 8:30am-7pm
Fees: Free

University of Nevada Herbarium & Arboretum
1000 Valley Road, Route 100a
Reno, NV 89512
Email: unherb@unr.edu
(702)784-1105 *Fax:* (702)784-4583
Established in the 1840s and devastated by a fire in 1904, the UNR Herbarium has been built back up to over 85,000 specimens, most from the Great Basin region of the U.S. Located within the Agriculture Experiment Station, the facility has a park area with educational signage and miles of sidewalks to view the mature trees and gardens. Self-guided tree walk maps are available at the information kiosk, 9th and Center Streets.
Hours: Herbarium 10am-4pm Mon-Thurs
Fees: Free

Wilbur D. May Arboretum & Botanical Garden
1502 Washington Street
Reno, NV 89503
(702)785-4153 *Fax:* (702)785-4707

This 10-acre site is devoted to native species of the Great Basin and Sierra Mountains.
Hours: Sunrise-sunset
Fees: Free

Selected Events

Las Vegas

Mid April
Spring Flower Show
More than 200 locally grown specimens of iris, as well as succulents, annuals and perennials. Sponsored by the Las Vegas Iris Society, the Nevada Garden Clubs and the Las Vegas Council of Garden Clubs. Call for exact dates.
Hours: 1-5pm Sat; 10am-5pm Sun
Fee: Free
Nevada Garden Club Center, Lorenzi Park, 3333 W. Washington Blvd, PO Box 27624, Las Vegas, NV 89126
(702)648-9494

April 24
Rose Society Show
A judged show sponsored by the Las Vegas Rose Society.
Hours: 1-8pm
Fee: Free
Meadows Mall, Valley View & Expressway, Las Vegas, NV
For information: **Las Vegas Rose Society**, 6840 Sierra Trail, Las Vegas, NV 89102
(702)369-8127 ext 7673

June 26, 27
Bearded Iris Sale
All plants are grown locally, with prices ranging from $12 to $50 and up. Held simultaneously at three locations in Las Vegas: Plant World Nursery at 5301 W. Charleston Blvd. (702)878-9485; Plant World Nursery at 1250 E. Tropicana

(702)739-6198; Dan's Plant World at 9040 Southeastern Avenue (702)361-1955.
Hours: Regular store hours
Fee: Free
For information: **Las Vegas Iris Society**, 2861 Channel Bay Drive, Las Vegas, NV 89128 (702)255-1263

October 2
🌿 Day with the Experts
Advice on arid gardening from experts.
Hours: 9am-3pm
Fee: Free
Desert Demonstration Garden *(See Nevada Guide to Gardens.)*

New Hampshire

Guide to Gardens

Fuller Gardens
10 Willow Avenue
North Hampton, NH 03862
(603)964-5414 *Fax:* (603)964-8901
🌿 This 2-acre Garden is on a seaside estate with several formal gardens and greenhouses. Collections include azaleas, rhododendrons, wisteria, spring bulbs and chrysanthemums in the fall.
Hours: May-Oct 10am-6pm; closed Nov-Apr
Fees: $4; $3.50 seniors

Selected Events

Conway

July 31, August 1
🌿 Garden Trail Tour
An unusual tour of gardens participating in a locally-sponsored competition, now in its 39th year, in three categories; gardens on commercial properties, gardens on public properties;

private flower and vegetable gardens. More than 60 entries, judged by local garden clubs with prizes funded by local businesses. Maps available from the sponsor on Main Street or at information booths and shops in the area.
Hours: 10am-5pm
Fee: Free
For information: **North Country Radio - WMWV**, PO Box 2008, Conway, NH 03818 (603)447-5988

Cornish

July 10
🌿 6th Annual Hidden Garden Tour
An annual tour of gardens in the Windsor-Cornish area. Call to confirm date and location.
Hours: 10am-4pm
Fee: $15 in advance; $18 day of tour
For information: **Historic Windsor, Inc.**, 54 Main Street, PO Box 1777, Windsor, VT 05089
Email: HistWinInc@aol.com
(802)674-6752

Keene

March 26-29
🌿 Flower Show
Breath of Spring. A regional show with half of the space devoted to garden displays, and half to educational booths, free gardening workshops, special presentations and vendors. Now in its fifth year. Benefits hospice care and child health programs in New Hampshire.
Hours: noon-5pm Fri; 9am-5pm Sat-Mon
Fee: $6
Cheshire Fairgrounds Arena, Route 12, South Keene, NH
For information: **Home Healthcare, Hospice & Community Services**, PO Box 564, 69L Island Street, Keene, NH 03431 (603)352-2253

North Hampton

May 8, 9
🌺 **Annual Plant Sale**
A celebration of Mother's Day with a sale of rosebushes, hardy perennials, unusual house plants and more.
Hours: 10am-3pm
Fuller Gardens *(See New Hampshire Guide to Gardens.)*

Portsmouth

May 8
🌺 **Annual Heritage Plant Sale**
Heirloom annuals raised in the greenhouse at Strawbery Banke, field dug perennials, flowering vines, shrubs, old roses, herbs and more.
Hours: 2-5:30pm Fri; 9:30am-2:30pm Sat
Fee: Free
Strawbery Banke Museum, 454 Court Street, Portsmouth, NH 03801
(603)433-1100

June 18, 19
🌺 **Pocket Gardens of Portsmouth Garden Tour**
A self-guided tour of eight to ten different private gardens open each day of the tour, plus a garden market featuring local artisans in the church courtyard on Saturday. Proceeds benefit the South Church general fund. Call to confirm dates.
Hours: 5-8pm Fri; 9am-2pm Sat
Fee: $10 in advance; $12 day of tour
For information: **Pocket Gardens of Portsmouth**, PO Box 628, Portsmouth, NH 03801
(603)436-4762

New Jersey

Guide to Gardens

Acorn Hall Gardens
68 Morris Avenue
Morristown, NJ 07960
(973)267-3465 *Fax:* (973)267-8773
🌺 The Acorn Hall Gardens are a recreation of gardens representative of the period of 1853-1888, using only plant materials available to the gardener of that time. It is a restoration project of the Home Garden Club of Morristown and features more than 30 different varieties of Victorian roses, an herb wheel and a spring bulb display.
Hours: Garden dawn-dusk; House 10am-4pm Mon & Thurs, 1-4pm Sun
Fees: Free

Deep Cut Gardens
352 Red Hill Road
Middletown, NJ 07748
(732)671-6050 *Fax:* (732)671-6905
🌺 The Gardens are designed as a demonstration site for the home gardener. The 40-acre site includes an orchard, vineyard, greenhouses and a variety of gardens, including vegetable, herb, rockery, azalea , perennial, shade and All-America Rose Selection gardens.
Web: www.monmouthcountyparks.com/parks/deepcut.html
Hours: Dawn-dusk
Fees: Free

Duke Gardens
Somerville, NJ
Mail: Duke Gardens Foundation, PO Box 2030, Route 206 South, Somerville, NJ 08876
(908)722-3700 *Fax:* (908)704-0004
🌺 The Gardens are comprised of eleven glass-enclosed gardens on the large estate of Doris Duke. There are Chinese, Colonial, English,

Edwardian, French, Italian, Japanese, Indo-Persion, desert, tropical and semi-tropical gardens. The collections of orchids, camellias, gardenias, jacarandas, tree ferns and cacti are outstanding. Advance reservations required.
Hours: Jun-Sep Noon-4pm by reservation

Frelinghuysen Arboretum

53 East Hanover Avenue
Morristown Township, NJ
Mail: PO Box 1295R, Morristown, NJ 07962
(973)326-7600 *Fax:* (973)644-9627
🌷 This 127-acre site, was developed as a country place for the Frelinghuysen family, called Whippany Farm. Its colonial Revival house is now the headquarters of the Morris County Park Commision. The estate was originally planted with trees and shrubs in the manner of an English landscape, and many of the plantings still exist. Among the many highlights are perennial, nurserymen's, winter, rock, blue, cottage and water gardens and the Rose Circle.
Web: www.parks.morris.nj.us
Hours: 9am-4:30pm
Fees: Free

Green Brook Sanctuary

Alpine, NJ 07620
(201)768-1360
🌷 The165-acre nature preserve atop the New Jersey Palisades includes a mature hardwood forest, wildflower trails, cliffside vistas of the Hudson River and a 250-foot waterfall. A new orientation center interprets the human history of the Sanctuary and the natural history of its six natural habitats. The Sanctuary can be seen by appointment only except on rare Open House days. See New Jersey Selected Events.
Hours: Open to members year round; to groups by appointment

Hartshorn Arboretum & Sanctuary

324 Forest Drive South
Short Hills, NJ 07078
(973)376-3587 *Fax:* (973)379-5058
🌷 The Arboretum is a 17-acre habitat with over 80 species of native wildflowers, common flowers and abundant bird life. The site is laced with woodland trails.
Web: www.hartshornarboretum.com
Hours: Dawn-dusk
Fees: Free

Herb & Botanical Alliance Garden

5916 Duerer Street
Egg Harbor, NJ
Mail: PO Box 93, Egg Harbor, NJ 08215
(609)965-0337 *Fax:* (609)965-4488
🌷 The Herb and Botanical Alliance Garden has an ethnobotanical fiber and dye collection, seed collections and several special gardens, including Wildlife, Native Plant, Tropical, Shade, Sun, Herb, Perennial, Community, Food and Children's Display Gardens.
Web: www.expresspages.com/h/herbbotanical/
Directions: 20 minute from Atlantic City, 40 minutes from Philadelphia
Hours: 9am-5pm
Fees: Donation requested

Leaming's Run Gardens

1845 Route 9 North
Cape May Court House, NJ 08210
(609)465-5871
🌷 Leaming's Run Gardens are set in 20 acres of pine and oak woodlands in the New Jersey Pine Barrens. Thousands of annuals in the woods along a mile-long path. There are 26 separate gardens, many devoted to single colors, plus the English Cottage and Serpentine Gardens.
Hours: 9:30am-5pm
Fees: $5 garden

Leonard J. Buck Garden

11 Layton Road
Far Hills, NJ
Mail: Somerset County Park Commission, 156 Mettler's Road, Somerset, NJ 08873
(908)234-2677 *Fax:* (908)234-9409
☙ This 33-acre site has 13 acres of cultivated gardens and landscaping, with notable trees of various species, including very large dawn redwoods from China. Other displays include royal azaleas, ferns and primroses.
Web: www.park.co.somerset.NJ.us
Hours: Mar-Nov 10am-4pm Mon-Fri; 10am-5pm Sat; noon-5pm Sun; Dec-Feb 10am-4pm
Fees: $1 suggested donation

New Jersey State Botanical Garden at Skylands

Morris Road
Ringwood, NJ
Mail: PO Box 302, Ringwood, NJ 07456
(973)962-9534 *Fax:* (973)962-1553
☙ Skylands is the culmination of two eras of landscape architecture under the direction of Francis Lynde Stetson, owner of Skylands from 1891-1922, and Clarence McKenzie Lewis, 1922-1953. The Garden contains an extensive variety of plants, shrubs and evergreens and deciduous trees in specialty areas. Highlights are the Crabapple Allée, terraced gardens, lilac garden, perennial and annual gardens, and woodland paths. The extensive vistas and view of the Ramapo Mountains frame this 96-acre botanical garden.
Web: www.njskylandsgarden.org
Hours: 8am-8pm
Fees: $3 per car weekends, holidays, summer season

Presby Memorial Iris Garden

474 Upper Montclair Avenue
Upper Montclair, NJ 07043
(973)783-5974 *Fax:* (973)746-0887
☙ The Garden displays over 4,000 iris varieties from all over the world, arranged to form a living history of irises. The plantings are arranged in a curve in Mountainside Park and are maintained by a variety of local groups and volunteers. Peak bloom season is generally from May 20 to June 10, with dwarf and median iris blooms around May 10 and beardless irises from late May into July.

Reeves-Reed Arboretum

165 Hobart Avenue
Summit, NJ 07901
(908)273-8787 *Fax:* (908)273-0359
☙ The Reeves-Reed Arboretum was first created in 1889 by John Hornor Wisner as his country estate. Calvert Vaux, the partner of Frederick Law Olmsted in the creation of Central Park, was the first landscape designer of the property, followed by Ellen Biddle Shipman in 1924 and Carl F. Pilat, 1924-25. Its renowned daffodil collection was started by Mrs. Wisner and expanded by the next owners, the Reeves. The rose garden, rock-pool garden and Italian-style cascading stone steps were added in the 1920s. In the late 1960s the Reeves added the herb garden and opened the woodland trails.
Web: www.reeves-reedarboretum.org
Hours: Dawn-dusk
Fees: Free

The Rutgers Gardens

Cook College, 112 Ryders Lane
New Brunswick, NJ 08901
(732)932-8451 *Fax:* (732)931-7060
☙ The 50-acre Arboretum features a holly collection, azaleas and rhododendrons, dogwoods, shade trees and trails. The site includes an All-America Selections garden and water conservation, sun and shade, shrub, evergreen and children's gardens, and dream turf plots.

Web: aesop.rutgers.edu/~floriculture/
Garden/rutgard.html
Hours: 8am-dusk
Fees: Free

Sayen Botanical Garden
155 Hughes Drive
Hamilton Township, NJ 08610
(609)890-3543 *Fax:* (609)581-4122
The 30-acre Garden is known for its large
and rare azalea and rhododendron collections, gathered from all over the world. It's
currently introducing a new native azalea.
Features include extensive trails, a pond
stocked with koi and water plants, and a bulb
display from early March through June. The
Garden was started in 1915, purchased by
Hamilton Township in 1987 and opened for-
mally in 1992.
Hours: Dawn-dusk
Fees: Free

Trailside Nature & Science Center
Watchung Reservation, 452 New Providence
Road
Mountainside, NJ 07092
(908)789-3670 *Fax:* (908)789-3270
This site contains a butterfly garden, back-
yard wildlife habitat, meadows, trails and a 5-
acre rhododendron garden.
Hours: Grounds open daylight hours; build-
ings 1-5pm
Fees: Donation requested

van der Goot Rose Garden
Colonial Parkway Arboretum
Somerset, NJ
Mail: 156 Mettler's Road, Somerset, NJ
08873
(732)873-2459 *Fax:* (732)873-0327
The Rudolf W. van der Goot Rose Garden
has a wide variety of types, sizes and colors of
roses, including All-America Rose Selections.

As designed and developed by van der Goot,
the one-acre Garden is divided into three areas:
the Mettler Garden, the Center Garden and the
Dutch Garden. Collectively these gardens display 3,000 roses representing over 200 varieties. Additional features include the collection
of species roses outside the main gardens and
the Fragrance and Sensory Garden.
Web: www.park.co.somerset.NJ.us
Hours: 8am-sunset
Fees: $1 suggested donation

Willowwood Arboretum
300 Longview Road, Chester Township
Morristown, NJ
Mail: PO Box 1295, Morristown, NJ 07960
(973)366-7600
On 130-acres of rolling farmland, the
Arboretum contains 3,500 kinds of native and
exotic plants, many dating back to 1908 and
the original plantings of the Tubbs brothers.
Two small formal gardens flank the 18th century residence on the site, but most of the
property is devoted to open areas and woodland with informal paths through oaks,
maples, willows, lilacs, magnolia, hollies,
cherries and conifers. Part of the Morris
County Park System.
Hours: 9am-dusk
Fees: Free

Selected Events

Alpine

May 2
Open House
One of the few times the Sanctuary is open to
the public.
Hours: 10am-2pm
Fee: Free
For information: **Green Brook Sanctuary** *(See*
New Jersey Guide to Gardens.)

Egg Harbor

20 minutes from Atlantic City, 40 minutes from Philadelphia

June 5, 6
❦ Spring Botanical Exposition

Workshops on herbs and their uses, organic agriculture and gardening, plant conservation, and more. Plus children's programs, herbal crafters, plants for sale, educational displays, herbal food and garden tours.

Hours: 11am-4pm
Fee: Free
Herb & Botanical Alliance Garden *(See New Jersey Guide to Gardens.)*

September 11
❦ Fall Herb & Garden Festival

Focuses on the uses of herbs, organic agriculture and gardening, native plant conservation, horticultural therapy, nutrition and wellness. Includes plants for sale, children's programs and garden tours. Held in the Shade Garden.

Hours: 10am-5pm
Fee: Free
Herb & Botanical Alliance Garden *(See New Jersey Guide to Gardens.)*

Far Hills

April 24, 25
❦ Earth Day Celebration & Plant Sale

Lectures at the Buck Garden Visitor's Center, guided tours of the woodland garden and plant rock outcroppings, and a plant sale.

Hours: 10am-5pm Sat; noon-5pm Sun
Fee: $1 suggested donation
Leonard J. Buck Garden *(See New Jersey Guide to Gardens.)*

Hamilton Township

10 miles from Trenton

April
❦ Daffodil Days

Lectures, tours and special events, plus 250,000 daffodil bulbs in full bloom. Call for exact dates.

Hours: 9am-6pm
Fee: Free
Sayen Botanical Garden *(See New Jersey Guide to Gardens.)*

May 9
❦ Mother's Day Azalea Festival

A craft show, food, entertainment and more with the azaleas at their peak of bloom. This is the one day of the year that the large estate home, typifying the arts and crafts style, is open to the public.

Hours: 9am-6pm
Fee: Free
Sayen Botanical Garden *(See New Jersey Guide to Gardens.)*

Madison

June 22
❦ Madison Garden Tour

Tour of private gardens in Madison. Benefits the restoration of Acorn Hall Gardens in Morristown. Call for more information and tickets.

For information: **Garden Club of Madison**, 11 Park Lane, Madison, NJ 07940 (973)377-1381

Middletown

Late April
❦ Spring Festival

Lectures on aquatics, orchids and gardening techniques, a raffle and auction of aquatic supplies and garden items, vendors selling koi and goldfish, pond items, garden plants, plus food for people and fish. Call for exact date.

Fee: Free
Deep Cut Gardens *(See New Jersey Guide to Gardens.)*

Morristown

April 17, 18
⚘ Annual New Jersey Daffodil Society Show
A popular standard judged show with educational exhibits.
Hours: 1-4pm Fri; 10am-4pm Sat
Fee: Free
Frelinghuysen Arboretum (See New Jersey Guide to Gardens.)

May 1, 2
⚘ Annual Plant Sale
Rare and unusual perennials, annuals, herbs, hardy perennials, shrubs and trees. Sponsored by the Friends of the Frelinghuysen Arboretum.
Hours: 10am-4pm
Fee: Free
Frelinghuysen Arboretum (See New Jersey Guide to Gardens.)

June 5
⚘ Great Swamp Bonsai Society Show & Exhibition
An annual event. Includes information on training bonsai.
Hours: 10am-3pm
Fee: Free
Frelinghuysen Arboretum (See New Jersey Guide to Gardens.)

July 25
⚘ Garden State Iris Society Sale
A sale of quality iris plants including beardless, Japanese, Siberian and more.
Hours: 1-5pm
Fee: Free
Frelinghuysen Arboretum (See New Jersey Guide to Gardens.)

September 17-19
⚘ 11th Annual Harvest Show & Plant Sale
A judged show of flower arrangements, vegetables and flowers, with a children's division, plus horticultural lecture-demonstrations daily, and a plant sale. Sponsored by the Morris County Park Commission, Friends of the Arboretum, in cooperation with the New Jersey Committee of the Garden Club of America.
Hours: 12:30-8pm Fri; 11am-5pm Sat, Sun
Fee: Free
Frelinghuysen Arboretum (See New Jersey Guide to Gardens.)

October 9, 10
⚘ 46th Annual Chrysanthemum Show
A standard, judged show which includes a special exhibit and sale of chrysanthemum plants, many grown by Chrysanthemum Society members.
Hours: 2-6pm Sat; 1-5pm Sun
Fee: Free
Frelinghuysen Arboretum (See New Jersey Guide to Gardens.)

November 6, 7
⚘ 37th Annual Tristate African Violet Council Show & Sale
A standard judged show and popular sale of African violets.
Hours: 1:30-5pm Sat; 10am-4pm Sun
Fee: Free
Frelinghuysen Arboretum (See New Jersey Guide to Gardens.)

Mountainside
Near Elizabeth

May 16
⚘ Spring Garden Fair & Plant Sale
Talks, demonstrations and displays on various garden topics and problems, plus Q&A with garden experts and soil testing kits. A plant sale of annuals, unusual perennials, native plants, house plants and shrubs. Sponsored by the Master Gardeners, Rutgers Cooperative Extension of Union County.

Hours: Noon-5pm
Fee: $1 suggested donation
Trailside Nature & Science Center *(See New Jersey Guide to Gardens.)*

New Brunswick

May 8, 9
🌺 Spring Flower Fair
Tours, children's activities and an extensive landscape plant sale of thousands of plants. Timed to the peak bloom of the Gardens' large and unusual rhododendron and azalea collection.
Hours: 10am-4pm
Fee: Free
The Rutgers Gardens *(See New Jersey Guide to Gardens.)*

July 31
🌺 Open House
Garden tours, display garden walks, lectures, plant sale, "Ask the Experts" table, children's activities.
Hours: 9am-3pm
The Rutgers Gardens *(See New Jersey Guide to Gardens.)*

October 16
🌺 Fall Foliage Festival
Landscape plant sales, tours, lectures, demonstrations, children's activities.
Hours: 10am-3pm
The Rutgers Gardens *(See New Jersey Guide to Gardens.)*

Ringwood

May 8, 9
🌺 Spring Flower Festival
Display of spring flowers and shrubs, self-guided tour of Skylands Manor, art show and sale.
Hours: Noon-5pm
Fee: $5; $4 seniors; $2 children

New Jersey State Botanical Garden at Skylands *(See New Jersey Guide to Gardens.)*

May 1, 2
🌺 Plant Sale
An extensive collection of woody shrubs, unusual perennials and annuals.
Hours: 10am-3:30pm
Fee: Free
New Jersey State Botanical Garden at Skylands *(See New Jersey Guide to Gardens.)*

December 2-5
🌺 Holiday Open House
Skylands Manor House decorated for the season by local garden clubs and florists. Self-guided tours available.
Hours: Noon-4pm Thurs; noon-7pm Fri-Sun
Fee: $5; $4 seniors; $2 children
New Jersey State Botanical Garden at Skylands *(See New Jersey Guide to Gardens.)*

Somerset

February 25-28
🌺 33rd Annual New Jersey Flower & Patio Show
A large regional show featuring professionally landscaped gardens, a large market area, floral design demonstrations and seminars. New this year, a botanical art display presented by the American Society of Botanical Artists.
Hours: 10am-9pm Thurs-Sat; 10am-6pm Sun
Fee: $7.50; $6 seniors & children
Garden State Exhibition Center, 50 Atrium Drive, Exit 6 off Route 287, Somerset, NJ
For information: **New Jersey Flower & Patio Show**, PO Box 548, Allenwood, NJ 08720
Web: www.gsec.com
(732)469-4000

June 12
🌺 Rose Day
An annual celebration honoring America's national flower. Lectures, demonstrations,

Q&A with staff members against a backdrop of thousands of roses at peak bloom.
Hours: 10am-4pm
Fee: $1 suggested donation
van der Goot Rose Garden *(See New Jersey Guide to Gardens.)*

Summit

May 22
🎴 The Complete Home Gardener Workshop
A celebration of Reeve-Reed's 25th Anniversary with a full day of at least twenty workshops, plus gardening equipment and book displays and Q&A opportunities with experts from New Jersey and New York.
Hours: 9am-5pm
Fee: Fee charged
Reeves-Reed Arboretum *(See New Jersey Guide to Gardens.)*

June 11, 12
🎴 A Garden Weekend & Garden Tour
A self-guided tour of up to six private gardens in Summit and Short Hills on both days, plus a plant auction and supper on Friday night, June 11, to benefit Reeve-Reed.
Hours: Tours 10am-4pm Fri, Sat; auction & supper 6pm Fri
Fee: Fee charged
For information: **Reeves-Reed Arboretum** *(See New Jersey Guide to Gardens.)*

October 2
🎴 Family Harvest Festival
An event for the whole family, with entertainment, children's activities, pony rides, crafts, food, pumpkin patch, hay-bale maze, woodland trail walks.
Hours: 10am-4pm
Reeves-Reed Arboretum *(See New Jersey Guide to Gardens.)*

December 2
🎴 Holiday House Tour
A tour of up to six private homes in Summit and Short Hills, decorated with fresh greens and natural materials. Includes the Arboretum's 1889 Wisner House and the Summit Historical Society's Carter House with crafts bazaar.
Hours: 10am-3pm
Fee: Fee charged
For information: **Reeves-Reed Arboretum** *(See New Jersey Guide to Gardens.)*

Upper Montclair

July & August
🎴 Donators' Day Sale of Iris Rhizomes
Friday and Saturday sales of bags of six rhizomes, many from the Presby Garden itself, at a cost of $15-$20 depending on the variety. A fund raiser for the Garden. Call for dates.
Hours: 10am-4pm
Presby Memorial Iris Garden *(See New Jersey Guide to Gardens.)*

New Mexico

Guide to Gardens

Living Desert State Park, Zoo & Gardens
1504 Miehls Drive
Carlsbad, NM
Mail: PO Box 100, Carlsbad, NM 88221
(505)887-5516 *Fax:* (505)885-4418
🎴 The Park covers 1,100 acres, with thousands of varieties of cacti and cultivars of southwestern plants, many native to the Chihuahuan Desert. The site is beautifully landcaped and has a greenhouse. The hiking trail through the Park takes about 1.5 hours, through gypsum hills, arroyos, sand dunes and pine trees.
Web: http://carlsbadnm.com

Hours: May 14-Labor Day 8am-8pm; Sep 7-May 13 9am-5pm
Fees: $3

Rio Grande Botanic Garden
2601 Central Avenue NW
Albuquerque, NM 87104
(505)764-6200 *Fax:* (505)848-7192
⚜ The Rio Grande Botanical Garden is part of the Albuquerque Biological Park, also home to the Zoo and Aquarium. The Garden opened in December 1996 on ten acres of a 52-acre site along the Rio Grande River. It includes a Demonstration Garden and a trio of walled gardens, the Spanish-Moorish Court, the Round Garden and the Ceremonial Rose Garden. The Desert Conservatory exhibits plant life from other arid zones of the Southwest, while the Mediterranean Conservatory houses native plants of South Africa, Australia, Chile, the Mediterranean Basin and Southern California. The Chihuahuan Desert Exhibit wraps around the Desert Conservatory.
Web: www.cabq.gov/biopark/
Hours: 9am-5pm; weekends Jun-Aug 9am-6pm
Fees: $4.50; $2.50 seniors & children

Santa Fe Botanical Garden
6401 Richards Avenue
Santa Fe, NM
Mail: PO Box 23343, Santa Fe, NM 87502
Email: bot_gardens@santa-fe.cc.nm.us
(505)428-1684 *Fax:* (505)428-1237
⚜ Still in the development stage, this 35-acre property was acquired 1993 and has since been managed as a preserve. Ecological restoration is underway and a trail with handicapped accessibility is being constructed.

Albuquerque

April 24
⚜ Garden Fair & Plant Sale
A Garden Center-wide sale, featuring hundreds of locally grown, garden-dug and acclimated bedding plants, annuals, perennials, daylilies, mini-roses and rooted chrysanthemum cuttings. Sponsored by the Council of Albuquerque Garden Clubs.
Hours: 9am-4pm
Fee: Free
Albuquerque Garden Center, 10120 Lomas NE in Los Altos Park , Albuquerque, NM 87112
Email: GardenCenter@juno.com
(505)296-6020

May 22, 23
⚜ Albuquerque House & Garden Tour
A tour of approximately six gardens in the Albuquerque area. Benefits the Rio Grande Botanic Garden.
For information: **Friends of Rio Grande Botanic Garden**, 1219 Los Arboles NW, Albuquerque, NM 87107
(505)848-7147

Late November-December 30
⚜ River of Lights
Three-dimensional light sculptures, scenes and stories created with millions of lights throughout the gardens, plus live entertainment, carolers, tree and wreath displays.
Hours: 6-9:30pm
Fee: $3; $1.50 seniors, children
Rio Grande Botanic Garden *(See New Mexico Guide to Gardens.)*

December 3, 4
⚜ Annual Holiday Fair
Poinsettias, fresh wreaths, garlands and

Christmas cactus for sale plus hand-crafted gifts and decorations from New Mexico's artisans and home-baked goodies. Sponsored by the Council of Albuquerque Garden Clubs.
Hours: 9am-5pm Fri; 9am-4pm Sat
Albuquerque Garden Center, 10120 Lomas NE in Los Altos Park , Albuquerque, NM 87112
Email: GardenCenter@juno.com
(505)296-6020

Carlsbad

May 13-16
🌿 **Mescal Roast & Spirit Dance**
Authentic Mescalero and Apache ceremonies associated with harvesting, roasting and sharing of the Agave plant, a staple and ceremonial food. Includes dinner and Indian dances.
Fee: $12
Living Desert State Park, Zoo & Gardens
(See New Mexico Guide to Gardens.)

Santa Fe

June 13, July 11, September 5
🌿 **Garden Tours**
Gardens for Gardeners. Self-guided tours of three-four private gardens, tended primarily by their owners, some with help from designers.
Hours: 2-5pm
Fee: $15
For information: **Santa Fe Botanical Garden**
(See New Mexico Guide to Gardens.)

July 20, 27 & August 3, 10
🌿 **Home & Garden Tour**
A series of guided bus tours of outstanding private and historic properties in Santa Fe. Four gardens per tour with Santa Fe Garden Club members as guides. Tours are extremely popular, so call early for tickets.
Hours: 1pm starting time for all tours
Fee: Fee charged

For information: **Recursos Travel**, 826 Camino Del Monte Rey, Santa Fe, NM 87501 (505)982-9301

New York
Guide to Gardens

Bailey Arboretum
194 Bayville Road
Locust Valley, NY 11560
(516)571-8020
🌿 The Bailey Arboretum was the summer estate of Mr. and Mrs. Frank Bailey and was given to Nassau County in 1968. Mr. Bailey collected more than 600 kinds of shrubs and trees which now make up a great part of the Arboretum. Among the many species are the Paper Bark Maple, Dawn Redwood and Long Island's largest Korean Pine and Black Walnut. In addition, there are gardens with collections of perennials, irises, annuals and flowering shrubs. A Sensory Garden has recently been added.
Hours: Daylight hours
Fees: $3; $1 Nassau County residents

Bayard Cutting Arboretum
NY State Parks, Montauk Highway
Oakdale, NY
Mail: PO Box 466, Oakdale, NY 11769
(516)581-1002 *Fax:* (516)581-1031
🌿 Designed by Frederick Law Olmsted in 1886, the 700-acre Arboretum contains a Pinetum and 75 acres landscaped with azalea, laurel, dogwood, rhododendron, holly and lilac. There are many exceptional tree specimens, a rose garden, perennial and annual beds and a grove of swamp cypress.
Hours: 10am-sunset Tues-Sun & holidays:
Fees: $4 per vehicle

Brooklyn Botanic Garden
1000 Washington Avenue
Brooklyn, NY 11225
(718)622-4433 *Fax:* (718)622-7839
🌺 The Brooklyn Botanic Garden blooms in the middle of one of the world's largest cities, with 52 acres of formal and informal gardens and the Steinhardt Conservatory. BBG boasts many firsts and unique garden sites, including the first Fragrance Garden, the Japanese Hill-and-Pond Garden, the Starr Bonsai Museum, the Plant Family Collection and the Trail of Evolution. The daffodil and cherry blossom displays are well-known highlights of the spring season.
Web: www.bbg.org
Hours: Apr-Sep 8am-6pm weekdays, 10am-6pm weekends & holidays; Oct.-Mar 8am-4:30pm weekdays, 10am-4:30pm weekends & holidays
Fees: $3; $1.50 seniors & students; $.50 children

Buffalo & Erie County Botanical Gardens
2655 South Park Avenue
Buffalo, NY 14218
Email: gardens@buffnet.net
(716)696-3555 *Fax:* (716)828-0091
🌺 These Gardens feature floral and plant displays in twelve greenhouses with special collections of cacti, ferns and palms, and outdoor gardens. The Conservatory was founded in 1899.
Hours: 9am-4pm
Fees: Free

Clark Botanic Garden
193 I U Willets Road
Albertson, NY 11507
(516)484-8600 *Fax:* (516)625-2718
🌺 The 12-acre Garden is situated on three lakes with special collections of roses, rhodo-

dendrons, herbs, wildlflowers and ferns. Special gardens include a children's garden and herb, rock, daylily and marsh gardens.
Hours: 10am-4:30pm
Fees: Free

The Cloisters of the Metropolitan Museum
Fort Tryon Park
New York, NY 10040
(212)923-3700 *Fax:* (212)795-3640
🌺 The flower and herb gardens have more than 250 species of plants grown in the Middle Ages. The Cloisters conducts tours of their medieval gardens in September, Tuesday through Sunday at 1pm.
Web: www.metmuseum.org
Hours: Mar-Oct 9:30am-5:15pm Tues-Sun; Nov-Feb 9:30am-4:45pm Tues-Sat
Fees: $8 suggested donation; $4 seniors & students

Cornell Plantations
One Plantation Road
Ithaca, NY 14850
(607)255-3020 *Fax:* (607)255-2404
🌺 This is the botanial garden, arboretum and natural areas of Cornell University. The Plantations feature herbs, vegetables, crop and weed plants, peonies, perennials, rock garden, native wildflowers, and more. The Newman Arboretum specializes in hardy rees and shrubs native to New York State.
Web: www.plantations.cornell.edu
Hours: Sunrise-sunset
Fees: Free

Donald M. Kendall Sculpture Gardens
700 Anderson Hill Mill Road
Purchase, NY 10577
(914)253-3000
🌺 Situated on 120 acres of landscaped grounds, the Sculpture Gardens were originally

executed by the architect Edward Durrell Stone, Sr. and his son, landscape architect Edward Stone, Jr. In 1980, ten years after the grounds opened, garden designer Russell Page reshaped the landscape in his style, placing the sculpture against rolling lawns and landscape features. Francois Goffinet continues the Garden's development today. A "Golden Path" winds through the site and leads past much of the sculpture. Features along the way include rectangular pools, azalea garden, perennial border and water lily pond.
Hours: Dawn-dusk
Fees: Free

Ellwanger Garden

625 Mt. Hope Avenue
Rochester, NY
Mail: The Landmark Society of Western New York, 133 South Fitzhugh Street, Rochester, NY 14608
(716)546-7029 *Fax:* (716)546-4788
🌿 The Garden has been continuously cultivated since 1867 by the family of one of Rochester's most prominent nurserymen, George Ellwanger. The half-acre site represents a historic period landscape and has noteworthy collections of perennials, roses and trees. Open to the public two days a year (see New York Selected Events).

George Landis Arboretum

Lape Road
Esperance, NY
Mail: PO Box 186, Esperance, NY 12066
(518)875-6935 *Fax:* (518)875-6394
🌿 This 100-acre Arboretum has special collections of lilacs, rhododendrons and southern Appalachian plants. Special gardens include a rose garden, iris, spring bulb, woodland plant, fern, annual and perennial gardens. Highlights include the Beal Peony Garden and the Quarry Rock Garden.

Hours: Dawn-dusk
Fees: Free

Hammond Museum Japanese Stroll Gardens

Deavau Road
North Salem, NY 10560
(914)669-5033 *Fax:* (914)669-8221
🌿 On the grounds of Hammond Museum is this unique Japanese Garden, featuring a Zen garden, bamboo grove and a lotus pond. There's a path with stepping stones that meanders through the garden and benches along the way. May and early June are good times to visit, when the azaleas, cherry trees and iris are in bloom.
Hours: May-Oct noon-4pm Wed-Sat
Fees: $4; $3 seniors & students

Highland Park Botanical Garden

180 Reservoir Avenue
Rochester, NY 14620
(716)244-9023 *Fax:* (716)256-4968
🌿 Designed by Frederick Law Olmsted, Highland Park appears to be a completely natural setting, when in fact it was carefully planned and completely planted with trees. It features over 1200 lilac bushes representing 500 varieties, a Japanese Maple collection, magnolias, rhododendrons, azaleas, mountain laurel and andromeda, spring bulbs and more. The Park's pansy bed of over 10,000 blooms is planted in a new pattern each year. The Park is the site of Warner Castle, home of the Rochester Civic Garden Center, with many display gardens. It is also the site of the Lilac Festival (see New York Selected Events).
Web: www.co.monroe.ny.us/parks/highland/
Hours: May-Oct 10am-6pm daily, 10am-8pm Wed; Nov-Apr 10am-4pm
Fees: Free

Holtsville Park & Ecology Site
249 Buckley Road
Holtsville, NY 11742
(516)758-9664
🏛 The Site has a variety of special gardens, including Butterfly and Bee, Herb, Perennial and Rose Gardens, as well as the Compost Trial bed and many different plantings of annuals.
Hours: Daylight hours
Fees: Free

Innisfree Gardens
Tyrell Road
Millbrook, NY 12545
(914)677-8000
🏛 Formerly the private garden of Walter and Marion Beck, Innisfree was opened to the public in 1960. Walter Beck devised the term "cup garden" to draw attention to something rare or beautiful, and Innisfree is a series of these framed, segregated pictures. Although influenced by the Chinese aesthetic, this is an American garden, with mostly native plant materials and rocks from the adjacent forest.
Directions: From Taconic Parkway, exit at Millbrook, Route 44
Hours: May1-Oct 20 10am-4pm Wed-Fri, 11am-5pm weekends & holidays; closed Mon & Tues except legal holidays
Fees: $2 weekdays, $3 weekends & legal holidays

Institute of Ecosystem Studies
Route 44A
Millbrook, NY
Mail: Box R, Millbrook, NY 12545
(914)677-5359 *Fax:* (914)677-6455
🏛 The Institute of Ecosystems, located at the 2,000-acre Mary Flagler Cary Arboretum, is an ecological and educational facility. Public attractions include display gardens, greenhouse, walking trails. The greenhouse is a great place to visit in the middle of an upper

New York State winter.
Web: www.ecostudies.org
Hours: 9am-5pm Mon-Sat; 1-5pm Sun; Oct-Apr to 4pm; closed major public holidays; Greenhouse open til 3:30pm
Fees: Free; pick up permit at Visitor's Center

LongHouse Reserve
133 Hands Creek Road
East Hampton, NY 11937
(516)329-3568 *Fax:* (516)329-4299
🏛 LongHouse Reserve is the creation of Jack Lenor Larson, textile designer and advocate of traditional and contemporary crafts. The entrance drive, lined with cryptomerias, leads to lawns, ornamental borders, plant collections and sculpture. All the areas are domestic in scale and applicable to home gardening. There are good collections of conifers, flowering trees and shrubs, bamboos, ornamental grasses, daylilies, perennials and roses. The April - May daffodil display includes more than 200 cultivars in a variety of settings.
Web: www.hamptons.com/longhouse/
Hours: Late Apr-mid Sep 2-5pm Wed & 1st & 3rd Sats of the month
Fees: $10 suggested donation

Lyndhurst
635 South Broadway
Tarrytown, NY 10591
(914)631-4481 *Fax:* (914)631-5634
🏛 Overlooking the Hudson River, the Gothic mansion called Lyndhurst sits on 67 landscaped acres which include an outstanding fern garden and a rose garden, maintained today by the Garden Club of Irvington.
Web: www.nthp.org
Hours: Apr 15-Oct 10am-5pm Tues-Sun; Nov 1-Apr 14 10am-4pm weekends only
Fees: $9; $8 seniors; $3 students

Madoo Conservancy

Sagaponack, NY
Mail: PO Box 362, Sagaponack, NY 11962
(516)537-8200 *Fax:* (516)537-8201
🌱 Madoo, on the south shore of Eastern Long Island, is the garden of the artist Robert Dash. Among its special features are mirrored sheds, a woodland garden, knot garden, pleached hornbeam, a user-friendly maze, and many more whimsical and unique designs.
Hours: May-Sep 1-5pm Wed & Sat
Fees: $10

Montgomery Place – Historic Hudson Valley

River Road
Annandale-on-Hudson, NY
Mail: PO Box 32, Annandale-on-Hudson, NY 12504
(914)758-5461 *Fax:* (914)758-0545
🌱 One of the most significant and well-preserved of the great American country estates, Montgomery Place is situated on 434 acres of rolling lawns, woodlands and formal gardens with scenic views of the Hudson River and the Catskill Mountains.
Web: www.hudsonvalley.org
Hours: 10am-5pm; closed Tues; Nov-mid Dec weekends only
Fees: Grounds $3; mansion & grounds $6

New York Botanical Garden

200th Street & Kazimiroff (Southern) Blvd
Bronx, NY 10458
(718)817-8700 *Fax:* (718)220-6504
🌱 The New York Botanical Garden was founded in 1891 on a 250-acre site in the northern section of the Bronx. The property includes a 40-acre tract of the original forest that once covered all of New York City, dramatic rock outcroppings, wetlands, ponds and a waterfall. Among the many horticultural features are the Peggy Rockefeller Rose Garden, Rock Garden,

Irwin Perennial Garden and outstanding collections of daylilies, orchids, hardy ferns, flowering trees, conifers and cherry trees. The NYBG is also home to the newly restored Enid A. Haupt Conservatory, the nation's largest Victorian glass house with distinguished collections of tropical, Mediterranean and desert plants.
Web: www.nybg.org
Hours: 10am-6pm Tues-Sun & Holiday Mon; Nov-Mar to 4pm
Fees: Grounds $3, $2 seniors & students, $1 children 2-12, free all day Wed & 10am-noon Sat; Conservatory $3.50, $2.50 seniors & students

Old Westbury Gardens

71 Old Westbury Road
Old Westbury, Long Island, NY 11568
(516)333-0048 *Fax:* (516)333-6807
🌱 Formerly the estate of John Phipps, these Gardens are set in a100-acre 18th century-style park with wide avenues leading to the house. Among the specialty gardens are a 2-acre Italian garden and boxwood, cottage, rose and wild gardens. There are also demonstration gardens, a pinetum, a large variety of rhododendrons and azaleas, and many fine tree specimens.
Hours: Apr-Dec 10am-5pm Wed-Mon; closed Tues & winter months
Fees: Gardens $6, $4 seniors, $3 children; House $4 additional, $3 additional seniors & children

Planting Fields Arboretum

Planting Fields Road
Oyster Bay, NY 11771
(516)922-9200 *Fax:* (516)922-0058
🌱 Established in 1916, the Arboretum is comprised of more than 400 acres with many special gardens. The Synoptic Garden is an alphabetical catalog of ornamental trees and shrubs. Collections include more than 600

varieties of rhododendrons and azaleas, as well as hollies and dwarf conifers. The conservatory contains one of the largest collections of camellias, plus cacti and succulents, begonias, orchids and other tropical plants.
Hours: 9am-5pm
Fees: $4 per vehicle Labor Day-Memorial Day & weekends year round

Queens Botanical Garden
43-50 Main Street
Flushing, NY 11355
(718)886-3800 *Fax:* (718)463-0263
🌱 The Garden is a 38-acre site with an arboretum, pinetum and eighteen special gardens, including formal display gardens, an extensive rose garden, teaching gardens, a wedding garden and a greenhouse.
Directions: New York City area
Hours: Apr-Oct 8am-6pm; Nov-Mar 8am-4:30pm; closed Mon year-round except legal holidays
Fees: Free

Robin Hill Arboretum
11556 Platten Road
Lyndonville, NY 14098
(716)765-2614
🌱 Robin Hill is a family-planted, 43-acre Arboretum started in 1935 by William and Mary Smith and their son, George Smith, oldest brother of the current owner. Over the years the other four children have helped to maintain and plant over 450 species of trees and shrubs. The collection includes giant sequoias, cypress, and metasequoias which are over fifty years old, large rhododendrons, dogwoods and small flower beds.
Hours: Adult visitors always welcome
Fees: Free

Rochester Civic Garden Center
5 Castle Park
Rochester, NY 14620
Email: garden@mcls.rochester.lib.ny.us
(716)473-5130 *Fax:* (716)473-8136
🌱 Located at Warner Castle in Highland Park, the Center's display gardens include a sunken garden and shady border, rock, courtyard and iris gardens, a daylily bed, rose beds and a 13th century herb garden.
Hours: Gardens dawn-dusk; building 9:30am-3:30pm Tues-Thurs, 9:30am-12:30pm Sat
Fees: Free

Sonnenberg Gardens
151 Charlotte Street
Canandaigua, NY 14607
(716)394-4922 *Fax:* (716)394-2192
🌱 The 50-acre Gardens surround an historic mansion at the foot of Lake Canandaigua in the heart of the Finger Lakes region. Special gardens include butterfly, Japanese, rose, Italian, moonlight, old-fashioned and rock gardens, as well as color-theme gardens and a reflecting pond. The Sonnenberg Conservatory is a greenhouse complex built between 1903-1915 by Lord and Burnham.
Web: www.sonnenberg.org
Hours: 9:30am-5:30pm
Fees: $7.50; $6.50 seniors; $3 children

Staten Island Botanical Garden
1000 Richmond Terrace
Staten Island, NY 10301
(718)273-8200 *Fax:* (718)442-3645
🌱 Located on 83 acres in the Snug Harbor section of Staten Island, the Garden features 19 special gardens, including the Lion's Sensory Garden, Glade of Shade, and the Neil Vanderbilt Orchid collection, as well as a 20-acre wetland. 1999 marks the opening of two new features: the only operating and producing vineyard in the five boroughs of New York

City, and the formal opening of SIBG's one-acre New York Chinese Scholar's Garden.
Directions: New York City area
Hours: 8am-dusk
Fees: Free

Stonecrop Gardens
Cold Spring, NY
Mail: RR2 PO Box 371, Cold Spring, NY 10516
(914)265-2000 *Fax:* (914)265-2405
🌺 Frank and Anne Cabot, founders of The Garden Conservancy, built this garden on a rocky hillside with views across the Hudson Highlands. It features an outstanding cliffside rock garden, English-style flower garden, beds with flowers and vegetable, a woodland garden, grass garden, and a new conservatory for miniature alpines and bulbs. The Gardens can be seen by appointment only.
Hours: Mid Apr-Oct Tues, Wed, Fri by appointment only

Trask Garden
Saratoga Springs, NY
Mail: Yaddo Garden Association, c/o Jane Wait, PO Box 395, Saratoga Springs, NY 12866
(518)583-1236
🌺 The Yaddo Garden Association is restoring the 100-year old private garden of Mr. and Mrs. Spencer Trask, which has over 1,000 roses in a formal bed, a pergola with climbers and a rock garden. The Garden will be one hundred years old in 1999 and a grand opening is targeted for the spring when the roses are in full bloom. Visitors are always welcome.

Vassar College Arboretum
Raymond Avenue
Poughkeepsie, NY 12601
(914)473-5370
🌺 Vassar College Arboretum is the 1,000-acre campus of the college, with more than 200 species of trees. HIghlights of the property include the Shakespeare Garden, Sculpture Garden, Native Plant Preserve and Ecological Preserve.
Web: www.vassar.edu
Hours: Dawn-dusk
Fees: Free

Wave Hill
West 249th and Independence Avenue
Riverdale, The Bronx, NY
Mail: 675 West 252nd Street, The Bronx, NY 10471
(718)549-3200 *Fax:* (718)884-8952
🌺 Wave Hill is set on 28 acres overlooking the Hudson River, and contains an English-style informal garden, a rock garden, herb garden, aquatic garden and arbor, a small alpine garden, roses, annuals and perennials, and greenhouse displays with cacti, succulents and tropical plants.
Web: www.wavehill.org
Directions: New York City area
Hours: 9am-5:30pm Tues-Sun, until dusk Fri; mid Oct-mid Apr 9am-4:30pm Tues-Sun
Fees: $4; $2 seniors & students; under 6 free; Tues, Sat am, Fri evenings & winter months free

Selected Events

Albertson

Mid May
🌺 **Sale of Outdoor Plants**
Annuals and perennials and more. Call for exact date.
Hours: 10am-3pm
Fee: Free
Clark Botanic Garden (See New York Guide to Gardens.)

Mid October
🌸 28th Annual Fall Plant Sale
A sale of dried arrangements made from materials grown by the Auxiliary members, plus bulbs, house plants, home-made vinegars and soup mixtures, dried herbs, pumpkins and more. Call for exact date.
Hours: 10am-3pm
Fee: Free
Clark Botanic Garden (See New York Guide to Gardens.)

Annandale-on-Hudson
Near Kingston

May 16
🌸 Festival
Out of the Garden. The fourth year for this festival which includes horticultural lectures all day, workshops, tours of Montgomery Place.
Hours: 10am-5pm
Fee: $7
Montgomery Place - Historic Hudson Valley (See New York Guide to Gardens.)

May 30-31, June 28-29, July 28-29, August 25-26, September 24-25
🌸 Twilight Garden Walks
A moonlit stroll through Montgomery Place's gardens with landscape curator Timothy Steinhoff. Includes desert afterwards. Coincides with the full moon. Reservations required.
Hours: May 6:30pm; Jun, Jul 7pm; Aug 6:30pm; Sep 6pm
Fee: $10
Montgomery Place - Historic Hudson Valley (See New York Guide to Gardens.)

Buffalo

March 27-April 11
🌸 Spring Flower Show
The annual spring bulb show with hyacinths, tulips, lilies, daffodils and hydrangeas.

Hours: 9am-4pm
Buffalo & Erie County Botanical Gardens (See New York Guide to Gardens.)

May 8
🌸 Rare Plant Garage Sale & Auction
Unusual plants donated by area nurseries and garden centers. Benefits the Gardens.
Hours: 9am-noon
Fee: Free
Buffalo & Erie County Botanical Gardens (See New York Guide to Gardens.)

July 24, 25
🌸 5th Annual Garden Walk
A self-guided tour of more than one hundred private gardens and a spectacular corporate English garden in the tree-lined residential area of mansions and restored Victorian homes on the historic West Side. Shuttle bus rides available. For map & guide, send contribution to the sponsor.
Hours: 10am-4pm
Fee: Contribution requested
For information: **Forever Elmwood Garden Walk**, 231 Norwood Avenue, Buffalo, NY 14222
Email: mlunenfe@sescva.esc.edu
(716)884-2195

November 6-21
🌸 Annual Chrysanthemum Show
The oldest flower show at the Buffalo and Erie County Botanical Gardens, featuring over ninety-five varieties of chrysanthemums, some dating back to the first show nearly a century ago.
Hours: 9am-4pm
Buffalo & Erie County Botanical Gardens (See New York Guide to Gardens.)

Canandaigua
30 miles from Rochester

May 8, 9
❧ Mother's Day Weekend
Kickoff for the opening of the Garden with a plant sale and auction. No charge for Moms when accompanied by their families.
Hours: 9:30am-5pm
Fee: $7.50
Sonnenberg Gardens *(See New York Guide to Gardens.)*

June 19-27
❧ Rose Week
Scheduled to coincide with the height of the rose blooming period. Call for schedule of events.
Hours: 9:30am-5:30pm
Fee: $7.50
Sonnenberg Gardens *(See New York Guide to Gardens.)*

Esperance
25 miles from Albany

May 15, 16
❧ Rare Plant Sale
Rare and unusual shrubs, trees and perennials.
Hours: 10am-4pm
Fee: Free
George Landis Arboretum *(See New York Guide to Gardens.)*

September 11, 12
❧ Fall Plant Sale
Rare and unusual shrubs, trees and perennials.
Hours: 10am-4pm
Fee: Free
George Landis Arboretum *(See New York Guide to Gardens.)*

Holtsville

March 6-14
❧ Brookhaven Indoor Landscape & Garden Show
Backyard landscapes with ponds, walkways, gazebos, trees and flower displays, plus a marketplace with everything from garden equipment to plants and ornaments and a variety of free workshops and demonstrations on the weekend. Benefits the Holtsville Ecology Site's Animal Preserve which houses many handicapped wild and domestic animals.
Holtsville Park & Ecology Site *(See New York Guide to Gardens.)*

Hudson

June 5
❧ 10th Annual Garden Sale & Plant Exchange
Open day at Hudson Bush Farm Garden, plus a plant sale and exchange by local Garden Clubs and societies, individual gardeners and small nurseries. Master Gardeners from the local coop extension on hand to answer questions, and homemade food available.
Hours: 10am-3pm
Fee: Free
Hudson Bush Farm, 154 Yates Road off Route 9H, Hudson, NY 12534
(518)851-7066

June
❧ 6th Annual Garden Tour
A tour of eight private gardens in rural Columbia County, the heart of the Hudson Valley. Benefits the Hudson Opera House. Call for exact date and information.
For information: **Hudson Opera House**, 554 Warren Street, Hudson, NY 12534
(518)822-1438

Millbrook

May
✿ Perennial Sale
Divisions from the Perennial Garden, select stock plants and common and unusual perennials. Gardeners on hand to answer questions. Call for exact date.
Fee: Free
Institute of Ecosystem Studies (See New York Guide to Gardens.)

September
✿ Fall Plant Sale
Asters, sedums, buddelia, grasses, daylily, garden divisions - all plants that do well in the Fall garden. Call for exact date.
Fee: Free
Institute of Ecosystem Studies (See New York Guide to Gardens.)

New York City
See also Old Westbury, Oyster Bay, Tarrytown, Westbury

February 12, 13
✿ Floral Design Competition
A special exhibition of the floral design work of the students and friends of the HSNY, including edible arrangements and Ikebana. Lectures and demonstrations.
Hours: Noon-6pm Fri; Noon-5pm Sat
Fee: $5
The Horticultural Society of New York, 128 West 58th Street, New York, NY 10019 (212)757-0915

March 14
✿ Making Brooklyn Bloom
A full day of seminars and workshops for community gardeners getting a head-start on spring.
Hours: 10am-4pm
Fee: Admission $3; $1.50 seniors & students; $.50 children

Brooklyn Botanic Garden (See New York Guide to Gardens.)

March 25-28
✿ Annual Greater New York Orchid Show
Displays by orchid growers from all parts of the world, lectures on orchid-related subjects, demonstrations on orchid culture, a large sales area and individual exhibits of thousands of varieties of orchids - all in the spectacular viewing space of the Winter Garden at the World Financial Center. Sponsored by the Greater New York Orchid Society and one of the largest such events in the U.S.
Hours: 10am-7pm Thurs-Sat; 10am-5pm Sun
Fee: Free
Winter Garden, World Financial Center, Battery Park City, West Street between Vesey & Liberty, New York, NY (212)945-0505

April 3, 4
✿ Spring Plant Information Weekend
Q&A sessions with experts and a plant sale.
New York Botanical Garden (See New York Guide to Gardens.)

Mid April
✿ Gardening Day
A day devoted to getting started in the garden, with lectures and demonstrations. Call for exact date and information.
Fee: Free
Queens Botanical Garden (See New York Guide to Gardens.)

Late April
✿ NY African Violet Show
A display and sale, plus demonstrations and advice from experts. Call for exact date.
Hours: Noon-7pm
Fee: $1
The Horticultural Society of New York, 128

West 58th Street, New York, NY 10019
(212)757-0915

April 23-25
⚘ Antique Garden Furniture Show & Sale
A yearly event held in a tent, with over twenty
dealers of antique garden accessories.
New York Botanical Garden (See New York
Guide to Gardens.)

April 24, 25
⚘ African Violet Show
Sponsored by the African Violet Society.
Fee: Free
Queens Botanical Garden (See New York
Guide to Gardens.)

April 30
⚘ 25th Anniversary Arbor Day
Celebration
Many environmental exhibits plus a petting
zoo and activities for all. Call for exact date.
Hours: 10am-1pm
Fee: Free
Queens Botanical Garden (See New York
Guide to Gardens.)

May 1, 2
⚘ Sakura Matsuri Cherry Blossom
Festival
Taiko drumming, music, dance performances,
demonstrations, exhibitions and guided tours
of the Japanese Garden when the cherry trees
are in full bloom. Call for schedule.
Hours: 10am-6pm
Fee: Admission $3; $1.50 seniors & stu-
dents; $.50 children
Brooklyn Botanic Garden (See New York
Guide to Gardens.)

May 1, 2
⚘ Annual Spring Plant Sale
Vegetables, perennials, herbs, ornamental grass-
es and annuals. Proceeds benefit the Garden's
horticultural and educational programs.
Hours: 10am-4pm Sat; noon-4pm Sun
Staten Island Botanical Garden (See New
York Guide to Gardens.)

May 5, 6
⚘ Spring Plant Sale
Loads of everything, from marigold seedlings
for children to trees, shrubs and rare perenni-
als, spread out over the Garden and under
tents. One of the country's largest plant sales.
Sponsored by the Auxiliary of the BBG.
Hours: 8am-6pm
Fee: Free
Brooklyn Botanic Garden (See New York
Guide to Gardens.)

May 9
⚘ Mother's Day
An orchestra concert and plant sale.
New York Botanical Garden (See New York
Guide to Gardens.)

May 12-15
⚘ Urban Garden Festival
A Festival in downtown Brooklyn focusing on
container plantings. Includes demonstrations
applicable to small urban gardens, children's
activities and a plant sale.
Hours: 10am-5pm
Fee: Free
MetroTech Commons, MetroTech Center,
Brooklyn, NY
For information: **MetroTech Business
Improvement District**, 4 Metrotech Center,
Brooklyn, NY 11201
Email: Metrobid@idt.net
(718)488-8200

June 5-13
⚘ Roses! Roses! Roses!
A celebration of roses with experts on hand to

answer questions during peak bloom in the Peggy Rockefeller Rose Garden.
New York Botanical Garden *(See New York Guide to Gardens.)*

Early June
✿ Garden Day at The Cloisters
An all-day Saturday event devoted to gardens, with lectures and demonstrations. Call for exact date.
The Cloisters of the Metropolitan Museum *(See New York Guide to Gardens.)*

Mid June
✿ Queens Rose Society Show & Sale
Sponsored by the Queens Rose Society. Call for exact date.
Fee: Free
Queens Botanical Garden *(See New York Guide to Gardens.)*

September 18
✿ Harvest Fair
Produce sales, vegetable and flower contests, and activities for the whole family. Co-sponsored by Brooklyn Green Bridge, the BBG's Children's Garden and Green Thumb.
Hours: 10am-4pm
Fee: Admission $3; $1.50 seniors & students; $.50 children
Brooklyn Botanic Garden *(See New York Guide to Gardens.)*

October
✿ Fall Festival
Activities for everyone. A great time to see the fall color at Wave Hill. Call for exact date.
Hours: Noon-4:30pm
Fee: Admission $4; $2 seniors & students; under 6 free
Wave Hill *(See New York Guide to Gardens.)*

October 2-9
✿ Gardens & Fall Colors along the Hudson
A cruise aboard the clipper ship Yorktown sponsored by the American Horticulture Society.
For information: **American Horticultural Society**, 7931 East Boulevard Drive, Alexandria, VA 22308
Email: info@haerttertravel.com
(800)942-6666

October 3
✿ Chili Pepper Fiesta
A celebration of all the cultures that use or grow chili peppers. Crafts, food, cooking demonstrations, entertainment and more.
Hours: 10am-5:30pm
Fee: Admission $3; $1.50 seniors & students; $.50 children
Brooklyn Botanic Garden *(See New York Guide to Gardens.)*

Mid December- Early January
✿ Christmas in the Middle Ages
A holiday celebration with decorations typical of the Middle Ages, including wreaths and garlands woven of herbs, berries and greens. Call for dates.
The Cloisters of the Metropolitan Museum *(See New York Guide to Gardens.)*

Newark
30 miles east of Rochester

May 22
✿ St. Mark's Garden Faire & Tea Room
A Faire featuring perennials, annuals, herbs, hanging baskets, garden wares and handmade crafts on the church lawn. An English-style tea available in the Parish House of scones, shortbread, tea sandwiches, cakes and tarts served with silver, china, chintz, palms and music.
Hours: 10am-3pm

Fee: Sale free; tea $5
St. Mark's Episcopal Church, 400 South
Main Street, Newark, NY 14513
(315)331-3610

Oakdale

Late September
❀ Plant & Harvest Display
A harvest and flower show is sponsored by the
Horticultural Society. Call for exact dates.
Hours: 10am-5pm
Bayard Cutting Arboretum (See New York
Guide to Gardens.)

Old Westbury
25 miles from New York City on Long Island

April 24, 25
❀ Plant Sale & Arbor Day Celebration
To celebrate the Gardens' opening, an Historic
and Perennial Plant Sale throughout the
weekend, plus garden lectures and demonstrations. Tree planting on Sunday, Arbor Day.
Hours: 10am-5pm
Old Westbury Gardens (See New York Guide
to Gardens.)

Oyster Bay
Greater New York City area

April 24, 25
❀ Arbor Day Celebration
A weekend celebration with a wildlife show by
the Theodore Roosevelt Bird Sanctuary, tours
of the Arboretum, children's activities, tree
planting and more.
Hours: 10am-5pm
Fee: Parking fee
Planting Fields Arboretum (See New York
Guide to Gardens.)

September 18, 19
❀ Dahlia Society Flower Show
A judged competition and display, plus

exhibits by most of the top growers in the
region. Sponsored by the Mid Island Dahlia
Society. The largest America Dahlia Society
show in the Northeast.
Hours: 10am-5pm; 1-6pm Sat; Noon-5pm Sun
Fee: Parking fee
Planting Fields Arboretum (See New York
Guide to Gardens.)

October 2-11
❀ Fall Garden Festival
A large show, now in its 94th year, featuring
landscaped gardens by the Long Island
Nurserymen's Association under and outside
the huge tent, plus exhibits by the 2nd
District Federated Garden Clubs and other
amateur plant societies and educational
groups. Lots of family activities on the two
weekends. Open house at the Greenhouses
and Coe Hall mansion.
Planting Fields Arboretum (See New York
Guide to Gardens.)

December 4, 5, 11, 12
❀ Winter Festival
Museum and Greenhouse decorated for the
season. On December 4-5, a juried crafts fair,
with over sixty exhibitors in the Hay Barn.
Special activities for children.
Fee: $5; children under 12 free.
Planting Fields Arboretum (See New York
Guide to Gardens.)

Rochester
See also Canandaigua, Newark, Webster

March 11-14
❀ The Greater Rochester Flower &
Garden Show
A large regional show featuring floral exhibits,
landscape displays, demonstrations and seminars, information on careers in horticulture,
and a sale of garden equipment, plants and
plant-related materials.

Hours: 9am-9pm Thurs-Sat; 9am-5pm Sun
Fee: $7; $4 children
Dome Center, 2695 East Henrietta Road,
Henrietta, NY
For information: **Genesee Finger Lakes
Nursery & Landscape Association**, 305
Hemlock Trail, Webster, NY 14580
Web: www.plantamerica.com/newyork/
region.htm
(716)265-9018

May 14-23
❧ Lilac Festival
Demonstrations, guided walking tours, a plant
sale, entertainment day and night timed to
coincide with peak bloom of the lilacs. Plus
open house at the historic castle, home to the
Garden Center of Rochester. Call for a complete schedule.
Highland Park Botanical Garden *(See New
York Guide to Gardens.)*

May 14-23
❧ Open Garden Day at Ellwanger Garden
One of the only two times (see "Peony
Weekend" below) that Ellwanger Garden is
open to the public. Basket of gold, bleeding
heart, candytuft, checkered lily, forget-me-not,
tulips and woodland phlox all in full bloom.
Part of Rochester's Lilac Festival.
Hours: 10am-4pm
Fee: $2
For information: **Ellwanger Garden** *(See New
York Guide to Gardens.)*

May 14-23
❧ Lilac Week
Historic house and garden tours, sale of
antiques and collectibles, activities for chil-
dren, lectures, and more.
Hours: 9am-4pm
Rochester Civic Garden Center *(See New
York Guide to Gardens.)*

June 5, 6
❧ 29th Landmark Society House & Garden Tour
A tour of one of Rochester's historic
neighborhoods.
Hours: 11am-4pm
Fee: $12 in advance; $15 day of tour
For information: **The Landmark Society of
Western New York**, 133 South Fitzhugh
Street, Rochester, NY 14608
(716)546-7029

June 12, 13
❧ Peony Weekend at Ellwanger Garden
Open weekend at Ellwanger Garden, with its
priceless collection of tree peonies, fern
peonies and Caucasian peonies in bloom,
some more than fifty years old and several
varieties unique to this garden. Loosestrife,
foxglove, Harrison's yellow rose, gas plant and
bearded iris also in bloom.
Hours: 10am-4pm
Fee: $2
For information: **Ellwanger Garden** *(See New
York Guide to Gardens.)*

June 19
❧ Greater Rochester Rose Show
The 80th anniversary celebration of the Rose
Society, with exhibitions of roses and arrange-
ments, classes, sale of miniature roses.
Hours: 2-5pm
Fee: $2
Cornell Cooperative Extension, 149 Highland
Avenue, Rochester, NY
For information: **Greater Rochester Rose
Society**, 816 Lindsey Circle, Webster, NY
14580

July 17, 18
❧ Garden Tour & Treasure Hunt
A tour of six to ten gardens plus refreshments,
art show and sale, and treasure hunt with prizes.

For information: **Rochester Civic Garden Center** *(See New York Guide to Gardens.)*

Saratoga Springs

March 28, 29
❦ Flower & Garden Show
Workshops, demonstrations, lectures, a floral design competition and a marketplace. Benefits the Children's Museum.
Hours: 10am-9:30pm Sat; 11am-6pm Sun
Fee: Fee charged
Wilton Mall at Saratoga, 3065 Route 50, Saratoga Springs, NY
For information: **The Children's Museum at Saratoga**, 36 Phila Street, Saratoga Springs, NY 12866
(518)584-6059

Southampton

Mid June
❦ Tour & Symposium
Landscape Pleasures. A day of presentations by well-known speakers on Saturday. Tours of outstanding gardens on Sunday. Call for schedule.
Hours: Symposium 9:45am-3pm Sat; reception 6-8pm Sat; tour 10am-3pm Sun
Fee: $125
For information: **Parrish Art Museum**, 25 Job's Lane, Southampton, NY 11968
(516)283-2118

Tarrytown
North of New York City, 1/2 mile south of Tappan Zee Bridge

May 8
❦ Plant Sale
A sale sponsored by the Garden Club of Irvington-on-Hudson when the rose garden is in full bloom. Includes advice from Garden Club members, music and refreshments.
Hours: 1-4pm

Fee: Free
Lyndhurst *(See New York Guide to Gardens.)*

June 6
❦ Rose Day
Music, refreshments and advice from experts on the care and cultivation of roses. Sponsored by the Garden Club of Irvington-on-Hudson.
Hours: 1-4pm
Fee: Free
Lyndhurst *(See New York Guide to Gardens.)*

Troy

March 11-14
❦ Capital District Garden & Flower Show
A large Albany-area show featuring a flower arranging competition, garden lectures, demonstrations and workshops. Benefits Wildwood Programs, an organization which serves neurologically impaired, learning disabled and autistic individuals and their families.
Hours: 4-9pm Thurs; 10am-5pm Fri; 10am-8pm Sat; 10am-6pm Sun
Fee: $7; $6 seniors & children over 10
Hudson Valley Community College, Vandenburgh Avenue - Route 4, Troy, NY
For information: **Wildwood Programs**, 2995 C Curry Road Extension, Schenectady, NY 12303
Email: neshowpro@aol.com
(518)786-1529

Webster
Near Rochester

June 13, 14
❦ Horticulture Faire
An event for the serious horticulturist and home gardener, with seminars, plant sales, an English Tea and tours through the Arboretum.
Hours: Starts 10am
Fee: Free

Webster Arborertum, 1700 Schlegel Road, 983 Ebner Road, Webster, NY 14580
(716)872-2911 *Fax:* (716)872-7111

Westbury
Greater New York City area

March 12-21
Spring Flower & Garden Show
A preview of spring in the indoor display gardens where annuals, perennials and flowering shrubs are in peak bloom. Demonstrations and creative ideas for garden design and care, plus free seminars and a children's show. On the second weekend, an *Horticultural Fair* with exhibits and seminars by local Horticultural Societies and other groups. Held rain or shine.
Hours: 8am-6pm
Fee: Free
Hicks Nurseries, 100 Jericho Turnpike, Westbury, NY 11590
(516)334-0066

North Carolina

Guide to Gardens

Biltmore Estate
Asheville, NC
Mail: 1 North Pack Square, Asheville, NC 28801
(800)543-2961
Biltmore is the 1895 French Renaissance residence of George Washington Vanderbilt. The Estate has over 8,000 acres with grounds and gardens designed by Frederick Law Olmsted.
Web: www.biltmore.com
Hours: 9am-5pm; open for selected candlelight evenings during Spring Festival and at Christmas (see North Carolina Selected Events)
Fees: $29.95; $22.50 youth

The Botanical Gardens at Asheville
151 W.T. Weaver Boulevard
Asheville, NC 28804
(704)252-5190
The Garden specializes in native plants of the South Appalachian region, with collections of rhododendron, azaleas and wildflowers.
Hours: 9:30am-4:30pm
Fees: Free

Cape Fear Botanical Garden
536 North Eastern Blvd
Fayetteville, NC
Mail: PO Box 53485, Fayetteville, NC 28305
(910)486-0221 *Fax:* (910)486-4209
Located on 85 acres, the Garden includes a large urban forest, a natural amphitheater, formal gardens and trails leading to bluffs overlooking Cross Creek and the Cape Fear River.
Web: www.artswire.org/artcncl/cfbg/index/
Hours: 10am-5pm; noon-5pm Sun except mid Dec-mid Feb
Fees: $2

Daniel Boone Native Gardens
Horn in West Drive
Boone, NC 28607
(828)264-6390
The Gardens were opened in 1966 and feature a collection of native North Carolina plants in an informal landscape design, with pools, sunken garden, rock garden and meadows.
Hours: 9am-6pm; noon-6pm Sun
Fees: Nominal fee charged

Daniel Stowe Botanical Garden
6500 South New Hope Road
Belmont, NC 23012
(704)825-4490 *Fax:* (704)825-4492
Daniel Stowe Botanical Garden is still early in its development. The focal points are the large Perennial Garden and the extensive collection of daylilies, with more than 275 vari-

eties offering cvontinuous blooms from late May through October.

Web: www.stowegarden.org

Hours: 9am-5pm Mon-Sat; noon-5pm Sun

Fees: Free

Elizabethan Gardens

Highway 64/264

Roanoke Island, NC

Mail: 1411 Highway 64/264, Manteo, NC 27954

Email: elizgrdn@interpath.com

(252)473-3234 *Fax:* (252)473-3244

🪴 Thie Gardens are on the site of the first English colony in the New World, and were created by the Garden Club of North Carolina in 1951. There are many seasonal highlights, including azaleas, dogwoods, gardenias, roses and magnolias. Features include a Sunken Garden, Shakespeare's Herb Garden, Woodland Garden and Wildlife Garden.

Fees: Fee charged

JC Raulston Arboretum at NCSU

4301 Beryl Road

Raleigh, NC 27606

(919)515-3132

🪴 The Arboretum is dedicated to the discovery, evaluation and promotion of well-adapted plants for the home landscape. The 8-acre garden includes a White Garden, Japanese Garden and 450-foot perennial border.

Fees: Free

North Carolina Botanical Garden

University of North Carolina, Laurel Hill Road

Chapel Hill, NC

Mail: CB Box 3375, Totten Center, UNC, Chapel Hill, NC 27599

(919)962-0522 *Fax:* (919)962-3531

🪴 The display gardens feature wildflowers, ferns, aquatics, carnivorous and poisonous plants, and an extensive herb garden. The

arboretum contains a woodland of mature pines, some virgin forest, a collection of indigenous trees, shrubs, and flowers of the southeast. There are two miles of nature trails.

Web: http://ils.unc.edu/hiking/NCBOT.HTM

Hours: Dawn-dusk

Fees: Free

Orton Plantation Gardens

9149 Orton Road, SE

Winnabow, NC 28479

Email: ortngarden@aol.com

(910)371-6851 *Fax:* (910)371-6871

🪴 The Gardens consist of formal and informal gardens surrounding an ante-bellum house. Special features include impressive oaks and other native trees and lawns with scenic vistas over the old rice fields and Cape Fear River. Spring is the best time to visit, with the blooming of camellias, azaleas, flowering trees and ornamentals.

Hours: 8am-6pm; Sept-Nov 10am-5pm

Fees: $8; $7 seniors

Reynolda Gardens of Wake Forest University

100 Reynolda Village

Winston-Salem, NC 27106

(336)758-5593 *Fax:* (336)758-4132

🪴 This 129-acre facility was originally part of the estate of Richard Joshua Reynolds and his wife. The Gardens include an early Lord and Burnham Greenhouse and formal gardens designed by Thomas Sears, divided into Northern and Southern segments. There are theme gardens, a Rose Garden, border gardens, display gardens, and vegetable and flower gardens.

Web: www.wfu.edu/gardens/

Hours: Dawn-dusk; Greenhouse 10am-4pm Mon-Fri, closed Sat, Sun

Fees: Free

Sarah P. Duke Gardens
Duke University
Durham, NC
Mail: PO Box 90341, Durham, NC 27708
(919)684-3698 *Fax:* (919)684-8861
🌺 The Gardens comprise 55 acres of land-scaped and woodland gardens located on Duke University's West Campus, adjacent to the Medical Center. There are five miles of allées, walks and pathways to formal and informal garden elements. Special features include The Terraces, designed by Ellen Biddle Shipman, the Blomquist Garden of Native Plants and the Asiatic Arboretum.
Web: www.hr.duke.edu/dukegardens/
Hours: 8am-dusk
Fees: Free

Tryon Palace Historic Sites & Gardens
610 Pollock
New Bern, NC
Mail: PO Box 1007, New Bern, NC 28563
Email: tryon_palace@coastalnet.com
(800)767-1560 *Fax:* (252)514-4876
🌺 The Gardens of Tryon Palace reflect a variety of styles, from the simple gardens of Colonial times to the complex landscaping of the high Victorian era. Features include the Entrance Allée, the Kitchen Garden, the Kellenberger Garden, an example of 18th century ornamental planting, the Wilderness Garden and the Hawks Allée.
Hours: 9am-5pm Mon-Sat; 1-5pm Sun
Fees: Fee charged

UNC Charlotte Botanical Gardens
Mary Alexander Road & Craver Road, UNC Campus
Charlotte, NC 28223
(704)547-4055 *Fax:* (704)547-3128

🌺 There are several outstanding special collections in this 9-acre Garden, including hardy ornamentals, rhododendron hybrids and Carolina natives. There are additional collections of orchids and succulents in the greenhouse.
Hours: Gardens daylight hours every day; Greenhouse 9am-4pm weekdays
Fees: Free

Wilkes Community College
Wilkesboro, NC
Mail: PO Box 120, Wilkesboro, NC 28697
(910)838-6294 *Fax:* (910)838-6277
🌺 The WCC Gardens are planted in collections as an integral part of the 140-acre campus. Some of the special gardens are the Rose Garden, Japanese Garden, Sensory Garden and Native Garden.
Web: 204.84.96.72/wcc/general_information/gardens.htm
Hours: Dawn-dusk
Fees: Free

Wing Haven Gardens & Bird Sanctuary
248 Ridgewood Avenue
Charlotte, NC 28209
(704)331-0664 *Fax:* (704)331-9368
🌺 This unique 3-acre Sanctuary is enclosed on all sides by brick walls, in the heart of a residential neighborhood. All the Gardens are designed to attract birds, with water elements and plants that provide food, cover and nesting sites. Beyond the formal gardens are wooded areas with ferns and wildflowers.
Hours: Gardens 2-5pm Sun, 3-5pm Tues, 10am-noon Wed
Fees: Free

Asheville

April 2-May 1
❀ Festival of Flowers
An annual spring festival featuring family activities, music, lavish Victorian floral arrangements in Biltmore House, one-hour guided garden walks on the weekends, and more. Timed to coincide with the blooming of the thousands of tulips, iris, flowering dogwoods, Japanese cherry trees and azaleas in the Gardens.
Hours: 9am-5pm; open for selected candlelight evenings during this time; call for schedule and advance reservations
Biltmore Estate *(See North Carolina Guide to Gardens.)*

May 1
❀ Day in the Gardens
Plant sales, tours of the Gardens, entertainment, arts and crafts, food and more.
Hours: 9am-5pm
Fee: Free
The Botanical Gardens at Asheville *(See North Carolina Guide to Gardens.)*

November 6-January 2
❀ Christmas at Biltmore
An annual holiday celebration in the Mansion with thousands of poinsettias, thousands of feet of evergreen roping, wreaths, imported, handcrafted trees, stately boughs and twinkling lights.
Hours: 9am-5pm; open for selected candlelight evenings during this time; call for schedule and advance reservations
Biltmore Estate *(See North Carolina Guide to Gardens.)*

Belmont
West of Charlotte

August 14, 15
❀ Hummingbird Mornings
A morning with Bill Hilton, the garden's Director of Education and Research and authority on capturing, banding and releasing wild hummingbirds, a skill he shares during these sessions.
Daniel Stowe Botanical Garden *(See North Carolina Guide to Gardens.)*

Boone
75 miles from Winston-Salem

July 10
❀ Home Garden Tour & Plant Sale
A tour of unique local homes and gardens, plus a plant sale at the Gardens.
Hours: 10am-3pm
Fee: Tour $10
For information: **Daniel Boone Native Gardens** *(See North Carolina Guide to Gardens.)*

August 13, 14
❀ Flower Show
A show sponsored by the Watauga Garden Club Council, with a different theme each year. Call to confirm date.
Hours: 9am-8pm
Fee: Free
Daniel Boone Native Gardens *(See North Carolina Guide to Gardens.)*

Cary
Just west of Raleigh

September 11, 12
❀ 58th Annual Gourd Festival
Exhibits of gourd traditions around the world and demonstrations of how to grow and dry gourds, attract birds and more. Includes displays of Chinese cricket cages, Peruvian acid-

burned bowls, Mexican lacquer ware, Japanese wine bottles, African musical instruments, an Indian sitar, and many crafts from the U.S. Sponsored by the Cary Gourd Village Garden Club and the Parks & Recreation Department.
Hours: 10am-5pm Sat; 1-5pm Sun
Fee: $1
Cary Community Center, 404 North Academy Street, Cary, NC
For information: **Gourd Village Garden Club**, 4008 Green Level Road West, Apex, NC 27502
(919)362-4357

Chapel Hill

March 27, 28
♫ Annual Daffodil Society Show
A standard judged show presented by the local chapter of the Society held in Totten Center.
Hours: 2-6pm Sat; 2-5pm Sun
North Carolina Botanical Garden *(See North Carolina Guide to Gardens.)*

Charlotte
See also Belmont

February 27-March 7
♫ Southern Spring Show
Spring Reflections. Everything for home and garden, including dozens of professionally landscaped gardens, judged flower show, Orchid Pavilion, Bonsai Pavilion, speakers and demonstrations, and a large marketplace.
Hours: 10am-9pm Mon-Sat; 10am-6pm Sun
Fee: $7 in advance; $8 at door; children under 12 free
Charlotte Merchandise Mart, 2500 East Independence Blvd, Charlotte, NC
For information: **Southern Shows, Inc**, PO Box 36859, Charlotte, NC 28236
(800)849-0248 or (704)376-6594

April 14-17
♫ Wing Haven Gardens Tour
A rare opportunity to tour the grounds, which are not normally open so as not to disturb the birds.
Hours: 10am-4pm
For information: **Wing Haven Gardens & Bird Sanctuary** *(See North Carolina Guide to Gardens.)*

April 22
♫ Plant Sale & Greenhouse Tour
A Greenhouse tour featuring hundreds of orchids, a rain forest Conservatory, hybrid carnivorous pitcher plants and more, plus a sale of common and unusual bedding plants, house plants and native plants.
Hours: 8am-3pm
Fee: Free
UNC Charlotte Botanical Gardens *(See North Carolina Guide to Gardens.)*

May 1, 2
♫ Gardener's Gardens Tour
A tour of private gardens tended by their owners.
For information: **Wing Haven Gardens & Bird Sanctuary** *(See North Carolina Guide to Gardens.)*

New Bern

April 9-11
♫ Tryon Palace Gardeners' Weekend
Free open garden day plus the second annual Historic Plant Sale featuring plants from the Tryon Palace Greenhouse and selected southeastern nurseries.
Hours: 9am-5pm
Fee: Free
Tryon Palace Historic Sites & Gardens *(See North Carolina Guide to Gardens.)*

April 9, 10
≈ New Bern Spring Historic Homes & Gardens Tours

A tour of approximately twelve historic homes and gardens not usually open to the public, plus eight churches and other semi-public buildings, with guides at each location. Walk or drive from site to site. Free walking tours of the Tryon Palace Gardens and New Bern Academy Museum gardens on this weekend, with thousands of tulips in bloom.
Hours: 10am-5pm
Fee: $13.50 in advance; $15 day of tour
For information: **New Bern Preservation Society**, PO Box 207, New Bern, NC 28563
(919)633-6448

October 8-10
≈ Chrysanthemum Festival

Free admission and a free lecture on the 9th, part of a city-wide festival celebrating the thousands of chrysanthemum blooms.
Hours: 9am-5pm
Fee: Free
Tryon Palace Historic Sites & Gardens *(See North Carolina Guide to Gardens.)*

November 26-December 22
≈ Candlelight, Deck the Doors & Holiday Secrets Tours

Special tours in celebration of the holidays. Call for exact schedule and reservations.
Hours: Candlelight tours 5-8pm; other tours 2pm by reservation
Fee: Fee charged
Tryon Palace Historic Sites & Gardens *(See North Carolina Guide to Gardens.)*

Raleigh
See also Cary

September 18
≈ Giant Growers Association Weigh-Off

A competition with awards for the biggest pumpkins, watermelons, cantaloupe, dipper gourd, bushel gourd, sunflower head and more.
Fee: Free
North Carolina State Farmers Market, Raleigh, NC
For information: **Giant Gardeners Association, Inc.**, 259 Fletcher Avenue, Fuquay-Varina, NC 27526
(919)557-5946

Wilkesboro
55 miles from Winston-Salem

April 29-May 2
≈ Merle Fest

Wildflower tours and a music festival in the gardens.
Wilkes Community College *(See North Carolina Guide to Gardens.)*

Wilmington

April 8-11
≈ Azalea Gardens Tour

A tour of ten private gardens during peak azalea time. Proceeds benefit community beautification projects. Part of Wilmington's Azalea Festival, with activities for everyone.
Hours: 10:30am-6pm
Fee: Fee charged
For information: **Cape Fear Garden Club**, PO Box 5214, Wilmington, NC 28403
(910)763-0905

Winston-Salem

March 27
≈ Orchid Auction

An auction of divisions from the Garden's collection in the Education wing of the Greenhouse.
Hours: 9am
Fee: Free
Reynolda Gardens of Wake Forest University *(See North Carolina Guide to Gardens.)*

April 24
❀ Spring Plant Sale
Annuals, perennials, and herbs grown at Reynolda Gardens. Held in the greenhouse.
Hours: 8am-noon
Fee: Free
Reynolda Gardens of Wake Forest University *(See North Carolina Guide to Gardens.)*

North Dakota

International Peace Garden
Dunseith, ND
Mail: PO Box 116, Route 1, Dunseith, ND 58329
(701)263-4390 *Fax:* (701)263-3169
❀ Located on the border between North Dakota and Manitoba, the International Peace Garden plants more than 150,000 flowers each summer in different displays, including a floral clock. The entire 2,300 acres is an official wildlife refuge and wildlife viewing area, with native forests, hiking trails, bike paths, camp grounds and other attractions.
Web: www.peacegarden.com
Hours: Always open
Fees: $7 per vehicle parking fee Jun-Sep 15 only

Dunseith

May 9
❀ International Peace Garden Open House
Mother's Day tours of the greenhouses and thousands of annuals in bloom.
Hours: 1-4pm
Fee: Free

International Peace Garden *(See North Dakota Guide to Gardens.)*

August 1
❀ International Peace Garden's 67th Anniversary Celebration
Tours of the gardens, musical entertainment, and more
Hours: 1-4pm
Fee: Free
International Peace Garden *(See North Dakota Guide to Gardens.)*

Grand Forks

July 17, 18
❀ Garden Tour
Tour of five local gardens.
Hours: Afternoon
Fee: $5
For information: **Grand Forks Horticultural Society**, 1406 South 17th Street, Grand Forks, ND 58201
(701)775-2174

Ohio

Cincinnati Zoo & Botanical Garden
3400 Vine Street
Cincinnati, OH 45220
(513)281-4701
❀ Excellent plantings of bamboos, palms dwarf conifers and other exotic plants are used to replicate the animals' natural habitats. April heralds an outstanding bulb display.
Web: cinci.com/recreation/parks.html
Hours: 9am-5pm
Fees: $8.00; $5.75 seniors; $4.75 children

Cleveland Botanical Garden
11030 East Boulevard

Cleveland, OH 44106
(216)721-1600 *Fax:* (216)721-2056
🌿 Located in downtown Cleveland, the Garden combines formal gardens, woodland walks and open areas. It features a rose garden, a Japanese garden, and the Herb Garden, originally planted by the Western Reserve Herb Society.
Web: www.cbgarden.org
Hours: 9am-5pm Mon-Sat; noon-5pm Sun
Fees: Free

Cox Arboretum
6733 Springboro Pike
Dayton, OH 45449
(937)434-9005 *Fax:* (937)434-4361
🌿 The Arboretum includes crabapples, a synoptic shrub garden, an herb garden, ivies and demonstration and test gardens. The greenhouses have cacti and succulent collections.
Web: aabga.mobot.org/AABGA/
Member.pages/cox.arb.html
Hours: 8am-dusk
Fees: Free

The Dawes Arboretum
7770 Jacksontown Road SE
Newark, OH 43055
(888)443-2937 *Fax:* (740)323-4058
🌿 This arboretum has over 1100 acres of plant collections and natural areas, featuring trees and shrubs tolerant of the Central Ohio climate.
Web: www.dawesarb.org
Hours: Dawn-dusk
Fees: Free

Fellows Riverside Gardens
Mill Creek Metro Parks
Youngstown, OH
Mail: PO Box 596, Canfield, OH 44406
(330)740-7116 *Fax:* (330)740-7129
🌿 Located in Mill Creek Park, Fellows Riverside

Gardens includes various special gardens, such as the Shade Garden, Perennial Border Walk and Climbing Rose Allée, Formal Rose Garden, Blue Garden, as well as special collections and a wonderful bulb display in spring.
Web: www.neont.com/millcreek/
Hours: 10am-dusk
Fees: Free

Franklin Park Conservatory & Botanical Garden
1777 East Broad Street
Columbus, OH 43203
(614)645-8733 *Fax:* (614)645-5921
🌿 The Conservatory is a replica of one built for the Chicago World's Fair of 1893. It has good collections of orchids, gesneriads, palms, tropical and subtropical plants, carnivorous plants, cacti and succulents, and offers seasonal displays throughout the year.
Web: www.fpconservatory.com
Hours: 10am-5pm Tues-Sun; 10am-8pm Wed; closed Mon except holidays
Fees: $5; $3:50 seniors & students; $2 children 2-12

The Holden Arboretum
9500 Sperry Road
Kirtland, OH 44094
(440)946-4400 *Fax:* (440)256-1655
🌿 The 3200-acre Arboretum has many outstanding collections. May and June are the best times to see the rhododendron, crabapple and lilac collections. There is also an excellent collection of nut trees. Holden has woodlands, bogs, prairies, dry creek beds, sand barrens and rocky cliffs, all planted appropriately to the individual ecosystems. Autumn is a good time to visit when the color of the trees is brilliant.
Web: www.holdenarb.org
Hours: 10am-5pm; closed Mon
Fees: $4; $3 seniors; $2 children; under 6 free

Inniswood Metro Gardens

940 Hempstead Road
Westerville, OH 43081
(614)895-6216 *Fax:* (614)895-6352
🌺 Inniswood Metro Gardens was the 37-acre estate of Grace and Mary Innis. The Gardens include rose, herb, woodland and rock gardens, and collections of daylilies, hostas and daffodils in the perennial beds. There are trails through the nature preserve and alongside the gardens.
Hours: 7am-dusk
Fees: Free

Kingwood Center

900 Park Avenue West
Mansfield, OH 44906
(419)522-0211 *Fax:* (419)522-0211
🌺 The Center includes an old, beautifully landscaped 47-acre garden surrounding an estate, with formal and natural gardens and lawns bordered by flower beds. Highlights include the Herb, Rose, Perennial and Iris Gardens. There is also a complex of six greenhouses with seasonal exhibitions and collections of orchids, cacti and succulents.
Web: www.virtualmansfield.com/kingwood/
Hours: Garden 8am-1/2 hr before sunset
Fees: Free

Krohn Conservatory

950 Eden Park Drive
Cincinnati, OH 45202
(513)421-5707 *Fax:* (513)421-6007
🌺 The 1902 Conservatory was rebuilt in 1933 and contains good collections of tropical plants, tree ferns, orchids, palms and desert plants.
Web: www.cinci.com/recreation/parks/krohn/krohn.html
Hours: 10am-5pm daily
Fees: Free

Rockefeller Park Greenhouse

750 East 88th Street
Cleveland, OH 44108
(216)664-3103 *Fax:* (216)664-3233
🌺 The Greenhouses shelter one acre of indoor exhibit space and offer eight seasonal shows per year. Displays include tropical plants, ferns, palms, cacti and succulents, orchids and more. The outdoor gardens include a Japanese-style garden and collections of azaleas and rhododendrons.
Hours: 10am-4pm
Fees: Free

Schoepfle Garden

11106 Market Street
Birmingham, OH
Mail: 12882 Diagonal Road, Sa Grange, OH 44050
Email: arb@centuryinter.net
(440)965-7237 *Fax:* (440)458-8924
🌺 The Garden provides a 70-acre preserve of natural woodlands, gardens, ponds and river valley donated to Lorain County Metro Parks in 1969. In addition to flowering shrubs, trees and perennials, there are special collections of rhododendrons, roses, cannas, hostas and topiaries.
Hours: 8am-dusk
Fees: Free

Secrest Arboretum

OSU, 1680 Madison Avenue
Wooster, OH 44691
(330)263-3761 *Fax:* (330)202-3504
🌺 Part of Ohio State Agricultural Research & Development, the 85-acre Arboretum is a display facility for trees and shrubs, with special collections of crabapples, rhododendrons and azaleas, and evaluation plots for more than 500 types of trees. There are a variety of flowering trees, old garden roses and educational displays.

Hours: Dawn-dusk
Fees: Free

Stan Hywet Hall & Gardens
714 North Portage Path
Akron, OH 44303
(888)836-5533 or (330)836-5533 *Fax:*
(330)836-2680
🦜 Stan Hywet Hall, one of the finest exam-
aples of Tudor Revival architecture, sits on 70
acres of garden landscaping designed by
Warren Manning. Among the special gardens
is the English Garden, designed by Ellen
Biddle Shipman, the Japanese Garden, the
Rose Garden, the Great Meadow, formal gar-
dens, Birch and London Plane Tree Allées.
Web: www.stanhywet.org
Hours: 9:30am-4:30pm
Fees: Gardens $4

Toledo Botanical Garden
5403 Elmer Drive
Toledo, OH
Mail: PO Box 7430, Toledo, OH 43615
(419)936-2986 *Fax:* (419)936-2987
🦜 Toledo Botanical Garden, formerly Crosby,
is on 70 acres in suburban Toledo. Highlights
include a woodland shade garden with aza-
leas and wildlflowers, an English Perennial
Garden, herb garden and fragrance garden.
Hours: 8am-5pm
Fees: Free

Wegerzyn Horticultural Center
1301 East Siebenthaler Avenue
Dayton, OH 45414
(937)277-9028 *Fax:* (937)277-6546
🦜 Wegerzyn Horticultural Center is part of the
46-acre Stillwater Park. It contains special
gardens, including a Rose Garden, Victorian
Garden and Children's Garden.
Fees: Free

Whetstone Park & Park of Roses
3923 North High Street
Columbus, OH
Mail: Columbus Recreation & Parks
Department, 440 West Whittier Street,
Columbus, OH 43215
(614)645-6640 *Fax:* (614)645-3384
🦜 From March into April in Whetstone Park,
about 1500 varieties of daffodils are on display,
representing one of the largest public plantings
of daffodil cultivars in the United States. The
Columbus Park of Roses is 13 acres with more
than 11,000 rose bushes representing 350 varieties, an Heirloom garden with 58 antique
varieities, some of them centuries old, and a test
garden. Peak bloom is generally in June and is
celebrated with the Park of Roses Festival (see
Ohio Selected Events). There are also rhododendrons, narcissus, wildflowers and herbs.

Selected Events

Akron

February 18-21
🦜 **Akron-Canton Home & Garden Show**
Regional show featuring eleven display gar-
dens, floral displays, seminars, more.
Hours: 11am-9:30pm Thurs-Sat;
11am-6pm Sun
Fee: $6
John S. Knight Center, 77 East Mill Street,
Akron, OH
For information: **St. Anthony's Productions**,
1540 West Market, Suite 302, Akron, OH
44333
(800)865-8859

May 8, 9
🦜 **May Garden Mart**
A sale of plants, flowers, garden ornaments
and more by area garden clubs and vendors,
plus lectures and demonstrations. Experts on

hand to answer questions and provide tips on gardening. Co-sponsored with the Garden Forum of Akron.

Hours: 10am-4pm
Fee: Admission $4
Stan Hywet Hall & Gardens *(See Ohio Guide to Gardens.)*

July
✿ Akron Gardens Tour

A tour of area gardens, now in its twelfth year. Sponsored by The Volunteer Center, a non-profit agency which recruits and refers volunteers to 300 local agencies. Call for exact dates.

Hours: 9am-4pm
For information: **The Volunteer Center**, 425 West Market Street, Akron, OH 44303
Email: volsummit@aol.com
(330)762-8991

October 2, 3
✿ Wonderful World of Ohio Mart

Thousands of mums displayed and for sale, plus crafts backyard herbs, food baskets, entertainment.

Hours: 10am-5pm
Fee: $5
Stan Hywet Hall & Gardens *(See Ohio Guide to Gardens.)*

Alliance

August 13-21
✿ Carnation City Festival

A celebration of the scarlet carnation held in Alliance, the home of Ohio's State Flower. Includes a variety of activities culminating in *Days In The Park* at Silver Park. Over 10,000 carnations in bloom throughout the city.

For information: **Alliance Chamber of Commerce**, 210 East Main Street, Alliance, OH 44601
Email: allcham@alliancelink.com
(330)823-6260

Cincinnati

February 27-March 7
✿ Cincinnati Home & Garden Show

Dozens of landscaped gardens, and what's said to be the Midwest's largest Garden Market for garden-related products. Sponsored by the Junior League of Cincinnati and other organizations.

Fee: $7
Cincinnati Convention Center, Cincinnati, OH
For information: **Cincinnati Home & Garden Show**, 3307 Clifton Avenue, Suite 4, Cincinnati, OH 45220
Web: www.hartproductions.com
(513)281-0022

April 21-April 25
✿ Cincinnati Flower Show

The Road Less Traveled. Features a display garden paying tribute to Sissinghurst Garden, children's gardens, formal sitting gardens, window box competitions, container gardens, urban gardens. floral arrangements, horticultural exhibitions, an amateur flower show by local clubs and a large market. plus information and tips from experts and celebrities. Said to be the nation's largest open-air horticultural exhibition of its kind and recipient of an endorsement from the Royal Horticultural Society of Great Britain. Sponsored by the Cincinnati Horticultural Society.

Hours: 9am-8pm Wed-Sat; 9am-6pm Sun
Fee: Fee charged
Ault Park, Herschel and Observatory Avenues, Cincinnati, OH
For information: **Cincinnati Horticultural Society**, 2625 Reading Road, Cincinnati, OH 45206
Email: CHSevents@aol.com
(513)763-7752 or 1-800-670-6808 for advance ticket purchases

August
☙ 16th Annual Neighborhood Gardens Tour

A bus tour of the best of Cincinnati's community gardens, including vegetable gardens, school gardens, summer youth gardens, seniors' gardens and more. Call for exact date and information.

For information: **Civic Garden Center of Greater Cincinnati**, 2715 Reading Road, Cincinnati, OH 45206
Email: civgard@fuse.net
(513)221-0991

Cleveland

February 6-14
☙ National Home & Garden Show

Bella Italia! Over 30 feature gardens, demonstrations, lawn and garden equipment. Sale of plants from show displays on Sunday, February 14, from 7-9pm.

Hours: 10am-6pm Sat; 10am-8pm Sun, 11am-9:30pm Mon-Thurs; 11am-10pm Fri; 10am-6pm last Sat, Sun
International Exposition Center, 6200 Riverside Drive, Cleveland, OH
For information: **Expositions, Inc**, PO Box 550, Cleveland, OH 44107
Web: www.expoinc.com
(800)600-0307

October 9
☙ Herb Fair

Products grown in the garden of the Western Reserve Herb Society, plus culinary items, potpourri, wreaths, tussy mussies two lectures on herbs. Sponsored by the Western Reserve Herb Society. Call (216)229-2226 for information.
Hours: 9am-3:30pm
Fee: Free
Cleveland Botanical Garden *(See Ohio Guide to Gardens.)*

Columbus
See also Westerville

February 27-March 7
☙ Columbus Dispatch Charities Home & Garden Show

Place in Time. Landscapes by members of the Columbus Landscape Association, plus an HerbFest '99, Garden Stage with national and local experts, and a large sales and services area. Benefits Ohio children's funds.
Hours: 4-9pm; noon-9pm Wed, Sat; noon-6pm Suns
Fee: Fee charged
Ohio State Fairgrounds, Columbus, OH
For information: **Columbus Dispatch Charities**, 34 South Third Street, Columbus, OH 43215
Web: www.dispatch.com
(614)461-5257

May 7, 8
☙ Garden Fair & Plant Sale

Ivy, hosta, holly and daylily boutiques, unusual herbaceous perennials, trees and shrubs, herbs and grasses, native plants, plus gardening materials, gardening books, a garden raffle, food, music and entertainment. An auction each day of rare and specimen plants. Benefits the operations of the OSU Chadwick Arboretum.
Hours: 7am-7pm Fri; 9am-5pm Sat
Fee: Free
Lawn of Dakan Hall, 674 West Lane Avenue, OSU, Columbus, OH
For information: **OSU Chadwick Arboretum**, 2001 Fyffe Court, Columbus, OH 43210
(614)688-3479

June 12, 13
☙ Park of Roses Festival

A celebration of the peak bloom season in the Park of Roses. Includes entertainments, demonstrations and exhibits by horticultural organizations and businesses. A good time also to visit the Topiary Garden in downtown Columbus at 408 East Town Street, a garden based on George Seurat's painting "Un dimanche a la Grande Jatte" and featuring topiary people, boats, dogs and a monkey. Opened in 1992 and growing every year.

Hours: 10am-7pm
Fee: Free
Whetstone Park & Park of Roses (See Ohio Guide to Gardens.)

Dayton

February 4
❧ Annual Native Plant Symposium
At Home with Native Plants: Creating Natural Habitats. An all-day event with lunch. Large reference manual supplied.
Fee: $39
Wegerzyn Horticultural Center (See Ohio Guide to Gardens.)

March 6
❧ Miami Valley Gardening Conference
A Day of Learning, A Year of Growing. A conference with Elsa Bakalar as the keynote speaker and eleven additional local experts.
Fee: $39
Wegerzyn Horticultural Center (See Ohio Guide to Gardens.)

May 1, 2
❧ Annual Mayfair Plant Sale
A major fund-raiser for the Garden, with displays, vendors, plant sales and more.
Hours: 1:30-5pm
Fee: Free
Wegerzyn Horticultural Center (See Ohio Guide to Gardens.)

May 8, 9
❧ Spring Flower Sale
A Mother's Day weekend sale timed for spring planting.
Hours: 10am-4pm
Cox Arboretum (See Ohio Guide to Gardens.)

May 15-October 30, Saturdays
❧ Farmer's Market
An open-air market held in the parking lot every Saturday.
Hours: 7am-noon
Fee: Free
Wegerzyn Horticultural Center (See Ohio Guide to Gardens.)

September 1-6
❧ Flower Show at Montgomery County Fair
A regional show, part of the annual county fair. Call to confirm dates.
Hours: 10am-10pm
Fee: $4
Montgomery County Fairgrounds, 1043 South Main Street, Dayton, OH 45409 (937)224-1619

September 18, 19
❧ Annual Rose Show
A statewide show of the Buckeye District of the American Rose Society.
Hours: 1:30-5pm
Fee: Free
Wegerzyn Horticultural Center (See Ohio Guide to Gardens.)

Delta
25 miles West of Toledo

May 15
❧ 6th Annual Green Thumb Fair
Held on Main Street, a sale of plants from the greenhouse and a crafts fair.
Hours: 9am-5pm
Fee: Free

For information: **Delta Chamber of Commerce**, 201 Wood Street, Delta, OH 43515
(419)822-4676

Kirtland

May 1, 2
🌺 Annual Tree & Plant Sale
Hundred of trees and plants for spring planting, plus expert advice and refreshments. Benefits the Arboretum.
The Holden Arboretum (See Ohio Guide to Gardens.)

Westerville
Near Columbus

May 1, 2
🌺 Perennial Plant Sale
Annual sale conducted by the Inniswood Volunteers
Hours: 9am-5pm Sat; noon-4pm Sun
Fee: Free
Inniswood Metro Gardens (See Ohio Guide to Gardens.)

September 24-26
🌺 Horticulture Fair
A flower show, speakers, food, entertainment, children's activities, vendors and more. Sponsored by the Inniswood Garden Society and the Volunteers.
Hours: 5pm-dark Fri; 9am-dark Sat; noon-5pm Sun
Fee: Free
Inniswood Metro Gardens (See Ohio Guide to Gardens.)

Youngstown

February 25-28
🌺 Youngstown Home & Garden Show
Eight landscaped gardens and floral displays.
Hours: 11am-9pm Thurs-Sat; 11am-6pm Sun

Fee: $5
Eastwood Expo Center, Niles, OH
For information: **St. Anthony's Productions**, 1540 West Market, Suite 302, Akron, OH 44333
(800)865-8859

May 8, 9
🌺 Mother's Day Weekend Springfest
Week-end long family entertainment, plant sales, garden photography exhibit, and six acres of floral displays in the Gardens. Free shuttles from remote parking area.
Hours: 10am-5pm Sat; noon-5pm Sun
Fee: Free
Fellows Riverside Gardens (See Ohio Guide to Gardens.)

Oklahoma

Guide to Gardens

Cann Botanical Gardens
14th & Grand
Ponca City, OK
Mail: Parks & Recreation Department, 905 West Hartford Avenue, Ponca City, OK 74601
(580)767-0430 *Fax:* (580)767-0471
🌺 The site is comprised of a formal garden with open areas and 1/2 mile of walkways. It includes many varieties of trees, over 250 varieties of perennials and annuals, a well-shaded patio with water display and several vine-covered arbors.
Hours: Always open
Fees: Free

Honor Heights Park
Muskogee, OK
Mail: Muskogee Parks & Recreation Department, 641 Park Drive, Muskogee, OK 74403

Email: parkrec@ok.azalea.net
(918)684-6302 *Fax:* (918)684-6211
🌿 The122-acre Honor Heights Park has 40 acres of hillside gardens, a rose garden, a lily pond and over 30,000 azaleas representing more than 650 varieties. The three arboreta at the park contain a variety of landscape trees, a native tree collection and a dogwood collection.
Hours: 8am-dusk
Fees: Free

Lendonwood Gardens
1308 West 13th Street
Grove, OK 74345
(918)786-2938
🌿 The oak-shaded Gardens are divided into five sections: Display, Oriental, English Terrace, Japanese, and American Backyard. Mid June to early July is peak bloom for more than 500 daylilies in the Gardens.
Web: www.greencis.net/^shack/lendonwood/
Hours: 8am-8:30pm
Fees: $5

Myriad Botanical Gardens
100 Myriad Gardens
Oklahoma City, OK 73102
(405)297-3995 *Fax:* (405)297-3175
🌿 At the heart of Myriad Botanical Gardens, located in downtown Oklahoma City, is the Crystal Bridge Tropical Conservatory, a translucent cylinder of acrylic and steel, housing tropical displays, streams and a towering waterfall.
Web: www.okc-cityhall.org/botanicalgardens/
Hours: 9am-6pm
Fees: $4; $3 seniors & students; $2 children

Will Rogers Garden & Exhibition Building
3400 NW 36th Street
Oklahoma City, OK 73112
(405)943-0827

🌿 The Garden consists of a 30-acre garden and arboreta. Highlights include a rose garden, a large perennial garden with a peony collection, and many cannas and irises. There's an azalea trail with redbuds, native trees, holly, crape myrtle and hibiscus. The Exhibition Building houses special shows and sales sponsored by various plant societies.
Hours: Garden 7am-sunset; Building 8am-5pm
Fees: Free

Selected Events

Muskogee

April 3-18
🌿 **Azalea Festival**
Entertainment and activities for all, including a parade on April 3rd. Timed to peak bloom of the azaleas.
Hours: Daylight hours
Fee: Donation requested
Honor Heights Park (*See Oklahoma Guide to Gardens.*)

November 25-January 1
🌿 **Garden of Lights**
A drive-through display of illuminated gardens and trees, plus animated light displays throughout the Park.
Hours: 5:30-10pm
Fee: Donation requested
Honor Heights Park (*See Oklahoma Guide to Gardens.*)

Oklahoma City

May 2
🌿 **Oklahoma Iris Society Exhibition**
The kickoff show for the Iris Society Convention, May 4-8.
Hours: 1-5pm

Will Rogers Garden & Exhibition Building
(See Oklahoma Guide to Gardens.)

June 6-12
⚘ National Garden Week & Summer Festival in the Park
A week-long celebration of National Garden Week, including opening of local gardens, a major Bonsai exhibition, an herb show, a mini rose show, and a large Festival in the Park on the final day.
Fee: Free
For information: **Will Rogers Garden & Exhibition Building** *(See Oklahoma Guide to Gardens.)*

Ponca City

June 5
⚘ Ponca City Herb Festival
An annual event featuring fresh herbs, demonstrations, samples and seminars, herbal crafts and products, food, music, and more.
Hours: 9am-4pm
Fee: Free
Cann Memorial Botanical Gardens, 14th & Grand, Ponca City, OK
For information: **Sage Rosemary & Thyme Garden Club**, 3644 Ashbury, Ponca City, OK 74604
Web: www.onlineshops.com/herbfest/
(580)767-1076

Stillwater
55 miles from Oklahoma City

April 24
⚘ Spring Garden Show
Features tours of the studio set "Oklahoma Gardening," the weekly gardening telecast on OETA, programs on turf management, bedding plants, grasses, gardening for wildlife, lawn care, and more, plus plant sales and seminars.

Hours: noon-4:30pm Sat
Fee: Free
OBGA Headquarters Garden, Virginia Avenue & Sangre Road, Stillwater, OK
Mail: Oklahoma State University, 360 Agriculture Hall, Stillwater, OK 74078
(405)744-5414 *Fax:* (405)744-9709

Tulsa

March 20, 21
⚘ Glasshouse Gardeners Show & Sale
Plants for the greenhouse and indoor gardener.
Tulsa Garden Center, 2435 Peoria Avenue, Tulsa, OK 74114
(918)746-5125

April 17, 18
⚘ 49th Annual Tulsa Garden Club Spring Tour
A tour of local gardens sponsored by the Tulsa Garden Club.
Hours: 10am-5pm Sat; noon-5pm Sun
Fee: Fee charged
For information: **Tulsa Garden Center**, 2435 Peoria Avenue, Tulsa, OK 74114
(918)746-5125

May 16, 17
⚘ Tulsa Garden Club Spring Show
A judged show of designed horticultural and special exhibits.
Hours: 1-5pm Sun; 11-5 Mon
Fee: Free
Tulsa Garden Center, 2435 Peoria Avenue, Tulsa, OK 74114
(918)746-5125

October
⚘ Annual Fall Garden Tour
A tour of local gardens sponsored by the Tulsa Garden Center. Call for exact date and ticket information.

For information: **Tulsa Garden Center**, 2435 Peoria Avenue, Tulsa, OK 74114
(918)746-5125

Oregon

Berry Botanic Garden

11505 SW Summerville Avenue
Portland, OR 97219
(503)636-4112 *Fax:* (503)636-7496
🌿 This Garden, started as a home garden, is a six-acre species garden, with a special collection of rare plants from the Pacific rim, obtained by the founder who sponsored major plant expeditions. Its collections include lilies, rhododendrons, primulas and alpines. The Garden can be seen by appointment only.
Web: www.berrybot.org
Hours: By appointment only
Fees: $5

Cecil & Molly Smith Garden

5065 Ray Bell Blvd
St. Paul , OR 97137
(503)625-6331 *Fax:* (503)625-6331
🌿 This Garden is the creation of a man who loved rhododendrons, sponsored collecting expeditions in the Himalayas, and participated in early seed exchanges and hybridizing. The wooded setting of native firs creates an ideal environment for a natural garden featuring superior forms of species and hybrid rhododendrons, complemented by wildflowers, bulbs, other trees and shrubs. The Garden can be seen by appointment only.
Web: www.rhododendron.org/portland/
Hours: 10am-3:30pm by appointment only
Fees: $3 for non American Rhododendron Society members

Connie Hansen Garden

1931 NW 33rd Street
Lincoln City, OR
Mail: PO Box 776, Lincoln City, OR 97367
(541)994-6338
🌿 The Garden was created over a twenty-year period by Constance P. Hansen, a well-known iris hybridizer and enthusiast. The 1-acre plus garden has meadow and woodlands, with a creek and two ponds and species that thrive in cool, wet coastal climates, such as rhododendrons and azaleas, irises, primroses, various perennials, maples, viburnums, magnolia and styrax japonica.
Hours: 9am-5pm
Fees: Free

Crystal Springs Rhododendron Garden

SE 28th Avenue, one block north of Woodstock
Portland, OR
Mail: PO Box 86424, Portland, OR 97286
(503)823-8358 *Fax:* (503)777-2048
🌿 This unique 7-acre Garden contains an outstanding collection of rare species and hybrid rhododendrons, azaleas and other lesser know ericaceous plants, as well as companion plants and unusual trees.
Hours: Mar 1-Labor Day dawn-dusk Thurs-Mon
Fees: $2

Greer Gardens

1280 Goodpasture Island Road
Eugene, OR 97401
Email: greergard@aol. com
(541)686-8266 *Fax:* (541)686-0910
🌿 Renowned for its collection of rare and unusual plants, Greer Gardens offers 4 acres of display gardens in a natural woodland setting of over 14 acres. Paths lead through the grounds, with Japanese maples, magnolias, conifers and extensive rhododendron collections, many of which were developed here.

Hours: 8:30am-5:30pm; 11am-5pm Sun
Fees: Free

Hoyt Arboretum
4000 SW Fairview Blvd
Portland, OR 97221
(503)823-3655
The Hoyt Arboretum, owned by the City of Portland, straddles a ridgetop in the Tuality Mountains west of Portland. The original Douglas Firs, Western Hemlocks, Red Cedars and Big Leaf Maples have been selectively clreared in order to plant 4,300 trees and shrubs representing over 800 species, varieties and cultivars.
Hours: 6am-10pm
Fees: Free

International Rose Test Garden
Washington Park, 400 SW Kingston Street
Portland, OR 97201
(503)823-3636 *Fax:* (503)823-1667
The oldest public garden of its kind in the United State, the Garden contains 8,000 roses representing 550 varieties on its 4-acre site. near the Japanese Garden and Hoyt Arboretum in Washington Park. There are two other rose gardens in the Portland Parks District: the sunken Rose Garden at Peninsula Park, North Ainsworth and Albiona, and Ladd's Addition Rose Garden at SE 16th & Harrison.
Web: www.parks.ci.portland.or.us
Hours: 7am-10pm
Fees: Donation requested

Japanese Garden
611 SW Kingston Avenue
Portland, OR
Mail: Japanese Garden Society of Oregon, PO Box 3847, Portland, OR 97208
Email: jgso@transport.com
(503)223-1321 *Fax:* (503)223-8303
The Garden is one of the finest Japanese gardens in this country, and features five traditional gardens, a pavilion and a good view of Mt. Hood. Many of the plants are imported from Japan.
Hours: Sep 10am-6pm; Oct-Mar to 4pm; Apr-May 10am-6pm; Jun-Aug 10am-8pm
Fees: $6; $4 seniors, $3.50 students

Leach Botanical Garden
6704 SE 122nd Avenue
Portland, OR 97236
(503)761-9503 *Fax:* (503)762-4659
The 9-acre Garden was planted by John and Lila Leach. The collection includes over 2,000 species, hybrids and cultivars on a site that's been described as "an oasis in an urban setting," with towering firs, lush shrubbery and wildflowers. The collections may be enjoyed on a self-guided tour that winds through the grounds.
Web: www.parks.ci.portland.or.us
Hours: 9am-4pm Tues-Sat; 1-4pm Sun; closed Mon
Fees: Free

Mount Pisgah Arboretum
33735 Seavey Loop Road
Eugene, OR 97405
Email: mtpsgah@efn.org
(541)747-3817
The Arboretum is comprised of 118 acres with large collections of native trees and herbs.
Hours: Sunrise-sunset
Fees: Free

Selected Events

Albany

January 30, 31
Annual Orchid Show & Sale
A display and sale with visiting societies and vendors.
Hours: 10am-6pm Sat; 11am-6pm Sun

Heritage Mall, 14th Avenue SE, Albany, OR
For information: **Mary's Peak Orchid Society**, 39127 Griggs Drive, Lebanon, OR 97355
Fax: (541)451-2613

Brookings

May 28-31
🌸 60th Annual Azalea Festival
Many events, including a Bonsai demonstration, flower show and sale, art shows, parade and lots of entertainment. Held at parks throughout the community, including Azalea Park, home of spectacular 300-year old native azalea plants with some over fifteen feet high. Wild rhododendrons also in bloom at this time.
For information: **Brookings Harbor Chamber of Commerce**, 16330 Lower Harbor Road, PO Box 940, Brookings, OR 97415
(541)469-3181

Eugene

May 8, 9
🌸 Mother's Day Weekend
A celebration when rhododendrons are at their peak.
Greer Gardens *(See Oregon Guide to Gardens.)*

May 16
🌸 Wildflower Festival & Plant Sale
Hundreds of wildflowers on display, walking tours of the Arboretum, a plant sale, fresh-baked goods, children's activities and a chance to bring your own wildflowers and have them identified by members of the Native Plant Society of Oregon.
Hours: 10am-4pm
Fee: $2 suggested donation
Mount Pisgah Arboretum *(See Oregon Guide to Gardens.)*

Early June
🌸 Rhododendron Sale
A sale considered one of the best by rhododendron fanciers. Call for exact date.
Greer Gardens *(See Oregon Guide to Gardens.)*

October 24
🌸 Mushroom Show & Plant Sale
A display and sale of hundreds of mushrooms and dried plants, plus a live plant sale, guided walks through the Arboretum, family activities and the chance to find out what's edible and what's not.
Hours: 10am-4pm
Fee: $2 suggested donation
Mount Pisgah Arboretum *(See Oregon Guide to Gardens.)*

Florence

May 14-16
🌸 92nd Annual Rhododendron Festival
A three-day annual event with a rhododendron show and displays of common and hybrid blooms by local growers, plus many events for everyone sponsored by the "City of Rhododendrons." Call for the "Rhody" brochure, or write the Chamber of Commerce.
Hours: 9am-10am
For information: **Florence Area Chamber of Commerce**, PO Box 26000, Florence, OR 97439
(800)524-4864 or (541)997-3128

Hillsboro

April 10, 11
🌸 Plant Sale
A sale of perennials, natives, herbs, ornamental grasses, small trees and shrubs and bulbs by over 75 specialty nurseries. Sponsored by the Hardy Plant Society of Oregon and benefiting community gardens and educational projects.

Hours: 10am-3pm
Fee: Free
Washington County Fairplex, NW Cornell Road between 28th & 37th, Hillsboro, OR
For information: **Hardy Plant Society of Oregon**, 1930 NW Lovejoy, Portland, OR 97209
Email: admin@hardyplant.com
(503)293-8225

September 11, 12
⚘ Plant Sale

The Fall version of the above event.
Hours: 10am-3pm
Washington County Fairplex, NW Cornell Road between 28th & 37th, Hillsboro, OR
For information: **Hardy Plant Society of Oregon**, 1930 NW Lovejoy, Portland, OR 97209
Email: admin@hardyplant.com
(503)293-8225

Hood River
60 miles from Portland

April 17, 18
⚘ Hood River Valley Blossom Festival

Orchard tours during blossom time, plus Columbia Gorge Blossom Bazaar, Country Faire Plant and Craft Fair, Pear Sampling and Sale, and the Fruit Blossom Special - Mt. Hood Railroad for a scenic excursion. For a complete schedule and map of the area and events, contact the Chamber.
For information: **Hood River Chamber of Commerce**, 405 Portway Avenue, Hood River, OR 97031
Web: www.gorge.net/hrccc/
(541)386-2000

October 15-17
⚘ Hood River Valley Harvest Festival

A festival featuring local produce and nursery stock, crafts and local entertainment. Now in its 17th year.

Hours: 1-9pm Fri; 10am-8pm Sat; 10am-5pm Sun
Fee: $2
For information: **Hood River Chamber of Commerce**, 405 Portway Avenue, Hood River, OR 97031
Web: www.gorge.net/hrccc/
(541)386-2000

Portland

February 24-28
⚘ Portland Home & Garden Show

Garden displays, seminars and talks, local garden and plant society exhibits and more.
Hours: noon-9pm Wed-Fri; 10am-9pm Sat; 10am-6pm Sun
Fee: $7
Portland Expo Center, Portland, OR
Email: obpr@aol.com
Web: www.oloughlintradeshows.com
For information: **Portland Home & Garden Show**, PO Box 25348, Portland, OR 97298
(503)246-8291 *Fax:* (503)246-1066

February 26-28
⚘ Yard, Garden & Patio Show

Four display gardens, a birdhouse exhibit, free seminars and lectures, local garden and plant society displays, plus over 200 exhibitors offering plant material, gardening supplies and equipment. Sponsored by the Oregon Association of Nurserymen.
Hours: 10am-9pm Fri, Sat; 10am-6pm Sun
Fee: $7; children under 12 free
Oregon Convention Center, 777 NE Martin Luther King, Jr. Blvd, Portland, OR
For information: **Oregon Association of Nurserymen**, 2780 SE Harrison, Suite 102, Milwaukie, OR 97222
Web: www.nurseryguide.com
(800)342-6401 or (503)653-8733

April 3
⚘ Early Flower Show
Rhododendron truss show and plant sale. Sponsored by the Rhododendron Society.
Hours: 8am-5pm
Fee: Admission $2
Crystal Springs Rhododendron Garden *(See Oregon Guide to Gardens.)*

April 4-10
⚘ Oregon Arbor Week
A week of activities, including tree plantings, guided hikes, exploring tours, walking the Tree Trail.
Fee: Free
Hoyt Arboretum *(See Oregon Guide to Gardens.)*

April 10, 11
⚘ Ikebana Show-Hana Matsuri
A celebration of flowers in honor of Buddha's birthday.
Hours: 10am-6pm
Fee: Free
Japanese Garden *(See Oregon Guide to Gardens.)*

April 20
⚘ Oregon Fuchsia Society Plant Auction & Sale
A plant auction and sale sponsored by the Oregon Fuchsia Society.
Hours: 7:30pm
United Methodist Church, SE 61st & Stark, Portland, OR
For information: **Oregon Fuchsia Society**, 16851 South Bradley Road, Oregon City, OR 97045
(503)235-5844

April 24
⚘ Spring Plant Sale
A large selection of Northwest natives, unusual, and drought-tolerant perennials, ferns, alpines, small shrubs, trees, bonsai, along with plants propagated from the Leach collection. Held at the Floyd Light Middle School; call Leach for directions.
Hours: 9am-3pm
Fee: Free
Leach Botanical Garden *(See Oregon Guide to Gardens.)*

April 24-May 2
⚘ Spring Open House
Free garden tours during this time. Call for reservations.
Hours: 10am, 2pm
Fee: Free
Berry Botanic Garden *(See Oregon Guide to Gardens.)*

May 8, 9
⚘ Mother's Day Show & Plant Sale
A large cut flower show and plant sale featuring a huge selection of rhododendrons at good prices, plus other rare and unusual plants. Now in its 41st year. Sponsored by the Portland Chapter of the Rhododendron Society.
Hours: 8am-5pm
Fee: Admission $2
Crystal Springs Rhododendron Garden *(See Oregon Guide to Gardens.)*

May 8, 9
⚘ Bonsai Exhibition
Forty examples of the best in miniature tree pruning, Japanese style.
Hours: 10am-6pm
Fee: Free
Japanese Garden *(See Oregon Guide to Gardens.)*

June 3-27
🌺 Portland Rose Festival
More than 80 events in 25 days, including three different rose shows and the Rose Festival's signature event, the Grand Floral Parade on June 9.
For information: **Portland Rose Festival Association**, 220 NW Second Avenue, Portland, OR 97209
Web: www.rosefestival.org
(503)227-2681

June 12, 13
🌺 Ikebana Rose Show
A display of Japanese flower arranging using roses in honor of the Rose Festival.
Hours: 10am-6pm
Fee: Free
Japanese Garden *(See Oregon Guide to Gardens.)*

June 30-July 4
🌺 International Bonsai Convention
Demonstrations by masters, hands-on workshops, lectures, exhibits, a bazaar and tours of local gardens for convention registrants. Hosted by the Bonsai Clubs International and the Bonsai Society of Portland.
Doubletree Hotel, Lloyd Center, Portland, OR
For information: **Bonsai Clubs International**, PO Box 1176, Brookfield WI 53008
Web: www.bonsai-bci.com
Email: myrthine@worldnet.ett.net

July 7
🌺 Tanabatta Star Festival
The annual Japanese Festival honoring two stars that come together only on the 7th day of the 7th month.
Hours: 7:30pm
Fee: Free
Japanese Garden *(See Oregon Guide to Gardens.)*

July 16-19
🌺 Summer Open House
Free garden tours during this time. Call for reservations.
Hours: 10am, 2pm
Fee: Free
Berry Botanic Garden *(See Oregon Guide to Gardens.)*

August
🌺 Oregon Fuchsia Society Show & Sale
A judged show and sale of locally-grown plants. Call for exact date.
Portland Nursery, 5050 SE Stark Street, Portland, OR
For information: **Oregon Fuchsia Society**, 16851 South Bradley Road, Oregon City, OR 97045
(503)235-5844

September 25
🌺 Fall Plant Sale
A sale of established perennials for next year, plus a selection similar to that at Spring Sale and plants propagated from the Leach collection. Held at the Floyd Light Middle School; call Leach for directions.
Hours: 9am-3pm
Leach Botanical Garden *(See Oregon Guide to Gardens.)*

October 22-24
🌺 Fall Open House
Free garden tours during this time. Call for reservations.
Hours: Tours 10am, 2pm
For information: **Berry Botanic Garden** *(See Oregon Guide to Gardens.)*

Pennsylvania

Guide to Gardens

Arboretum at Haverford College
Haverford, PA 19041
(610)896-1101
The 216-acre Arboretum, located on the campus, was inspired by 19th century English parks. It features nature trails, a duck pond, a Pinetum, three Pennsylvania State Champion Trees, a Japanese Zen Garden and Herb Garden. Over 1000 trees and shrubs are labeled.

Bowman's Hill Wildflower Preserve
River Road, Route 32
New Hope, PA
Mail: PO Box 685, New Hope, PA 18938
Email: bhwp@bhwp.org
(215)862-2924 Fax: (215)862-1846
Bowman's Hill Wildflower Preserve is comprised of 100 acres devoted to preserving the native flora of Pennsylvania. Walk the two dozen trails through woodlands, meadows and along Pidcock Creek where seasonal changes, birds and wildlife can be viewed.
Web: www.bhwp.org
Hours: 10am-5pm
Fees: Free

Chanticleer
786 Church Road
Wayne, PA 19087
(610)687-4163
Thirty acres of gardens, lawns, meadows and wooded areas. Highlights include the Summer Perennial Garden, Formal Garden, Hemlock Hedge, Woodland Garden and wonderful views.
Hours: Apr-Oct 10am-3:30pm Wed-Sat
Fees: $5; $3 children

Demuth Foundation
120 East King Street
Lancaster, PA 17602
(717)299-9940 Fax: (717)299-9749
This city garden of the 18th century brick home where the artist Charles Demuth lived (1881-1925) was the subject of many of his watercolors. A highlight of the garden is the white rosa rugosa "Souvenir de Philmon Chachon." It is believed that Demuth brought the plant from Paris as a gift to his mother.
Web: www.demuth.org
Hours: Dawn-dusk
Fees: Free

The Gardens Collaborative
9414 Meadowbrook Avenue
Philadelphia, PA 19118
(215)247-5777
The Gardens Collaborative is a consortium of some 50 gardens and historic houses in the Delaware Valley. The Collaborative offers a Guidebook and Map to all the sites. The Philadelphia area encompasses all the major gardens in the area, from the Morris Arboretum and Historic Bartram's Garden to the Haverford College campus, Swarthmore's Scott Arboretum, Tyler Arboretum, Chanticleer and many more. Send a check for $8.95 to The Gardens Collaborative and receive their Guidebook.

The Gardens of Temple University
580 Meeting House Lane
Ambler, PA
Mail: Horticulture/Landscape Department, Temple University, Ambler, PA 19002
(215)643-1200 Ext 3
The Gardens at the Ambler Campus of Temple University include the formal perennial garden, originally designed by James Bush-Brown and Beatrix Farrand, which now has a more modern plant palette. There is also a

woodland garden, ground cover garden, herb garden, sustainable wetland garden, propagation center, Class of 1990 Courtyard and Louise Stine Fisher Garden, showcasing dwarf evergreens and Japanese maples.
Hours: Dawn-dusk
Fees: Free

Henry Foundation for Botanical Research

801 Stony Lane
Gladwyne, PA
Mail: PO Box 7, Gladwyne, PA 19035
(610)525-2037 *Fax:* (610)525-4024
Dedicated to the preservation of American plants, these 50 acres are maintained in their natural form with many rare and endangered species, as well as varieties of rhododendron, magnolia, holly and others.
Hours: 10am-4pm Mon-Fri; by appointment Sat, Sun
Fees: Free

Henry Schmieder Arboretum

Delaware Valley College, Route 202 & New Britain Road
Doylestown, PA
Mail: 700 East Butler, Doylestown, PA 18901
(215)345-1500 *Fax:* (215)345-5277
This is a large preserve with a number of special gardens. Highlights are a woodland garden, hedge demonstration garden, herb garden, the Kerr orchid collection in greenhouses, and mature specimen trees.
Web: aabga.mobot.org/AABGA/Member.pages/Schmeider/schmeider.html
Hours: Dawn-dusk
Fees: Free

Hershey Gardens

Hotel Road
Hershey, PA
Mail: PO Box 416, Hershey, PA 17033
(717)534-3492 *Fax:* (717)534-8940
Hershey Gardens started as a 3.5-acre rose garden in 1937 and has now expanded into a 23-acre botanical display. In addition to the award-winning rose garden, it includes collections of conifers, hollies, rhododendrons, Japanese maples and dramatic specimen trees such as giant sequoias, blue atlas cedar and European beech.
Hours: Mid Apr-Oct 9am-6pm
Fees: $5; $4.50 seniors; $2.50 youths

Historic Bartram's Garden

54th Street & Lindbergh Blvd
Philadelphia, PA 19143
Email: bartram@libertynet.org
(215)729-5281 *Fax:* (215)729-1047
The oldest living botanical garden in the U.S., the Garden is situated in Fairmont Park in the middle of Philadelphia. It features a wildflower meadow, river trail, wetlands, stone house and farm buildings, all overlooking the Schuykill River. This was the garden of John Bartram, America's first botanist and the country's best known plant collector and explorer, and has been restored and replanted with material known to its original owner.
Web: www.libertynet.org/~bartram/
Hours: 10am-4pm
Fees: Free

Jenkins Arboretum

631 Berwyn Baptist Road
Devon, PA 19333
(610)647-8870
The Arboretum consists of a 46-acre preserve with collections of azaleas, rhododendrons, daylilies and wildflowers. The site also includes demonstration gardens and test gardens for daylilies and woody ornamentals.
Hours: Dawn-dusk
Fees: Free

Longwood Gardens
US Route 1
Kennett Square, PA 19348
(610)388-1000 *Fax:* (610)388-2294
Longwood Gardens is one of the premier gardens in North America, evoking the great pleasure gardens of Europe. Eleven thousand different types of plants flourish throughout the 1,050 acres of formal gardens, fountains, idea gardens, meadows and woodlands, with nearly four acres inside the Conservatory. Among the many highlights are a topiary garden, a maze, rose garden, heather garden, wildflower garden, lily pond and more.
Web: www.longwoodgardens.org
Hours: 9am-6pm; Nov-Mar 9am-5pm
Fees: $12 ($8 Tues); $6 youths; $2 children 6-15

Morris Arboretum
University of Pennsylvania, 100 Northwestern Avenue
Philadelphia, PA 19118
(215)247-5777 *Fax:* (215)248-4439
Morris Arboretum has 92 public acres with thousands of rare and lovely woody plants, including many of Philadelphia's oldest, rarest and largest trees. This Victorian landscape garden of winding paths, streams and special garden areas is the official arboretum of the state and is listed on the National Register of Historic Places.
Web: www.upenn.edu/morris/
Hours: 10am-4pm; Apr-Oct weekends 10am-5pm
Fees: $5; $4 seniors; $3 students

Phipps Conservatory & Botanical Gardens
Schenley Park
Pittsburgh, PA 15213
(412)622-6914 *Fax:* (412)622-7363
Phipps is one of the older conservatories in the country, a thirteen-room Victorian glasshouse with an Oriental garden, cacti and succulents, a formal garden, palm court, orchids, ferns, seasonal displays and butterflies. The outdoor gardens include perennials, annuals, herbs and medicinal plants, aquatics, the Japanese Courtyard with a premier collection of bonsai, and the Discovery Garden.
Web: phipps.conservatory.org
Hours: 9am-5pm; closed Mon
Fees: $5; $3.50 seniors, students; $2 children

The Pittsburgh Civic Garden Center
1059 Shady Avenue
Pittsburgh, PA 15232
Email: garden@trfn.clpgh.org
(412)441-4442 *Fax:* (412)665-2368
The Pittsburgh Civic Garden Center is located in Mellon Park in Shadyside, and maintains over fifteen teaching gardens on the grounds. These include the Daffodil and Daylily Walk, Ornamental Grass Garden, Butterfly Garden, Herb, Ground Cover, and Rock Gardens.
Web: trfn.clpgh.org/garden/
Hours: Daylight hours
Fees: Free

Rodale Institute Experimental Farm
611 Siegfriedale Road
Kutztown, PA 19530
(610)683-1400 *Fax:* (610)683-8548
Set on a 1732 farm, Rodale features a demonstration garden showcasing organic principles in growing vegetables, flowers and herbs. There are also mini-gardens, including the native plants and grasses garden, the salad garden, the Children's Garden and the Community Projects Garden.
Web: www.envirolink.org/seel/rodale/
Hours: 9am-5pm; noon-5pm Sunday
Fees: Free; guided tours $6; $3 children

Rodef Shalom Biblical Botanical Garden

4905 Fifth Avenue
Pittsburgh, PA 15213
(412)621-6566

This is the largest Biblical Botanical Garden of its kind in North America. It features more than 100 temperate and tropical plants in a setting of the land of the Bible, with a waterfall, a desert, a bubbling stream, and a replication of the Jordan River meandering through the garden from Lake Kineret to the Dead Sea.
Web: trfn.pgh.pa.us/rodef/garden/
Hours: Jun 1-Sep 15
Fees: Free

Scott Arboretum

Swarthmore College, 500 College Avenue
Swarthmore, PA 19081
(610)328-8025

The Scott Arboretum at Swarthmore encompasses a beautiful woodland, with an excellent rhododendron collection, and collections of daffodils, azaleas, hollies, flowering cherries, crabapples, tree peonies, lilacs, magnolias and conifers. Special gardens include a rock garden, a woodland garden and rose garden.
Hours: Dawn-dusk
Fees: Free

Tyler Arboretum

515 Painter Road off Route 352
Media, PA 19063
Email: tylerarb.aol.com
(610)566-9134 *Fax:* (610)891-1490

The Arboretum is a 700-acre preserve containing collections of rhododendrons, azaleas, dogwoods, dwarf conifers, crabapples, cherries, magnolias and more. About twenty miles of trails wind through the grounds.
Hours: 8am-dusk
Fees: $3; $1 children

Selected Events

Allentown

See also Kutztown

February 19-21
Lehigh Valley Flower & Garden Show
A large regional show featuring twelve landscape exhibits by area designers, demonstrations by florists, a retail sales area, food and more. Also a sale of remaining plants after Sunday closing at 5pm.
Hours: 10am-9pm Fri, Sat; 10am-5pm Sun
Fee: $7
Agriculture Hall, Allentown Fair Grounds,
17th & Chew Streets, Allentown, PA
For information: **The Waterworks**, 111 East Fairmont Street, Coopersburg, PA 18036
(610)433-7541 *Fax:* (610)433-4005

Brookville

June 16-20
Western Pennsylvania Laurel Festival
Carnival games for all, concerts, crafts, a fiddler contest, and Queen's Pageant and Parade at the height of the laurel bloom.
For information: **Laurel Festival**, PO Box 142, Brookville, PA 15825
(814)849-8448

Chadds Ford

14 miles from Wilmington, Delaware

May 8, 9
Wildflower, Native Plant & Seed Sale
Hundreds of native plants, shrubs and wildflowers, many propagated by Conservancy volunteers, as well as hand-collected and sorted wildflower seeds. Plus tours of the wildflower gardens and expert advice on landscaping with native plants and wildflowers. Sponsored by the Brandywine Conservancy.
Hours: 9:30am-4:30pm
Fee: Free

Brandywine River Museum, Brandywine Conservancy, Routes 1 & 100, PO Box 141, Chadds Ford, PA 19317
Web: www.brandywinemuseum.org
(610)388-2700

Early June
🌸 14th Annual Bonsai Show
An exhibit and demonstration of pruning techniques by members of the Brandywine Bonsai Society. Call for exact date.
Hours: 9:30am-4:30pm
Fee: $5; $2.50 seniors, students
Brandywine River Museum, Brandywine Conservancy, Routes 1 & 100, PO Box 141, Chadds Ford, PA 19317
Web: www.brandywinemuseum.org
(610)388-2700

Doylestown
Near Philadelphia

March 13, 14
🌸 Bucks Beautiful Garden Fair
Eighty exhibitors, including small gardens and several museums, plant and related materials for sale, informal workshops and seminars on a wide range of topics, such as low maintenance perennials, water gardening, gardening in the shade, home composting and more. Co-sponsored by the Central Bucks Chamber of Commerce and Delaware Valley College. Call the Chamber at (215)348-3913 for information.
Hours: 10am-5pm
Fee: Free (nominal parking fee)
Henry Schmieder Arboretum *(See Pennsylvania Guide to Gardens.)*

April 24, 25
🌸 Annual "A" Day Country Fair
A weekend event which includes a major flower show, garden tours, nature exhibits and activities for the whole family. Call for schedule of events.

Hours: 9am-5pm
Fee: Free (nominal parking fee)
Henry Schmieder Arboretum, Delaware Valley College, 700 East Butler Avene, Doylestown, PA 18901
Web: aabga.mobot.org/AABGA/ Member.pages/Schmeider/schmeider.html
(215)345-1500

Gladwyne
Near Philadelphia

May
🌸 Rare Plant Sale
Call for exact date and directions.
Henry Foundation for Botanical Research
(See Pennsylvania Guide to Gardens.)

Greensburg
Near Pittsburgh

May 15
🌸 May Mart
A garden fair on the grounds of the Greensburg Garden & Civic Center, with educational presentations, a plant sale, garden items for sale, homemade lunch, a bake sale and lots of family fun. Features the Horticultural Committee's Perennial Sale of top nursery stock and participation by twenty-six garden organizations.
Hours: 9am-1pm
Fee: Free
Greensburg Garden & Civic Center, 951 Old Salem Road, Greensburg, PA 15601
(724)836-1123

July 10
🌸 Garden Tour
A tour of five to ten private gardens in the greater Greensburg area.
For information: **Greensburg Garden & Civic Center**, 951 Old Salem Road, Greensburg, PA 15601
(724)836-1123

Hershey

12 miles from Harrisburg

September 19
❧ Annual Hershey Community Gardenfest

A free community day at Hershey Gardens when local organizations share their knowledge and enthusiasm for gardening with everyone. Lots of activities and displays, musical entertainment, picnic fare, a scavenger hunt and tours.
Hours: 11am-6pm
Fee: Free
Hershey Gardens *(See Pennsylvania Guide to Gardens.)*

Kennett Square

14 miles from Wilmington

January 23-February 28
❧ Exhibition of Botanical Illustrators

Women of Flowers. An exhibit of botanical illustrations by Victorian women featured in the book of the same name by Jack Kramer.
Hours: 9am-5pm
Longwood Gardens *(See Pennsylvania Guide to Gardens.)*

March 6, 7
❧ North American Viewing Stone Society

Over thirty stones collected locally and from afar in a display of this ancient art, whereby stones evoke miniature landscapes and objects in the eyes of the viewer.
Hours: 10am-5pm
Longwood Gardens *(See Pennsylvania Guide to Gardens.)*

April 17, 18
❧ Delaware Valley Daffodil Society Show

Competitive show with over 1,000 blooms.
Hours: 1-5pm Sat; 10am-5pm Sun
Longwood Gardens *(See Pennsylvania Guide to Gardens.)*

April 30
❧ 21st Annual Rare Plant Auction

A nationally renowned event eagerly awaited each year by many aficionados of rare and unusual plants. Features silent and live auctions of newly introduced and exceptionally grown plants that are difficult to find on the commercial market. Cocktails and an extensive buffet complete the evening. Sponsored by the Delaware Center for Horticulture.
Fee: $150 Subscriber; $175 Patron; $250 Benefactor
Longwood Gardens, US Route 1, Kennett Square, PA
For information: **Delaware Center for Horticulture**, 1810 North DuPont, Wilmington, DE 19806
(302)658-6262

May 9
❧ Rhododendron Society Flower Show

A show of rhododendrons and azaleas sponsored by the Valley Forge Chapter of the American Rhododendron Society.
Hours: 1-5pm
Longwood Gardens *(See Pennsylvania Guide to Gardens.)*

May 22
❧ Home & Garden Tour

A tour of about eight outstanding private gardens rarely open to the public in the Kennett Square and historic Chester County area. Includes artists painting in the gardens, musicians, experts to answer horticultural questions and chefs preparing tastings. Benefits the Bayard Taylor Memorial Library. Call for tickets and lunch reservations.
Hours: 10am-4pm
Fee: $25; lunch may be ordered at additional cost

For information: **Bayard Taylor Memorial Library**, PO Box 730, Kennett Square, PA 19348
(610)444-2702

June 12
✿ Del-Chester Rose Society Show
A competitive show of over 1000 blooms, with modern and old-fashioned roses and nine artistic classes of flower arrangements.
Hours: 1-6pm
Longwood Gardens *(See Pennsylvania Guide to Gardens.)*

October 9, 10
✿ Delaware Chrysanthemum Society Show
A competitive show of over 400 blooms, with 115 classes.
Hours: 1-5pm Sat; 10am-5pm Sun
Longwood Gardens *(See Pennsylvania Guide to Gardens.)*

Kingston
Near Wilkes Barre

April 23-25
✿ Northeastern Pennsylvania Flower Show
Over 500 entries of both amateur horticulture and design and professional landscape and floral exhibits. Also a garden market, educational exhibits and demonstrations. Presented by the Back Mountain Bloomers Federated Garden Club in conjunction with the Northeastern Pennsylvania Philharmonic.
Hours: 10am-9pm Fri, Sat; 10am-6pm Sun
Fee: $6; $3 children
109 Field Artillery Armory, 280 Market Street, Kingston, PA
For information: **Back Mountain Bloomers Federated Garden Club**, PO Box 125, Dallas, PA 18612
(800)836-3413 or (717)457-8301

Lancaster
See also Marietta

June 12, 13
✿ 16th Annual Garden Tour
A tour of over a dozen private gardens, including small city gardens and large country and suburban gardens, the Charles Demuth family garden, and gardens of other artists. Benefits the Demuth Foundation.
Hours: 10am-5pm Sat; 11am-6pm Sun
Fee: $10 (tickets good for both days)
For information: **Demuth Foundation** *(See Pennsylvania Guide to Gardens.)*

Lebanon

July 17
✿ Garden Tour
A tour of ten private gardens which each year visits a different area of Lebanon County. Held rain or shine. Benefits the restoration projects of the Trust.
Hours: 9am-4pm
Fee: $10
For information: **Lebanon County Historic Preservation Trust**, PO Box 844, Lebanon, PA 17042
(717)274-5933

Marietta
10 miles from Lancaster, 25 miles from Harrisburg

June 20
✿ Marietta Garden Tour
A tour of eight local gardens, most within walking distance of each other, in the historic town of Marietta. Plus a mystery plant contest for tour-goers, an outdoor garden cafe and a barbershop quartet.
Hours: 10am-5pm
Fee: $6 in advance; $8 day of tour
For information: **Marietta Area Business Association**, PO Box 67, Marietta , PA 17547

Web: www.marietta.net/gardentour/
(717)426-4533

Media
Near Philadelphia

April 24
✿ Arbor Day Plant Sale
A variety of trees, shrubs, and perennials, plus unusual annuals for sale. Experts on hand to answer questions.
Hours: 9am-3pm
Fee: Free
Tyler Arboretum *(See Pennsylvania Guide to Gardens.)*

October 16, 17
✿ Pumpkin Days
A fall festival for the whole family, with a craft show, hayrides, scarecrow-making, music and entertainment.
Hours: 10am-5pm
Fee: $3; $1 children 3-15
Tyler Arboretum *(See Pennsylvania Guide to Gardens.)*

Morrisville

September 11, 12
✿ Manor Faire
A garden display and recreation of an English Garden Fair, with events for everyone.
Fee: $6; $5.50 seniors; $4 students (includes Manor admission)
Pennsbury Manor, 400 Pennsbury Memorial Road, Morrisville, PA 19067
(215)946-0400

New Hope
30 miles from Philadelphia

May 8, 9
✿ Mother's Day Plant Sale
A wide selection of plant species native to Pennsylvania, such as creeping phlox,

columbine, foam flower and fire pink. All plants propagated by staff and volunteers or donated by private gardeners; none collected from the wild.
Hours: 10am-4pm
Fee: Free
Bowman's Hill Wildflower Preserve *(See Pennsylvania Guide to Gardens.)*

September 11, 12 & 18, 19
✿ Fall Plant Sale
An excellent selection of Pennsylvania native plants for the fall planting season.
Hours: 10am-4pm
Fee: Free
Bowman's Hill Wildflower Preserve *(See Pennsylvania Guide to Gardens.)*

Philadelphia
See also Doylestown, Gladwyne, Media, New Hope, Swarthmore

March 7-14
✿ Philadelphia Flower Show
Design on Nature...The Art of Gardening. The country's oldest and largest indoor flower show. Ten acres of space celebrating this year's theme, gardens as beautiful and distinguished works of art. Proceeds benefit programs that provide assistance to neighborhood greening programs and the restoration and revitalization of Philadelphia's downtown green spaces and gateways. Note: Three- and four-day tours which include the Flower Show available through Philadelphia Hospitality, Inc. (800)714-3287.
Hours: 8am-6pm Sun; 10am-9:30pm Mon-Fri; 8am-9:30pm Sat
Fee: Weekdays $16; Weekends $18; $8 children under 12; 2-day SuperPasses $27 available by booking reservations at area hotels; contact PHS for advance and group sales
Pennsylvania Convention Center, 12th & Arch Streets, Philadelphia, PA

For information: **Pennsylvania Horticultural Society**, 100 North 20th Street, 5th floor, Philadelphia, PA 19103
Web: www.libertynet.org/flowersho/
(215)988-8800

April 23-May 16
🌿 Philadelphia Open House
A series of thirty tours of some of Philadelphia's most beautiful, unusual and interesting homes and gardens. By foot and by bus, guided and self-guided, in Philadelphia neighborhoods as well as the surrounding suburbs. Early reservations suggested. Now in its 21st year and sponsored by the Friends of Independence National Historical Park.
Fee: $20-$75
For information: **Philadelphia Open House**, 313 Walnut Street, Philadelphia, PA 19106
Email: finhp@aol.com
(215)928-1188

April 25
🌿 Arbor Day
An Arbor Day celebration with special festivities and family programs, including tree planting and tree climbing.
Hours: 1-4pm
Morris Arboretum *(See Pennsylvania Guide to Gardens.)*

April 25, May 2, 9
🌿 Open Garden Days
Open garden days at the beautiful 100-acre gardens of the nation's first private psychiatric hospital.
Hours: Noon-5pm
Fee: $2 per car
Friends Hospital Gardens, 4641 Roosevelt Blvd & Adams Avenue, Philadelphia, PA 19124
(215)831-7817

May 1
🌿 Annual Native Plant Sale
Native plants, wildflowers, herbs, small flowering trees and shrubs and sapling historic trees for sale. Plus gardening workshops and tours of the historic house and gardens.
Hours: 10am-4pm
Historic Bartram's Garden *(See Pennsylvania Guide to Gardens.)*

Early May
🌿 Spring Plant Sale
A sale of harder-to-find and unusual plants for the home landscape, including perennials, small trees and shrubs, antique roses, ornamental grasses, landscape roses, wildflowers and ferns. Arboretum's horticultural staff on hand to answer questions, make suggestions and recommend their favorites. Call for exact date.
Fee: Admission $5; $4 seniors; $3 students
Morris Arboretum *(See Pennsylvania Guide to Gardens.)*

May 19, 20
🌿 Rittenhouse Square Flower Market
Booths set up around the Square offer annuals, herbs and refreshments. Activities for children as well. Benefits children's charities in the area. Call to confirm dates.
Hours: 8am-6pm
Rittenhouse Square, Philadelphia, PA
For information: **Rittenhouse Association Charity**, 314 Catherine Street, #401, Philadelphia, PA 19147
(215)271-7149

May 22, 23
🌿 Bartram 300 Living History Festival
A festival celebrating the 300th anniversary of the birth of John Bartram, America's first botanist, with 18th century crafters, music, dance, reenactments and food. Also, tours of

Bartram House, the botanical garden and the world's newest tall ship, children's events and more.
Fee: Free
Historic Bartram's Garden *(See Pennsylvania Guide to Gardens.)*

Mid September
⚘ The Harvest Show
An annual harvest competition where more than 700 local gardeners show off their best, from colossal cabbages and titanic tomatoes, to garlic braids, botanically correct carrots and fall flowers. Plus educational exhibits, demonstrations and lots of family activities, especially for kids under the Children's tent. Call for exact dates.
Hours: 10am-5pm
Fee: $4
Horticultural Center, West Fairmont Park, Belmont Avenue & Horticulture Drive, Philadelphia, PA
For information: **Pennsylvania Horticultural Society**, 100 North 20th Street, 5th floor, Philadelphia, PA 19103
Web: www.libertynet.org/phs/
(215)988-8800

Mid September
⚘ Rare Plant Auction
Call for date and information.
Morris Arboretum *(See Pennsylvania Guide to Gardens.)*

Late September
⚘ Healing Plants Festival
Call for date and information.
Morris Arboretum *(See Pennsylvania Guide to Gardens.)*

Pittsburgh
See also Greensburg

February 20
⚘ Western Pennsylvania Gardening & Landscaping Symposium
An all-day symposium with distinguished speakers, including Holly Shimizu, Gordon Hayward, Stephanie Cohen, Art Kulak, Dr. Frank Gouin and Marco Polo Stufano. Sponsored by the Civic Garden Center, the Horticultural Society of Western Pennsylvania and Penn State Cooperative Extension.
Fee: $85 by January 31; $95 thereafter
The Pittsburgh Civic Garden Center *(See Pennsylvania Guide to Gardens.)*

April 17-May 30
⚘ Planning a Butterfly Garden
An exhibit of plants that attract butterflies to gardens and information on planning a butterfly garden.
Phipps Conservatory & Botanical Gardens *(See Pennsylvania Guide to Gardens.)*

April 22, 23
⚘ National Daffodil Show
The annual show of the American Daffodil Society featuring over 3000 daffodils from all over the United States, England, Northern Ireland, the Netherlands and Canada.
Hours: 2-6pm Thurs; 8am-10pm Fri
Fee: Free
Pittsburgh Marriott City Center, 112 Washington Place, Pittsburgh, PA
For information: **American Daffodil Society**, 4126 Winfield Road, Columbus, OH 43220
Email: nliggett@compuserve.com
(412)831-1672

April 23-25
⚘ Daffodil Society Show
Sponsored by the Daffodil Society. Call to confirm dates.

Phipps Conservatory & Botanical Gardens
(See Pennsylvania Guide to Gardens.)

May 1, 2
⚜ Bonsai Weekend
Demonstrations, classes and critiques throughout the weekend. A tour behind the scenes to see hundred of plants under cultivation.
Phipps Conservatory & Botanical Gardens
(See Pennsylvania Guide to Gardens.)

May 7
⚜ The Great Garden Auction
An annual fund-raiser and chance to bid on coveted varieties of plants, trees and unique garden accessories and artifacts. Reservations required.
Hours: Silent auction 6-7:30pm; live auction 7:40pm
The Pittsburgh Civic Garden Center *(See Pennsylvania Guide to Gardens.)*

May 8, 9
⚜ Mother's Day Weekend Plant Sale
A sale timed to spring planting.
Phipps Conservatory & Botanical Gardens
(See Pennsylvania Guide to Gardens.)

May 15, 16
⚜ African Violet Society Show
Sponsored by the African Violet Society. Call to confirm dates.
Phipps Conservatory & Botanical Gardens
(See Pennsylvania Guide to Gardens.)

May 21-23
⚜ May Market
An annual event, now in its 60th year, featuring a huge selection of perennials, annuals, vegetables, native plants, trees and shrubs. Also lectures, floral arranging demonstrations, experts on hand, live entertainments, food and more. Family Day on Sunday.

Hours: 10am-5pm Fri, Sat; call for Sunday hours
Fee: Free
The Pittsburgh Civic Garden Center *(See Pennsylvania Guide to Gardens.)*

June 5, 6
⚜ 7th Annual Hosta Cut-leaf Show
An annual show of these shade-loving plants.
Phipps Conservatory & Botanical Gardens
(See Pennsylvania Guide to Gardens.)

June 27
⚜ Open Gardens Day Tour
A self-guided tour of about thirty private gardens selected for their horticultural, botanical, historical or design excellence and located in various areas of Pittsburgh. Tour booklet, maps and parking instructions available from sponsor.
Hours: 9am-6pm
Fee: $45; $35 members
For information: **The Horticultural Society of Western Pennsylvania**, PO Box 5126, Pittsburgh, PA 15206
(412)361-8677

July 10
⚜ Enchanted Garden Tour
A tour of six private gardens with lunch and transportation included. Advance reservations required.
Hours: 9am-4pm
Fee: $40
For information: **Passavant Hospital Foundation**, 9100 Babcock Blvd, Pittsburgh, PA 15237
(412)367-6640

July 24, 25
⚜ Victorian Houses & Gardens Tour
A tour of private homes and gardens on the North Side. Starts at the Gazebo, Beech

Avenue and Galveston near the Community College.

Hours: Noon-5pm

For information: **Allegheny West Civic Council**, 845 Lincoln Avenue, Pittsburgh, PA 15233

(412)323-8884

Pottsville

June 27

🌿 **Schuykill County Garden Tour & Tea**

A tour of seven Schuykill County gardens, plus demonstrations and talks on ideas, techniques and culinary arts related to gardening. A Victorian Tea served throughout the day at the Schuykill County Council for the Art.s.

Hours: 1-5pm

Fee: $8

Schuykill County Council for the Arts, 1440 Mahantongo Street, Pottsville, PA

For information: **Orwigsburg Historical Society**, 100 East Market Street, Orwigsburg, PA 17961

(717)366-8713

Swarthmore

Near Philadelphia

April 24

🌿 **Arbor Day Celebration**

A celebration of Arbor Day at the Scott Offices with activities for the whole family. Rain or shine. Call for complete information.

Hours: 10:30am-1:30pm

Fee: Free

Scott Arboretum *(See Pennsylvania Guide to Gardens.)*

Rhode Island

Blithewold Mansion, Gardens & Arboretum

101 Ferry Road (Route 114)

Bristol, RI 02809

Email: info@heritagetrust.org

(401)253-2707 *Fax:* (401)253-0412

🌿 Blithewold was built at the turn of the century in the style of a 17th century English manor house and is an example of the gracious lifestyle of that bygone era. The property still retains the original design by New York landscape architect John DeWolf and overlooks Narragansett Bay. Blithewold's collection of exotic and native plants includes a Chinese Toon Tree, the first known to flower in this country, and a 90 year-old Giant Sequoia, the largest of its kind East of the Rocky Mountains. Highlights include the rose garden, rock garden and the Great Lawn reaching down to the water's edge.

Hours: 10am-5pm

Fees: Grounds $5, $3 children; house & grounds tour $8; $5 children

Green Animals

Cory's Lane

Portsmouth, RI

Mail: Preservation Society of Newport County, 424 Bellevue Avenue, Newport, RI 02840

(401)847-1000

🌿 One of the properties administered by the Preservation Society of Newport County, Green Animals is distinguished by its collection of 80 topiaries in the shapes of animals, birds, arches, spirals and various geometric forms set in flower beds. Green Animals is one of the oldest topiary gardens in the U.S. and a rare example of a country estate which combines formal topiaries, vegetable and herb

gardens, orchards and changing displays in the flower beds.
Web: www.newportmansions.org
Hours: May-Oct 10am-5pm
Fees: $8; $6 seniors, students $4 children (combination tickets for various Newport properties available)

Selected Events

Bristol
25 miles from Providence

April 25
⚘ Arbor Day
Arborists on hand to answer questions on the care and planting of trees. Plus frequent tours of Blithewold's thirty-three landscaped acres.
Blithewold Mansion, Gardens & Arboretum
(See Rhode Island Guide to Gardens.)

November 26-December 30
⚘ Christmas at Blithewold
A turn-of-the-century celebration at the Mansion with an 18-foot tree in the entrance hall and beautiful seasonal plants throughout.
Hours: Noon-8pm
Blithewold Mansion, Gardens & Arboretum
(See Rhode Island Guide to Gardens.)

Newport
35 miles from Providence

June 18-20
⚘ Secret Gardens of Newport
An annual tour of wonderful private gardens in the Historic Point section. Includes entry to The Hunter House, Floral Festival at St. John's Church and a plant sale.
Hours: noon-4pm Fri, Sun; 10am-4pm Sat
Fee: $15 in advance; $18 day of tour (ticket good for all 3 days)

For information: **The Secret Garden Tour**, 33 Washington Street, Newport, RI 02840 (401)847-0514

July 10, 11
⚘ The Newport Flower Show
Held at Rosecliff, one of the most elegant of the Newport mansions overlooking the Atlantic Ocean. Features horticultural classes, a garden marketplace, original artistic classes. Benefits the Garden Fund for the Newport Mansions.
Hours: 10am-6pm
Fee: $10 in advance; $12 at door; $6 children
Rosecliff, Newport, RI
For information: **The Preservation Society of Newport County**, 424 Bellevue Avenue, Newport, RI 02840
Web: www.newportmansions.org
(401)847-1000

November 26-January 2
⚘ Christmas at the Newport Mansions
Three of the Newport mansions, The Breakers, Chateau-sur-Mer and The Elms, decorated for the holidays with poinsettias from the Society's greenhouse, floral arrangements and other period decorations. On Sundays in December, special family activities at each house in turn.
Hours: 10am-4pm
The Breakers, Chateau-sur-Mer, The Elms, Newport, RI
For information: **The Preservation Society of Newport County**, 424 Bellevue Avenue, Newport, RI 02840
Web: www.newportmansions.org
(401)847-1000

Portsmouth

35 miles from Providence

July 14
🌿 Green Animals Children's Garden Party

Clowns, mimes, magicians, kiddies' rides, refreshments and entertainment in a topiary garden. Sponsored by The Preservation Society.

Hours: 4-8pm
Fee: $10; $5 children 6-12
Green Animals Topiary Gardens, Cory's Lane, Portsmouth, RI
For information: **The Preservation Society of Newport County**, 424 Bellevue Avenue, Newport, RI 02840
Web: www.newportmansions.org
(401)847-1000

Providence

See also Bristol, Newport, Portsmouth

February 18-21
🌿 Annual Rhode Island Spring Flower & Garden Show

Gardens of the Future. More than 30 display gardens, garden club exhibits, children's gardens, educational and environmental booths, competitions, garden talks and workshops, and the Garden Marketplace.

Hours: 10am-9pm Thurs-Sat; 10am-6pm Sun
Fee: $9 in advance; at door $11, $10 seniors & students, $3 children
Rhode Island Convention Center, One Sabin Street, Providence, RI
For information: **Rhode Island Flower & Garden Show**, PO Box 370, Camden, ME 04843
Web: www.flowershow.com
(800)766-1670

South Carolina

Brookgreen Gardens

1931 Brookgreen Gardens Drive, Highway 17S
Pawley's Island, SC
Mail: PO Box 3368, Pawley's Island, SC 29585
Email: info@brookgreen.org
(843)246-4218 Ext 250 *Fax:* (843)237-1014

🌿 Set on 300 acres in the midst of a 9,100 preserve stretching from the Atlantic Ocean to the historic rice fields of the Waccamaw River, Brookgreen Gardens is the work of the sculptor Anna Hyatt Huntington and her husband, Archer Huntington. The Huntingtons' design features an allée of 200-year old live oaks leading to a series of informal, connecting gardens, following a butterfly-shaped plan as background for the sculpture. The sculpture on display is largely the work of American artists, such as Daniel Chester French, Frederic Remington, Carl Milles, Gutzon Borglum and Anna Hyatt Huntington. The gardens are planted with dogwoods, azaleas, orchids and over 2,000 species native and adapted to the Southeast. The wildlife sanctuary covers many acres and is rich in bird and animal life.

Hours: 9:30am-4:45 pm
Fees: $7.50; $3 children

Cypress Gardens

3030 Cypress Gardens Road
Moncks Corner, SC 29461
(843)553-0515 *Fax:* (843)569-0644

🌿 Cypress Gardens was originally part of one of the Cooper River's most important rice plantations. Today the 163-acre swamp garden can be seen by hiking the nature trails or exploring in a flat-bottomed boat. In spring the gardens are full of azaleas, dogwoods, daf-

fodils and wisteria. A small working rice field was recently recreated at Cypress Gardens and rice is again planted and harvested using centuries-old methods.
Hours: 9am-5pm
Fees: Fee charged

Edisto Memorial Gardens
Highway 301 South
Orangeburg, SC
Mail: PO Box 863, Orangeburg, SC 29115
(803)534-6376
⚜ The Gardens encompass over 150 acres, with a wetlands park traversed by a boardwalk, a butterfly garden, a sensory garden and a terrace garden. The highlight of Edisto is the rose garden, with over 50 beds of roses ranging from miniatures to grandifloras and climbers. The site is an All-America Rose Selections test garden. It's the main site of the South Carolina Festival of Roses, held during the last weekend in April. See South Carolina Selected Events.
Hours: Dawn-dusk
Fees: Free

Kalmia Gardens of Coker College
1624 West Carolina Avene
Hartsville, SC 29550
(843)383-8145 *Fax:* (843)383-8149
⚜ Kalmia Gardens, located on the bluffs of Black Creek, consist of 30 acres on the site of the early 19th century plantation of Capt. Thomas E. Hart. Walking trails wind through a black water swamp, laurel thickets, pine, oak and holly uplands, and a collection of ornamentals. The site includes a AHS Daylily Display Garden.
Web: www.coker.edu/kalmia/
Hours: Dawn-dusk
Fees: Free

Magnolia Plantation & Its Gardens
3550 Ashley River Road
Charleston, SC 29414
(800)367-3517 or (843)571-1266 *Fax:* (843)571-5346
⚜ America's oldest continually-planted garden, circa 1680, this informal British-style garden estate was acquired in 1676 by the Drayton family, whose heirs still own it. The Gardens feature one of the largest collections of azaleas and camellias in the country. Highlights include the horticultural maze, Barbados Tropical garden, Biblical garden, herb and topiary gardens, Audubon Swamp garden and more.
Web: www.magnoliaplantation.com
Hours: Mar 8am-5pm; Apr-Oct 8am-5:30pm; more limited winter hours
Fees: $10; $9 seniors; $8 teens; $5 children; under 6 free

Middleton Place
4300 Ashley River Road
Charleston, SC 29414
(843)556-6020 *Fax:* (843)766-4460
⚜ The Gardens which Henry Middleton began in 1741 reflect the grand classic style and principles of Le Notre, with attention to woods, water, vistas, focal points and surprises. Rare camellias bloom in winter and azaleas cover the hillside in spring. Summer blooms include kalmia, magnolias, crape myrtle and roses. The site is a National Historic Landmark.
Web: www.middletonplace.org
Hours: 9am-5pm
Fees: fee charged

Riverbanks Zoo & Botanical Gardens
500 Wildlife Parkway
Columbia, SC
Mail: PO Box 1060, Columbia, SC 29202
(803)779-8717 *Fax:* (803)253-6381
⚜ The 70-acre Botanical Garden is located on the west bank of the Saluda River, across

from Riverbanks Zoo, and features a flood plain valley, slopes and upland areas that can be viewed from trails. The Walled Garden is part of the first phase of development, and within this 12-acre tract are several theme gardens, including the Berry Garden, Art Garden, Midnight Garden and seasonal beds. The Rose Garden was opened recently.
Web: www.riverbanks.org
Hours: 9am-4pm; til 5pm summer weekends, holidays
Fees: $5.75; $3.25 children; reduced fee for seniors, students

Singing Oaks Garden

1019 Abell Road
Blythewood, SC 29016
(803)786-1351
🌸 A private garden, Singing Oaks is an accredited AHS Display Garden, with over 2,000 different daylily cultivars in a garden setting amidst many companion trees, shrubs and perennials.
Hours: May 15-July 15, or by appointment
Fees: Free

The South Carolina Botanical Garden

1 Perimeter Road
Clemson, SC
Mail: Poole Agriculture Center, Clemson University, Clemson, SC 29634
(864)656-3405 *Fax:* (864)656-4960
🌸 Highlights of this 270-acre site are the many niche gardens, including Camellia Garden, Wildlife Habitat, Wildflower Meadow, Conifer Garden, Xeriscape Garden, the Woodland Wildflower Garden and the Nature Trail, plus many more. The Garden offers First Friday nature walks and various annual celebrations for families and children.
Web: virtual.clemson.edu/groups/scbg/
Hours: Dawn to dusk
Fees: Free

Swan Lake Iris Gardens

822 West Liberty Street
Sumter, SC
Mail: PO Box 1449, Sumter, SC 29151
Email: sumter@usc.net
(800)688-4748 *Fax:* (803)775-0915
🌸 With over 160 acres, this park creates a natural setting for azaleas, camellias and one of the largest iris gardens in the country. It's the main site for the Iris Festival held in Sumter each year. See South Carolina Selected Events.
Hours: 8am-dusk
Fees: Free

Selected Events

Charleston

February
🌸 **Camellia Walks**

Guided tours of the Specimen Garden every Tuesday, Thursday and Saturday during this month, with emphasis on the varieties, flower types, propagation and cultivation of the camellias. Lunch at the Middleton Place Restaurant included. Reservations required.
Hours: Tours begin at 11am
Fee: $18
Middleton Place *(See South Carolina Guide to Gardens.)*

Mid February-end of February
🌸 **Daffodil Days at Magnolia Plantation**

A celebration of spring at America's oldest continually-planted garden (circa 1680) with millions of daffodils, flowering fruit trees, early azaleas, full-blooming camellias, spirea, iris, anemones, roses, atamasco lilies and redbud. Tour of Revolutionary Greek Revival Plantation House included.

Hours: 9am-4pm
Fee: $16 adults; $15 seniors; $14 teens; $11 children 6-12
Magnolia Plantation & Its Gardens (See South Carolina Guide to Gardens.)

February 20, 27 & March 6, 13, 20
☙ Nature Walks

A tour of the outer areas of Middleton Place, including forest, marsh and flooded rice field, home of winter nesting bald eagles. Opportunity to learn about birds and the river/swamp ecosystem of the Low country.
Hours: 10-11:30am
Fee: gate admission
Middleton Place (See South Carolina Guide to Gardens.)

March 18-April 17
☙ 52nd Annual Festival of Houses & Gardens

Tours of Charleston's historic district, an area going back to the 1670's containing many period buildings that represent the major architectural styles of many eras. Glorious Gardens guided tours every Thursday of the public and private gardens in this historic district. On the other days, tours of different areas, each visiting eight to ten houses and one to three gardens. Some candlelight tours offered.
Fee: $35 per ticket for each event
For information: **Historic Charleston Foundation**, 51 Meeting Street, PO Box 1120, Charleston, SC 29402
Web: www.historiccharleston.org
(803)722-3405

April 3, 10
☙ House & Garden Tours

Annual tours of private homes and gardens, with floral arrangements in the homes done by Garden Club members. Refreshments served.

Call for information and tickets. Sponsored by the Garden Club of Charleston.
Hours: 2-5pm
Fee: $25
For information: **The Garden Club of Charleston**, PO Box 20652, Charleston, SC 29412
(843)795-1420

September 23-October 30
☙ Fall Candlelight Tours of Homes & Gardens

Evening walking tours of historic houses, gardens and churches in Charleston on Thursdays, Fridays and Saturdays. Afternoon Garden Tours on Sundays.
Hours: Evening tours 7-10pm; Sunday afternoons 2-5pm
Fee: $30 each
For information: **Preservation Society of Charleston**, PO Box 521, Charleston, SC 29402
Web: www.preservationsociety.org
(843)722-4630

September 30-October 3
☙ Charleston Garden Festival

Charleston-Barbados Connections. Ten major events including a two-day symposium featuring nationally known speakers, tours of the city's finest gardens, horticultural tours of four private plantations rarely open to the public, lectures, workshops, a market place with over 60 nurseries and garden vendors, indoor show gardens and landscapes, water gardens and floral arrangements. Tickets for the plantation tours, garden tours and lectures sold separately. Proceeds from the show benefit Florence Crittenton Programs, offering shelter, education, medical care and counseling to pregnant women and their children. Many events at Gaillard Auditorium.

Gaillard Auditorium, 77 Calhoun Street, Charleston, SC
For information: **Charleston Garden Festival**, 19 St. Margaret Street, Charleston, SC 29403
(803)722-0661

December 4
🌿 Manigault House Christmas
A holiday celebration at Manigault House, decorated for Christmas with plant material and flowers in keeping with the period when the Manigaults lived there.
Hours: 10am-5pm
Fee: $6
Manigault House, Charleston, SC
For information: **The Garden Club of Charleston**, PO Box 20652, Charleston, SC 29412
(843)795-1420

December 5-19
🌿 Camellia Christmas at Magnolia Plantation
Billed as America's most extensive outdoor Camellia display. Admission includes Plantation House tour. Audubon Swamp Garden walking tours and Nature Train rides available at additional charge.
Hours: 9am-4:30pm
Fee: $10; $9 seniors; $8 teens; $5 children 6-12
Magnolia Plantation & Its Gardens *(See South Carolina Guide to Gardens.)*

Clemson
30 miles from Greenville

Mid April
🌿 Spring Plant Sale
Select varieties of ornamental plants particularly suited to Zone 7, but difficult to find, are offered. Call for exact date.
Hours: 9am-1pm

The South Carolina Botanical Garden *(See South Carolina Guide to Gardens.)*

May
🌿 3rd Annual Herb Festival
A festival featuring lectures throughout the day, tours of the woods, vendors. Hosted by the Friends of the South Carolina Botanical Garden. Call for exact date.
Hours: 9am-5pm
Fee: fee charged
The South Carolina Botanical Garden *(See South Carolina Guide to Gardens.)*

Mid October
🌿 Fall Plant Sale
Call for exact date.
Hours: 9am-1pm
The South Carolina Botanical Garden *(See South Carolina Guide to Gardens.)*

Columbia

June 5
🌿 Annual Daylily Show
A judged show with literature and information on growing daylilies of all kinds. Sponsored by the Mid-Carolina Daylily Society.
Hours: 1-5pm
Fee: Admission. $5.75; $3.25 children; reduced fee for seniors, students
Riverbanks Zoo & Botanical Gardens *(See South Carolina Guide to Gardens.)*

Greenwood

June 18-20
🌿 South Carolina Festival of Flowers
A popular festival with lots to offer garden enthusiasts, including tours of private gardens and the Park Seed Company's famous Trial Gardens, plus music, arts and crafts, sports, food and more.
Fee: Free for most events

For information: **South Carolina Festival of Flowers**, PO Box 980, Greenwood, SC 29648
Email: Chamber@AIS.AIS-GWD.com
(864)223-8411

Orangeburg
45 miles from Columbia

April 23-25
❧ South Carolina Festival of Roses
A family-oriented festival in the Edisto Memorial Gardens, planned to coincide with the beginning of the rose blooming season. Includes all kinds of live entertainment, sports tournaments, races, arts and crafts, and more, plus a display at least 75 varieties of roses in this official test garden for the All-American Rose Selection, Inc. For complete information, contact the Chamber.
Hours: 10am-5pm
Fee: Free
Edisto Memorial Gardens, Highway 301 South, Orangeburg, SC
For information: **Orangeburg County Chamber of Commerce**, PO Box 328, Orangeburg, SC 29116
Web: www.orangeburgsc.net
(803)534-6821

Sumter

April 3
❧ Secret Backyard Tour & Garden Picnic
A tour through the gardens of Sumter's historic homes, plus a garden picnic. Sponsored by the Council of Garden Clubs in Sumter.
Hours: 10am-4pm; picnic 11:30am-1:30pm
Fee: $15
For information: **Sumter Convention & Visitors Bureau**, 32 East Calhoun Street, PO Box 1229, Sumter, SC 29151
Web: www.sumter.sc.us
Email: tourism@ftc-i.net
(800)688-4748

May 27-30
❧ Iris Festival
A festival celebrating the blooming of Swan Lake Iris Gardens, 150 acres of gardens and lake with one of the world's most spectacular array of Japanese irises and twenty-four other varieties. Over 6,000,000 plants in bloom along the banks of the lake, home to the eight known species of swans. Event sponsored by the Sumter Garden Club Council.
Hours: 6:30-9pm Thurs; 8:30am-9:30pm Fri; 1:30-6:30pm Sun
Fee: Free
Alice Boyle Garden Center in Swan Lake, Sumter, SC
For information: **Sumter Convention & Visitors Bureau**, 32 East Calhoun Street, PO Box 1229, Sumter, SC 29151
Web: www.sumter.sc.us
Email: tourism@ftc-i.net
(800)688-4748

May 27-30
❧ Spring Fling Bicycle & Walking Tour
A self-guided walking or bicycle tour along Sumter's bike trail which offers views of private gardens that are in peak bloom at this time.
For information: **Sumter Convention & Visitors Bureau**, 32 East Calhoun Street, PO Box 1229, Sumter, SC 29151
Web: www.sumter.sc.us
Email: tourism@ftc-i.net
(800)688-4748

Tennessee

Guide to Gardens

Cheekwood, Nashville's Home of Art & Gardens
1200 Forrest Park Drive
Nashville, TN 37205

(615)356-8000 *Fax:* (615)353-2168

� The Botanical Garden at Cheekwood includes such specialty gardens as the Japanese Garden and herb, perennial and wildflower gardens. The new Seasons Garden opened in the fall of 1998, and the Woodland Sculpture Trail opens in spring 1999.
Web: www.cheekwood.org
Hours: 9am-5pm Mon-Sat; 11am-5pm Sun
Fees: $9; $7 seniors; $5 children 3-17

Dixon Gallery & Gardens
4339 Park Avenue
Memphis, TN 38117
(901)761-5250 *Fax:* (901)682-0943
🌷 Created out of 17 acres of native Tennessee woodland, the Gardens are landscaped in the English park style, with open vistas and formal gardens. The site includes a woodland garden, cutting garden, Camellia Conservatory and greenhouse.
Web: www.dixon.org
Hours: 10am-5pm Tues-Sat; 1-5pm Sun
Fees: $5; $4 seniors; $1 children

The Hermitage: Home of President Andrew Jackson
4580 Rachel's Lane
Hermitage, TN 37076
(615)889-2941 *Fax:* (615)889-9909
🌷 In 1819 Andrew Jackson employed English gardener William Frost to plan and plant this garden. During the 1820s his wife, Rachel Jackson, developed the ornamental plantings. Laid out as a near perfect one-acre square, the garden features the same old-fashioned flowers and shrubs that bloomed in it over 170 years ago.
Web: www.thehermitage.com
Hours: 9am-5pm; closed 3rd week Jan
Fees: $9.50; $8.50 seniors; $4.50 children

Memphis Botanic Garden
750 Cherry Road
Memphis, TN 38117
(901)685-1566 *Fax:* (901)682-1561
🌷 The Garden contains many special areas, including a Japanese garden, and iris, magnolia, rose, daffodil, dahlia and wildflower gardens. It features very good specimens of Japanese cherry trees, holly, crabapples and shrubs of the region. It also has a conservatory with crotons, orchids and bromeliads.
Web: aabga.mobot.org/AABGA/ Member.pages/memphis.bot.gdn.html
Hours: 9am-6pm Mon-Sat; 11am-6pm Sun; Nov-Feb close at 4:30pm
Fees: $2; $1.50 seniors; $1 children 2-11

Reflection Riding
400 Garden Road
Chattanooga, TN 37419
(423)821-9582
🌷 Reflection Riding is a 300-acre botanical garden, home to a variety of trees, shrubs and flowers. Visitors can walk, bike or drive the three mile loop or hike many miles up Lookout Mountain or along Lookout Creek.
Hours: 9am-5pm; 1-5pm Sun
Fees: $3; $2 seniors, children

University of Tennessee Arboretum
901 Kerr Hollow Road
Oak Ridge, TN 37830
(615)483-3571 *Fax:* (615)423-3572
🌷 The 260-acre Arboretum features woody plants, dogwoods, conifers, vibernums, hollies, landscape and native plants.
Hours: 8am-sunset
Fees: Free

University of Tennessee Trial Gardens
Agriculture Campus
Knoxville, TN

Mail: University of Tennessee Institute of Agriculture, PO Box 1071, Knoxville, TN 37901 (423)974-7324 *Fax:* (423)974-2947

🌺 The Trial Gardens are open for the public to enjoy, and consist of 500 perennials, 600 annuals, herbs and hundreds of trees growing along a winding brick path.

Web: web.utk.edu/~hort/
Hours: Daylight hours
Fees: Free

Selected Events

Chattanooga

April 10, 11 & 17, 18
🌺 **Spring Wildflower Festival & Native Plant Sale**
Guided wildflower tours, programs, sale of native plants at the greenhouse, and wildlife exhibit at Chattanooga Nature Center.
Hours: 9am-5pm Sat; 1-5pm Sun
Fee: Free
Reflection Riding *(See Tennessee Guide to Gardens.)*

April 16, 17
🌺 **Garden Fest**
Plants With A Purpose. A sale of native plants and organic vegetables plus workshops on gardening for wildlife and programs for adults and children.
Hours: 10am-7pm Fri; 9am-5pm Sun
Fee: $5 per car
Greenway Farms, Hixson, TN
For information: **Chattanooga Nature Center**, at Reflection Riding, 400 Garden Road, Chattanooga, TN 37419
Web: www.cdc.net/~nature
(423)821-1160

September
🌺 **Native Plant Sale**

Hundreds of selections of native plants available at the greenhouse. Call for exact date.
Hours: 9am-5pm Sat; 1-5pm Sun
Fee: Free
Reflection Riding *(See Tennessee Guide to Gardens.)*

Gatlinburg

April 22-24
🌺 **Spring Flower Pilgrimage**
Over 100 guided walks to see the wildflowers, birds and other wildlife in the Great Smokies, all led by subject-matter experts. Attracts 1500 visitors annually. Call for details and a brochure.
For information: **Great Smoky Mountains National Park**, 107 Park Headquarters Road, Gatlinburg, TN 37738
(423)436-1255

Hermitage
12 miles from Nashville

May 15, 16
🌺 **Spring Garden Fair**
Tours of historic Hermitage Garden and a once-a-year opportunity to purchase old-fashioned and antique plants from the Garden. Plus bird watching walks, archeological site tours, tree treks, lectures and crafts demonstrations.
Hours: 9am-5pm
Fee: Admission $9.50; $8.50 seniors; $4.50 children
The Hermitage: Home of President Andrew Jackson *(See Tennessee Guide to Gardens.)*

Knoxville

Late May
🌺 **Secret Garden Tour**
A tour of private gardens in the Knoxville area to benefit the Trial Gardens at the University of Tennessee, Knoxville. Call for exact date and information.

Hours: 1-6pm
Fee: $15
For information: **Friends of Trial Gardens at University of Tennessee**, PO Box 51394, Knoxville, TN 37950
Web: funnelweb.utcc.utk.edu/~uthort/
Email: mcweaver@usit.net
(423)525-4555

Memphis

April 16-18
✿ Annual Spring Plant Sale
Thousands of plants especially tested to grow well in the region, including perennials, annuals, vines, salvia, ferns, roses, trees and garden accessories. Billed as the Mid-South's largest plant sale, now in its 24th year.
Hours: 10am-6pm Fri, Sat; 11am-4pm Sun
Fee: Free
Memphis Botanic Garden *(See Tennessee Guide to Gardens.)*

May 20, June 17, July 15, August 19, September 9
✿ Japanese Garden & Candlelight Tours
Candlelight tours of the Japanese Garden of Tranquility with hundreds of luminarias edging the lake. Plus stories of Japanese folklore.
Hours: Tours start at sundown and vary; call for start times
Fee: $5; $1 children
Memphis Botanic Garden *(See Tennessee Guide to Gardens.)*

Nashville
See also Hermitage

February 11-14
✿ The Antiques & Garden Show of Nashville
A popular annual show featuring dealers from around the country and specialty gardens created by area landscapers.

Nashville Convention Center, Nashville, TN
(615)352-1282
For information: **Cheekwood, Nashville's Home of Art & Gardens** *(See Tennessee Guide to Gardens.)*

February 27, 28
✿ Middle Tennessee Society Camellia Show
Sponsored by the Middle Tennessee Society.
Cheekwood, Nashville's Home of Art & Gardens *(See Tennessee Guide to Gardens.)*

March 4-7
✿ Nashville Lawn & Garden Show
Gardening at the Edge. Features a one-acre display of 24 specialty gardens, a lecture series and hundreds of exhibit booths with gardening products, services and equipment.
Hours: 10am-9pm Thurs-Sat; 10am-5pm Sun
Fee: $6; $5 seniors; $1 children
Tennessee State Fairgrounds, Nashville, TN
For information: **Nashville Lawn & Garden Show**, 5711 Old Harding Road, Suite 4, Nashville, TN 37205
(615)352-3863

April 8-11
✿ Wildflower Fair
An annual three-day fair featuring a sale of native wildflowers, ferns, native trees and shrubs as well as garden-related items and tours of the Howe Wildflower Garden.
Sponsored by the Garden Club of Nashville.
Cheekwood, Nashville's Home of Art & Gardens *(See Tennessee Guide to Gardens.)*

May 13-16
✿ Community Flower Show
An opportunity to see the latest in floral design.
Cheekwood, Nashville's Home of Art & Gardens *(See Tennessee Guide to Gardens.)*

September 24, 25
🌿 Perennials Conference
Two days devoted to perennials with nationally known speakers.
Hours: 8:30am-4pm
Fee: fee charged
Cheekwood, Nashville's Home of Art & Gardens *(See Tennessee Guide to Gardens.)*

Texas

Guide to Gardens

Amarillo Botanical Gardens
Harrington Medical Center Park, 1400 Streit Drive
Amarillo, TX 79106
(806)352-6513 *Fax:* (806)352-6227
🌿 This garden has a fragrance garden for the blind and seasonal displays.

Bayou Bend Collection & Gardens
1 Westcott Street
Houston, TX
Mail: PO Box 6826, Houston, TX 77265
(713)639-7750 *Fax:* (713)639-7770
🌿 This urban oasis, the creation of Miss Ima Hogg, is just five minutes from downtown Houston and consists of 14 acres of formal gardens and natural woodlands. There are eight distinctive gardens each featuring a variety of plants of the region. Today the gardens are maintained by the River Oaks Garden Club and the Bayou Bend Gardens Endowment.
Hours: 10am-5pm Tues-Sat; 1-5pm Sun
Fees: $3 for Garden; children under 11 free

Beaumont Botanical Gardens
6090 Babe Zaharias Drive
Beaumont, TX
Mail: PO Box 7962, Beaumont, TX 77726
(409)842-3135 or (409)892-1137

Hours: Conservatory 10am-5pm Sat, 1am-5pm Sun
Fees: Garden is free; Conservatory $3, $2 seniors, $1 children 6-12

Chihuahuan Desert Arboretum
Texas Highway 118
Ft. Davis, TX
Mail: Chihuahuan Desert Research Institute, PO Box 905, Ft. Davis, TX 79734
(915)364-2499
🌿 The 20-acre Arboretum is a tool for scientists, students and naturalists, with over 200 species of trees and shrubs. The Cactus and Succulent Greenhouse has over 240 species from the Chihuahuan Desert. The Modesta Canyon Trail descends into a hidden canyon, with large cherry, hawthorn and Madrone trees as well as clear pools, making this a birder's paradise.
Web: www.cdri.org
Hours: 9am-5pm
Fees: Free

Corpus Christi Botanical Gardens
8545 South Staples Street
Corpus Christi, TX 78413
(512)852-2100 *Fax:* (512)852-7875
🌿 This 180-acre site along Oso Creek combines natural mesquite forest, wetlands and landscaped vistas with special gardens and exhibits. Highlights include the Orchid House, Plumeria collection, Sensory Garden, Bird and Butterfly Trail, Gator Lake and Children's Garden.
Hours: 9am-5pm; closed Monday
Fees: $2; $1.50 seniors; $1 children

Dallas Arboretum & Botanical Gardens
8525 Garland Road
Dallas, TX
Mail: 8617 Garland Road, Dallas, TX 75218
Email: DABS@ONRAMP.NET

(214)327-8263 *Fax:* (214)324-9801

🌺 The 66-acre Gardens are on the grounds of the former DeGolyer and Camp estates on White Rock Lake. There are ornamental gardens and woodlands, and a large azalea collection. Autumn is the time to see 15, 000 chrysanthemums in bloom.

Hours: 10am-6pm; Nov-Feb 10am-5pm
Fees: $6; $5 seniors; $3 children; under 6 free

Dallas Horticulture Center

3601 Martin Luther King Blvd, Fair Park
Dallas, TX
Mail: PO Box 152537, Dallas, TX 75315
(214)428-7476 *Fax:* (214)428-5338

🌺 Highlight of these gardens, the second oldest in Texas, is the Texas Native Plant Collection, which includes the wildflowers and native flora of the Edwards Plateau and Texas Hill Country. Other features include the Contemporary Garden, the Shakespeare Garden, Xeriscape, Earthkeeper's, Butterfly, and Rose Gardens, and the Physic Garden for the visually impaired. The Conservatory contains the Plants of Africa Collection.

Hours: Daylight hours; Visitor's Center 10am-5pm, 1-5pm Sun; closed Monday
Fees: Free

The Earle-Harrison House & Pape Gardens

1901 North 5th Street
Waco, TX 76708
Email: earleharrison@texnet.net
(254)753-2032 *Fax:* (254)756-3820
Hours: 9am-4:30pm Mon-Fri; 1:30-5pm Sat, Sun
Fees: $2

El Paso Municipal Rose Garden

1702 North Copia Street
El Paso, TX
Mail: Parks & Recreation Department, 4640

Delta Street, El Paso, TX 79905
Email: rosestar78@aol.com
(915)532-7318 or (915)566-0014

🌺 The 1.5-acre Garden was planted in 1958 by the El Paso Rose Society. From its start of 200 plants the garden has grown to more than 1,400 bushes, representing approximately 200 varieties. It is maintained by the City Parks & Recreation Departments and volunteers from the Rose Society.

Hours: 8am-2pm Tues-Sat

Fort Worth Botanic Garden

3220 Botanic Garden Blvd
Fort Worth, TX 76107
(817)871-7689 or (817)871-7673 *Fax:* (817)871-7638

🌺 The oldest botanic garden in Texas, the Garden contains thousands of native and exotic species on 110 acres. The Rose Garden was the first garden constructed, and many others have been added, including the Japanese Garden, the Perennial Garden, the Exhibition Greenhouse, the Conservatory and more. The Garden is home to the Texas Garden Clubs, Inc. and all affiliated garden clubs. The City of Fort Worth also maintains the Fort Worth Water Gardens, 1501 Commerce Street, a spectacular water display on over 4 1/2 acres with excellent tree specimens.

Hours: 9am-7pm Tues-Sat; 1-7pm Sun
Fees: Free; $1 Conservatory; $2 Japanese Garden weekends

Heard Museum & Wildlife Sanctuary

One Nature Place
McKinney, TX 75069
Email: heardmuseum@texoma.net
(972)562-5566 *Fax:* (972)548-9119

🌺 The Heard's Native Plant Display Garden is approached by walking through the cedar arbor entry, down the Redbud allée, through the collection of Native Texas plants and

trees. The wildlife sanctuary offers the Walnut Trail, Hoot Owl trail, and Hilltop and Red-tailed Guided Trails.
Web: www.heardmuseum.org
Hours: 9am-5pm Mon-Sat; 1-5pm Sun
Fees: $3; $2 children

Houston Arboretum & Nature Center
4501 Woodway
Houston, TX 77024
Email: hanc@compuserve.com
(713)681-8433 *Fax:* (713)681-1191
🌱 The Arboretum comprises a nature preserve of 155 acres with five miles of trails through forest and past ponds. The Discovery Room houses interactive educational exhibits.
Web: www.neosoft.com/~arbor/
Hours: Grounds 8:30am-6pm; Building 9am-5pm
Fees: Free

Lady Bird Johnson Wildflower Center
4801 La Crosse Avenue
Austin, TX 78739
(512)292-4100 *Fax:* (512)292-4627
🌱 The site was designed to emphasize a landscape illustrative of the beauty of the Central Texas Hill country and its native plants. Some areas are left natural, others more formal, with a Wildflower Meadow, Display Gardens and Home Comparison Gardens.
Web: www.wildflower.org
Hours: 9am-5:30pm Tues-Sun
Fees: $4; $2.50 seniors, students; $1children

Mercer Arboretum & Botanic Gardens
22306 Aldine Westfield
Humble, TX 77338
(281)443-8731
🌱 On 250 acres of East Texas piney woods along Cypress Creek, Mercer offers twelve major display gardens, including daylilies, an exceptional ginger collection, a dry land garden with many plants native to East Texas, a tropical garden that survives miraculously well in a subtropical zone. Five miles of trails traverse the different ecosystems of the site.
Hours: 8am-5pm; 8am-7pm during daylight savings time
Fees: Free

Moody Gardens
One Hope Blvd
Galveston, TX 77554
(800)582-4673 *Fax:* (409)744-1631
🌱 This 242-acre site has more than 25 acres of indoor and outdoor gardens, and offers individuals with disabilities the unique opportunity to engage in gardening activities for short stays or extended periods of time. The outdoor displays include many tropical and subtropical plants, such as hibiscus and crotons. The Rain Forest Pyramid is a unique place to visit, with its collections of rain forest plants from South America, Africa and Asia as well as wildlife native to these regions.
Web: www.moodygardens.com
Hours: 9:30am-6pm Sun-Thurs; 9:30am-9pm Fri, Sat
Fees: $6; $5 seniors, children

San Antonio Botanical Garden
555 Funston Place
San Antonio, TX 78209
(210)207-3262 *Fax:* (210)829-4866
🌱 The 33-acre Garden includes formal gardens, a sacred garden, rose, herb, old-fashioned, Japanese gardens, xeriscape and wildlife pants gardens, and more. The Conservatory is a complex of five glass houses. Native areas are an East Texas forest with lake, Hill Country and South Texas scrub country.
Hours: 9am-6pm
Fees: $4; $2 seniors; $1 children

Tyler Municipal Rose Garden & Rose Museum

420 Rose Park Drive
Tyler, TX
Mail: PO Box 8224, Tyler, TX 75711
(903)597-3130 *Fax:* (903)597-3031
🌹 Tyler calls itself the Rose Capital of the Nation. The 14-acre Tyler Municipal Rose Garden has 30,000 bushes with over 400 varieties. The Garden is groomed to perfection for the annual Rose Festival (See Texas Selected Events). The one-acre Heritage and Sensory Garden has antique roses dating from before the Civil War. Local growers are a mainstay of support and founded the Texas Rose Research Foundation in Tyler. The Rose Museum has a wide range of exhibits, from antebellum to computer roses.
Web: www.tylertexas.com
Hours: 9am-4pm Tues-Fri; 10am-4pm Sat; 1:30-4pm Sun
Fees: Garden is free; Rose Museum $3.50, $2 children

Zilker Botanical Gardens

2220 Barton Springs Road
Austin, TX 78746
(512)477-8672 *Fax:* (512)481-8253
🌹 Zilker Botanical Gardens are located in the center of the capital city of Texas, on a site with handsome trees, natural grottos and aquatic habitats. Highlights of the gardens are a Xeriscape Garden, Cactus, Oriental and Rose Gardens, a Butterfly Garden and Trail, bedding and floral displays, and a Dinosaur Trackway discovered in 1992.
Web: www.zilker-garden.org
Hours: Gardens 7am-6pm
Fees: Free

Selected Events

Amarillo

May 9
🌹 **Mother's Day Iris Show**
Presented by members of the North Plains Iris Society and billed as one of the largest iris shows in the region.
Hours: 1-30-5pm
Fee: Free
Amarillo Botanical Gardens *(See Texas Guide to Gardens.)*

June 5
🌹 **Bouquet of Gardens Tour**
A tour of private gardens in the area. Benefits the Gardens.
Hours: 10am-4pm
Fee: $10
For information: **Amarillo Botanical Gardens** *(See Texas Guide to Gardens.)*

Arlington

Between Dallas and Ft. Worth

February 26-28
🌹 **Neil Sperry's All Garden Show**
A large regional show with display gardens, lectures and demonstrations, many garden-related products and services for sale. An on-site broadcast of Neil Sperry's Gardening Radio Show each morning.
Hours: 3-8pm Fri; 8am-8pm Sat; 8am-6pm Sun
Fee: $7.50
Arlington Convention Center, Arlington, TX
For information: **Neil Sperry's Gardens Magazine**, PO Box 864, McKinney, TX 75070
Web: www.neilsperry.com
(800)752-4769

Austin

February 14
☙ Rose Pruning Demonstration
Spring rose pruning demonstration and step-by-step lessons by members of the Austin Rose Society. Covers hybrid teas, grandifloras, floribundas, miniatures, climbing roses and old garden roses. Call the Society at (512)452-1495 for information.
Hours: 1-4pm
Zilker Botanical Gardens *(See Texas Guide to Gardens.)*

March 13
☙ Men's Garden Club Spring Bulb Sale
Hundreds of large #1 grade caladium bulbs, gladioli, elephant ears and a variety of other bulbs on sale. Sponsored by the Men's Garden Club of Austin.
Hours: 9am-5pm
Zilker Botanical Gardens *(See Texas Guide to Gardens.)*

April weekends
☙ Wildflower Days Festival
An annual festival celebrating spring at the National Wildflower Research Center. Special events every weekend, featuring speakers, authors, storytellers and outdoor demonstrations, plus food, music and fun activities. Includes one-on-one sessions with gardening experts, tours of the gardens, hikes on the Nature Trail, and views from the Observation Tower. Call for schedule of events.
Hours: 9am-5:30pm
Fee: $5 subject to change
Lady Bird Johnson Wildflower Center *(See Texas Guide to Gardens.)*

April 3, 4
☙ Cactus & Succulent Society Show & Sale
A display and sale of cactus and succulents

from South, Central and North America, and Africa by enthusiasts from Central Texas and Oklahoma.
Hours: 10am-5pm
Zilker Botanical Gardens *(See Texas Guide to Gardens.)*

April 18
☙ Austin Rose Show
A display of some of the finest roses grown in Central Texas, including old garden roses, miniatures, hybrid teas, multifloras and grandifloras. Timed to coincide with peak bloom in the Mabel Davis Rose Garden.
Hours: 1-5pm
Zilker Botanical Gardens *(See Texas Guide to Gardens.)*

May 1, 2
☙ Garden Festival
A large outdoor flower festival and plant sale with many garden clubs and plant societies participating. Live music, food, arts and crafts exhibits and games for children. A fund-raiser for the Garden Center.
Hours: 10am-6pm
Fee: $4; children under 12 free
Zilker Botanical Gardens *(See Texas Guide to Gardens.)*

Beaumont

April 24, 25
☙ Neches River Festival & Flower Show
A show of floral arrangements and horticultural displays sponsored by Milady Garden Club.
Hours: 3-5pm Sat; 1-5pm Sun
Fee: Free
Beaumont Botanical Gardens *(See Texas Guide to Gardens.)*

May 1, 2
☙ Beaumont Spring Gardens Tour
Tour of four private gardens and the

Beaumont Botanical Gardens. Plus a plant sale at the Garden Center and an "Ask the Expert" panel in the Gardens.
Hours: 1-5pm
Fee: $6
For information: **Beaumont Botanical Gardens** *(See Texas Guide to Gardens.)*

December 4
Christmas Homes Tour
An annual event featuring three private homes, the Garden Center and the Gardens, all decorated for the season with holiday plants and flowers. All decorations for sale.
Hours: 10am-5pm
Fee: $8
For information: **Beaumont Botanical Gardens** *(See Texas Guide to Gardens.)*

Corpus Christi

April 17
Spring Plant Sale & Garden Festival
A sale of propagations and divisions from some of the Garden's rare collections, including orchids, cacti, tropicals, as well as selections from local plant societies. Also seminars on plant care, refreshments and more.
Hours: 9am-5pm
Fee: Free
Corpus Christi Botanical Gardens *(See Texas Guide to Gardens.)*

October 23
Aunt Flora's Gigantic Fall Plant Sale
A sale of propagations and divisions from the Garden's collections, including bromeliads, plumeria, orchids, cacti, tropicals, as well as selections from local plant societies and vendors.
Hours: 9am-5pm
Fee: Free
Corpus Christi Botanical Gardens *(See Texas Guide to Gardens.)*

Dallas
See also Arlington, Fort Worth

March 6-April 11
Dallas Blooms
Birds in Paradise. Billed as the Southwest's largest spring floral display with over 200,000 bulbs, including daffodils, tulips, narcissus and one of the largest collections of azaleas, all in full bloom. Weekend events include a plant sale, horticultural demonstrations, exhibits, entertainment and children's activities.
Dallas Arboretum & Botanical Gardens *(See Texas Guide to Gardens.)*

El Paso

Early October
El Paso Rose Society Show
A judged show presented by the El Paso Rose Society and held at the garden they help to maintain. For information and exact date, write the Society c/o Lyle Hosmer, 10132 Camwood, El Paso, TX 79925, call (915)598-4970 or email rosestar78@aol.com.
El Paso Municipal Rose Garden *(See Texas Guide to Gardens.)*

Fort Worth
See also Arlington, Dallas

April 10, 11
Japanese Garden Spring Festival & Flowercade
Traditional Japanese music and dance, martial art demonstrations, bonsai and calligraphy demonstrations.
Hours: Festival 11am-4pm Sat, noon-4pm Sun; Flowercade 9am-5pm
Fort Worth Botanic Garden *(See Texas Guide to Gardens.)*

May 7, 8, 9
Begonia, Perennials, & Madonna Lily Shows

A weekend of three events: Friday through Sunday, the Southwest Region Begonia Show; Saturday and Sunday, the Madonna Lily Show and *Perennials on Parade* in the Trial Garden.
Hours: Begonias 9am-5pm; Perennials 8am-3pm; Madonna Lilies 8am-7pm
Fort Worth Botanic Garden *(See Texas Guide to Gardens.)*

October 16, 17
⚘ Garden Fun Fest '99
A flower show, plant sale, pumpkin party, scarecrow exhibition, live entertainment, food vendors and more. Fun for the whole family. Held in the Japanese Garden. Call to confirm dates.
Fee: Free
Fort Worth Botanic Garden *(See Texas Guide to Gardens.)*

Ft. Davis

April 24, 25
⚘ Annual Native Plant Sale
A sale of over 1000 container plants, cacti and succulents, all native to the Chihuahuan Desert Region of North America.
Hours: 9:30am-4pm
Fee: Free
Chihuahuan Desert Arboretum *(See Texas Guide to Gardens.)*

Galveston

March 19-21
⚘ Spring Caladium Bulb Sale
A sale of "Mammoth" grade Caladium bulbs by the Galveston Garden Club. Now in its 31st year.
Hours: 10am-6pm
Fee: Free
Moody Gardens Hotel & Convention Center, Two Hope Blvd, Galveston, TX
For information: **Galveston Garden Club**,

Powhatan House, 3427 Avenue O, Galveston, TX 77550
(409)763-0077

November 11
⚘ Powhatan Pansy Potpourri
Galveston Garden Club's annual garden party where presold flats of pansies are distributed to buyers. Orders taken from October through November 4. Held on the beautiful lawn of the historic 1847 club headquarters, covered with hundreds of flats of pansies which disappear by day's end.
Hours: Noon-6pm
Galveston Garden Club, Powhatan House, 3427 Avenue O, Galveston, TX 77550
(409)763-0077

Houston
See also Humble

January 14
⚘ Annual Saide Gwin Blackburn Environmental Seminar
Conservation by Design. A seminar featuring Larry McKinney, Director of Resource Protection, Texas Parks and Wildlife, as speaker.
Hours: 9:30am
Houston Museum of Natural Science, One Herman Circle Drive, Houston, TX
For information: **River Oaks Garden Club**, 2503 Westheimer Road, Houston, TX 77098
Web: www.riveroaksgardenclub.org
(713)526-6228

January 16
⚘ Texas Arbor Day
To honor the state's Arbor Day, distribution of over 2,000 tree seedlings on a first-come basis. Also winter woods walks, exhibits, lectures on tree care and pruning, music and family events.
Hours: 10am-4pm
Fee: Free

Houston Arboretum & Nature Center *(See Texas Guide to Gardens.)*

March 6, 7, 13, 14
꧁ Azalea Trail Home & Garden Tour
A well-known tour, now in its 64th year, of some of Houston's finest private homes and gardens, plus the historic Forum of Civics Building, home of the River Oaks Garden Club, and the Bayou Bend Collection and Gardens, once the estate of the late Houston philanthropist and collector Ima Hogg. Sponsored by the River Oaks Garden Club. Benefits civic beautification, conservation and horticultural efforts in the Houston area.
Hours: 11am-6pm
Fee: $12 in advance; $15 after March 5
For information: **Bayou Bend Collection & Gardens** *(See Texas Guide to Gardens.)*

April 9-11
꧁ African Violet Society of America Exhibition
A show and sale held in conjunction with the Society's annual convention.
Hours: 9am-5pm
Fee: Display is free
Adams Mark Hotel, Westheimer, Houston, TX
For information: **African Violet Society of America**, 2375 North Street, Beaumont, TX 77702
Web: www.avsa.org
Email: offmgr@avsa.org
(800)770-2872

April 24
꧁ Earth Day
A celebration that includes wildflower tours, crafts and music.
Hours: 10am-4pm
Houston Arboretum & Nature Center *(See Texas Guide to Gardens.)*

April 26-28
꧁ Florescence: The Arts in Bloom
A National Garden of America Flower Show, sponsored by the River Oaks Garden Club, the Garden Club of Houston and the Museum of Fine Arts, Houston.
Museum of Fine Arts, 1001 Bissonnet, PO Box 6826, Houston, TX 77265
(713)523-2483 River Oaks Garden Club

November 13
꧁ Arboretum Amble
A walk in the woods over a naturalistic obstacle course and a nature trail, plus sessions on "who's who" in the woods, music, refreshments and live animals.
Hours: 10am-4pm
Houston Arboretum & Nature Center *(See Texas Guide to Gardens.)*

Humble
Near Houston

March 19, 20
꧁ March Mart Plant Sale
A sale that emphasizes hard-to-find plants that do well in the Gulf Coast area. Includes perennials, trees and shrubs, vines, shade plants and tropicals. Experts on hand to answer questions. A major fund raiser sponsored by the Mercer Arboretum Advisory Committee.
Hours: 8am-4pm
Mercer Arboretum & Botanic Gardens *(See Texas Guide to Gardens.)*

March 27, 28 & April 3, 4
꧁ Iris Tours
Guided tours of Mercer's outstanding collection in bloom.
Hours: 10am Sat; noon Sun
Mercer Arboretum & Botanic Gardens *(See Texas Guide to Gardens.)*

August 13, 14
⚜ Ginger Program & Sale
A program and sale of these exotic-looking, hardy flowering plants which comprise one of the highlights of Mercer's collections.
Hours: 10:30 am
Mercer Arboretum & Botanic Gardens (See Texas Guide to Gardens.)

McKinney

April 17, 18
⚜ Native Plant Festival & Sale
Billed as the largest native plant sale in Texas. Features trees, shrubs, vines, ground covers, annuals, perennials and accent plants. Rare and unusual native species available in limited quantities, and experts on hand to answer questions.
Hours: 9am-5pm
Fee: Free
Heard Museum & Wildlife Sanctuary (See Texas Guide to Gardens.)

Round Top

March 10, 17, April 3, 21, May 14
⚜ Herb Days at Round Top
Guided tours of the Herb Gardens, lunch and lecture. Call for registration.
Hours: 11am-2pm
For information: **Institute at Round Top**, PO Drawer 89, Round Top, TX 78954 (409)249-3973

March 27
⚜ Round Top Herb Symposium
An all-day celebration of herbs with lectures, demonstrations, exhibits, delicious food, music and more. Preregistration required; call to register.
For information: **Institute at Round Top**, PO Drawer 89, Round Top, TX 78954 (409)249-3973

May 5
⚜ National Herb Day Celebration
A special day featuring the 1999 Herb of the Year, Lavender. Programs about its cultivation, usage, recipes, lore and legends.
Hours: 11am-2pm
For information: **Institute at Round Top**, PO Drawer 89, Round Top, TX 78954 (409)249-3973

San Antonio

March
⚜ Annual Plant Sale
A sale timed to spring planting. Call for date.
Hours: 9am-5pm
San Antonio Garden Center, 3310 North New Braunfels, San Antonio, TX 78209 (210)824-9981

April 10, 11
⚜ Viva Botanica
A family fair featuring horticultural presentations, plant sales, environmental exhibits, music and food, at a time when the wildflowers and gardens should be at peak bloom.
Hours: 10am-6pm
San Antonio Botanical Garden (See Texas Guide to Gardens.)

September 25
⚜ Gardens by Moonlight
Music and food in the gardens by lantern light and the light of the full moon.
Hours: 7-11pm
San Antonio Botanical Garden (See Texas Guide to Gardens.)

October
⚜ Fall Family Garden Fair
An October vegetable show with children's activities. Call for exact date and information.
San Antonio Botanical Garden (See Texas Guide to Gardens.)

Tyler

October 14-17
66th Texas Rose Festival
Something for everyone, including rose shows, floral shows, arts and crafts, fine art, historic reenactments, a doll, bear and toy show, rambling rose square dance and the Rose Parade. Call or write for schedule.
Tyler Municipal Rose Garden & Rose Museum *(See Texas Guide to Gardens.)*

Waco

March 20, 21
State Garden Show of Texas
A series of seminars by horticulturists and experts on vegetables, organics, landscaping with native plants, canning and more. Includes more than one hundred exhibits of plants, seeds and equipment, as well as garden-related educational exhibits.
Hours: 9am-5pm Sat; noon-5pm Sun
Fee: $5
Heart of Texas Coliseum, 4601 Bosque Blvd, Waco, TX
For information: **Texas Gardener Magazine**, PO Box 9005, Waco, TX 76714
(254)848-9393 *Fax:* (254)848-9779

April 17, 18
Gardening on 5th Street
Features gardening and lawn products, lots of plants and noted speakers, plus tours of the antebellum house.
Hours: 9am-6pm Sat; 10am-6pm Sun
Fee: Free; $2 house tour
The Earle-Harrison House & Pape Gardens *(See Texas Guide to Gardens.)*

Utah

Guide to Gardens

Red Butte Garden & Arboretum
University of Utah, 300 Wakara Way
Salt Lake City, UT 84108
(801)581-4747 or (801)581-5322 *Fax:* (801)585-6491
The site is comprised of hundreds of acres of natural area, mountain trails and display gardens. Highlights include the Four Seasons Garden with views of the valley, the Terrace Gardens with the herb, medicinal and fragrance gardens, the Floral Walk, the Wildflower Meadow and Oak Tunnel.
Web: www.utah.edu/redbutte/
Hours: May-Sep 9am-dusk; Oct-Apr 10am-5pm Tues-Sun
Fees: $3; $2 seniors, children & students

Selected Events

Salt Lake City

March 5-April 12
Equinox Light Show
Lights throughout the Garden to celebrate the Equinox and the coming of spring. Call for information
Red Butte Garden & Arboretum *(See Utah Guide to Gardens.)*

May
Grand Opening of the Children's Garden
Call for the date and a schedule of special events.
Red Butte Garden & Arboretum *(See Utah Guide to Gardens.)*

May 22
❧ 20th Annual Plant Sale
A sale of annuals, perennials, trees and shrubs, vegetables. Experts on hand to give advice and answer questions.
Hours: 9am-5pm
Red Butte Garden & Arboretum (See Utah Guide to Gardens.)

Vermont

Selected Events

Burlington
See also Stowe, Vergennes

September 11
❧ Intervale Festival
A day of events celebrating the renewal of the Intervale, the flood plain region of the Winooski River, now restored to its original fertility by Gardener's Supply and the non-profit Intervale Foundation. Includes a harvest festival, music and hayrides, tours of organic growers, electric car rides, performances by Bread and Butter Theater and more. Participation by many of the region's growers and non-profit organizations.
Hours: 10am-4pm
Fee: $3 per car; walkers & bike riders free
For information: **Gardener's Supply**, 128 Intervale Road, Burlington, VT 05401
Web: www.gardeners.com
Email: info@gardeners.com
(802)660-3505 Fax: (802)660-3501

Putney

July 17
❧ 12th Annual Yellow Barn Garden Tour
An extremely popular day-long self-guided tour of ten private gardens. Several landscape designers on hand at gardens to answer questions. Chamber music and refreshments at selected gardens and a chamber music concert in the evening following the tour. Tickets available by phone or mail in advance from The Yellow Barn or at The Yellow Barn and outlets in the area. Optional gourmet boxed picnic lunch available by reservation, a good idea in this rural area. Benefits The Yellow Barn Music School and Festival, a professional training center for young musicians. Rain date following day. Call to confirm date.
Hours: 9:30am-3:30pm
Fee: $15; $8 boxed lunch; $12 concert
For information: **The Yellow Barn Music School**, Main Street, RR2, PO Box 371, Putney, VT 05346
Web: members.aol.com/ybarn/
Email: ybarn@aol.com
(802)387-6637

Shelburne

May 22, 23
❧ Lilac Festival
The pleasures and pastimes of a Victorian Sunday afternoon when Shelburne's renowned lilac collection is at its peak, with blooms on more than 400 bushes in shades from deep purple and lavender to pink and white.
Hours: 10am-5pm
Shelburne Museum, US Rte 7, Shelburne, VT
Mail: PO Box 10, Shelburne, VT 05482
Web: www.shelburnemuseum.org
(802)985-3346

Stowe
35 miles from Burlington

June 25-27
❧ Stowe Flower Festival
Free tours of many area gardens, talks, demonstrations and goods for sale. Stop at the information tent for maps, schedules, brochures and directions. Call for complete

information on the Festival and lodging.
For information: **Stowe Flower Festival**, PO
Box 1320, Stowe, VT 05672
Web: www.stoweinfo.com
(800)247-8693

Vergennes

30 miles from Burlington

July & August
🌿 6th Annual Flower Days Festival

A summer-long series of garden events,
including a sale of unusual annuals, an auction of plants and garden items, a "mystery
box" flower arranging contest, garden tours,
English High Tea. For schedule and complete
information call or visit the web site.
Fee: Free; parking fee
Basin Harbor Club, Seven miles west of
Vergennes off Rte 22A, Vergennes, VT 05491
Web: www.basinharbor.com
(802)475-2311

Windsor

July 10
🌿 6th Annual Hidden Garden Tour

A tour of a number of the most lovely and spec-
tacular private gardens in the Windsor, Vermont-
Cornish, New Hampshire area. Catered lun-
cheon optional. Call to confirm date.
Hours: 10am-4pm
Fee: $15 in advance; $18 day of tour
For information: **Historic Windsor, Inc.**, 54
Main Street, PO Box 1777, Windsor, VT 05089
Email: HistWinInc@aol.com
(802)674-6752

Virginia
Guide to Gardens

American Horticultural Society
7931 East Boulevard Drive
Alexandria, VA 22308
Email: info@ahs.org
(800)777-7931 *Fax:* (703)768-8700
🌿 AHS headquarters is located at River Farm,
once owned by George Washington, with 25
acres of lawns, gardens, meadows and woods
on the banks of the Potomac River. Open
daily for self-guided tours. Pick up map at
River Farm.
Web: www.ahs.org
Hours: 8:30am-5pm

The Arboretum at James Madison University
Harrisonburg, VA
Mail: 18 Medical Arts East MSC 5701,
Harrisonburg, VA 22807
(540)568-3194 *Fax:* (540)568-1886
🌿 The Arboretum consists of 125 acres of
native oak-hickory forest, with miles of wind-
ing trails leading to diverse habitats, including
a pond with aquatic plants and pond wildlife,
the Andre Viette Perennial Bulb Garden, the
April Walk with fifty-two varieties of daffodils,
a bog garden, rhododendron collection, fern
valley, herb and rock gardens, and one of
Virginia's largest wildflower gardens.
Web: www.jmu.edu/external/arb/
Hours: Dawn-dusk
Fees: Free

Ashlawn Highland
James Monroe Parkway
Charlottesville, VA 22902
Email: ashlawnjm@aol.com
(804)293-9539 *Fax:* (804)293-8000
🌿 Originally the home of James Monroe, the

estate and gardens of Ashlawn Highland have been restored. The site includes an old box-wood garden with specimen plants, an herb garden and kitchen garden.
Web: avenue.org/ashlawn/
Hours: Mar-Oct 9am-6pm; Nov-Feb 10am-5pm
Fees: $7; $6.50 seniors; $4 children

Ben Lomond Manor House
10311 Sudley Manor Drive
Manassas, VA 22110
Email: oldrosegarden@yahoo.com
The Rose Garden at Ben Lomond House was the antique rose collection of Jim Syring, and represents 160 varieties of roses grown between the 1400s and 1867. Bequeathed by Syring to the Lake Jackson Garden Club in 1995, the collection was then donated to the Ben Lomond site and planted there in 1996. It is now maintained and developed by the Garden Club, the Ben Lomond Advisory Board and other organizations. Email the facility for visiting information.
Web: www.geocities.com/~oldrosegarden/

Colonial Williamsburg Foundation
Williamsburg, VA
Mail: PO Box 1776, Williamsburg, VA 23187
(800)447-8679 *Fax:* (757)565-8630
There are ninety residential gardens within this restoration, and twenty-five are open to the public without reservation. The gardens range from small cottage gardens to formal gardens of various styles, including boxwood designs, vegetable gardens, topiaries and espaliered fruit trees.

Glen Burnie Historic House & Gardens
530 Amherst Street
Winchester, VA 22601
Email: glenburn@shentel.net
(540)662-1473 *Fax:* (540)662-8756

There are 25 acres of formal gardens at Glen Burnie, with a series of garden rooms, each with its own character. The spaces range from a small herb garden to a Grand Allée of flowering crabapple trees. Other highlights include a Chinese Garden, formal vegetable garden, perennial cutting garden, rose gardens, water gardens and magnificent lawns.
Hours: Apr-Oct 10am-4pm Tue-Sat, noon-4pm Sun
Fees: $8; $6 seniors, students; $5 gardens only

Green Spring Gardens Park
4603 Green Springs Road
Alexandria, VA 22312
(703)642-5173 *Fax:* (703)642-8095
Green Spring Gardens Park is a 27-acre park located in Alexandria. There are two dozen gardens, an 18th century manor house and a Horticulture Center that offers classes and research facilities.
Web: www.fairfaxcounty-management.com/greenspr.htm
Hours: Dawn-dusk
Fees: Free

Gunston Hall Plantation
10709 Gunston Road
Lorton, VA 22079
(800)811-6966 or (703)550-9220 *Fax:* (703)550-9480
Gunston Hall was built by George Mason, framer of the United States Constitution and author of the Virginia Declaration of Rights. The estate is surrounded by 550 acres, with restored formal gardens containing plants from the colonial period. Twelve-foot high boxwood form an allée in the garden's center, and English box outlines the four parterres. East of the formal gardens are modern plantings including cutting gardens and herb garden.
Web: www.gunstonHall.org

Hours: 9:30am-5pm
Fees: Fee charged

Lewis Ginter Botanical Garden
1800 Lakeside Avenue
Richmond, VA 23228
(804)262-9887 *Fax:* (804)262-9934
The Garden is situated on 90 acres surrounding a lake, and has a large perennial garden, a Japanese tea house garden, children's garden, narcissus and daylily collections, over 850 varieties of daffodils and more.
Hours: 9:30am-4:30pm
Fees: $4; $3 seniors; $2 children 2-12

Mary Washington House & Garden
1200 Charles Street
Fredricksburg, VA
Mail: Association for the Preservation of Virginia Antiquities, 1200 Charles Street, Fredricksburg, VA 22401
(540)373-1569
The Garden reflects Mrs. Washington's planting, and features the same sundial from her time. The large boxwoods she planted line a brick walkway that separates the vegetable garden from the English-style flower garden. Today the house is headquarters for the Mary Washington Branch of the Association for the Preservation of Virgina Antiquities, which administers this house, Saint James' House (open by appointment only), Hugh Mercer Apothecary Shop and Rising Sun Tavern.
Hours: Mar-Nov 9am-5pm; Dec-Feb 10am-4pm
Fees: House & garden $4; garden $2

Maymont Foundation
1700 Hampton Street
Richmond, VA 23220
(804)358-7166 *Fax:* (804)358-9994
An intact 100-acre late Victorian country estate, Maymont is on the banks of the James River in the heart of Richmond. Features include beautifully landscaped grounds, Italian, Japanese and herb gardens, and a Children's Farm.
Web: www.maymont.org

Norfolk Botanical Garden
Azalea Garden Road
Norfolk, VA 23518
(757)441-5830 *Fax:* (757)853-8294
The 155-acre Garden has a huge collection of azaleas representing 700 varieties, plus rhododendron, dogwood and camellia collections. Theme gardens include the Camellia Garden, the 3.5-acre Rose Garden, the Fragrance, English Border, Sunken, Healing and Four Seasons gardens, and Wildflower Meadows.
Web: www.communitylink.org/nbg/
Fees: $4; $3 seniors; $2 children

Oatlands Plantation
20850 Oatlands Plantation Lane
Leesburg, VA 22075
(703)777-3174 *Fax:* (703)777-4427
This Federal style mansion of 1800 has been completely restored with formal gardens, terraced gardens with a 150-year old boxwood gazebo, reflecting pool, specimen oaks planted by the original owner, plus magnolias, a boxwood allée, a bowling green and many species of trees and flowering shrubs.
Hours: 10am-4:30pm; 1-4:30pm Sun
Fees: $6; $5 seniors, students

Orland E. White Arboretum
State Arboretum of Virginia, US Route 50
Boyce, VA
Mail: Route 2, Box 210, Boyce, VA 22620
(540)837-1758 *Fax:* (540)837-1523
The Arboretum features the largest collection of boxwood in North America, and more than

half the world's pine species, as well as the Virginia native plant trail, herb garden, perennials, daylilies and azaleas. A three mile loop drive winds through a grove of 350 ginkgo trees.
Web: www.virginia.edu/~blandy/
Hours: Dawn-dusk every day
Fees: Free

Stratford Hall Plantation
Route 214
Stratford, VA
Mail: Robert E. Lee Memorial Association
Stratford, VA 22558
(804)493-8038 or (804)493-8371 weekends & holidays *Fax:* (804)493-0333
🌿 The birthplace of Robert E. Lee, this plantation is operated as it would have been in the mid-19th century. In addition to cultivated fields, woodlands and meadows, there are formal gardens with boxwood, a rose garden, herb and kitchen gardens and flowering shrubs.
Web: www.stratfordhall.org
Hours: 9:30am-4:30pm
Fees: $7; $6 seniors; $3 children

Woodlawn Plantation
9000 Richmond Highway
Alexandria, VA 22309
(703)780-4000 *Fax:* (703)780-8509
🌿 Woodlawn was built on land overlooking the Potomac and given to George Washington's foster daughter as a wedding gift. The 20 acres of gardens are beautifully restored, with parterre gardens of old fashioned roses which are at their peak in late May. Nature trails wind through the estate.
Hours: 10am-4pm; noon-4pm Sun
Fees: $6; $4 seniors, students

Woodrow Wilson Birthplace & Gardens
18-24 North Coalter Street
Staunton, VA
Mail: PO Box 24, Staunton, VA 24402

Email: woodrowwilson@juno.com
(540)885-0897 *Fax:* (540)886-9874
🌿 These gardens were restored in the early 1930s by Charles F. Gillette, with boxwood beds and terraced gardens.
Hours: 9am-5pm
Fees: Fee charged

Selected Events

Statewide

April 17-24
🌿 **Historic Garden Week in Virginia**
Tours of more than thirty areas of the state, from the Atlantic to the Appalachians. A detailed Guidebook available by sending a $4 donation to the Historic Garden Week Headquarters. Tickets can be obtained on day(s) of tour at each house or the local tour center. Call or visit the HGW web site for more information. Billed as "America's largest open house," now in its 66th year. Sponsored by The Garden Club of Virginia and its local garden clubs. Proceeds fund grounds and gardens restorations of Historic Landmarks in Virginia.
Hours: 10am-5pm unless otherwise noted in Guidebook
Fee: $15-$20 block tickets; $3-$5 single house admission
For information: **Historic Garden Week Headquarters**, 12 East Franklin Street, Richmond, VA 23219
Web: www.VAGardenweek.org
Email: gdnweek@erols.com
(804)644-7776

Alexandria

May 9-13
🌿 **Rose Garden Teas**
An annual tea in the Underwood Dining Room

when the Woodlawn heritage rose collection is in full bloom, one of the largest and oldest collections in the area. Includes tours of the Mansion guided by the property director and garden tours led by the site rosarian. Reservations required.

Fee: $20

Woodlawn Plantation (See Virginia Guide to Gardens.)

June 20
✿ River Farm Discovery Day & Daylily Day

Events for adults and children. Tours of the gardens, demonstrations, activities, food, plant sale. Held at George Washington's Farm at the AHS site.

American Horticultural Society (See Virginia Guide to Gardens.)

October 3
✿ River Farm Discovery Day & Harvest Festival

Tours of the gardens, demonstrations, activities, food, plant sale, events for adults and children. Held at George Washington's Farm at the AHS site.

American Horticultural Society (See Virginia Guide to Gardens.)

Boyce
9 miles east of Winchester

May 8, 9
✿ Garden Fair & Plant Sale

Free garden lectures, educational programs for children, an enormous array of woody and herbaceous plant material for sale, plus gardening supplies, seeds and books. One of Northern Virginia's largest horticultural events. Sponsored by the Foundation of the State Arboretum of Virginia.

Hours: 10am-4:30pm

Fee: $3 donation for parking

Orland E. White Arboretum (See Virginia Guide to Gardens.)

October
✿ Arborfest

An annual celebration focusing on different aspects of arborculture and horticulture each year. Free guided tours of the ginkgos and maples, lots of demonstrations, lectures, food and activities for everyone. Call for exact date.

Hours: Noon-5pm

Fee: Donation requested

Orland E. White Arboretum (See Virginia Guide to Gardens.)

Charlottesville

April 17-24
✿ Historic Garden Week

Tours of the house and gardens of Ashlawn Highland, the home of President James Monroe. Other activities include a Champagne and Candlelight event on Sunday, April 18, with the house and gardens illuminated and period music performed. Part of a state-wide celebration of Historic Garden Week.

Hours: 9am-6pm; candlelight tour 7:30-9:30pm

Fee: $7; $6.50 seniors; $3.00 children 6-11; $8 candlelight tour

Ashlawn Highland (See Virginia Guide to Gardens.)

Fredricksburg

September 17-19
✿ Our Living Legacies

A tour of Mary Washington House and Garden, as well as the Rising Sun Tavern, Mercer Apothecary Shop and St. James House, all with small gardens. Special exhibits and demonstrations honoring crafts of the 18th and 19th centuries.

Hours: 9am-5pm

Fee: $4; $1.50 children
Mary Washington House & Garden *(See Virginia Guide to Gardens.)*

Leesburg

April 18, 19
❧ Catoctin Rural Historic District

Open days at seven properties with interesting architectural and horticultural features: Temple Hall, Sunnyside, Rockland, Noland's Ferry, Montresor, Christ Church and Daydream. Part of Historic Garden Week in Virginia.
Hours: 1-5pm Sun; 10am-5pm Mon
Fee: $20 block ticket; $4 single site admission
For information: **Leesburg Garden Club**, PO Box 49, Leesburg, VA 20160
Web: www.leesburggardenweek.com
(703)777-6281 or (800)752-6118

April 24, 25
❧ Leesburg Flower & Garden Festival

A festival with landscape displays, retail booths, guided walking tours of historic downtown Leesburg, musical entertainment, food and drink, children's activities and more.
Hours: 10am-6pm Sat; 10am-4pm Sun
Fee: $3; $2 children; under 6 free
Historic Downtown Leesburg, King & Market Streets, Leesburg, VA
For information: **Leesburg Flower & Garden Festival**, 50 Ida Lee Drive NW, Leesburg, VA 22075
Web: www.idalee.org
(703)777-1262

May 1
❧ May Herb Fair

Sponsored by the Goode Creek Herb Guild.
Hours: 10am-4pm
Fee: Admission $6; $5 seniors & students
Oatlands Plantation *(See Virginia Guide to Gardens.)*

Middleburg

June 15, 16
❧ Middleburg Gardens Tours

A self-guided driving tour of five private estate gardens located in the beautiful countryside of this renowned horse and hunt country.
For information: **Middleburg Beautification & Preservation Society, Inc.**, PO Box 2034, Middleburg, VA 20118
(540)687-3360

Mount Vernon

April 17-May 2
❧ Gardening Days at Mount Vernon

An annual outdoor plant, gift and garden sale in George Washington's historic upper garden, when the magnificent formal and vegetable gardens are at their best. Plus horticultural and agricultural displays in the greenhouse and greenhouse tours on Tuesdays and Thursdays.
Hours: 9am-5pm
Fee: fee charged
George Washington's Mount Vernon, GW Memorial Parkway, PO Box 110, Mount Vernon, VA 22121
(703)780-2000

New Castle

June-September
❧ Fenwick Mines Wetland Trail

Self-guided tour along the trail, past the Scented Herb Garden planted by the New Castle Garden Club, nestled between two old wash ponds from mining days. Good place to view wildflowers, mountain laurel and rhododendron in spring and fall foliage in the fall.
Hours: Always open
Fee: Free
For information: **New Castle Garden Club**, PO Box 30, New Castle, VA 24127
(540)864-5195

October 9
✿ Fall Festival Day
Activities on Main Street in New Castle, including crafts, homemade breads, jams and jellies, tours of the Old Brick Hotel. A good time to walk the Fenwick Mines Wetlands Trail. Sponsored by the Craig County Historical Society.
Hours: 8am-5:30pm
Fee: Free
For information: **New Castle Garden Club**, PO Box 30, New Castle, VA 24127 (540)864-5195

Norfolk

May 7-9
✿ Spring Plant Sale
An annual sale of a large variety of spring annuals, perennials, rare plants, shrubs, trees, grasses and herbs. Plus a gift shop sale, "Ask the Plant Doctor" booth, plant society members on hand, vendors, food and more.
Fee: Free
Norfolk Botanical Garden *(See Virginia Guide to Gardens.)*

May 9
✿ Mother's Day
Free entry for any mother when accompanied by her child on this special day.
Norfolk Botanical Garden *(See Virginia Guide to Gardens.)*

June 20
✿ Father's Day
Free entry for any father when accompanied by his child on this special day.
Norfolk Botanical Garden *(See Virginia Guide to Gardens.)*

Richmond

February 18-21
✿ Maymont Flower & Garden Show

Once Upon A Garden. Dozens of exhibition landscapes, displays by garden clubs and organizations, vendors of horticultural items, and lectures by garden experts. Now in its 10th year. Benefits Maymont Foundation, a park encompassing formal gardens, a house museum and native wildlife.
Hours: 9am-8pm Thurs-Sat; 9am-6pm Sun
Fee: $10 in advance; $12 at door; $18 2-day pass; $30 4-day pass
Richmond Centre, 400 East Marshall Street, Richmond, VA
For information: **Maymont Foundation** *(See Virginia Guide to Gardens.)*

April 16, 17
✿ Spring Garden Fair & Plant Sale
Plants offered by over 40 vendors, books and gifts, plus children's activities and door-prizes. Organized by the Garden's corps of volunteers.
Hours: 10:30am-6pm Fri; 9am-3pm Sat
Fee: Free
Lewis Ginter Botanical Garden *(See Virginia Guide to Gardens.)*

April 24
✿ Maymont's Herbs Galore
A full day of herb-related seminars and sales. Includes cooking class with an expert and a chance to gather herbs and ideas at the Market on the Lawn. Early registration is advisable as seminars fill up faster every year.
Hours: 9am-5pm
Fee: Free admission; seminar fees vary
Maymont Foundation *(See Virginia Guide to Gardens.)*

July 31
✿ Gardenfest for Children
A day of learning for everyone focusing on the importance of plants in day-to-day life.
Hours: 9:30am-4pm

Fee: Admission $4; $3 seniors; $2 children 2-12
Lewis Ginter Botanical Garden (*See Virginia Guide to Gardens.*)

September
❦ Fall Garden Fair & Plant Sale
Great deals from over 40 vendors on plants, books, and gifts in time for the best planting season. Activities for children. Call for exact date.
Hours: 10:30am-6pm Fri; 9am-3pm Sat
Fee: Free
Lewis Ginter Botanical Garden (*See Virginia Guide to Gardens.*)

Roanoke

April 17
❦ A Friendly Street Tour
A tour of local homes and gardens sponsored by the Roanoke Valley Garden Club as part of Virginia's Historic Garden Week. Lunch available.
Hours: 10am-5pm
Fee: $12 tour; $7 lunch
For information: **Roanoke Valley Garden Club**, 3260 Allendale Street, Roanoke, VA 24014
(540)343-4519

Staunton

April 24
❦ Open Garden Day
Open garden day, part of Historic Garden Week in Virginia.
Hours: 9am-5pm
Fee: fee charged
Woodrow Wilson Birthplace & Gardens (*See Virginia Guide to Gardens.*)

Upperville

April 13
❦ Daffodil Show & Tea
Blends Virginia style and hospitality with exhibitions of the latest high tech hybrids and floral designs in a show that attracts exhibitors from the Tristate area and beyond. Open to amateur growers, with entries accepted Wednesday, April 12, from 2-5pm and Thursday, April 13, from 8-10:30am. Now in its 36th year and accredited by the American Daffodil Society for its horticulture competition. Sponsored by the Upperville Garden Club.
Hours: 2-5pm
Fee: Donation requested
Trinity Parish House, US Route 50, Upperville, VA
For information: **Upperville Garden Club**, 301 Archer Court, Berryville, VA 22611
(540)955-0428

Virginia Beach

January 22-24
❦ Virginia Flower & Garden Show
Landscape display gardens, judged displays, seminars, lectures and demonstrations, speakers, garden marketplace, activities, the show of the Tidewater District of the Virginia Federation of Garden Clubs, floral photography and more. Special packages available for out-of-town visitors. Call for complete information.
Hours: 10am-6pm Fri; 10am-8pm Sat; 10am-5pm Sun
Fee: $6
Virginia Beach Pavilion, Route 44, Virginia Beach, VA
For information: **Virginia Flower & Garden Show**, 1271-330 Great Neck Village, Virginia Beach, VA 23454
Web: www.virginiagardens.org
(757)853-0057

April 20
✿ Historic Garden Week House & Garden Tour

A tour of five homes and a garden with refreshments in the garden from 1-4pm. Sponsored by the Virginia Beach Garden Club.
Hours: 10am-6pm
Fee: $15 block ticket; $5 single house tour
For information: **Virginia Beach Garden Club**, 1220 Crystal Lake Circle, Virginia Beach, VA 23451
(757)425-0419

Warrenton

April 21, 22
✿ House & Garden Tour

A tour of approximately six local homes and gardens sponsored by the Warrenton Garden Club as part of Virginia's Historic Garden Week.
Hours: 10am-5pm
Fee: $15 block tickets; $5 single house admission
For information: **Warrenton Garden Club**, 8481 Lock Lane, Warrenton, VA 20186
(540)347-5138

July 4
✿ 6th Annual Fair at Airlie

A farmer's market, antique show and crafters booths, demonstrations, food and children's activities. Plus nature walks through the grounds at Airlie, fly fishing on the lake, and a tour through the butterfly gardens. Sponsored by the Piedmont Environmental Council.
Hours: Noon-5pm
Fee: $10 car
Airlie Conference Center, Warrenton, VA
For information: **Piedmont Environmental Council**, 45 Horner Street, PO Box 460, Warrenton, VA 22186
Email: pec@mnsinc.com
(540)347-2334

Williamsburg

March 28-31
✿ Symposium

Celebrating American Garden Design. The 53rd annual symposium with lectures, tours, Master Classes, demonstration classes and a faculty of well-known garden lecturers, horticulturists and writers. Attracts over 200 horticultural professionals and home gardening enthusiasts annually. Co-sponsored by the American Horticultural Society. For complete symposium information call (757)220-7255.
Fee: $250.
For information: **Colonial Williamsburg Foundation** *(See Virginia Guide to Gardens.)*

Winchester
See also Boyce

June 4, July 2, August 6
✿ Gardens at Night

Gardens illuminated on these three nights.
Hours: 6-10pm
Fee: $5; $3 seniors, students
Glen Burnie Historic House & Gardens *(See Virginia Guide to Gardens.)*

June 19
✿ How Does Your Garden Grow?

An interactive tour for children of Glen Burnie's gardens and chance to create a decorative box garden to take home.
Hours: 11am-3pm
Fee: fee charged
Glen Burnie Historic House & Gardens *(See Virginia Guide to Gardens.)*

Washington

American-Japanese Garden
Reton Avenue South & 55th Avenue
Seattle, WA
Mail: Kubota Garden Foundation, PO Box
78338 , Seattle, WA 98178
(206)725-5060
🌸 This extraordinary Garden on 20 acres of
hills and valleys is the work of Fujitaro
Kubitaro, an entirely self-taught gardener who
wanted to display the beauty of the Northwest
in the Japanese manner. The site was his family home and landscape business and has
since been acquired by the city of Seattle and
declared an Historic Landmark.
Hours: Dawn-dusk
Fees: Free

Bellevue Botanical Garden
12001 Main Street
Bellevue, WA
Mail: PO Box 40536, Bellevue, WA 98005
(425)452-2750 *Fax:* (425)452-2748
🌸 The Bellevue Botanical Garden comprises
36 acres of display gardens, rolling hills,
woodlands, meadows and wetlands in
Wilburton Hill Park. The most famous feature is
the Northwest Perennial Alliance Border,
designed, planted and maintained by a dedicated group of volunteers. The Alliance also
maintains a 6,000 square-foot mixed border of
shade plants and an adjacent shrub border.
Other highlights include an Alpine and Rock
Garden, featuring native alpine meadow and
bog plants as well as introduced species, a
Waterwise Demonstration Garden and the first
phase of a new Eastern Garden. The Garden
includes noteworthy collections of rhododendrons, ground covers and other natives.

Hours: 7:30am-dusk
Fees: Free

The Bloedel Reserve
7571 NE Dolphin Drive
Bainbridge Island, WA 98110
(206)842-7631 *Fax:* (206)842-8970
🌸 This former private residence on
Bainbridge Island in Puget Sound combines
second-growth forest on one half of the prop-
erty and landscaped spaces on the other half.
Among its features are a Bird Sanctuary,
English-style landscaped lawn areas looking
out to the sound, a Moss Garden, a Japanese
Garden designed by Kubota, a Reflection
Garden and Woodland Garden. Reservations
required.
Web: www.bloedelreserve.org
Hours: 10am-4pm Wed-Sun by reservation
Fees: $6; $4 seniors, children

Carl S. English, Jr. Garden
3015 NW 54th Street
Seattle, WA
Mail: Seattle District US Army Corps of
Engineers, PO Box C-3755, Seattle, WA 98124
(206)783-7059 *Fax:* (206)783-7001
🌸 The 7-acre Garden and arboretum is situated alongside the Hiram M. Chittenden Locks of
the Lake Washington Ship Canal. It is the work
of Carl S. English, Jr. who grew many of the
more than 500 species of trees, shrubs and
woody plants from seeds he gathered from all
over the world. A quarter mile self-guided tour
leads through a good sample of the collections.
Hours: 7am-8pm; Visitor Center Jun 15-Sep
14 11am-8pm, Sep 15-Jun 14 11am-5pm
Thur-Mon
Fees: Free

Conservatory at Volunteer Park
Seattle, WA
Mail: Friends of the Conservatory at Volunteer

Park, 1402 East Galer Street, Seattle, WA
98112
Email: marylamb@msn.com
(206)322-4112
🌿 This Victorian glass Conservatory was
designed in 1912 in the style of London's
Crystal Palace and is a focal point of the north
end of Volunteer Park. The Conservatory con-
sists of five spaces: The Palm House, the
Seasonal Display House, the Cactus and
Succulent House, the Fern House and the
Bromeliad House.
Hours: 10am-4pm
Fees: Free

Elisabeth C. Miller Botanical Gardens
Olympic Drive, The Highlands
Seattle, WA
Mail: PO Box 77377, Seattle, WA 98177
Email: 104343.561@compuserve.com
(206)362-8612 *Fax:* (206)362-4136
🌿 This garden is known for its fine collection
of trees, shrubs and woody plants.
Reservations required.
Hours: 10am-1pm Wed, Thurs by
appointment only
Fees: Free

Lakewold Gardens
12317 Gravelly Lake Drive SW
Lakewood, WA 98499
(888)858-4106 *Fax:* (253)584-3021
🌿 Lakewold is a 10-acre public estate garden, with formal gardens and naturalistic displays. Highlights include woodland areas,
aquatic displays, rock and alpine gardens,
shade, rose and fern gardens. The collections
feature hundreds of species of Rhododendron
and over thirty varieties of Japanese maples.
Lakewold was designed by the landscape
architect Thomas Church.
Web: www.lakewold.org
Hours: Apr-Sep 10am-4pm Thurs-Mon, noon-

8pm Fri; Oct-Mar 10am-3pm Fri-Sun
Fees: $5; $3 seniors & students; under 6 free

Manito Park
South Grand Blvd at 18th
Spokane, WA
Mail: Spokane Parks & Recreation
Department, West 808 Spokane Falls Blvd,
Spokane, WA 99201
(509)625-6622
🌿 Highlights of this Park include the formal
Duncan Garden, the Gaiser Conservatory with
seasonal shows and collections of tropical
plants, the Perennial Garden, Rose Hill,
Japanese Garden, Lilac Garden and Duck Pond.
Hours: Dawn-dusk
Fees: Free

Point Defiance Park
5600 North Pearl Street
Tacoma, WA
Mail: Metro Park Tacoma Administration,
4702 South19th Street, Tacoma, WA 98405
(253)591-5328 *Fax:* (206)591-2049
🌿 Point Defiance Park has several special
gardens including the Japanese Garden, the
Herb Garden, Rhododendron Garden, Rose
Garden, Iris Garden, Dahlia Trial Garden, and
Northwest Native Garden. It's managed by
Metro Park Tacoma, a city agency that also
maintains The Ouget Gardens, the Nature
Center, and the W. W. Seymour Botanical
Conservatory at Wright Park. (See other listing
in this Guide.)
Web: www.tacomaparks.com
Hours: Dawn-dusk
Fees: Free

The Rhododendron Species Foundation Garden & Pacific Rim Bonsai Garden
Weyerhaeuser Headquarters, 2525 South
336th Street
Federal Way, WA

Mail: PO Box 3798, Federal Way, WA 98063
Email: rsf@halcyon.com
(253)838-4646; Bonsai Garden
(253)924-3153 *Fax:* (253)838-4686
🌺 This garden, dedicated to the conservation of Rhododendron species, has many special features, including a a woodland garden, hardy fern collection, alpine and pond gardens, heather display, magnolia grove, greenhouse and excellent collections of rhododendrons and azaleas. Adjacent to this site is a bonsai collection owned and maintained by the Weyerhaeuser Company which can be visited by appointment.
Web: www.halcyon.com/rsf/
Hours: Mar-May 10am-4pm, closed Thurs; Jun-Feb 11am-4pm, closed Thurs, Fri
Fees: $3.50; $2.50 seniors, students

W. W. Seymour Botanical Conservatory
316 South G Street
Tacoma, WA
Mail: Metro Park Tacoma Administration, 4702 South 19th Street, Tacoma, WA 98405
(253)591-5330
🌺 Situated in Wright Park, the Conservatory features seasonal flower displays, orchids, cacti and tropical plants.
Web: www.tacomaparks.com
Hours: 10am-4:30pm
Fees: Free

Washington Park Arboretum
2300 Arboretum Drive East
Seattle, WA 98112
(206)325-4510 *Fax:* (206)325-7426
🌺 The Washington Park Arboretum encompasses 230 acres on the shores of Lake Washington, with collections of oaks, conifers, camellias, Japanese maples, hollies and woody plants from the Pacific Northwest and around

the world. Highlights include the Japanese Garden, the Waterfront Trail and Azalea Way.
Web: weber.u.washington.edu/~wpa/index.html
Hours: 10am-4pm
Fees: Free; fee for Japanese Garden

Yakima Area Arboretum
1401 Arboretum Drive
Yakima, WA 98901
(509)248-7337 *Fax:* (509)248-8197
🌺 A botanical oasis in the arid desert of central Washington, the Arboretum is a 35-acre irrigated test site for plants tolerant of this extreme climate. The Arboretum has an eleven-acre native wetland, research and community outreach activities.
Web: www.ahtrees.org
Hours: 9am-5pm Tue-Fri; 9am-4pm Sat
Fees: Free

Selected Events

Bainbridge Island
30 minutes by ferry from Seattle

July 10, 11
🌺 **Bainbridge in Bloom Garden Tour**
A tour of six private gardens on Bainbridge Island. Includes a plant sale, garden art and crafts fair, book sale and lectures. Benefits the Bainbridge Island Arts and Humanities Council.
Hours: 11am-5pm
Fee: $20
For information: **Bainbridge Island Arts & Humanities Council**, 261 Madison Avenue South, Bainbridge Island, WA 98110
Email: biahc@linknet.kitsap.lib.wa.us
(206)842-7901

Bellevue

Near Seattle

May 1
🌼 Plant Sale
Annual sale timed to spring planting.
Bellevue Botanical Garden *(See Washington Guide to Gardens.)*

May-September
🌼 Northwest Perennial Alliance Open Gardens Days
Open garden days at approximately 50 private gardens of Northwest Perennial Alliance members in the greater Seattle area. Self-guided mini-tours on some weekends, when several gardens are featured in one geographic area. A booklet containing dates, times, a brief description and driving directions available from the sponsor.
Fee: $20; includes membership in NPA & quarterly newsletter
For information: **Northwest Perennial Alliance**, 8830 Points Drive, Bellevue, WA 98004
Email: mraitz@accessone.com
(206)324-0179

May 9
🌼 Mother's Day Plant Sale
An annual sale with refreshments and entertainment at a time when the rhododendrons are at their peak.
Hours: 1-3pm
Fee: Free
Bellevue Botanical Garden *(See Washington Guide to Gardens.)*

December
🌼 Garden D'Lights
A festival of lights when the gardens are illuminated for the holidays.
Bellevue Botanical Garden *(See Washington Guide to Gardens.)*

Bellingham

June 26, 27
🌼 13th Annual Tour of Private Gardens
A tour of six of Bellingham's finest private gardens.
Hours: 11am-5pm
Fee: $8; $4 children
For information: **Whatcom in Bloom Garden Society**, PO Box 4443, Bellingham, WA 98227
(360)738-6833

Federal Way

April 9, 10
🌼 Annual Spring Plant Sale
Thousands of rare and unusual plants of all sizes, including landscape-size, with a wide variety of rhododendrons, azaleas, ferns, heather, maples, dwarf conifers, bonsai, alpines.
Hours: 3-6pm Fri; 9am-3pm Sat
Fee: Free
The Rhododendron Species Foundation Garden & The Pacific Rim Bonsai Garden *(See Washington Guide to Gardens.)*

September 19
🌼 Fall Plant Sale
Thousands of unusual plants of all sizes, including landscape-size, with a wide variety of rhododendrons, azaleas, ferns, heather, dwarf conifers, alpines and more.
Hours: 9am-3pm
Fee: Free
The Rhododendron Species Foundation Garden & The Pacific Rim Bonsai Garden *(See Washington Guide to Gardens.)*

Okanogan

July 10
🌼 Shady Creek Pond & Garden Tour
A self-guided tour of outstanding gardens in Okanogan Valley. Ticket price includes a

catered luncheon at Shady Creek Gardens & Ponds. Proceeds benefit Okanogan Valley Master Gardener Foundation and its Native Plants of Okanogan County Garden, 130 2nd Avenue North, open from May-August.

Hours: 9am-4pm
Fee: $12
For information: **Okanogan Valley Master Gardener Foundation**, 1989 Old 97 Road, Okanogan, WA 98840
(509)422-4272

Port Townsend

May 9-17
🌿 Rhododendron Festival

A celebration of the state flower which includes a rhododendron show, carnival, craft fairs and a parade the last Saturday.

Fee: Most events free
For information: **Port Townsend Chamber of Commerce**, 2437 East Sims Way, Port Townsend, WA 98368
(888)365-6978

Pt. Hadlock

June
🌿 Secret Garden Tour

A tour of private gardens which have been prepared and plants labeled for identification by the Master Gardeners. Call for exact date.

Hours: 11am-4pm
Fee: $8
For information: **Jefferson County Master Gardeners**, 201 West Patison, Pt. Hadlock, WA 98339
(360)379-5610

Puyallup

April 16-18
🌿 American Primrose Society National Flower Show

Held in conjunction with the Spring Fair. Exhibitions by members and nonmembers, plus Rock Garden Society exhibitions and plant sale. Hosted by the Tacoma Chapter and the Rock Garden Society.

Western Washington Farigrounds, Expo Building, Puyallup, WA
For information: **American Primrose Society**, 6911 104th Street East, Puyallup, WA 98373
(253)841-4192

Seattle

See also Bainbridge Island & Bellevue

Center for Urban Horticulture

E.C. Miller Library, 3501 NE 45th Street
Seattle, WA
Mail: PO Box 354115, Seattle, WA 98195
(206)685-8033
🌿 The Center for Urban Horticulture holds many of its programs at the Miller Library. Call for a schedule of their monthly lectures, symposia, workshops, tours and classes.

February 17-21
🌿 11th Annual Northwest Flower & Garden Show

The third largest spring flower show in North America. Features thirty designed gardens, acres of educational and commercial exhibits, an expanded orchid show, lectures and demonstrations.

Hours: 9am-9:30pm Wed-Sat; 9am-7pm Sun
Fee: Fee charged
Washington State Convention and Trade Center, 9th & Pike Streets, Seattle, WA
For information: **Northwest Flower & Garden Show**, 1515 NW 51st Street, Seattle, WA 98107
Web: www.gardenshow.com
(800)229-6311

April
⚜ Fuchsia Spring Plant Sale
Many fuchsias plus other plants. Call for exact date and for sales in July and August.
Hours: 9am-2pm
Lake City Community Center, 12531 28th NE, Seattle, WA
For information: **Northwest Fuchsia Society**, PO Box 33071, Seattle, WA 98133
(206)364-7735

April 24, 25
⚜ 50th Annual Plant Sale
Florabundance. Held this year in an airplane hangar that holds "three tennis courts of sale plants." More than 50 participating nurseries. One of the largest plant sales in the region.
Hours: 10am-5pm
Fee: Free
Sand Point Naval Air Station, Seattle, WA
For information: **Washington Park Arboretum** (*See Washington Guide to Gardens.*)

May
⚜ Annual Plant Sale
A great variety of plants, including those similar to plants found at the Garden. Call for exact date.
Fee: Free
American-Japanese Garden (*See Washington Guide to Gardens.*)

May 8
⚜ Spring Plant Sale
A selection of plants like those in the Conservatory, including blooming orchids, bromeliads, flowering and foliage plants and, for Spring, a selection of hardy perennials and fuchsia baskets. Held in front of the Conservatory and sponsored by the Friends of the Conservatory.
Hours: 10am-4pm
Fee: Free

Conservatory at Volunteer Park (*See Washington Guide to Gardens.*)

May 15
⚜ Fuchsia & Perennial Sale
Sponsored by the Greater Seattle Fuchsia Society.
Hours: 9am-3pm
Fee: Free
Greater Seattle Fuchsia Society, 12735 1st Avenue NW, Seattle, WA 98177
(206)364-7735

July 17
⚜ West Seattle Garden Tour
An annual tour of eight gardens, with artists and music. Proceeds benefit Art West, West Seattle's community-based non-profit arts organization. Advance tickets available May 1.
Hours: 9am-5pm
Fee: $12
For information: **West Seattle Garden Tour**, PO Box 16152, Seattle, WA 98136
(206)938-0963

July 24, 25
⚜ Annual Fuchsia Society Show
A judged show presented by the Greater Seattle Fuchsia Society
Hours: 9am-4pm
Fee: Free
Swanson's Nursery, 9701 15th Avenue, NW, Seattle, WA
For information: **Greater Seattle Fuchsia Society**, 12735 1st Avenue NW, Seattle, WA 98177
(206)364-7735

September
⚜ Fall Plant Sale
The Autumn version of the May event. Call for exact date.
Fee: Free

American-Japanese Garden *(See Washington Guide to Gardens.)*

September 18
❧ Spring Plant Sale
A selection of plants like those in the Conservatory, including blooming orchids, bromeliads, flowering and foliage plants. Held in front of the Conservatory and sponsored by the Friends. Call to confirm the date.
Hours: 10am-4pm
Fee: Free
Conservatory at Volunteer Park *(See Washington Guide to Gardens.)*

Early October
❧ Fall Bulb Sale
An opportunity to plan your Spring garden from a wide selection of bulbs and plants, including many hard-to-find varieties. Held at the Graham Visitors Center. Call for exact date.
Hours: 11am-5pm
Washington Park Arboretum *(See Washington Guide to Gardens.)*

Spokane

May 15
❧ 61st Armed Forces Lilac Festival Torchlight Parade
A torchlight parade which ends in the park, where lilacs are in full bloom. Part of the annual festival of the "The Lilac City." A fundraiser for senior high school scholarships.
Hours: 7:45pm
For information: **Spokane Lilac Festival Association**, 315 W Mission, Suite 24, Spokane, WA 99201
(509)326-3339

Tacoma

February 3-7
❧ Tacoma Home & Garden Show
Garden products, new bulbs, garden society exhibits, landscaped gardens, plus speakers and demonstrations at every hour of the show.
Hours: noon-9pm Wed-Thurs; 11am-10pm Fri-Sat; 11am-6pm Sun
Fee: $7
Tacoma Dome, Tacoma, WA
For information: **Tacoma Home & Garden Show**, PO Box 110849, Tacoma, WA 98411
Web: otstacoma.org
(253)756-2121

February 13, 14
❧ Winter Plant Sale
Flowering annuals, perennials and foliage plants for sale. Held in the Seymour Botanical Conservatory.
Hours: 10am-4pm
Fee: Free
W. W. Seymour Botanical Conservatory, 316 South G Street, Tacoma, WA
For information: **Point Defiance Park** *(See Washington Guide to Gardens.)*

May 1
❧ Spring Garden Fair & Plant Sale
Potted perennials, house plants, used books and horticultural displays. Refreshments available. Sponsored by Capital District garden clubs. Held inside the Pagoda Building.
Hours: 10am-3pm
Point Defiance Park *(See Washington Guide to Gardens.)*

May 29, 30
❧ Spring Plant Sale
A good chance to purchase flowering annuals and perennials for the summer garden. Proceeds benefit the W.W. Seymour Botanical Conservatory.

Hours: 10am-4pm
Fee: Free
Point Defiance Greenhouse, 5400 North Shirley, east of go-cart track, Tacoma, WA
For information: **Point Defiance Park** *(See Washington Guide to Gardens.)*

June 18, September 17
🌿 A Morning in the Herb Garden
Share plants, information and use of herbs. Held at the Herb Garden, near the Rose Garden, at Point Defiance Park. Sponsored by the Horticulture Study Club, which planted and maintains the Herb Garden.
Hours: 10am-1pm
Fee: Free
Point Defiance Park *(See Washington Guide to Gardens.)*

August 14, 15
🌿 Fuchsia Display
A display of many hardy fuchsias, put on by the Tacoma Fuchsia Society and held in the Pagoda.
Hours: 10am-3pm
Point Defiance Park *(See Washington Guide to Gardens.)*

Fall Plant Sale
🌿 Spring Plant Sale
A good chance to purchase fall annuals, garden mums, perennials and house plants. Proceeds benefit the W.W. Seymour Botanical Conservatory.
Hours: 10am-4pm
Fee: Free
Point Defiance Greenhouse, 5400 North Shirley, east of go-cart track, Tacoma, WA
For information: **Point Defiance Park** *(See Washington Guide to Gardens.)*

September 25, 26
🌿 Chrysanthemum Show
A show presented by the Capitol District Garden Club. Held inside the Pagoda Building.
Hours: 10am-3pm
Point Defiance Park *(See Washington Guide to Gardens.)*

Yakima

April 24
🌿 Spring Plant Sale
Climate-tested plants for an instant garden. Sponsored by the Friends of the Arboretum, Bonsai Society, Master Gardeners and Native Plant Society.
Hours: 9am-sellout
Fee: Free
Yakima Area Arboretum *(See Washington Guide to Gardens.)*

May 8, 9
🌿 Mother's Day Weekend
The planting of 5000 petunias along the banks of Jewett Pond. Petunias on sale at $10 a dozen for Mother's Day.
Hours: 9-11am
Fee: Free
Yakima Area Arboretum *(See Washington Guide to Gardens.)*

June 20
🌿 Father's Day Bonsai Exhibit
Sponsored by the Yakima Valley Bonsai Society.
Hours: 10am-4pm
Fee: Free
Yakima Area Arboretum *(See Washington Guide to Gardens.)*

West Virginia

Guide to Gardens

Core Arboretum
Monongahela Blvd, WVU Evansdale Campus
Morgantown, WV
Mail: WVU Department of Biology, PO Box
6057, Morgantown, WV 26506
(304)293-5201 ext 528 *Fax:* (304)293-6363
🐚 The 75-acre Arboretum along the
Monongahela River presents a number of natural habitats and environments, including open
fields, wooded hillside and low, moist bottom
land. It emphasizes species native to West
Virginia, with special collections of viburnums,
heaths, ferns, herbs and wildflowers. Several
trails wind through the Arboretum, an excellent
place for observing birds and other wildlife.
Hours: Dawn-dusk
Fees: Free

Sunshine Farm & Gardens
Route 5GT
Renick, WV 24966
(304)497-3163 *Fax:* (304)497-2698
🐚 Renick is the site of Sunshine Farm and
Gardens, an Arboretum which has special collections of perennials and four greenhouses,
sells plants and conducts tours of the location
daily, by appointment only. Call the proprietor,
Barry Glick, for directions.

Selected Events

Charlestown

April 24, 25
🐚 44th Annual House & Garden Tour
A tour of about ten homes and gardens in historic Berkeley and Jefferson Counties. Call for
reservations.
Fee: $10; $5 children under 13

For information: **Shenandoah Potomac
Garden Council**, 105 Jerry Court,
Charlestown, WV 25401
(800)498-2386; (304)264-8801 in WV

April 11, 18, 25
🐚 Wildflower Walks
Sunday wildflower walks through an old-growth hardwood forest, with masses of
Virginia bluebells, and other wildflowers.
Covers about one mile.
Hours: 2-3:30pm
Fee: Free
Core Arboretum *(See West Virginia Guide to
Gardens.)*

Wisconsin

Guide to Gardens

Boerner Botanical Gardens
5879 South 92nd Street in Whitnall Park
Hales Corners, WI 53130
(414)425-1130 *Fax:* (414)425-8679
🐚 Boerner is a major arboretum and garden
on 680 acres. Highlights include a lilac garden of over 400 species surrounded by vast
numbers of tulips in 100 varieties, a collection
of flowering crabapples, a pinetum, wildflower
garden and trails. Special gardens, all with
large numbers of species and varieties,
include a formal rose garden, walled tree
peony garden, rock garden, perennial and
annual gardens, water lily pools, bog gardens,
a prairie garden and a large herb garden. The
rose garden is the site of the annual Rose
Festival. See Wisconsin Selected Events.
Web: www.uwm.edu/Dept/Biology/Boerner/
Hours: 8am-sunset
Fees: Free; parking fee

Green Bay Botanical Garden

2600 Larsen Road
Green Bay, WI
Mail: PO Box 12644, Green Bay, WI 54307
(920)490-9457 *Fax:* (920)490-9461
🌷 The Garden is still a work in progress. The Visitors' Center opened in 1995 and in 1996 an official Grand Opening was held, with most of the lawn and bed areas in place. At this time thirteen of a potential sixty acres are under development.
Web: www.itol.com/botanical/
Hours: May-Oct 10am-6pm, closed Mon; Nov-Apr 9am-4pm Mon-Fri
Fees: Free

Mitchell Park Conservatory

524 South Layton Blvd
Milwaukee, WI 53215
(414)649-9830 *Fax:* (414)649-8616
🌷 The Mitchell Park Conservatory has three glass-domed spaces: the Tropical Dome, the Arid Dome, and the Show Dome. The Show Dome has five elaborate themed seasonal shows each year. The Tropical Dome contains 1200 species from five continents, including more than 500 species of orchids, fruits, nuts and spices, as well as birds who nest in this miniature rain forest. The Arid Dome contains an excellent collection of cacti, succulents, shrubs, bulbs and other native plants in their natural environments.
Web: www.uwm.edu/Dept/Biology/domes/
Hours: 9am-5pm
Fees: $4; $2.50 children

Olbrich Botanical Gardens

3330 Atwood Avenue
Madison, WI 53704
(608)246-4550 *Fax:* (608)246-4719
🌷 Olbrich Gardens feature Perennial, Wildflower, Herb and Rock Gardens. In 1997 the Rose Garden was designated as the most outstanding AARS public rose garden in the country. There is also a Sunken Garden with reflecting pool and perennials, and the Bolz Conservatory, a 50-foot glass pyramid with tropical and orchid collections, and seasonal displays.
Web: www.ci.madison.wi.us/olbrich/olbrich.html
Hours: Grounds 8am-5pm (to 8pm June-Aug & to 4pm Nov-Mar); Conservatory 10am-4pm Mon-Sat, 10am-5pm Sun
Fees: Conservatory $1 (free Wed & Sat am); children under 5 free; grounds free to all

Paine Art Center & Arboretum

1410 Algoma Boulevard
Oshkosh, WI 54901
(920)235-4530 *Fax:* (920)235-6303
🌷 The Arboretum of 15 acres surrounds the Paine Art Center, and is planted with native and exotic trees, shrubs and herbaceous plants. The four acres directly encircling the manor house are in the formal 18th century English style, with flower beds, herb and rose gardens. The Arboretum continues across Algoma Boulevard, with crabapples, woodlands and prairie.
Web: focol.org/~paineart/
Hours: 11am-4pm Tues-Sun; 11am-7pm Fri; closed Mon
Fees: Free

Rotary Gardens

1455 Palmer Drive
Janesville, WI
Mail: PO Box 8023, Janesville, WI 53545
(608)752-3885 *Fax:* (608)752-3853
🌷 The 15-acre site has theme gardens representing international styles, including formal gardens with French fragrances, an English Cottage Garden, an American Perennial Garden, and others.
Web: www.jvlnet.com/~gardens/

Hours: Dawn-dusk
Fees: Free; donations encouraged

University of Wisconsin at Madison Arboretum

1207 Seminole Highway
Madison, WI 53711
(608)263-7888 *Fax:* (608)262-5209
🌿 This extensive Arboretum of over 1200 acres contains the state's largest woody plant collection in its Longnecker and Viburnum Gardens. The Arboretum's native plant and animal communities consist of prairie, wetland and woodland habitats, including the Curtis and Greene Prairies, the Wingra Oak Savanna, three deciduous forests, two conifer forests and two marshes in the wetlands. The Arboretum has special events on most weekends, classes, tours and special events. Call them for a schedule.
Web: www.wisc.edu/arboretum/
Hours: 7am-10pm; drive-through gate open noon-6pm Sun
Fees: Free

Selected Events

Green Bay

June 5, 6
🌿 15th Annual Garden Fair

A plant sale by area nurseries, gardening demonstrations and advice from Master Gardeners and garden clubs. Free parking and entertainment. Held on the sixty-acre tract of land that is now the home of the recently-opened Garden.
Hours: 9am-5pm Sat; 9am-4pm Sun
Fee: $2
Green Bay Botanical Garden *(See Wisconsin Guide to Gardens.)*

July 11, 12
🌿 11th Annual Garden Walk

A self-guided tour of six outstanding private gardens plus the Green Bay Botanical Garden. Optional bus tour available.
Hours: 10am-6pm
Fee: $12 in advance; $15 day of walk
For information: **Green Bay Botanical Garden** *(See Wisconsin Guide to Gardens.)*

August 14
🌿 Renaissance Herb Fair

Demonstrations of the uses of herbs, a food table, vendors, participants in period costumes, games for children, jugglers, tarot readings, and more.
Hours: 10am-4pm
Fee: Fee charged
Green Bay Botanical Garden *(See Wisconsin Guide to Gardens.)*

Janesville

February 7
🌿 Horticulture Show
Fee: Donation requested
Rotary Gardens *(See Wisconsin Guide to Gardens.)*

May 15, 16
🌿 10th Anniversary Celebration

An anniversary celebration when tens of thousands of bulbs are at peak bloom in the garden.
Rotary Gardens *(See Wisconsin Guide to Gardens.)*

May 16, June 6, 20, July 4, 18, August 1, 15, September 5
🌿 Rotary Gardens Tours

Guided tours of the gardens available on these days.
Hours: 1pm
Fee: Free

Rotary Gardens *(See Wisconsin Guide to Gardens.)*

July 17
⚘ Garden Walk
Tour of outstanding local private gardens.
Hours: 10am-4pm
Fee: $9 in advance; $11 day of walk
For information: **Rotary Gardens** *(See Wisconsin Guide to Gardens.)*

September 19
⚘ Annual Harvest Fest & Plant Sale
A family day with a plant sale, music, food, arts and crafts, children's activities and more. Rain date: September 26.
Hours: 11am-4pm
Fee: $2; $1 children 6-12
Rotary Gardens *(See Wisconsin Guide to Gardens.)*

Madison

February 6, 7
⚘ Orchid Quest '99
The 12th winter show of the Orchid Growers Guild, an American Orchid Society judged show with more than 30 venders and exhibits. Many varieties of orchids in beautiful displays, and for sale, plus lectures on home orchid growing. A great exotic tropical retreat in the middle of winter in Wisconsin. Vendors from 5 different states and visitors from 3 states.
Hours: 10am-6pm Sat; 10am-5pm Sun
Fee: $5; children under 13 free
Dane County Exhibition Hall, 1919 Expo Way, Madison, WI
For information: **Orchid Growers Guild**, PO Box 5432, Madison, WI 53705
Email: greed@itis.com
(608)831-2877

May 7, 8
⚘ Spectacular Spring Plant Sale
A huge selection of annuals, perennials, grasses, herbs, plants for sun and shade, butterfly gardens, daylilies and old-fashioned roses. Staff on hand to give suggestions and advice.
Hours: 7am-6pm Fri; 8am-4pm Sat
Fee: Free
Olbrich Botanical Gardens *(See Wisconsin Guide to Gardens.)*

May 8
⚘ Native Plant Sale
A great opportunity to purchase woodland and prairie plants for the home landscape.
Hours: 9am-2pm
University of Wisconsin at Madison Arboretum *(See Wisconsin Guide to Gardens.)*

July 6-August 15
⚘ Butterfly Bonanza
Hundreds of live butterflies of all colors in the tropical Conservatory.
Hours: 10am-5pm
Fee: $4
Olbrich Botanical Gardens *(See Wisconsin Guide to Gardens.)*

July 16, 17
⚘ Olbrich Home Garden Tour
A tour of eight private gardens, including the garden of national garden writer Marilyn Sachtjen.
Hours: 10am-4pm
Fee: $10 in advance; $14 day of tour
For information: **Olbrich Botanical Gardens** *(See Wisconsin Guide to Gardens.)*

August 15
⚘ Garden Open House & Festival
Sundae in the Gardens. Coincides with the

last day of Butterfly Bonanza. Plant information from more than a dozen area plant societies, live entertainment, food and children's activities. An annual festival for everyone.
Hours: Noon-4pm
Fee: Fee charged
Olbrich Botanical Gardens (See Wisconsin Guide to Gardens.)

Milwaukee

March 26-April 3
⚘ Realtors' Home & Garden Show
Gardens designed by top landscapers in the area plus everything of interest to the gardener, and a European Flower Market and Garden Promenade.
Hours: 11am-9pm Fri, Sat; 4-9pm Mon-Thurs; 11am-6pm Sun
Fee: $6; $3 seniors
Wisconsin State Fair Park, 8100 West Greenfield Avenue, West Allis, WI 53214
(414)778-4929

June 12-22
⚘ Rose Festival
A nine-day celebration which includes garden walks, workshops, demonstrations, music, food and more. Set in a forty-acre English-style garden, with 50,000 rose blooms of 350 varieties. For a brochure or more information call The Friends at (414)529-1870.
Boerner Botanical Gardens (See Wisconsin Guide to Gardens.)

September 25, 26
⚘ Mid-America Orchid Society Fall Show
Hundreds of species of orchids filling the Show Dome and exhibits by growers from all over the country, Canada and Europe. Billed as the largest orchid festival in the Mid West.
Mitchell Park Conservatory (See Wisconsin Guide to Gardens.)

Oshkosh

May 8
⚘ Spring Plant Sale
Perennials, annuals, trees and shrubs for sale, plus gardening demonstrations and garden experts are on hand to answer questions.
Paine Art Center & Arboretum (See Wisconsin Guide to Gardens.)

September 11
⚘ Fall Bulb Sale
Bulbs and other plants for sale, along with garden-related materials. Plus demonstrations, garden experts to answer questions, and a farmer's market.
Paine Art Center & Arboretum (See Wisconsin Guide to Gardens.)

Racine

May 24
⚘ Chinese Medicinal Herb Garden Installation
The installation of this garden is the end result of a class held by the Wisconsin Institute of Chinese Herbology.
Hours: 10am-3pm
Fee: Free
Wisconsin Institute of Chinese Herbology, Racine, WI
Web: www.herbworld.com/herbschool/
Email: herbssch@execpc.com
(414)886-5858

Wyoming

Guide to Gardens

Cheyenne Botanic Gardens
710 South Lions Park Drive
Cheyenne, WY 82001
Email: botanicgarden@compuserv.com

(307)637-6458 *Fax:* (307)637-6453

The Cheyenne Botanic Gardens consist of 6,800 square feet of greenhouse. The facility is 100% passively solar-heated and partially solar-powered. It contains an herb garden, tropical trees and vines, a cactus garden and a variety of ornamental flowers. Seasonal displays are held in the conservatory, parts of which are also used to grow food year-round for volunteers and for distribution to low-income families.

Web: www.lcc.whecn.edu/scc/cheyenne/botanic_gardens/

Hours: 8am-4:30pm Mon-Fri; 11am-3pm weekends, holidays

Fees: Free

Canada

Alberta

Guide to Gardens

Calgary Zoo Botanical Gardens

1300 Zoo Road NE

Calgary, AB

Mail: PO Box 3036 Station B, Calgary, AB T2M 4R8

(403)232-9342 *Fax:* (403)237-7582

The Gardens feature a Conservatory and the Dorothy Harvie Garden in the center of St. George's Island, a formal garden of more than 4000 ornamental species acclimated to the growing conditions of Calgary. There are also seasonal blooming displays plus special areas devoted to water conservation, shade, woodland and alpine gardens. The Conservatory has three gardens of distinctive environments: the Arid Garden, Rainforest Garden and Butterfly Garden.

Web: www.calgaryzoo.ab.ca

Hours: 9am-4pm

Fees: May-Sep $9.50; $4.75 seniors Tues-Thurs only; $4.75 children 2-7; under 2 free; reduced rates off season

Devonian Botanic Garden

University of Alberta, Highway 60 north of Devon

Edmonton, AB T6G 2E1

(403)987-3054 *Fax:* (403)987-4141

With 80 acres of landscape and gardens on a 210-acre site, the Garden has among its many highlights an Orchid House, Plants of Alberta, Alpine Garden, Butterfly Garden, Iris and Primula Dells, lilac and peony collections, Native People's Garden and Nature Walks.

Web: www.discoveredmonton.com/devonian/dbg.html

Hours: 10am-6pm

Fees: $5; $4 seniors, student; $3 children

The Muttart Conservatory

9626-96 A Street

Edmonton, AB

Mail: PO Box 2359, Edmonton, AB T5J 2R7

(780)496-8755 *Fax:* (780)496-8747

Built in the late 1970s, the four pyramids of Muttart Conservatory are a landmark in Edmonton's Saskatchewan Valley. Diverse environments within the Conservatory range from a tropic jungle to arid desert and temperate forest. The fourth pyramid houses changing shows.

Hours: 9am-6pm; 11am-6pm Sat, Sun

Fees: $4.50, $3.50 seniors, students; $2 children

Selected Events

Edmonton

February 13-21
❧ 22nd Annual Orchid Show
In Search of Orchids. A judged show of the American Orchid Society, the most northerly of its kind, with displays, plants and flower arrangements, corsages, artwork and more.
Hours: 11am-6pm first weekend ; 9am-9pm Mon-Thur; 9am-6pm Fri-Sun
Fee: $4.50; $3.50 seniors, students; $2 children
The Muttart Conservatory *(See Alberta Guide to Gardens.)*

May 8
❧ Mother's Day in the Garden
Potting marigolds for Mom and children's choir performances.
Devonian Botanic Garden *(See Alberta Guide to Gardens.)*

June 20
❧ Father's Day
Craft demonstration and potting annuals for Dad.
Devonian Botanic Garden *(See Alberta Guide to Gardens.)*

July 1
❧ Canada Day & Garden Celebration
Music , birthday cake and crafts.
Devonian Botanic Garden *(See Alberta Guide to Gardens.)*

July 3, 4
❧ Martagon Lily Show
Sponsored by the Alberta Regional Lily Society.
Hours: 10am-7pm
Devonian Botanic Garden *(See Alberta Guide to Gardens.)*

July 11
❧ Raspberry Festival & Tasting
Over twenty varieties of raspberries.
Hours: 10am-7pm
Devonian Botanic Garden *(See Alberta Guide to Gardens.)*

July 24, 25
❧ Rose Show
An indoor display.
Hours: 10am-7pm
Devonian Botanic Garden *(See Alberta Guide to Gardens.)*

September 25, 26
❧ Crafters Fall Flower Fair
Botanical crafts using materials harvested from the Devonian.
Hours: 11am-4pm
Devonian Botanic Garden *(See Alberta Guide to Gardens.)*

British Columbia

Guide to Gardens

Bloedel Conservatory
Queen Elizabeth Park,33rd & Cambie Street
Vancouver, BC
Mail: 2099 Beach Avenue, Vancouver, BC
V6G 1Z4
(604)257-8570 *Fax:* (604)257-2412
❧ The centerpiece of Queen Elizabeth Park is the Bloedel Floral Conservatory, a radiant triodetic dome. It houses approximately 500 species and varieties of plants, from jungle to desert environments, with tropical birds flying freely. The Park has lovely landscaping and seasonal displays in Quarry Gardens, as well as an outstanding view of the city from Conservatory Plaza.

Hours: 9am-8pm summer, weekends to 10pm; 10am-5pm winter
Fees: $3:30; $2 seniors; $1.65 youth; under 6 free

The Butchart Gardens

800 Benvenuto Avenue
Brentwood Bay, BC
Mail: PO Box 4010, Brentwood Bay, BC V8X 3X4
Email: email@butchartgardens.bc.ca
(250)652-5256 or (250)652-4422
Fax: (250)652-3883
🌺 Butchart Gardens is a must for all garden travelers to Victoria. The Display Gardens are particularly beautiful from April through October. The huge number of varied plantings insures something special for everyone at any time. The Gardens are illuminated with Christmas lighting and decorations during December.
Web: butchartgardens.bc.ca/butchart/
Hours: Apr-Oct 9am-4pm; vary off peak
Fees: Apr-Oct $11.50; $5.75 ages 13-17; $1.50 children; off peak fees vary

Horticulture Centre of the Pacific

505 Quayle Road
Victoria, BC V8X 3X1
Email: hortcentre@bigfoot.com
(250)479-6162
🌺 This garden at the Centre consists of 15 acres of demonstration and teaching gardens and about 90 acres of undeveloped land, including wetlands. The main gardens at the entrance rotunda demonstrate vegetation suitable for Victorian gardens of all sizes, with mixed borders. Specialty gardens include water gardens, a Japanese garden, an outstanding heather garden, dahlia trial garden, native plant area, lilies, herbs and others.
Web: www.islandnet.com/~hcp/
Hours: Apr 1-Sep 30 8am-8pm; Oct 1-Mar 31

9am-4:30pm
Fees: $5; children under 12 free

Minter Gardens

52892 Bunker Road
Rosedale, BC
Mail: PO Box 40, Chilliwack, BC V2P 6H7
Email: minter@minter.org
(604)794-7191 or (604)792-3799 *Fax:* (604)792-8893
🌺 The Gardens comprise 27 acres of display gardens nestled against 7000-ft. Mt. Cheam. Eleven themed gardens include the Rose Garden, English Cottage Garden, rhododendrons, Victorian Topiary Ladies and a floral peacock, plus hundreds of thousands of spring bulbs and various displays in every season.
Web: www.minter.org
Hours: 9am-closing
Fees: May-Sep $9.50; $8.50 seniors; $6 children 6-18

University of British Columbia Botanical Garden

6804 Southwest Marine Drive
Vancouver, BC V6T 1Z4
(604)822-9666 *Fax:* (604)822-2016
🌺 Located on the cliffs overlooking the Strait of Georgia, these 70 acres are planted with over 10,000 different trees, shrubs and flowers, including one of Canada's largest collection of rhododendrons. Highlights include the Asian Garden, Native Garden, Alpine Garden, Perennial Borders, Food Garden, Winter Garden and Physick Garden.
Web: www.hedgerows.com/UBCBotGdn/index.htm
Hours: Mar 8-Oct 12 10am-6pm
Fees: $4.50; $2.25 seniors, students

VanDusen Botanical Garden

5251 Oak Street
Vancouver, BC V6M 4H1

(604)257-8666 *Fax:* (604)266-4236

🌹 The 55-acre Garden has collections of rhododendron, holly, ponds with water lilies, as well as a Sino-Himalayan garden, maze and a "walk in the forest" exhibition.
Web: www.hedgerows.com
Hours: 10am-seasonal closings
Fees: $11 family; $5.50 adults; $2.50 seniors, youth; off peak fees vary

Selected Events

Vancouver

February 19, 20
🌹 **Chinese New Year**
Festivities at the Garden.
Hours: 10:30am-9:30pm
Fee: Special Garden admission
VanDusen Botanical Garden (*See British Columbia Guide to Gardens.*)

April
🌹 **Plant Sale**
Over 35,000 plants for sale, plus an information booth with answers to garden questions. Call for exact date.
Hours: 10am-4pm
Fee: Free
VanDusen Botanical Garden (*See British Columbia Guide to Gardens.*)

May 9
🌹 **Mother's Day Perennial Plant Sale**
Plants from the Garden's collections and new, interesting cultivars from around the world. Many rare and unusual plants and experts on hand to provide advice.
Hours: 10am-4pm
Fee: Free
University of British Columbia Botanical Garden (*See British Columbia Guide to Gardens.*)

June 4-6
🌹 **VanDusen Flower & Garden Show**
One of the premier garden events in Canada. Features 200 plus displays on over seven acres, all under tents on the Great Lawn, corner of Oak Street and 37th Avenue.
Hours: 9am-6pm
Fee: $8; $5 seniors, children; $16 family
VanDusen Botanical Garden (*See British Columbia Guide to Gardens.*)

June 21
🌹 **Midsummer's Eve Celebration**
A medieval fair on the Great Lawn presented by Society for Creative Anachronism.
Hours: 7-9pm
Fee: $11 family; $5.50 adults; $2.50 seniors, youth
VanDusen Botanical Garden (*See British Columbia Guide to Gardens.*)

October 16, 17
🌹 **Apple Festival**
Over 50 varieties of apples to taste and buy, as well as unusual apple tree varieties. Expert advice available on identification, pruning and cultivation, plus apple cider, candy apples and more.
Hours: 11am-4pm
Fee: Free
University of British Columbia Botanical Garden (*See British Columbia Guide to Gardens.*)

December 10-January 1
🌹 **Festival of Lights**
Thousands of lights in the Garden.
Hours: 5-9:30pm
Fee: Regular garden admission
VanDusen Botanical Garden (*See British Columbia Guide to Gardens.*)

Victoria

May 8, 9
✿ Garden Tour
A self-guided tour of ten of Victoria's most beautiful gardens over a two-day period. Plus a tea garden with musical entertainment by Conservatory students and a plant sale. Tickets available at many local outlets. Sponsored by the Victoria Conservatory of Music.
Hours: 10am-5pm
Fee: $25
For information: **Victoria Conservatory of Music**, 839 Academy Close, Victoria, BC V8V 2X8
Email: mta@island.net
(250)386-5311

July 4
✿ Festival of Music & Flowers
Musical performances in the gardens with Master Gardeners on hand to answer questions. Lunch and refreshments availalbe.
Hours: 10am-4pm
Fee: $5; children under 12 free
Horticulture Centre of the Pacific *(See British Columbia Guide to Gardens.)*

July 9-11
✿ 6th Annual Royal Victoria Flower & Garden Festival
Demonstration gardens, Canadian and international speakers, nursery and garden accessory retailers, and ideas and information for gardeners at every level. This year at a new location with Hatley Castle and its gardens in the background on Vancouver Island.
Hours: 9am-8pm Fri; 9am-6pm Sat, Sun
Fee: Fee charged
Royal Roads University, 2005 Sooke Road, Victoria, BC

For information: **Royal Victoria Flower & Garden Festival**, 3721 Grange Road, Victoria, BC V8Z 4S9
Email: tradeshows@pccinternet.com
(250)881-7469

August 8
✿ Artists in a Country Garden
Over thirty artists in the gardens selling and demonstrating their art. Classical musicians and Master Gardeners also on hand.
Hours: 11am-4pm
Fee: $5; children under 12 free
Horticulture Centre of the Pacific *(See British Columbia Guide to Gardens.)*

Manitoba

Guide to Gardens

The Garden Gallery
Warren, MB
Mail: Box 25, Warren, MB R0C 3E0
Email: bhamlin@man.net
(204)322-5731
✿ These are the gardens of artist Bonnie Hamlin and include herb gardens, moon gardens, rose gardens, iris and lily gardens and a nature walk of a quarter mile through native oaks and poplars.
Directions: 1 mile east & 2 miles north of junction of Highways 6 & 67
Hours: End of May-Mid Sept 11am-4pm
Fees: $2

Selected Events

Warren
15 miles from Winnipeg

June 12, 13
✿ Iris Festival

Musicians playing amidst the flowers and craftspeople on hand to celebrate the blooming of thirteen large iris beds representing over 400 varieties.
Hours: 10am-5pm
Fee: $5
The Garden Gallery *(See Manitoba Guide to Gardens.)*

New Brunswick

Guide to Gardens

Fredericton Botanic Garden
Prospect Street
Fredericton, NB
Mail: PO Box 57, Fredericton, NB E3B 4Y2
(506)452-9269
The Fredericton Botanic Garden is a volunteer-run public garden under construction. Much of the land has been cleared and trees and hedges planted. Currently, there are extensive walking trails through woods and beside streams, as well as several large demonstration perennial beds. Plans are underway for the building of a rose garden in 1999-2000.

Kingsbrae Horticultural Garden
220 King Street
St. Andrew, NB E0G 2X0
Email: kinghort@nbnet.nb.ca
(506)529-3335 *Fax:* (506)529-4875
Set in the resort community of St. Andrews-By-The-Sea, Kingsbrae Garden is a new 27-acre site, with a white garden, knot garden, butterfly and bird gardens, collections of roses and daylilies, a labyrinth and maze, and a woodland trail leading through old-growth forest.
Web: www.townsearch.com/kingsbraegarden/
Hours: May-Oct 9am-dusk
Fees: $6; $4 seniors, students

Selected Events

Fredericton

May 31
Spring Plant Sale
A wide range of plants, including trees, shrubs, alpine plants, annuals, house plants and hardy perennials for zone 4b. Master Gardeners and Composters on hand to answer questions. An annual sale run by the volunteers of the Fredericton Botanic Garden.
Hours: noon-4pm
Fee: Free
Boyce Farmer's Market, 665 George Street, Fredericton, NB
For information: **Fredericton Botanic Garden** *(See New Brunswick Guide to Gardens.)*

St. Andrew

May 29, 30
Perennial Plant Exchange
Bring one perennial and take a new one home.
Hours: 9am-dusk
Kingsbrae Horticultural Garden *(See New Brunswick Guide to Gardens.)*

September 4, 5
Perennial Plant Exchange
The Fall version of the spring event. Bring one perennial and take a new one home.
Hours: 9am-dusk
Kingsbrae Horticultural Garden *(See New Brunswick Guide to Gardens.)*

Newfoundland

Memorial University Botanical Garden
306 Mount Scio Road
St. John's, NF A1C 5S7
Email: garden@morgan.ucs.mun.ca
(709)737-8590 *Fax:* (709)737-8596
✿ The 110-acre Garden offers diverse environments, including bog, boreal forest, lakeshore and rocky barrens. Special features include wildflowers, a rock garden, heritage garden, cottage garden, heather and rhododendron gardens, perennial border, vegetable garden, wildlife garden and the Alpine House.
Web: www.mun.ca/botgarden/
Hours: May1-Nov 30 10am-5pm
Fees: $2; $1 seniors, children

Selected Events

St. John's

May 29, 30
✿ **Newfoundland Horticultural Society Spring Flower Show**
Exhibits, information and more.
Hours: noon-5pm Sat; 10am-5pm Sun
Fee: Free
Memorial University Botanical Garden *(See Newfoundland Guide to Gardens.)*

August 7
✿ **Open House**
A day of activities. Call for schedule and information.
Hours: noon-5 Sat; 10am-5pm Sun
Fee: Free
Memorial University Botanical Garden *(See Newfoundland Guide to Gardens.)*

September 4
✿ **Friends of the Garden Plant Sale**
A chance to stock up for the fall planting season.
Hours: 10am-4pm
Fee: Free
Memorial University Botanical Garden *(See Newfoundland Guide to Gardens.)*

October 24
✿ **Dried Flower Sale**
Presented by Friends of the Garden.
Hours: noon-5pm Sat; 10am-5pm Sun
Fee: Free
Memorial University Botanical Garden *(See Newfoundland Guide to Gardens.)*

Nova Scotia

Annapolis Royal Historic Gardens
441 St. George Street
Annapolis Royal, NS
Mail: PO Box 278, Annapolis Royal, NS B0S 1A0
(902)532-7018 *Fax:* (902)532-7445
✿ Situated in the birthplace of Canada, the 10-acre Gardens and 50-acre wildflower sanctuary overlook the wetlands and meadows of a tidal river valley and feature displays that illustrate the history of gardening and horticulture in Nova Scotia. Highlights include a Rose Collection, Knot Garden, Acadian Section, Perennial Border, Governor's Garden, Victorian Garden and Innovative Garden.
Web: www.historicgardens.com
Hours: Mid May-Mid Oct 9am-dusk
Fees: $5

Ontario

Guide to Gardens

Allan Gardens Conservatory

Carleton Street between Jarvis & Sherbourne
Toronto, ON
Mail: Department of Parks & Recreation, 19 Horticulture Avenue, Toronto, ON M5A 2P2
(412)392-1111 *Fax:* (412)392-0318

Situated on the 13 acres of Allan Gardens is the Conservatory, with six specialized greenhouses: Arid House, Tropical Landscape House, Palm House, Cool Temperature House, Tropical House and a show area for four seasonal displays.
Hours: 9am-4pm Mon-Fri; 10am-5pm weekends
Fees: Free

The Arboretum at Guelph

University of Guelph
Guelph, ON N1G 2W1
(519)824-4120 *Fax:* (519)763-9598

The 402-acre Arboretum has collections of trees and shrubs and thematic gardens against the backdrop of old-growth forest and meadows. Forty-six collections range from the "World of Trees" to lilacs and rhododendrons. Gardens include the Japanese Garden, Formal English Garden and Wildlife Garden.
Web: www.uoguelph.ca/~arboretum/
Hours: Grounds dawn-dusk
Fees: Free

Gage Park

Gage Avenue South
Hamilton, ON
Mail: Hamilton Department of Works, 71 Main Street West, 4th floor, Hamilton, ON L8P 4Y5
Email: gagepark@interlynx.net
(905)546-2666 *Fax:* (905)546-4193

Gage Park is a horticultural park in the heart of Hamilton. It contains an extensive rose garden, perennial garden and large collection of indigenous and exotic trees. The greenhouse complex, site of the Annual Chrysanthemum Show (see Ontario Selected Events), includes a tropical greenhouse with collection of exotic plants.
Web: www.city.hamilton.on.ca
Directions: between Main Street East & Lawrence Road
Hours: Dawn-dusk
Fees: Free

Niagara Parks Commission

2565 Niagara Parkway North
Niagara Falls, ON
Mail: PO Box 150, Niagara Falls, ON L2E 6T2
Email: npinfo@niagaraparks.com
(905)354-8755; Greenhouse (905)354-1721 *Fax:* (905)356-9041

The Niagara Parks Commission oversees several sites. The Niagara Botanical Gardens has over 100 acres of gardens, including herb, vegetable, a major Canadian arboretum with collections of ornamental trees and shrubs, Rose Garden, Garden for the Visually Impaired, Native Butterfly Garden, and is also the site of the only residential school for horticulture students in Canada. The Greenhouses, which produce all of the bedding plants for the city, has palms and tropical plants and eight seasonal displays a year. Other sites managed by the Commission include the Butterfly Conservatory, the Centennial Lilac Gardens with ten acres of 1200 plus lilac bushes representing 200 varieties, the Floral Clock and Queen Victoria Park, with collections of native and international plant material, a rock garden, hybrid tea rose garden, and bedding displays with seasonal highlights.
Web: www.niagaraparks.com
Hours: Botanical Gardens Oct-May 9:30am-5pm, May-Sep until 8:30pm; Greenhouses July-Aug 9:30am-9pm; 9:30am-4:30pm rest of year

Fees: Free

Royal Botanical Gardens
680 Plains Road West
Burlington, ON
Mail: PO Box 399, Hamilton, ON L8N 3H8
Email: bloom@rbg; events@rbg
(905)527-1158 *Fax:* (905)577-0375
🌸 The Gardens, on more than 2700 acres, have 50 different collections in five different garden areas, as well as three sanctuaries traversed by trails, which protect a wilderness of high cliffs, deep ravines and wetlands. Special gardens include the more than two-acre Rose Garden, one acre of irises, the Rock Garden, the arboretum, as well as an extraordinarily large collection of lilacs.
Web: www.rbg.ca
Hours: Gardens 9:30am-6pm
Fees: $7; $5 seniors, students; $2 children

Wellington County Museum
RR #1
Fergus, ON N1M 2W3
Email: wcmchin@sentex.net
(519)846-0916 *Fax:* (519)846-9630
🌸 The Museum is the oldest House of Industry in Canada and overlooks the once mill-laden Grand River. Its gardens, designed by artist Cecily Moon, are maintained by volunteers of the Elora and Salem Horticultural Society and the Fergus Horticultural Society. The Nature Garden has communities of mixed hardwood trees plus wildflowers and a meadow. There is a Woods Edge Community with poplar, cedar, red osier dogwood and wildflowers, and a Prairie Community. The Cottage Garden is composed entirely of fruit bearing plants and herbs. The Victorian Garden has many popular flowers of Europe introduced to Canada by the late nineteenth century settlers.
Hours: Dawn-dusk
Fees: Free

Fergus

July 10
🌸 Grand Garden Tour & Herb Fair
A self-guided tour of five private gardens and three public gardens. Plus a Herb Fair with displays and a sale of herbs and related products, perennials and garden items. Light lunch available. A joint fund raiser for the Museum and Theatre on the Grand.
Hours: 10am-3pm
Fee: Herb Fair free; $7 tour; $6 lunch
For information: **Wellington County Museum** *(See Ontario Guide to Gardens.)*

Guelph

September 11
🌸 Plant Sale
Natives herbs and unusual plants for sale. Rare and one-of-a-kind specimens featured at a Silent Auction (9-11am). Catalog available in August.
Hours: 9am-3pm
Fee: Free
The Arboretum at Guelph *(See Ontario Guide to Gardens.)*

Hamilton

October 30-November 14
🌸 Hamilton's Annual Chrysanthemum Show
Mums and Sugarplums. Over 75,000 blooms representing over 240 varieties of mums in imaginative displays on a theme inspired by The Nutcracker ballet. Held in the Gage Park Greenhouse.
Hours: 9am-8pm
Fee: $3; $2 seniors, children
Gage Park *(See Ontario Guide to Gardens.)*

Niagara Falls

June 17
❧ Annual Rose Show
Presented by the Society. Held at the Niagara Falls Library, Victoria Avenue Branch.
Hours: 2:30-5pm
Fee: Free
For information: **Niagara Falls Horticultural Society**, 4223 Front Street, Niagara Falls, ON L2G 6G7
Email: rleavere@aol.com
(905)295-4632

July 17
❧ Garden Tour
A tour of private gardens in the area.
Hours: 1-5pm
Fee: $5
For information: **Niagara Falls Horticultural Society**, 4223 Front Street, Niagara Falls, ON L2G 6G7
Email: rleavere@aol.com
(905)295-4632

August 19
❧ Annual Flower & Vegetable Show
Presented by the Society. Held at the Niagara Falls Library, Victoria Avenue Branch.
Hours: 2:30-5pm
Fee: Free
For information: **Niagara Falls Horticultural Society**, 4223 Front Street, Niagara Falls, ON L2G 6G7
Email: rleavere@aol.com
(905)295-4632

Toronto

All year
❧ The Gardening Network
A program which includes visits to gardens, talks and presentations throughout the year, available to members and nonmembers.

All events free; newsletter comes with membership.
Fee: Free
For information: **The Gardening Network**, 3044 Bloor Street West, Suite 142, Toronto, ON M8X 2Y8
Web: www.interlog.com/~wezel/garden/garden1.htm
Email: thegardeningnetwork@usa.net
(416)233-3989

March 10-14
❧ Canada Blooms Flower Show
A Gardener's Getaway. The largest indoor flower and garden show in Canada, with six acres of gardens, displays, marketplace and educational programs. Sponsored by the Garden Club of Toronto and Landscape Ontario. Proceeds fund projects for the benefit of the Toronto community.
Hours: 10am-10pm Wed-Sat; 10am-6pm Sun
Fee: $9 in advance; at gate $10, $9 seniors, $5.50 students, children under 10 free
Metro Toronto Convention Centre, South Building, 222 Bremner Blvd, Toronto, ON
For information: **Toronto Flower & Garden Show**, 777 Lawrence Ave East, North York, ON M3C 1P2
(800)730-1020 or (416)593-0223

April 1-4
❧ 6th Annual Success With Gardening Show
A "hands on" gardening show, with over 200 exhibitors, seminars, display gardens and educational displays from the Ontario Horticultural Association and local garden clubs.
Hours: 10am-9pm Thurs; 10am-6pm Fri; 10am-9pm Sat; 10am-6pm Sun
Fee: $9; $7 seniors, students; $4 children; free parking
International Centre, 6900 Airport Road, Mississauga, ON

For information: **Success with Gardening Show**, 165 Royal Orchard Blvd, Thornhill, ON L3T 3E1
Web: www.oak.net/shobiz/gard/
(905)881-5708

April 9-11
⚜ Ontario Garden Show
Over 100 exhibitors offering everything from plants to gazebos and more. Lectures and educational exhibits. For information call (905)522-6117 ext 306.
Hours: noon-9pm Fri; 9am-9pm Sat; 9am-6pm Sun
Fee: $7
Royal Botanical Gardens *(See Ontario Guide to Gardens.)*

May 6, 8
⚜ RBG Auxiliary Plant Sale
RBG's annual offering of unique and rare plants.
Hours: 9:30am-12:30pm
Fee: Free
Royal Botanical Gardens *(See Ontario Guide to Gardens.)*

May 23, 24, 30
⚜ Lilac Festival
Music, guided tours and a food tent at peak bloom time of one of the world's largest lilac collections.
Royal Botanical Gardens *(See Ontario Guide to Gardens.)*

June 6, 13
⚜ Iris & Peony Festival
A festival in the Gardens blooming with 250,000 iris in every color, along with a spectacular collection of tree peonies and herbaceous garden peonies.
Royal Botanical Gardens *(See Ontario Guide to Gardens.)*

June 26, 27
⚜ Hamilton & Burlington Rose Show
Sponsored by local rose societies.
Hours: 1:30-5pm Sat; 10am-4pm Sun
Royal Botanical Gardens *(See Ontario Guide to Gardens.)*

June 27 & July 4, 11
⚜ Rose Festival
Music, food, guided tours and activities for children to celebrate two fragrant acres of blooming roses.
Royal Botanical Gardens *(See Ontario Guide to Gardens.)*

July 17, 18
⚜ Lily Society Show
Sponsored by the Ontario Regional Lily Society.
Hours: 2-5pm Sat; 10am-5pm Sun
Royal Botanical Gardens *(See Ontario Guide to Gardens.)*

August 28, 29
⚜ Herb Faire
An outdoor marketplace with vendors and a gourmet food and wine pavilion in the Rose Garden, Hendrie Park.
Hours: 10am-5pm
Royal Botanical Gardens *(See Ontario Guide to Gardens.)*

September 11. 12
⚜ Chrysanthemum & Dahlia Society Show
Presented by local societies.
Hours: 12:30-5pm Sat; 10am-5pm Sun
Royal Botanical Gardens *(See Ontario Guide to Gardens.)*

September 19
⚜ Ikenobo Ikebana Japanese Flower Show
Sponsored by the local society.
Hours: 1-5pm

Royal Botanical Gardens (*See Ontario Guide to Gardens.*)

November 4-13
❀ The Winter Garden Show at the Royal
Exhibits, retail boutiques and landscape displays, plus garden-related information via computer at the Education Centre and talks by garden experts. Part of the Royal Agricultural Winter Fair and a major horticultural exhibition in Canada.
Hours: 9am-9pm Mon-Sat; 9am-8pm Sun
Fee: $11; $8 seniors & youth
The Coliseum at the National Trade Centre, Exhibition Place, Toronto, ON M6K 3C3
Web: www.royalfair.org
Email: rwfair@ican.net
(416)393-6400

November 19-21
❀ RBG Auxiliary Christmas Show & Sale
A popular show and sale of holiday arrangements and unique gifts.
Royal Botanical Gardens (*See Ontario Guide to Gardens.*)

Quebec
Guide to Gardens

Belle Terre Botanical Garden & Arboretum
120 Milliken Road
Otter Lake, QC
Mail: PO Box 215, Otter Lake, QC J0X 2P0
(819)453-7270
❀ This bio-dynamic, completely organic Garden, together with the commercial garden center, is on 200 acres in the Laurentian Highlands. There are artesian mineral springs from pools, creeks and streams throughout the Garden, where herbs, annuals, perennials, vegetable and fruits are grown. The site offers

all kinds of family activities and workshops. Contact them for schedule.
Hours: 10am-dusk by reservation
Fees: Free

Jardin Roger Van den Hende
Univ Laval
Sainte-Foy, QC
Mail: Pavillon de l'Envirotron, Univ. Laval, 2480 Bl. Hochelaga, Sainte-Foy, QC G1K 7P4
(418)656-3410 *Fax:* (418)656-7871
❀ This is the botanical garden of the university, containing over 2000 species and cultivars grouped by families, with native and introduced species. Highlights include a Rose Garden, Water Garden, arboretum and woody plant collection.
Hours: May 1-Sep 30 9am-8pm
Fees: Free; parking fee

Les Jardin de Métis
200 Route 132
Grand-Métis, QC
Mail: CP 242, Mont Joli, QC G5H 3L1
Email: jarmetis@globetrotter.qc.ca
(418)775-2221 *Fax:* (418)775-6201
❀ The Gardens are located at a site high above the meeting of the Métis and St. Lawrence Rivers, with magnificent views over the Gaspe coastline to the mountains of the north shore. Of special interest is the July bloom of more than 500 of the magnificent Meconopsis Blue Poppies. Native to the steppes of the Himalayas, they flower at Grand-Métis as in no other garden in North America. There is also an exceptional display of lilies in August.
Hours: May-Oct 8:30am-8pm
Fees: $7.50 family; $3.20 adults; $1.65 seniors, children

Les Jardins du Domaine Howard
1350 Boul de Portland
Sherbrooke, QC

Mail: PO Box 426, Sherbrooke, QC J1H 5J7
Email: tourisme@sdrs.com
(819)821-1919 *Fax:* (819)822-6074
✿ This 6.5-acre park contains three historic mansions surrounded by woodlands, hiking paths, a lake, and gardens with more than 200 species of annuals and perennials. There is an excellent lily display at the end of June.
Web: www.sders.com/tourisme/
Hours: Grounds dawn-dusk; Greenhouses 8am-4pm Mon-Fri
Fees: Free

Montréal Botanical Garden
4101 Rue Sherbrooke Street, East
Montréal, QC H1X 2B2
(514)872-1400 *Fax:* (514)872-4917
✿ The Garden has ten exhibition greenhouses and some thirty outdoor gardens on 180 acres. Highlights of the special gardens are a shade garden, alpine garden, flowery brook, perennial garden, the Japanese and Chinese Gardens, and the Rose Garden with more than 10,000 rose bushes. The newest addition is the Garden of Innovations. The Tree House, an arboretum, includes a courtyard of miniature North American trees. The ten greenhouses have displays ranging from the tropical rain forest to the deserts of Africa, with noted collections of orchids, cacti, banana trees and seasonal exhibitions.
Web: www.ville.montreal.qc/ca/jardin/
Hours: 9am-5pm; open until 7pm in summer
Fees: $9; $6.75 seniors, students; $4.50 ages 6-17; reduced rates Nov 2-April 30

Selected Events

Grand-Métis

June 1-15
✿ **Crabapple Festival**
A festival signaling the opening of the Gardens for the season with the collection of more than 100 historic crabapples in bloom.
Les Jardin de Métis *(See Quebec Guide to Gardens.)*

Otter Lake
Near Ottowa, Ontario

July 4
✿ **Canadian American Day Friendship Celebration**
An annual event with flower exhibition, plant sales, tours, ecology, food.
Belle Terre Botanical Garden & Arboretum *(See Quebec Guide to Gardens.)*

Sherbrooke

October 24-31
✿ **45th Annual Floral Exhibition**
A very popular exhibition of flowers from around the world held in the Municipal Greenhouses in Howardeen Park.
Fee: $3; $2 seniors, students
For information: **Les Jardins du Domaine Howard** *(See Quebec Guide to Gardens.)*

Saskatchewan

Guide to Gardens

Saskatoon Civic Conservatory
Mendel Art Gallery
Saskatoon, SK
Mail: Building & Grounds Department, City Hall, Saskatoon, SK S7K 0J5
(306)975-2546
✿ The Conservatory is attached to the Mendel Art Gallery on the banks of the South Saskatchewan River. The display consists of a large variety of tropical, temperate and arid plants, featuring shows of seasonal blooms.

Far Away Places

Foreign Tours

January 10-February 10
❦ Summer Gardens of Australia & New Zealand
For information, call (800)942-6666 or visit www.haerttertravel.com.
This tour is sponsored by: **American Horticultural Society** *(See Virginia Guide to Gardens.)*

January 23-30
❦ Costa Rica, From Orchid Gardens to Cloud Forest
A tour led by the Horticultural Society of New York's Education Director, Scott Appell. Includes private gardens, Costa Flores Tropical Flower Plantation, Bosque de Paz Cloud Forest, the Rain Forest, Carrara Biological Preserve. For information, call (800)585-2489 or (718)457-0672.
This tour is sponsored by: **The Horticultural Society of New York**, 128 West 58th Street, New York, NY 10019

February 1-14
❦ Venezuela: From Amazonas to the Andes
A tour led by UC Botanical Garden Horticultural Manager David Brunner to one of the most biologically diverse countries in the world. Includes visits to "Lost World of the Tepuis" and the Orinoco Basin, often called the "Serengeti of South America." For complete information call (800)624-6633 or (707)579-2420.
This tour is sponsored by: **UC Berkeley Botanical Garden** *(See California Guide to Gardens.)*

February 4-14
❦ The Galapagos
A tour of these fascinating islands with Holden. For complete information call Holden's Education Department at (440)256-1110.
This tour is sponsored by: **The Holden Arboretum** *(See Ohio Guide to Gardens.)*

February 6-13
❦ Flora & Fauna of Costa Rica
For complete information call (800)448-2685.
This tour is sponsored by: **Chicago Botanic Garden** *(See Illinois Guide to Gardens.)*

May 10-23
❦ The Humanist Garden: Gardens & Villas of the Italian Renaissance
A tour of Tuscany, Venice and the Palladian villas near Verona led by Michael Bernsohn, landscape designer and owner of Las Baulines Nursery. For information call (800)624-6633 or (415)661-0668 ext 300.
This tour is sponsored by: **Strybing Arboretum & Botanical Gardens** *(See California Guide to Gardens.)*

April 6-17
❦ The Gardens of Morocco
Led by Elizabeth Scholtz, Director Emeritus of the Brooklyn Botanic Garden, this tour is an insider's view of Morocco. For complete information call (718)622-4433, ext 250 or ext 251.
This tour is sponsored by: **Brooklyn Botanic Garden** *(See New York Guide to Gardens.)*

April 15-25
🌺 Holland at Tulip Time
For information call (800)448-2685.
This tour is sponsored by: **Washington Park Arboretum** *(See Washington Guide to Gardens.)*

April 20-May 1
🌺 Spring Gardens of Amalfi, Naples, Rome & the Islands of Ischia & Capri
For information, call (800)942-6666 or visit www.haerttertravel.com.
This tour is sponsored by: **American Horticultural Society** *(See Virginia Guide to Gardens.)*

May 2-11
🌺 Secret & Spectacular Gardens of Holland
Tour highlights include the Flower Auction and Keukenhof Gardens, visits to private gardens, the de la Hazy garden in Zeeland, Apeldorn gardens, the Japanese garden in the Hague, and more. For information, call (800)585-2489 or (718)457-0672.
This tour sponsored by: **The Horticultural Society of New York**, 128 West 58th Street, New York, NY 10019

May 24-June 1
🌺 English Gardens & The Chelsea Flower Show
For information, call (800)448-2685.
This tour is sponsored by: **Cox Arboretum** *(See Ohio Guide to Gardens.)*

June 19-30
🌺 English Gardens
For information, call (800)448-2685.
This tour is sponsored by: **Riverbanks Zoo & Botanical Gardens** *(See South Carolina Guide to Gardens.)*

July 7-18
🌺 Gardens of Scotland
For information, call (800)942-6666 or visit www.haerttertravel.com.
This tour is sponsored by: **American Horticultural Society** *(See Virginia Guide to Gardens.)*

July 18-August 2
🌺 Gardens of China
For information, call (800)942-6666 or visit www.haerttertravel.com.
This tour is sponsored by: **American Horticultural Society** *(See Virginia Guide to Gardens.)*

September 13-21
🌺 Gardens of the Italian Lakes
For information, call (800)942-6666 or visit www.haerttertravel.com.
This tour is sponsored by: **American Horticultural Society** *(See Virginia Guide to Gardens.)*

September 21-October 5
🌺 Exploring China: Its Plants, Gardens, Art & History
A fourteen-day journey to the regions around Shanghai, Suzhou, Kunming and Lijiang led by Dr. William Wu with Richard Brown of the Bloedel Reserve as escort. Includes the International Horticultural Exposition in Yunnan Province. For complete information, call (415)929-0550 or (800)666-1288.
This tour sponsored by: **Pacific Horticulture Magazine**, 4104 24th Street, #111, San Francisco, CA 94114

Horticultural Events

Belgium

April 16-May 15
🌺 Royal Greenhouses Open House
Each year during a short period of time the Royal Greenhouses of the Royal Palace at Laeken are open to the public.
Royal Palace, Laeken, Brussels
For information: **Belgian National Tourist Office**, 780 Third Avenue, Suite 1501, New York, NY 10170
Web: www.visitbelgium.com
(212)758-8130 *Fax:* (212)355-7675

France

May 14-16, October 14-17
🌺 Journées des Plantes
A large plant show and sale held at the Domaine de Courson, Courson Monteloup, near Paris. With more than one hundred exhibitors. *For information:* **Domaine de Courson**, 91680 Courson Monteloup
Email: courson@wanadoo.fr
011 33 1 64 58 9012
Fax: 011 33 1 64 58 9700

The Netherlands

March 25-May 19
🌺 Keukenhof Gardens 50th Anniversary
The 50th anniversary of these remarkable gardens, founded by the leading bulb-growers and located in the middle of the three main bulb towns is celebrated with new theme gar-

dens and a new exhibition hall. The gardens offer an amazing Spring display of as many as 5-6 million bulbs and other flowering trees and plants, both out-of-doors and in several large greenhouses. It is best to visit Keukenhof in April and May when the blooms are at their peak on the beautiful grounds. For complete information contact Keukenhof directly.
Keukenhof Gardens, Lisse
(212)370-7360 US; 011 31 252 465-555 in The Netherlands

August 19-September 19
🌺 Summer Garden at the Keukenhof
One third of the Keukenhof grounds display summer flowers. Art exhibits are also part of this special summer garden.
Keukenhof Gardens, Lisse
(212)370-7360 US; 011 31 252 465-555 The Netherlands

United Kingdom

Below is a listing of major shows of the Royal Horticultural Society.

May 7-9
🌺 Malvern Spring Garden Show
Set against the spectacular backdrop of the Malvern Hills, this is one of the best of British flower shows. Highlights include floral art, around 500 sundries stands, courtyard gardens, a specialist society section and the RHS Advisory desk. Organized jointly by the RHS and the Three Counties Agricultural Society.

May 25-28
🌺 Chelsea Flower Show
This is the ultimate gardening event, held on the grounds of The Royal Hospital, Chelsea, London. It includes show gardens by the world's leading designers, displays by special-

ist nurseries, top gardening products and a range of conservation, education and science displays. All tickets are sold in advance. May 25 and 26 are members-days only, but many tour groups schedule visits on these days.
The Royal Hospital, Chelsea, London

June 16-20
✿ BBC Gardeners' World Live
Gardening showbiz meets the very best in horticulture at this large and energetic Birmingham show. It features gardening celebrities from BBC Gardeners' World Live, the BBC Gardeners' World Magazine Theatre and a number of imaginative show gardens. An RHS Flower Show is part of this event.
National Exhibition Centre, Birmingham, England

July 6-11
✿ Hampton Court Palace Flower Show
Highlights include 8 massive tents brimming with flowers, many show gardens, water gardens, plants and many gardening accessories for sale, and the Royal National Rose Society's British Rose Festival.
Hampton Court, East Molesey, Surrey

July 22-25
✿ RHS Flower Show
Held at Tatton Park.

July 25, 26
✿ Wisley Flower Show
This is an RHS Show and is held at the RHS Garden in Wisley.

September 25, 26
✿ Malvern Autumn Show
This show combines horticultural delights with rural crafts and skills in a celebration of the season. Displays feature dahlias and other fall flowers as well as harvest fruit. There are rural

crafts, identification clinics for apples, pears and fungi, horse logging championships, sheep dog trials and more. Organized by the RHS in conjunction with the Three Counties Agricultural Society.

December 14, 15
✿ RHS Christmas Show, Westminster
This is the annual celebration of the season. For recorded information 24 hours a day, call (0171) 649 1885. For tickets call Ticket hot line (0171) 316 4707.

✿ Westminster Flower Shows
Throughout the year the Royal Horticultural Society holds two-day flower shows featuring competitions organized by horticultural societies specializing in many areas. Call the 24 hour hot line at 011 44 71 316-4707 for current schedule and information.

Scotland

June 4-6
✿ Scotland's National Gardening Show
The youngest of the RHS shows, Scotland's National Gardening Show was launched two years ago in its charming setting beside the Loch in Strathclyde Country Park. It features show gardens geared specifically to Scotland's growing conditions, floral exhibits, a craft marquee and garden accessories sales areas.
Strathclyde Country Park, Strathclyde, Scotland

For information on all the above shows: **The Royal Horticultural Society**, 80 Vincent Square, London SW1P 2PE
Web: www.rhs.org.uk
011 44 71 630-7422 *Fax:* 011 44 71 630-600

Flower Shows

Following is a state-by-state listing of the major shows. The name of the city where the show is listed appears in bold type. Please see Selected Events for complete descriptions.

Alabama

March 25-28
🌺 Flower Show
Spring Hill College Campus, 4000 Dauphin Street, **Mobile**, AL 36602
(334)639-2050

Arkansas

February 19-21
🌺 1999 Arkansas Flower & Garden Show
State House Convention Center, **Little Rock**, AR
(800)459-SHOW

California

March 18-21
🌺 San Francisco Flower & Garden Show
The Cow Palace, **San Francisco**, CA
(800)829-9751 or (415)495-1769

April 17, 16
🌺 74th Annual Flower Show
Spreckles Park, **Coronado**, CA

April 30, May 1, 2
🌺 Carmel Garden Show
Quail Lodge Resort, **Carmel**, CA
(831)625-6026

July 27-August 9
🌺 Sonoma County Fair & Exposition Flower Show
Sonoma County Fairgrounds, 1350 Bennett Valley Road, **Santa Rosa**, CA 95402
(707)545-4200

August 14-22
🌺 Southern California Home & Garden Show
Anaheim Convention Center, **Anaheim**, CA
(714)978-8888

October 7-10
🌺 1999 Los Angeles Garden Show
Arboretum of Los Angeles County , 301 North Baldwin Avenue, Arcadia (**Los Angeles**), CA 91007
(626)447-8207

Colorado

February 6-14
🌺 Colorado Garden & Home Show
Colorado Convention Center, 700 14th Street, **Denver**, CO
(303)932-8100

Connecticut

February 18-21
🌺 18th Annual Connecticut Flower & Garden Show
Connecticut Expo Center, **Hartford**, CT
(860)529-2123

District of Columbia

March 4-7
🌺 Washington Flower & Garden Show
The Washington Convention Center, 900 Ninth Street NW at New York Avenue, **Washington**, DC
(703)569-7141

Florida

February 19-21
🌺 5th Annual Palm Beach Tropical Flower & Garden Show

Flagler Drive, Intracoastal Waterway between Evernia & Banyan Streets, **West Palm Beach**, FL
(561)655-5622

March 11-14
🌿 Garden & Leisure Lifestyles Show
Ocean Center, 101 North Atlantic Ave (Route A1A), **Daytona Beach**, FL
(904)252-1511

Georgia

January 28-31
🌿 Atlanta Garden & Patio Show
Cobb Galleria Centre, Two Galleria Parkway, **Atlanta**, GA
(770)998-9800

February 17-21
🌿 Southeastern Flower Show
City Hall East Exhibition Center, 640 North Avenue, **Atlanta**, GA
(404)888-5638

Idaho

March 25-28
🌿 U.S. Bank Boise Flower & Garden Show
Boise Center at The Grove, **Boise**, ID
(888)888-7631

Illinois

February 10-14
🌿 Festival of Flowers & Homes
Rosemont Convention Center, **Rosemont** (Chicago), IL
(847)888-4585

March 12-14
🌿 Lawn, Flower & Garden Show
QCCA Expo Center, 2621 4th Avenue, **Rock Island**, IL (near Davenport, IA)
(309)788-5912

March 13-21
🌿 Chicago Flower & Garden Show
Navy Pier, **Chicago**, IL
(312)321-0077

Indiana

February 24-28
🌿 Ft. Wayne Home & Garden Show
Memorial Coliseum, 4000 Parnell Avenue, **Ft. Wayne**, IN
(800)678-6652

March 13-21
🌿 41st Annual Indiana Flower & Patio Show
Indiana State Fair Grounds, **Indianapolis**, IN
(800)215-1700 or (317)576-9933

April 30, May 1, 2
🌿 Spring Gardening Show
Holliday Park, 64th & Spring Mill Road, **Indianapolis**, IN
(317)290-ROSE

Iowa

February 17-22
🌿 Des Moines Home & Garden Show
Veterans Memorial Auditorium, 838 5th Avenue, **Des Moines**, IA
(800)HOM-SHOW

March 12-14
See Lawn, Flower & Garden Show under Illinois

Kansas

March 4-7
🌿 32nd Annual Wichita Lawn, Flower & Garden Show
Century II Civic Center, **Wichita**, KS
(316)721-8740

Kentucky

March 4-7
🌺 The Home Garden & Remodeling Show
Kentucky Fair & Exposition Center,
Louisville, KY
(502)429-6000

Maine

March 11-14
🌺 Portland Flower Show
Portland Company Complex, 58 Fore Street,
Portland, ME
🌺 Portland Flower Show

Maryland

March 5-7 & March 12-14
🌺 Maryland Home & Flower Show
Timonium Fairgrounds, 2100 York Road,
Timonium, MD 21093
(410)863-1180

April 15-18
🌺 The Rites of Spring Home
 & Garden Exhibition
Timonium Fairgrounds, 2100 York Road,
Timonium, MD
(410)554-2662

October 15-17
🌺 Fall Maryland Home & Garden Show
Timonium Fairgrounds, 2100 York Road,
Timonium, MD 21093
(410)863-1180

Massachusetts

March 13-21
🌺 128th New England Spring Flower Show
Bayside Exposition Center, 200 Mt. Vernon,
Boston, MA
(617)536-9280

March 25-28
🌺 Central Massachusetts Spring Flower Show
Centrum Centre, 50 Foster Street,
Worcester, MA
(800)533-0229

Michigan

March 5-7
🌺 Kalamazoo County Flowerfest
Wings Stadium, I-94, Sprinkle Road exit,
Kalamazoo, MI
(616)381-3597

Minnesota

March 3-7
🌺 Minneapolis Home & Garden Show
Minneapolis Convention Center, 1301 South
2nd Avenue, **Minneapolis**, MN
(612)933-3850

Missouri

January 8-10
🌺 St. Louis Flower Show
America's Center, 701 Convention Plaza, **St.
Louis**, MO
(314)342-5036

New Hampshire

March 26-29
🌺 Flower Show
Cheshire Fairgrounds Arena, Route 12,
South Keene, NH
(603)352-2253

New Jersey

February 25-28
🌺 33rd Annual New Jersey
 Flower & Patio Show
Garden State Exhibition Center, 50 Atrium
Drive, Exit 6 off Route 287, **Somerset**, NJ
(732)469-4000

New York

March 6-14
Brookhaven Indoor Landscape & Garden Show
Holtsville Park & Ecology Site, 249 Buckley Road, **Holtsville**, NY 11742
(516)758-9664

March 11-14
The Greater Rochester Flower & Garden Show
Dome Center, 2695 East Henrietta Road, Henrietta (**Rochester**), NY
(716)265-9018

March 11-14
Capital District Garden & Flower Show
Hudson Valley Community College, Vandenburgh Avenue - Route 4, **Troy**, NY
(518)786-1529

North Carolina

February 27-March 7
Southern Spring Show
Charlotte Merchandise Mart, 2500 East Independence Blvd, **Charlotte**, NC
(800)849-0248 or (704)376-6594

Ohio

February 6-14
National Home & Garden Show
International Exposition Center, 6200 Riverside Drive, **Cleveland**, OH
(800)600-0307

February 18-21
Akron-Canton Home & Garden Show
John S. Knight Center, 77 East Mill Street, **Akron**, OH
(800)865-8859

February 25-28
Youngstown Home & Garden Show
Eastwood Expo Center, Niles (**Youngstown**), OH
(800)865-8859

February 27-March 7
Cincinnati Home & Garden Show
Cincinnati Convention Center, **Cincinnati**, OH
(513)281-0022

February 27-March 7
Columbus Dispatch Charities Home & Garden Show
Ohio State Fairgrounds, **Columbus**, OH
(614)461-5257

April 21-25
Cincinnati Flower Show
Ault Park, Herschel and Observatory Avenues, **Cincinnati**, OH
(513)763-7752 or (800)670-6808 for advance ticket purchases

Oregon

February 24-28
Portland Home & Garden Show
Portland Expo Center, **Portland**, OR
(503)246-8291

February 26-28
Yard, Garden & Patio Show
Oregon Convention Center, 777 NE Martin Luther King, Jr. Blvd, **Portland**, OR
(800)342-6401 or (503)653-8733

Pennsylvania

February 19-21
Lehigh Valley Flower & Garden Show
Agriculture Hall, Allentown Fair Grounds, 17th & Chew Streets, **Allentown**, PA
(610)433-7541

March 7-14
✿ Philadelphia Flower Show
Pennsylvania Convention Center, 12th & Arch
Streets, **Philadelphia**, PA
(215)988-8800

March 13, 14
✿ Bucks Beautiful Garden Fair
Henry Schmieder Arboretum, Delaware Valley
College, Route 202 & New Britain Road,
Doylestown, PA
(215)345-1500

April 23-25
✿ Northeastern Pennsylvania Flower Show
109 Field Artillary Armory, 280 Market Street,
Kingston (Wilkes Barre), PA
(800)836-3413 or (717)457-8301

Rhode Island

February 18-21
✿ Annual Rhode Island Spring
   Flower & Garden Show
Rhode Island Convention Center, One Sabin
Street, **Providence**, RI
(800)766-1670

South Carolina

September 30-October 3
✿ Charleston Garden Festival
Gaillard Auditorium, 77 Calhoun Street,
Charleston, SC
(803)722-0661

Tennessee

February 11-14
✿ The Antiques & Garden Show of Nashville
Nashville Convention Center, **Nashville**, TN
(615)352-1282

March 4-7
✿ Nashville Lawn & Garden Show

Tennessee State Fairgrounds, **Nashville**, TN
(615)352-3863

Texas

February 26-28
✿ Neil Sperry's All Garden Show
Arlington Convention Center, **Arlington**
(Dallas), TX
(800)752-4769

March 20, 21
✿ State Garden Show of Texas
Heart of Texas Coliseum, 4601 Bosque Blvd,
Waco, TX
(817)772-1270

Virginia

January 22-24
✿ Virginia Flower & Garden Show
Virginia Beach Pavilion, Route 44, **Virginia
Beach**, VA
(757)853-0057

February 18-21
✿ Maymont Flower & Garden Show
Richmond Centre, 400 East Marshall Street,
Richmond, VA
(804)358-7166

Washington

February 3-7
✿ Tacoma Home & Garden Show
Tacoma Dome, **Tacoma**, WA
(253)756-2121

February 17-21
✿ 11th Annual Northwest
   Flower & Garden Show
Washington State Convention and Trade
Center, 9th & Pike Streets, **Seattle**, WA
(800)229-6311

Wisconsin

March 26-April 3
❀ Realtors' Home & Garden Show
Wisconsin State Fair Park, 8100 West Greenfield Avenue, West Allis (**Milwaukee**), WI 53214
(414)778-4929

Canada

British Columbia

June 4-6
❀ VanDusen Flower & Garden Show
VanDusen Botanical Garden, 5251 Oak Street, **Vancouver**, BC V6M 4H1
(604)257-8666

July 9-11
❀ 6th Annual Royal Victoria Flower & Garden Festival
Royal Roads University, 2005 Sooke Road, **Victoria**, BC
(250)881-7469

Ontario

March 10-14
❀ Canada Blooms Flower Show
Metro Toronto Convention Centre, South Building, 222 Bremner Blvd, **Toronto**, ON
(800)730-1020 or (416)593-0223

April 1-4
❀ 6th Annual Success With Gardening Show
International Centre, 6900 Airport Road, Mississauga (**Toronto**), ON
(905)881-5708

April 9-11
❀ Ontario Garden Show
Royal Botanical Gardens, 680 Plains Road West, Burlington (**Toronto**), ON
(905)527-1158

November 4-13
❀ The Winter Garden Show at the Royal
The Coliseum at the National Trade Centre, Exhibition Place, **Toronto**, ON M6K 3C3
(416)393-6400

Useful Books

The following is a list of some useful publications. There are many regional guides on the shelves of a good bookstore, library or horticultural society. If you know of a good guide, please let us know.

National Geographic Guide to America's Public Gardens *Mary Zuazua Jenkins, National Geographic Society, Washington, DC.* A brand new guide, with beautiful photographs and detailed descriptions.

The Complete Guide to North American Gardens: The Northeast and The West Coast *(1991) William C. Mulligan, foreword by Linda Yang, Little, Brown & Co., New York, NY.* These two volumes cover gardens of major interest that are open to the public. They are beautifully designed and portable.

The Northwest Gardeners' Resource Directory, 7th ed. *(1997) Stephanie Feeney, Cedarcroft Press, Bellingham, WA.* This wonderful compendium lists everything that's going on horticulturally in the Northwest.

Gardener's On the Go!: Seattle *(1998) Stephanie Feeney. Cedarcroft Press, Bellingham, WA.* A must for visits to the Puget Sound area, with twenty tours and everything you need to know, from how to get there to where to have lunch.

Glorious Gardens to Visit: 58 Gardens Within 3 Hours of New York City *(1989) and* **Glorious Gardens to Visit in Northern California: 65 Gardens Within 3 Hours of San Francisco** *(1993) Priscilla Dunhill and Sue Freedman, Clarkson N. Potter, Inc., New York, NY.* Both of these paperback guides are entertainingly written and well-researched.

Gardenwalks *(1997) Marina Harrison & Lucy D. Rosenfeld, Michael Kesend, New York, NY.* Gardens from Maine to Virginia, with some unusual and off-beat selections that are favorites of the authors.

Gardens of the Wine Country *(1998) Molly Chappellet & Richard Tracy, Chronicle Books, San Francisco, CA.* Beautiful photographs of the gardens in the Napa Valley. Something all travelers to the Wine Country will enjoy.

10 Great Garden
Vacations for 1999

Great Ideas for a Los Angeles
Garden Vacation
by *Karen L. Dardick*

If you're planning a visit to the Los Angeles area, the public gardens reflect great diversity and range from formal to woodland, from elegance to simplicity itself.

Start at Descanso Gardens in La Canada, (near Pasadena), where more than 60,000 camellia shrubs thrive in an oak forest. A perfect time to visit is March 19 through April 18, when the Spring Festival of Flowers occurs and the gardens are in peak bloom. The Tulip Promenade features 15,000 named varieties, along with daffodils, lilies, hyacinths and other spring flowers. Special events at the Festival include flower shows, lectures, plant sales. This is a public garden that should not be missed. See *California Guide to Gardens* for more information.

For a look at private gardens, put April 11 on your calendar and the 40th Annual Garden Tour sponsored by the Santa Monica Auxiliary of the Children's Hospital of Los Angeles. It's a self-guided tour of five residential gardens in Santa Monica and West Los Angeles.

About 30 miles outside of LA, the wildflowers are blooming in Claremont. From March 16 through May 16 you can take a docent-led tour through the Rancho Santa Ana Botanic Garden on Saturday or Sunday afternoons.

From April 16-25 there's a Rose Festival at the Huntington Library and Botanical Garden, with tours, talks, demonstrations, plant sales and thousands of roses at the peak of their spring bloom. The Huntington is in a park-like setting with fifteen special gardens containing plants from around the world.

For more information on any of these events, see the *California Selected Events* section in this guide.

The Los Angeles County Arboretum in Arcadia is another major public garden for your list. See *California Guide to Gardens* for more information. The over one-hundred acres are also home ot colorful peacocks, a legacy from Lucky Baldwin, the original owner of the site.

The Getty Center, high on a hilltop in West Los Angeles with views of the Santa Monica Mountains, resembles an Italian village. Richard Meier's formal architecture is complemented by acres of geometric and precisely designed planting beds containing trees, shrubs and flowering plants. The controversial Robert Irwin Central Garden, with unbridled color and bold design, is attracting the most attention from local gardeners who either love it or hate it. Reservations are necessary, so be sure to call in plenty of time to coincide with your visit. (310)440-7300

Lummis Home in Los Angeles is a state historic monument. Built by Charles Lummis in the late 1800's, the stone house and garden consist of 1.8 acres and demonstrate water conservation and low maintenance gardening. (323)222-0546

Mildred E. Mathias Botanical Garden is on the sprawling UCLA campus in Westwood. Named for the garden director who had great impact on Southern California horticulture, the garden is home to more than 3,000 plant species, including rare cycads, Malaysian rhododendrons, eucalyptus trees, cacti and succulents, and California native plants. (310)825-1260

Self-Realization Fellowship Lake Shrine, Pacific Palisades, is a 10-acre meditation garden combining a wide variety of flowering plants, trees and shrubs, all planted around a natural lake. The serene gardens with meditation nooks attract thousands of visitors annually. (310)454-4114

Karen Dardick writes and gardens in Los Angeles.

Arizona in Spring

Spring is the time to be in Arizona, where the great attraction is the spectacular blooming of the wildflowers in the desert. Starting in late March, as the dry mountain canyons are transformed into veritable rock gardens, the Arizona-Sonora Desert Museum in Tucson offers Wildflower Walks. Join Desert Museum naturalists for an easy two-mile round-trip hike to identify and enjoy the wildflowers. Call (520)883-1380 for information and dates.

Also in Tucson, Tohono Chul Park gives Wildflower Tours from February 15 to April 16. Guides discuss the various wildflowers and what they need to grow, as you walk through the desert searching for these beauties. The tours are held Monday, Wednesday and Friday at 10am. (520)742-6455

In Phoenix, the Desert Botanical Gardens operate a Wildflower hotline from March 3 through April 28 Call (602)481-8134 seven days a week, 24 hours a day, to find out the best places in Arizona to see desert wildflowers.

At the Desert Botanical Gardens, February through May are the prime months to enjoy the different colored, brilliant cactus blooms. The Saguaro generally blooms in May. In the warmer summer months view the night blooming cactus, with blooms the size of trumpets that last for one night.

At Boyce Thompson Arboretum, 55 miles from Phoenix in Superior, Wildflower Month is celebrated in March, with displays of cultivated and native wildflowers throughout the month. Wildflower tours are conducted on Saturdays and Sundays. Call the Wildflower hotline at (520)689-2811 for the best times to visit.

Another special event during this time is the Spring Landscape Plant Sale at the Desert Botanical Garden in Phoenix on March 20, 21. This sale features more than 15,000 landscape plants, trees and shrubs for arid lands, as well as smaller plants for patio container gardening.

From March 19 to April 4 at Boyce Thompson in Superior, thousands of drought tolerant trees, shrubs, annuals, perennials, cacti and succulents are for sale. Horticulturists are on hand to answer questions and lead tours of the Demonstration Garden, where visitors can see mature species of plants, each Saturday and Sunday starting at 1:30pm.

On March 28 in Tucson's Tohono Chul Park there's a Wildflower Festival & Picnic, with a progressive dinner, wildflower walks, activities and musical entertainment.

And if you stay in Tucson until April 11, you can visit some of the most intriguing private gardens in Tucson, featuring everything from xeriscaping to wildflowers. The Home and Garden Tour is sponsored by The Tucson Botanical Gardens. Call (520)326-9686 for complete information.

See *Arizona Selected Events* in this guide for more information on any of these events.

Garden Openings and More in Indianapolis
by Jo Ellen Meyers Sharp

Three openings in Indianapolis make this a good city to visit for your garden vacation.

First, visit Oldfields at the Indianapolis Museum of Art. More than 19,000 plants have been added to the Ravine Garden at Oldfields, a 26-acre American country estate on the grounds of the Indianapolis Museum of Art overlooking the Indianapolis Canal and the White River Valley. The Garden will reopen May 23, following a two-year restoration, with more than 40 flowering trees, 800 flowering shrubs, 300 evergreens, 5,000 perennials, 7,000 bulbs and 4,000 ferns and wildflowers. Limestone pathways that descend 50 feet from the mansion to the Indianapolis Canal have been restored, along with other stone work, fountains and waterfalls. Oldfields also has a Formal Garden with rose covered trellises and arbors, restored in 1993, a Grand Allée and woodland garden. *Oldfields, 1200 West 38th Street, Indianapolis. (317)923.1331.*

Another place to take in is the Garfield Park and Conservatory. The Conservatory was established in 1872 and has just reopened following a renovation. It maintains large collections of tropical plants and holds four annual seasonal displays. In the adjacent Park is the Victorian style 2.5-acre Sunken Gardens where restoration was completed in October 1998 It has three lighted fountains, and seasonal displays of annuals and perennials. *Garfield Park and Conservatory, 2450 South Shelby Street, Indianapolis. (317)327-7184*

Scheduled to open June 13 is White River Gardens, a three-acre conservatory and garden complex and sister institution to the Indianapolis Zoo. The $14 million project includes a glass-enclosed conservatory, outdoor idea gardens, water garden, a wedding garden for ceremonies and receptions, a resource center and a half-mile of winding paths and walkways. The zoo and gardens are part of White River State Park.. The signature artwork for the gardens is the Midwestern Panorama, a 160-foot-long and 16-foot-tall circular mural by Andrew Reid of Miami in the Rotunda entrance. The mural is a 360-degree depiction of gardening activities and plants from winter through spring, summer, fall and back to winter. *White River Gardens at The Indianapolis Zoo, 1200 West Washington Street, Indianapolis. (317)630-2001*

If you have a chance, visit Altum's Horticultural Center and Gardens, a unique garden center with a decidedly European flavor, in the historic town of Zionsville just outside of Indianapolis. *Altum's Horticultural Center and Gardens, 11335 North Michigan Road, Zionsville, IN (317)733-4769*

You might also want to take in the Spring Gardening Show, *Orchard in Bloom*, held from April 30 through May 2 in Holliday Park. The proceeds from this fun-filled show benefit the Indy Parks Foundation and The Orchard School. See *Indiana Selected Events* in this guide for a complete description and information.

Jo Ellen Meyers Sharp is a freelance writer who gardens in Indianapolis.

Choice Events in St. Louis

St. Louis is home to one of the great horticultural institutions in the United States, the Missouri Botanical Garden. In addition to having wonderful collections, the MBG maintains a very active schedule, so there are usually events going on at all times of the year. See *Missouri Guide to Gardens* for more information.

If you visit in the winter, you should plan to attend the St. Louis Flower Show, *Because Life Should Be Beautiful*. It's held January 8 through 10 at the America's Center and hosted by the Junior League of St. Louis

For another winter treat, visit the Conservatory at the MBG, from January 30 to March 14. There you'll find dinosaurs lurking among one of the largest collections of orchids in North America.

Later, in spring, at a much more hospitable time for vacationing, the MBG holds its GardenExpo weekends from April 17 to May 9. They feature special garden tours, Society shows, hands-on workshops, demonstrations, vendors, entertainment, refreshments and children's activities.

On April 24 there's the Perennial Plant Sale in University City, just outside of St. Louis. You'll find plants from home gardens, including some unusual varieties, all in excellent condition and at reasonable prices. The sale is sponsored by University City in Bloom and proceeds support this volunteer group's efforts to maintain over 300 public gardens throughout the City.

For a chance to see private gardens, take the Annual House & Garden Tour on May 15 and 16. This is a self-guided tour of eight houses and gardens in the turn-of-the-century Kingsbury Place and Waterman Place neighborhoods of St. Louis.

Also on May 15, the Shaw Arboretum of the MBG, 35 miles west of St. Louis in Gray Summit, holds its Native Plant Sale. Twelve nurseries from Missouri and Illinois offer a wide selection of plants native to the Midwest, with hundreds of varieties of wildflowers, ferns, trees and shrubs, as well as seeds and plants of the prairie, wetland, woodland and savanna. The sale takes place at the Whitmore Wildflower Garden in the Arboretum.

For another chance to see private gardens, visit Hermann, about 70 miles west of St. Louis on the Missouri River. On May 22 and 23 the Hermann Garden Club holds a Town Tour and a Country Tour. The Town Tour is a walking tour of gardens in the Hermann Historic District, while the Country Tour visits gardens in the surrounding hills by car. You can take either or both. Other special events are held at this time by local wineries and bed and breakfasts.

For more information on these events, see *Missouri Selected Events*.

Unusual Gardens and Events
of Northern California
by Beth Benjamin

For a great garden vacation in Northern California, consider the following possibilities.

Just south of San Francisco is the Alan Chadwick Garden (5 acres) and Center for Agroecology and Sustainable Food Systems (25 acres) at University of California at Santa Cruz. Students and apprentices began the Garden under Chadwick's leadership in 1966, and added the Center (known as the Farm) in 1971. On a hill overlooking Monterey Bay, this is one of the most glorious horticultural sites, where organic, sustainable techniques for growing flowers, herbs and vegetables have created an inspiring and beautiful place to visit. (831)459-4140

Connected to the Farm by a meandering path is the University's Arboretum, filled with collections of Mediterranean, Australian, South African and New Zealand plants. Banksia, protea, grevillea and other exotics flourish in the California climate and attract ravenous hummingbirds. (831)427-2998

Filoli at Woodside is an exquisite formal garden, with 15 acres of perfectly tended garden beds and borders surrounded by more than 600 acres of oak forest and woodland watershed. Visiting Filoli is like taking a trip to some of the most famous gardens of England. See *California Guide to Gardens* for more information.

Just north of San Francisco is the wine country with lots of great events in May. From May 1-9 you can enjoy the Mt. Tamalpais Wildflower Festival, a week of lectures, hikes through the trails of Mt. Tamalpais, a walk through the garden of a noted rosarian, and more. The event raises money for Mt. Tamalpais State Park and is sponsored by the Mountain Home Inn.

On May 16, the Heritage Rose Group in El Cerrito holds their annual Celebration of Old Roses, with hundreds of roses – old, modern and miniature – from many growers, on display and for sale.

On May 22 the Petaluma Historical Museum holds a tour of ten private gardens in this Victorian town in the wine country, a not-to-be-missed event. For more information on any of these events, see *California Selected Events* in this guide.

Then you can visit some really special nurseries, garden tours in themselves.

Sierra Azul Nursery specializes in plants from the Mediterranean basin, South Africa, Australia, Chile and California natives, featuring species that are drought-tolerant and water conserving. They have created a beautiful and instructive two-acre demonstration garden alive with birds, including many hummingbirds and butterflies, that is watered only once a month. *Sierra Azul Nursery, 2660 E. Lake Avenue, Watsonville. Open daily 9am-5:30pm. (831)763-0939*

The Berkeley Horticultural Nursery offers more than two acres of a wide variety of plants in a beautifully laid out nursery. Specializing in natives, aquatics and perennials, with strong specimens of maples, rhododendrons and camellias, Berkeley Hort is a wonderful place to browse and get a sense of how the plants will look side by side. *Berkeley Horticultural Nursery, 1310 McGee Avenue, Berkeley. Open 9-5 every day except Thursday. (510)526-4705*

Maggie Wych of Western Hills Rare Plants continues the dream of the nursery's late founders, Marshall Olbrich and Lester Hawkins, to create both a world class garden and an eclectic nursery of unusual, rare and useful land-scape plants. This extraordinary three-acre nursery, set in the lovely country-side of Sonoma County, is an important destination for knowledgeable horti-culturists from around the world. *Western Hills Rare Plants, 16250 Coleman Valley Road, Occidental. Open Thurs-Sun 10am-4pm; by appointment only in December and January. (707)874-3731*

Beth Benjamin, a partner at Renee's Garden, writes and gardens in Felton, California.

Philadelphia in May

The Philadelphia area offers lots of garden vacation opportunities. The first thing to do, if you know you're going to be in the Philadelphia area, is to get your free map from The Gardens Collaborative in Philadelphia. You can also purchase their wonderful guidebook *Paradise Presented: Beautiful Gardens in Philadelphia and the Delaware Valley.* See *Pennsylvania Guide to Gardens* for information.

On May 19 and 20, be sure to take in the Rittenhouse Square Flower Market. Booths are set up around the Square and filled with annuals, herbs, food treats and lots of other items for sale. The event includes activities for children and benefits children's charities in the area.

On May 22 and 23 there's a festival at Historic Bartram's Garden to cele-brate the 300th anniversary of the birth of the founder of America's oldest botanical garden. There are 18th century crafters, music, dance, reenact-ments, children's events, food and a variety of tours.

For more information on both these events see *Pennsylvania Selected Events* in this guide. Round out your trip with visits to these three gardens.

Awbury Arboretum in the historic Germantown section of the city is the largest remaining piece of open land in this part of town – 55 acres of green space. The centerpiece of the Arboretum is the Francis Cope House with grounds planned by William Saunders, designer of the U.S. Capitol grounds. There are open meadows, ponds, woods, plantings and farmland in addition to the planted landscapes. *Awbury Arboretum, One Awbury Road, Philadelphia, PA 19138. (215)849-2855*

Cliveden (1763-67) is the National Trust for Historic Preservation property, originally built as the summer home for Chief Justice Benjamin Chew and occupied almost continuously by the Chew family until 1972. The largely twentieth-century garden contains a wide variety of mature trees and shrubs. Cliveden's Franklinia Tree is possibly the largest specimen in the Philadelphia area. You can wander through the formal garden, with espaliered fruit trees, annuals and perennials, and see the garden timeline along the carriage wall. *Cliveden, 6401 Germantown Avenue, Philadelphia, PA 19144. (215)848-1777*

The Morris Arboretum at the University of Pennsylvania is a must. The garden's 92 public acres contain thousands of rare and lovely woody plants, a Victorian landscape garden, a rose garden, glasshouse fernery and many more special horticultural treats. *Morris Arboretum, 100 Northwestern Avenue, Philadelphia, PA 19118. (215)247-5777*

Out on the Main Line you can visit the lovely campus of Haverford College, the Jenkins Arboretum in Devon, Chanticleer in Wayne, near St. David's and the Henry Foundation in Gladwyne. Or you can head towards Media and the Tyler Arboretum on the Swarthmore College Campus. See the *Pennsylvania Guide to Gardens* and the *Delaware Guide to Gardens* for more information and ideas.

Great Gardens in the Chicago Area
by Susan Crawford

Any garden vacation in the Chicago area has to start in Glencoe at the Chicago Botanic Garden. To visit the Chicago Botanic Garden is to be confronted with an embarrassment of riches. In order to have time to pause and savor the details, here are some personal favorites: the English walled garden and the Japanese islands.

The former is a large area divided into rooms enclosed within high walls of a soft-hued red brick. The plantings are sweeping and generous in the English style and include specimens marginally hardy in the Chicago area, that grow vigorously in this protected environment. Warm or cool colors prevail and water is present in various of the Garden's lagoons.

The Japanese Islands are spare, sculptured and calm, with carefully shaped deciduous trees and shrubs and conifers that have been elegantly pruned and tied. The arched bridge at the entrance has a wooden railing so smooth and lovely it demands to be touched. You can stroll on gravel paths around two of the islands, while the third only can be admired from a distance.

In the City of Chicago are two venerable conservatories. The Garfield Park Conservatory is one of the largest conservatories of its kind in the world, built by Jens Jensen in 1907. It has deteriorated from its glory days but an extensive renovation is planned. The Lincoln Park Conservatory, Stockton Drive at Fullerton, is almost as handsome as Garfield Park and better maintained. Each is the site of five large annual floral shows.

On Michigan Avenue and LaSalle Street in downtown Chicago, island beds have been planted with an expert eye for color and scale. Anchored by stately grasses and perennials, with bulbs, annuals, vines and mums providing seasonal changes, these are splendid additions to the vibrancy of the urban scene.

Two small gardens in the city, attractively planted and pleasant for a stroll or a picnic, are the Lincoln Garden behind the Chicago Historical Society and The Rosenbaum Garden, Oak Street just east of Michigan Avenue.
If you are near Grant Park, visit the Rose Gardens, North and South of the landmark Buckingham Fountain, with beds of many varieties of modern roses.

On the Northwestern University Campus in nearby Evanston, is the Shakespeare Garden. Designed by Jens Jensen in 1915 and maintained by the Evanston Garden Club, it offers a romantic and secluded sanctuary behind tall hedges, and represents a loose adaptation of the bard's planting list with additions such as ornamental grasses.

Also in Evanston is Merrick Park, at the corner of Lake Street and Oak Avenue, with a traditional rose garden of mostly modern cultivars. Its focal point is the extraordinary 1921 Centennial Fountain, a cast iron confection of three basins surrounded by painted white cranes spouting water.

A good time to visit these gardens is on June 27, after going on the Anniversary Garden Walk sponsored by Keep Evanston Beautiful. This tour visits twelve private gardens. Proceeds go to fund environmental education. Transportation is required.

For more tours of private gardens, check out the Annual Dearborn Garden Walk & Heritage Festival on July 18. Over fifty award-winning gardens are open, and the event includes a neighborhood street festival and architectural walking tours of this historic Chicago neighborhood. Proceeds are used to enhance and preserve the character of the neighborhood.

A different kind of experience is the Annual Parade of Ponds on July 24 and 25, offering self-guided tours to more than 125 water gardens and private landscapes throughout the Chicago suburbs

And on September 18, you can take the Housewalk and Gardens tour of six historic homes and gardens in Northwest Chicago.

For more information on any of these tours, see the *Illinois Selected Events* section in this guide.

Other wonderful garden spots in the Chicago area include: the Oak Park Conservatory with its wonderful spring Herb sale; the Ladd Arboretum in Evanston; the Morton Arboretum in Lisle. See the *Illinois Guide to Gardens* for more information on these sites.

Susan Crawford writes and gardens in Chicago.

Summer Gardens and Tours in Maine

If your vacation takes you to Maine and garden tours are on your wish list, there is plenty going on.

For example, on July 7 and 8 the Brunswick Topsham Land Trust sponsors *Gardening with Nature*, a tour of private gardens in and around Brunswick. Included are shade gardens, seaside gardens, perennial and annual displays, each the work of the owner.

The next weekend is packed with private garden viewing possibilities. On Friday, July 15, in the Camden-Rockport area, a tour sponsored by the Camden Garden Club features many private homes and gardens, including the Spite House Gardens.

On Saturday, July 17, there's a tour of six private gardens – usually three in Lewiston and three in Auburn – to benefit the Maine Music Society. Tickets can be purchased in advance by contacting the Society.

Or, if you are in the Kennebunk area, you can take in the *Private Gardens of the Kennebunks*. This tour of eight gardens benefits the York County Child Abuse Council.

On July 18, there's the annual tour of country gardens in the middle watershed towns of Warren, Union and Hope, sponsored by the Georges River Land Trust. Tickets, brochure and map can obtained in advance at area bookstores or by writing to GRLT.

For contact information on any of these tours, see the *Maine Selected Events* section in this guide. You can also pick up a copy of the magazine *People, Places, PLANTS; The Gardening Magazine of Maine*. This will tell you in a flash the garden tours and other garden doings in the area you're visiting – and generally there are lots!

Of course, summer is a great time to see any gardens in Maine, since their season is so short. So don't forget to check out the *Maine Guide to Gardens* earlier in these pages and make up your list.

Inner City Gardens of Toronto
by Lorraine Flanagan

There's lots doing almost year round in Toronto, starting with the *Canada Blooms* Flower and Garden Show in March, one of the largest indoor flower shows in Canada. Then there's the Ontario Garden Show in April at the Royal Botanical Garden in nearby Burlington, lilac festivals in May, iris and peony festivals in June, roses in July, herbs in August, mums in the fall, and the big Winter Garden Show at the Royal in November. See *Ontario Selected Events* in this guide for more information.

To see gardens that reflect the history and neighborhood flavor of Toronto, try these small gardens.

Up on a hill overlooking the city, you'll find Casa Loma. The gardens of this historic fairy tale castle have been beautifully restored by the Garden Club of Toronto. Take a stroll through the cool Carolinian woodland, the rhododendron dell, or any of the five perennial gardens. Discover the secret garden with its canopy of roses and clematis, and don't miss the Dancing Fountain, the Water Garden or the Meadow Gardens. *Casa Loma, 1 Austin Terrace, Toronto (416)923-1171*

Just across the street are the gardens of Spadina House. Dating from 1818, the restored gardens incorporate many of the plants cherished by the families who lived there. An old "Manitoba Rose" hugs the fence by the pierced stone pergola, a patch of Lily-of-the-Valley lies where the family's children picked bunches of flowers to earn pocket money, and some of the original Concord grapes grow over the Grape Arbor. *Spadina House Gardens, 285 Spadina Road, Toronto (416)392-6910*

In contrast to Victorian Toronto, two modern community gardens, the Village of Yorkville Parks and the Alex Wilson Community Garden, are very much rooted in today's Toronto. The result of an effort by Yorkville residents that began in 1973, Yorkville Park is designed as a series of gardens symbolic of the row houses that once stood on the site. The gardens feature many native plants, including an amelanchier grove, an Ontario marsh and walks through native bittersweet, birches and pine. *Village of Yorkville Parks, Yorkville Avenue at Bellair. Call Toronto Parks & Recreation for a brochure. (416)392-1111*

South and west of this garden, on Richmond Street, is a garden created and dedicated to the memory and vision of the revolutionary author of the Culture of Nature, Alex Wilson. Filled with native plantings of black-eyed Susan and wild bergamot, the Alex Wilson Community Garden hosts 40 allotment plots where neighborhood gardeners grow vegetables and flowers. *Garden at 552 Richmond Street West, half a block east of Bathurst. Call Toronto Parks & Recreation for a brochure. (416)392-1111*

A visit to Toronto in the summer almost always includes a trip to Harbourfront, a lakeside development of theater, crafts, shopping and open air music and markets. It's also home to the seven Artist's Gardens, designed by Ontario's artists and designers. Scheduled to open this summer at Harbourfront is the world's first "interactive" music garden. Designed by Boston garden designer Julie Moir Messervy, in collaboration with cellist Yo-Yo Ma, the garden will be composed of six sections, each designed to evoke a movement from Bach's Cello Suite No. 1, which Ma suggests is evocative of nature. *For a brochure, call (416)973-5379.*

Lorraine Flanagan gardens and writes from her city garden in Toronto.

A Do-It-Yourself
Garden Tour of Manhattan

If you are in Manhattan and feeling garden-deprived, you can satisfy your garden longings without leaving the island with this little do-it-yourself tour of small, special places.

In Greenwich Village stop by the Jefferson Market Courthouse Garden, right next to the Public Library that's housed in that wonderful building. This garden was created by local residents and is maintained and tended by volunteers. It is open to the public on weekends, but you can look through the fence and get some idea of this peaceful, lush garden blooming in the heart of the Village.

In Soho try to look in on the Liz Christy Garden, a community garden which stretches from Second Avenue to Bowery on Houston Street. This exuberant garden has plots of vegetables, flowers, vines, shady trees, all the work of the local artists and residents who live and garden there.

Another community garden is found on the northern end of the spacious esplanade in Riverside Park. Enter the Park at Riverside Drive and 91st Street, go down the hill and up to the riot of color which has been planted down the center of the esplanade. This garden is made up of small areas allotted to the participating gardeners, and is crammed full of all sorts of annuals and perennials and small garden ornaments.

Further uptown at the Cathedral of St. John the Divine, on Amsterdam Avenue and West 100th Street, you can visit the Biblical Garden and the Hope Rose Garden. The latter is planted with David Austin roses.

Visit the Conservatory Garden in Central Park at Fifth Avenue and 106th Street to see the lovely formal beds, beautiful plantings and fountains. Don't forget to visit Bryant Park, behind the New York Public Library on 42nd Street and Fifth Avenue. This recently restored site typifies a classic European-style park, with flower beds, terraces and huge arching London plane trees.

AMERICAN
HORTICULTURAL
SOCIETY

1999 TRAVEL STUDY PROGRAMS

**Summer Gardens of Australia
and New Zealand**
January 10 - February 10, 1999

**Spring Gardens of Amalfi,
Naples, Rome and the Islands
of Ischia and Capri**
April 20 - May 1, 1999

**Spring Gardens of Wales, with
optional extension to the
Royal Chelsea Flower Show**
May 16 - 24, 1999 and
May 24 - 28, 1999

**Wilderness Gardens of Alaska
exploration voyage on board
the M | V Yorktown Clipper.**
June 12 - 19, 1999

**Gardens of Scotland,
featuring the Royal Scotsman**
July 7-18, 1999

Gardens of China
July 18 - August 2, 1999

Gardens of the Italian Lakes
September 13 - 21, 1999

**Gardens and Fall Colors
along the Hudson,
an exploration voyage
on board the
M | V Nantucket Clipper**
October 2 - 9, 1999

**Details and Brochures from our
Travel Planners**

The Leonard Haertter Travel Co.
7922 Bonhomme Avenue
St. Louis, Missouri 63105
Tel: 314-721-6200
Fax: 314-721-8497
Nationwide Toll Free: 800-942-6666
email: info@haerttertravel.com
http://www.haerttertravel.com